BRITISH NAVAL PRIZE LAW IN THE SEVEN YEARS' WAR

BRITISH NAVAL PRIZE LAW IN THE SEVEN YEARS' WAR

A. B. McLeod

THE BOYDELL PRESS

First published 2025
The Boydell Press, Woodbridge

ISBN 978 1 83765 281 5

The Boydell Press is an imprint of Boydell & Brewer Ltd
PO Box 9, Woodbridge, Suffolk IP12 3DF, UK
and of Boydell & Brewer Inc.
668 Mt Hope Avenue, Rochester, NY 14620-2731, USA
website: www.boydellandbrewer.com

Our Authorised Representative for product safety in the EU is Easy Access
System Europe – Mustamäe tee 50, 10621 Tallinn, Estonia,
gpsr.requests@easproject.com

A CIP catalogue record for this book is available
from the British Library

To Claire and Alan, without whose love and support
this book would not have come to fruition

CONTENTS

ILLUSTRATIONS

Figures

Tables

ACKNOWLEDGEMENTS

The National Archives holds the documents which I photographed and transcribed for this book. The staff there were unfailingly helpful over the years it took me to gather the material I used. Amanda Bevan was the source of both advice and encouragement. Then just finishing her supervision of the work of many researchers who created the series HCA IND-18089 and HCA 32 0161-256, Amanda allowed me access to the huge databases thus created, which saved me years of toil.

Paul Bugden shared his professional understanding of the maritime world and maritime law and pointed me in the direction of useful research material. Jeremy Michell and I shared the delights to be found in HCA 32.

Chris Donnithorne has put his immense database to use on many occasions to help me understand postings, commissions and all the complexity of the Admiralty's administration.

The Drakeford family, present-day relations of the Richard Drakeford I found so useful, have been very supportive. The Staffordshire Archives, which hold the Richard Drakeford material, have been constantly helpful.

I have been grateful to Peter Sowden over many years, particularly for his vision of a legal spotlight being played on an obscure naval period nearly three hundred years ago. Hendrikje Dorussen has solved problems with speed and efficiency.

My husband and sons have, as always, been prepared to read, comment, question and commend the work. Without them nothing would have been achieved.

ABBREVIATIONS

ADM	Admiralty
HCA	High Court of Admiralty
LG	*London Gazette*
LL	Lloyds List
NMM	National Maritime Museum
TNA	The National Archives

GLOSSARY

adjudge pronounce judicially

advocate a professional pleader in a court of justice, in this context a member of Doctors Commons, with a doctorate from Oxford or Cambridge; an advocate with right of audience in the Civil Courts, the civilian equivalent of a common law barrister-at-law

appellant a person who applies (appeals) to a higher court against an adverse judgement of a lower court

arrest to seize by legal authority and take into custody

attachment a court order for money or property to be taken from someone in order to pay their debts

bail security given for the release of property in issue pending hearing of the case

bill of lading a document issued by a carrier to a shipper with multiple functions and evidencing the terms of, and parties to, a contract of carriage, describing the type, quantity and destination of the goods carried

blockade the interdiction by a blockading state of maritime transport to and from the blockaded country necessitating *inter alia* a neutral vessel's submission to inspection for contraband

bond a deed by which a person is bound to make payment to another

bottomry an arrangement by which the master of a ship borrows money on a bond, whereby the ship is the security, and forfeits it if the bond is not repaid

bounty *see* Gun and Head Money

bream to burn and scrape clean a ship's bottom

by day the by day was the first day of the new term, Michaelmas following Trinity etc.

cabotage coastal trade

cause a person or thing that occasions something

charter party contract for carriage by which the owner of a ship lets her or part of her to others for use in transporting a cargo

cite summons to appear in a law court

claimant the owner or agent of the captured vessel or cargo

cockett a certificate given to merchants warranting that goods have been duly entered through customs and all duties paid

colouring an attempt to disguise by the use of false papers the true ownership of a vessel, her cargo or the nature of her voyage

complaint a formal statement that someone has harmed someone else or done something illegal, which must be proved in court of law

condemn declare seized goods to be forfeited

condemnation judgement by court that a vessel and/or its cargo was lawful prize

contempt behaviour that is illegal because it does not obey or respect the rules of a law court

contraband cargo of war-like use destined for the enemy and forbidden to be supplied by neutrals to belligerents

contumacy wilful disobedience to a court order

court below Vice Admiralty Court

damages a sum of money claimed or awarded in compensation for a loss or injury

decree an official order issued by a legal authority as judgement

deferred put off to a later time

demurrage the amount payable to a shipowner by a charterer for failure to load or discharge a ship within the time agreed

Doctors Commons a self-governing body of professionals holding doctorates either of civil law from Oxford or of law from

Cambridge, working from a site south of St Paul's, in Knightrider Street

dogger North Sea coasting vessel working off the Dogger Bank fishing grounds

draft a small allowance for waste on goods sold by weight

droit a customary right of the Crown, belonging through him to the Lord High Admiral, being (at the time of the Seven Years' War) that part of the prize fund which accrued by right to the Lord High Admiral as comprised ships improperly brought in for adjudication in a prize court before declaration of war or reprisal; those brought in by those operating without a lawful commission or letter of marque; and those forced in to a British port by stress of weather or shipwrecked

embargo an order of state forbidding ships to leave its ports

en flute ships sailing *en flute* were warships employed as troop transports. The main gun deck was cleared of its battery, allowing space to berth troops, but the guns on the weather deck were retained along with the crew for the same; the number of retained guns was typically larger than found on a chartered merchant ship

enrol to enter a deed amongst the rolls of a court of justice

executor a person appointed by a testator to carry out the terms of his will

exemplification an attested copy of a legal document under an official seal

exhibited submitted as evidence to the court for consideration

furze dried branches of brushwood tied together to make a torch to clean a ship's bottom

guinea worth one pound and one shilling (£1.05)

Gun Money bounty paid early in eighteenth century at rate of £10 per gun for capture of warship or privateer, replaced by Head Money in 1708

Head Money prize bounty of £5 per head paid by the exchequer to Royal Naval warships based on persons alive at the beginning of an engagement on board vessels captured, burnt or driven on shore

impost a tax or other compulsory payment

in the premises 'taking into consideration all that has herein above been stated'

inhibition injunction

Inn of Court a College of Barristers empowered to call its members to the Bar, thereby conferring on them the right of audience in the higher courts. The four Inns are: Lincoln's Inn, the Inner and Middle Temples, and Gray's Inn

Instance Court a court empowered to try civil cases at first instance, such as the Admiralty Court or Vice Admiralty Court

interlocutory decree given during the course of a case being provisional on some other event, not the final judgement

interrogatory written (not oral) evidence obtained from questions in writing put to a witness

intimation act of making something known

Judge below Judge in Vice Admiralty Court

letter of marque a legal instrument issued by a state authorising a privateer to seize and bring in enemy property or contraband

libel the original claim in prize proceedings of the libellant asserting rights to the prize

liquidation to wind up the affairs of a company by ascertaining liabilities and apportioning assets

made post promoted from master and commander to captain in the Royal Navy. Seniority in the service was determined by the date on which the officer was 'made post'

manifest to make clear to the eye or the understanding

manifest (ship's) particulars of a ship's cargo

moiety each of the two parts into which a thing is divided

monition notice brought by the captor of the seizure of ship as prize, warning all interested parties to attend court and show why it should not be condemned as prize

navy agent a person who advanced money to seamen and officers against the eventual payment of wages or outcome of such prize claims as they might have

nullity something of no legal force or validity

order in Council a regulation issued by the sovereign on the advice of the Privy Council

oyer and terminer a commission issued to judges on a circuit to hold courts

petition application to a court for a writ

petition for desertion request, usually by defendant, that the action be abandoned

pipe office the pipe rolls recorded government income and expenditure

porrect to put forward a file for examination or correction at a later date

prejudice harm or injury that may result from some action

presents by this document

privateer an armed vessel owned and manned by private individuals holding a government commission and authority by a letter of marque to take prizes on the terms set out by the commission

prize ship or goods legally captured in time of war

prize agent the agent for a captor in a prize suit, whose duties were regulated by statute

prize jurisdiction civil trials heard by the court to establish whether or not a captured ship had been lawfully seized and what should happen to it and its contents

proctor a person managing causes in a court administering civil or canon law, the eighteenth-century equivalent in the civil courts of a solicitor

prohibition decree from a superior court to prevent another court from trying an action, as being outside its jurisdiction

quietus residue, remainder

ransomer individual held as hostage by the captor until payment was made for the ship that had been released on ransom

recall distribution of prize money to those who had missed the initial distribution

relaxed a partial remission or relaxation of a penalty

release remit a debt; deliver or liberate from a restriction

remembrancer the Sovereign's Remembrancer kept records of taxes, paid and unpaid

remission means by which a case is sent back to a lower court from which it was appealed for further findings of fact etc.

reprisal the act of taking a captured ship or more generally a war-like act outside of hostilities as a means of righting wrongs

restitution restoration of property previously taken away or surrendered

restore give back to the original owner

reverse change to the opposite decision

salvage reward paid to persons (salvors) who have saved a vessel or her cargo

schedule list of intended times

sea-brief a permission from a neutral state to the master to proceed on a certain voyage specifying the master's name and residence; the name, property, description, tonnage and destination of the ship; the nature and quantity of the cargo; the place from whence it comes, and its destination, together with such other matters as the practice of the place requires

sentence a decision of a law court

spoil goods taken from an enemy in time of war

surrogate a person appointed to act for another

tare allowance made for the weight of packaging

tare and tret arithmetical rule for computing a tare

tartan lateen-sailed single-masted fast ship used in the Mediterranean

turn-back having read the captain's letter, the secretary to the Admiralty turned back the corner of the letter and scribbled his reply there for the clerks to formulate an official response for his signature

Introduction

This is an investigation into an element of naval history which took place nearly three hundred years ago. It arose out of a study made of the thirty-seven men 'made post' or promoted to the rank of captain in 1757, just after the declaration of war between Britain and France. More than six thousand letters were written by these men to the Admiralty during their careers, and these were photographed and transcribed. These letters brought closer their hopes and fears, their triumphs and tragedies, their successes and failures. Although the letters were very formulaic, the characters and personalities of the writers became familiar. A great deal was learned about the strengths and weaknesses of 'the service', as it was known to those whose voices were recorded.

It was also clear that the officer corps from which the tranche was drawn had been created by changes brought about by administrators such as Samuel Pepys. In the seventeenth century, gentlemen who went to sea were not professionals – until Pepys's introduction of a passing certificate made certain that every lieutenant was professionally qualified. Pepys went further:

> Were it not to be wished that the seaman's trade be made so honourable and profitable that not only the younger brothers of England might be encouraged to seek their fortunes that way … but that even the elder might esteem it for the dignity of it.[1]

Officers' pay rates were established in 1700 and remained unchanged throughout the eighteenth century, until the mutinies of the fleet in the 1790s changed the way the Royal Navy was paid. Officers were paid by the day: admirals who were also commander-in-chief £5, admirals £3 10s, vice admirals £2 10s, rear admirals £1 15s. The young captains of my tranche earned six shillings a day, at a time when most of 'the people' on board earned less than £1 a calendar month.[2] Captains were paid at least one year in arrears, when their

1 J.R. Tanner, *Samuel Pepys's Naval Minutes* (Navy Records Society, 1926), 405–6.

2 Comparable pay rates today for an admiral £150,000 (£410 per day), a captain £110,000 (£300 per day) and an ordinary seaman £18,000 (£50 per day) when the currency was pounds, shillings and pence, with twelve pence in a shilling, and twenty shillings in a pound.

books had been passed, and the sailors were also often owed up to two years of pay.[3] As prize money was paid within weeks, not years, it was clear that there was an incentive to take prizes, and that these were taken by 'captains who managed to be in the right place, at the right time, with the right sort of ship, and the right set of instructions'.[4]

When they had triumphed over their adversaries, what happened next? What happened once their prizes had been brought into port? There was no simple solution to these questions. Nearly 8,000 further documents were located and identified as being worth transcribing, and gradually the picture became clearer. As databases were built up from the records, familiar names were recognised from time to time. Some of original tranche did themselves proud, others achieved nothing – but that is to be expected in a sample. One captain, John Lockhart, had to become an honorary member of the tranche as he featured in the story so often.

There are still gaps. Pages of some of the records are missing. Entire classes of documents were culled early in the twentieth century. Photographing some of the original documents was almost impossible because of their condition. But enough of the facts emerged for me to realise that this was a story worth telling. The naval prizes of the Seven Years' War had not been written about before, for good reason. It was not easy to uncover the facts. Admiral Richard Hill had written the definitive book on prizes of the Napoleonic War, as he followed in the footsteps of Lord Stowell at the Middle Temple and was able to use Stowell's notes on his decisions to show the way. I was not so fortunate. Sir Thomas Salusbury, Judge of the High Court of Admiralty throughout my period, was a very undistinguished man who left no hint of his reasoning for or against declaring a capture a legitimate prize. But there is more to the story than the final judgement, as I discovered to my delight.

Once the capture of the prize had been achieved, most of the rest of the action took place in Doctors Commons, with the final scene located in the dining room beside it. Illustrated in Chapter 5 (see Figure 4), this location will become familiar. The legal vocabulary of the proctors has to be embraced, and there can be no escape from a world which is very far from our own. To help with this, a glossary has been provided. The reader will be immersed in this very different word-bound world. The original documents, which have been used throughout, use spelling which is close to but not the same as our own, and the original spelling has been retained. Much of this legal world, whose vocabulary is arcane, might cause an unsuspecting reader to baulk at unfamiliarity. Uncomfortable or not, it is worth persevering.

3 Joseph Peyton asked for wages for his men to be paid. They were deliberately two years in arrears to reduce desertion. His men were paid wages to December 1754 before he left dock May 1756. TNA ADM 1/2293 Captains' Letters P 1757–58 Peyton 23 May 1756.

4 Daniel Baugh, *British Naval Administration in the Age of Walpole* (Princeton, 1965), 115.

There was social benefit in the fact that the wealth which resulted in total from the naval prizes of these years was spread amongst the thousands of officers and 'the people' in the navy. Some individuals received a great deal more than others. Thanks to the generosity and foresight of Queen Anne in her Act of 1708, the benefit was to the country rather than the Crown, and with wonderful success achieved its intention of boosting morale in the Royal Navy, and its provisions were unchanged for a century.[5] Head Money was designed to encourage captains to attack ships of force and not just merchantmen.[6] The result of this initiative was that by the end of the Seven Years' War nearly 75,000 French naval personnel had been taken off the sea. This will be discussed in later chapters. The financial cost of this to the Treasury of £374,940 indicates the degree to which the state supported the navy's endeavours.[7]

The legal framework also made clear the penalties for fraud. Any financial transaction could provide opportunities for fraud, and the authorities did their best to make certain that all those taking part had certainty about the benefits to which they were entitled, and the costs if absolute honesty was not observed. The substantial bond which agents had to deposit before undertaking responsibility for the captors' money is an example of this. The regulations also required agents' proceedings to be timely, again with financial penalties if they held on to money, perhaps for their own use. An example of each of the necessary legal documents is included in the Appendices.

The *London Gazette* was the official organ of the government. Other newspapers and periodicals of the period were also a means whereby ordinary people could become aware of the momentous happenings at sea. Those who could not read would be told the details, and the relatively small amounts of prize money due to 'the people' or their relatives would be eagerly pursued. The Secretary to the Admiralty ensured that captures were publicised, listing on the 'turn back' of the captors' letters the titles of newspapers to which extracts of interest would be sent. Readers of the present age will be charmed, both by the official announcements, and by the content of letters from naval officers published by the papers. Researchers will find them invaluable. Scrutiny of the dates of successive publications shows the rapidity with which mail coaches carried news away from London and the south coast to interested readers further north.

The speed with which the legal proceedings were concluded will amaze today's readers. All the legal provisions demanded rapid decisions. Accustomed as I was to the workings of the Admiralty secretariat, this was not a surprise. Lord Sandwich, head of the Admiralty, had promised that if a letter to him

5 N.A.M. Rodger, *Command of the Ocean: A Naval History of Britain, 1649–1815* (Allen Lane, 2004), 524.

6 Baugh, *British Naval Administration*, 142.

7 TNA ADM 43/20. CPI inflation calculator suggests that £1 in 1750 would be worth £278 today. The financial cost to the Treasury today would be over £104 million.

was written on one side of a piece of paper, he would reply the same day. His clerks, living in their cottages in Spring Gardens across the corner of Horse Guards Parade, worked from 10.00 am until the last letter was completed, sometimes as late as 11.15 pm. Urgent orders to Portsmouth or Plymouth were entrusted to dispatch riders, the 'gallopers', the envelopes endorsed with the times at which they changed horses during the night. Captains' letters from Chatham, Sheerness or Deal, written on Monday, were read in London on Tuesday, Sandwich's replies received by them on Wednesday. Is there a government department today which could match that?

Introducing the first volume of his *Law and Custom of the Sea*, Part 1, which covered the period 1205–1648, R.G. Marsden commented that: 'The advance made in the four centuries covered by the documents here collected towards the recognition of a common law and common usages to regulate war and fighting at sea is small, and its progress intermittent.'[8] After Queen Anne's Act, very little changed during the century. The prize records are in a fair state of preservation, and the prize sentences have been carefully filed and indexed. However, they do not throw any light on the growth of prize law, because there was none. Throughout the period they are framed in the same bare and technical terms, and reveal no more than a statement of the condemnation or order for restitution. The regulations surrounding prize didn't change at all.

Secondary sources on the earlier period, such as Baugh's *British Naval Administration*, made clear the importance of prize money, 'the chief attraction of the naval service'. Baugh lists all the evidence that he found from his period: an admiral confiding to a colleague that he has had 'a little pickings'; a young captain yearning to get into a smaller ship 'for the advantage of cruising'; a lucky captain making a fortune overnight; an admiral being almost assured of it. Admiral Anson's captures at Cape Ortegal in 1737 brought in £755,900, of which his share was £63,000, that of his second in command, Sir Peter Warren, £31,500. By the end of this war Anson had amassed £96,000, Warren £48,000.[9] During the period 1744–47 Rodney amassed over £10,000 from his prizes, buying farms and other property in Hampshire: 'the penniless captain had become one of the landed gentry'.[10] Writers about the navy in the eighteenth century had no doubt that 'the hope of prize-money looked large', and 'lucky captains' could make their sailors a fortune. Letters of seamen and officers alike are littered with mentions of prize money paid or prize money

8 R.G. Marsden, *Law and Custom of the Sea*, Vol. II AD 1649–1767 (Navy Records Society, 1916), xxix.

9 Julian Gwyn, *The Enterprising Admiral: The Personal Fortune of Admiral Sir Peter Warren* (McGill-Queen's University Press, 1974), 20. Warren made use of his fortune, lending it at interest and investing it, also at interest. His purchases in the Meon Valley totalled £15,768.

10 David Spinney, *Rodney* (London, 1969), 86–7.

calculated from recent captures.[11] Boscawen wrote to his wife Fanny, 'If these French gentry do not escape me this time, they will pay for the house and furniture too.' A later letter talked of the effect the hope of prize money had on his crew: 'You can't think how keen our men are, the hope of prize money makes them happy, a signal for a sail brings them all on deck.'[12]

Other sources didn't mention prize money at all. William Spavins recounted his experiences at sea capturing prizes in wonderful detail, but never mentions the rewards he would have been entitled to.[13] It has been estimated that 'at an all-round average, prize money brought in to the sailor approximately as much as his naval pay each year'.[14]

There is a feature of the legal world which is at present unresolved. The documents I found made clear the costs of each decision, passed on in due course to the agents for payment before the prize money was distributed. What is not clear is that behind the fees there was another dimension of patronage which involved funds on a large scale. I am indebted to John Ehrman for his insight into the social distinction between fees and a salary. If one charged a fee, one was being properly paid for services rendered. It was considered degrading to take the King's money as a salary, to be employed, to be a dependant with no position of your own. Ehrman quotes the Customs department as being 'less for the collection of revenue than for the collection of favours'.[15] I return to this distinction later.

This book is the result of reading the words of those whose lives were being described. It is 'out of their mouths', not at third hand.

Research such as this focuses on detail. Readers must not lose sight of the big picture, the part played by the navy as a whole during the eighteenth century. Mahan, writing about sea power during this period, concludes:

> The noiseless, steady, exhausting pressure with which sea power acts, cutting off the resources of the enemy while maintaining its own … the overwhelming sea power of England was the determining factor in European history … keeping its own people in prosperity at home, and building up the great empire which is now seen.[16]

[11] Roy and Lesley Adkins, *Jack Tar: The Extraordinary Lives of Ordinary Seamen in Nelson's Navy* (Abacus, 2008), 61, 237.

[12] G.J. Marcus, *Heart of Oak* (Oxford University Press, 1975), 124.

[13] William Spavins, *The Narrative of William Spavins a Chatham Pensioner by himself* (Chatham Publishing, 1998).

[14] Peter Kemp, *The British Sailor: A Social History of the Lower Deck* (London, 1970), 129.

[15] John Ehrman, *The Younger Pitt: The Years of Acclaim* (London, 1969), 174, 176.

[16] Alfred Thayer Mahan, *The Influence of Sea Power upon History 1660–1783* (Boston, 1944), 209.

1

The Legal Framework before 1756

The law of capture at sea probably had its beginnings in the eleventh century in the Mediterranean *Il Consolato del Mare*. This was a code of sea laws compiled by order of the ancient kings of Aragon. Originally written in the dialect of Catalonia, it has since been translated into every language of Europe. By this code, neutral goods in captured enemy ships were restored to their owners, and enemy goods in neutral ships could be seized, although neutral ships and neutral cargoes had to be restored.[1] Encapsulated in this and recognised by all the States of Europe as a common instrument between them, was the question of prize, from the Old French 'prise' meaning 'taken or seized'. In the Atlantic the *Rôles d'Oléron*, perhaps initiated by Eleanor of Aquitaine, were based on the maritime trade in wine from La Rochelle along the Atlantic coast from the end of the twelfth century, and were sanctioned by the immemorial usage and custom of the sea.[2]

The earliest recorded judicial proceedings regarding the legality of capture of foreign goods or vessels took place in 1357, and later proclamations through the centuries repeated the basic principles of legal obligation preserved within the legal system.[3] The laws of the sea were enshrined in *Liber Niger Admiralitatis*, originally in ancient French or Latin. The earliest manuscript version, held in the National Archives, dates from 1450.[4] This was a medieval

[1] D.P. O'Connell, *The Influence of Law on Sea Power* (Manchester, 1975), 19; Reginald G. Marsden, ed., *Law and Custom of the Sea*, Vol. II (Navy Records Society, 1916), 361; Andrew Clapham, 'Booty, Bounty, Blockade and Prize: Time to Reevaluate the Law', *International Law Studies* (Vol. 97 2021), 1219.

[2] Sir Christopher Robinson, *Collectanea Maritima* (White and Butterworth, 1801), iv; this invaluable little book was written in Doctors Commons in 1801 and explains in the postscript that as the 'celebrated Answer to the Prussian memorial delivered on behalf of the British Government A.D. 1753' (discussed in Chapter 2) was already in print in many editions, he had not included it. The book has been made available by Google. Richard Hill, *The Prizes of War: The Naval Prize System in the Napoleonic Wars 1793–1815* (Sutton Publishing, 1998), 5.

[3] Henry J. Bourguignon, *Sir William Scott, Lord Stowell: Judge of the High Court of Admiralty, 1798–1828* (Cambridge University Press, 1987), 10.

[4] Sir Travers Twiss transcribed *The Black Book of the Admiralty* between 1871 and 1876 (TNA HCA 12/1).

code of maritime law and included not just the Rolls of Oléron, but all the most important laws, ordinances, decisions and acts of the High Court of Admiralty. This code emerged as a separate entity probably after the battle of Sluys in 1340. It was established to deal with questions of piracy or spoil, but later developed a jurisdiction in prize, with a civil jurisdiction for such matters as salvage and collision which went back to Roman civil law. Actions could be taken against ships and goods as well as persons. Rule 10 in the Black Book stated:

> In the case of any ship or vessel of the enemy being taken as prize by any ship of our fleet, then the captors shall have for their own use all manner of goods and furniture found above the hatches, or the forecastle or the poop of the said vessels, saving always the ancient customs and usages of the sea.[5]

During the time of Queen Elizabeth, when the taking of foreign ships was a key source of income for the Crown, the laws of the sea justified taking prizes in law. Any prizes taken had to be legally justified. If the fleet met with foreign ships '*making resistence … then it is lawfull … to take them with strong hand*' but without despoiling, rifling or embezzling the goods. Moreover, any maritime case had to be heard by the Judge of the High Court of Admiralty, and could not be disposed of until the Judge had given his verdict. Any ship going after plunder without a licence from the Admiralty would incur 'her Majesties heavy displeasure'.[6]

Role of the Admiralty Court

It was not until 1589, following the Armada, that formal condemnation of prizes by sentence of the Admiralty Court became common, once the Privy Council had ordered that all prizes captured should be brought in for adjudication in the Admiralty Court.[7] Grotius's anonymously published treatises *De Jure Praedae* [On the Law of Spoils] 1604 and *Mare Liberum* [The Free Sea] 1609, on the sea as international territory, became the foundation of prize law which continued to develop throughout the subsequent centuries.[8] Grotius concluded that 'the ship of a neutral nation cannot protect the property of an enemy'.[9]

5 Clapham, 'Booty, Bounty, Blockade and Prize', 1208.

6 Robinson, *Collectanea Maritima*, 29.

7 Reginald G. Marsden, ed., *Law and Custom of the Sea*, Vol. 1 (Navy Records Society, 1915), xxi; Bourguignon, *Sir William Scott*, 9.

8 Andrew Blom, *Hugo Grotius (1583–1645)* (Internet Encyclopedia of Philosophy).

9 Martine Julia van Ittersum, ed., Gwladys Williams and Walter Zeydel, trans., Hugo Grotius, *De Jure Praedae Commentarius* (Liberty Fund, 2005), 68–9; Charles

At the time of the Armada, Spain depended on maritime goods from the Baltic, and the Privy Council urged the Hanseatic towns:

> ... to forbeare to send into Spayne or Portugal any kind of provision fitt for the maintenance of the king of Spayne for his warre against this realm upon paine of confiscation of the same goods and the shippes upon which they should be laden, in case they should be taken with any such warlyke provision by any of her majestie's shippes or of her subjects.[10]

The Dutch were similarly involved in the carrying trade. Charles I used some of the same language about war-like provisions or contraband when his Anglo-Dutch treaty forbade the transport of 'corne, victual, armes, or provision for his shipping, navye, or armes' from the Hanseatic towns, with the warning that their ships would be subjected to 'capture and condemnation as good prize'.[11]

The language used in Article 4 of the Prize Rules of 22 February 1664 is clear and unambiguous:

> ... that where any ship met withall by any of the King's royal navy, or other ship commissioned by his authority, shall fight or make resistance, or the said master or any of her company shall throw, burn, tear or conceal any of the ship's papers or documents, or shall have no papers at all found in the said ship, or shall bring and offer to the Court any false writings for evidence, thereby to clear her or her goods, or any of them, the said ship and goods shall be judged and condemned as good and lawful prize.[12]

If papers had been destroyed or concealed, that was considered conclusive of guilt. In 1672 it was again established that:

> The throwing away of paper is such an indication that they were material to the concerns of the ship and lading, that the proof of the contrary will hardly be admitted, for *cui bono* was the throwing them away, if it were not to save ship or goods, and missive letters are many times great evidences of the condition both of ships and lading.[13]

Jenkinson, *A Discourse on the Conduct of Great Britain with respect to Neutral Nations* (London, 1758).

10 Philip C. Jessup and Francis Deák, 'The Early Development of the Law of Contraband of War II', *Political Science Quarterly* (Vol. 48 no. 1 1933), 62–93.

11 Jessup and Deák, 'Contraband of War II'.

12 Francis Deák and Philip C. Jessup, 'Early Prize Court Procedure' Part 2, *University of Pennsylvania Law Review* (Vol. 82 May 1934), 819.

13 Sir Robert Wiseman in Deák and Jessup, 'Early Prize Court Procedure', 820.

The 1674 Anglo-Dutch Treaty on Commerce and Navigation contained the Article:

> … by which neither side would give aid, favour or council directly or indirectly by Land or by Sea or on fresh waters, nor shall furnish nor consent that the subjects and inhabitants of their Dominions and Countries shall furnish any ships, soldiers, mariners, provisions, money, instruments of war, gun-powder or any other thing necessary for making war, to the enemies of the other party.

The words of the Treaty were in Latin, so accessible to readers in every court of Europe. This Article was then repeated in the subsequent Treaties: James II's Treaty of Windsor, 17 August 1685; William III's Treaty of Whitehall, 14 August 1689; Queen Anne's Treaty of Utrecht, 29 January 1712; George I's Treaty of Westminster, 6 February 1715; George II's Treaty of Westminster, 27 May 1728; George II's Treaty of Vienna, 20 February 1731.[14]

Sir Leoline Jenkins (1625–85) is remembered as one of the most influential experts on prize law. He elucidated the principles and improved the practice of the law. In a letter to Sir Joseph Williamson in 1672 he explained the necessity of hearing from both sides: '… it is against the Law of all Courts, and the Rights of all Nations, not to hear the Party in Judgement before Sentence pass against them'.[15] His decisions as Judge of the Admiralty foreshadow the development of the doctrine of continuous voyage.[16] Jenkins asserted that the maritime character of the case, not its location, should determine Admiralty jurisdiction, but at the time no Act was passed.[17] Jenkins refused to let the government dictate what he considered to be decisions derived from international law. He was often called to the Privy Council to explain the reasons behind his decisions, giving researchers a useful summary of prize law of the period. A letter to him from Samuel Pepys dated 3 April 1675 says: 'I heartily beg your forgiving me the hourly interruptions you thus receive from your most affectionate and obedient servant.'[18]

In 1680 Jenkins advised the Crown that the fundamental maxim of neutrality was that 'a neuter prince being in peace when his neighbours are at war ought not to make the condition of one neighbour better than that of the other'. A neutral ship would in theory have no reason to resist being searched, whereas if

14 Sir James Marriott, *The Case of the Dutch Ships Considered* (London 1758), 18.

15 Deák and Jessup, 'Early Prize Court Procedure' Part 1, 686.

16 David James Llewelfryn Davies, Dictionary of Welsh Biography, https://biography.wales/article/s-JENK-LEO-1625 (accessed 11 September 2024).

17 Bourguignon, *Sir William Scott*, 24.

18 Llewelfryn Davies, 'The Development of Prize Law under Sir Leoline Jenkins', *Transactions of the Grotius Society* (Vol. 21 1935), 149–60.

she fled or resisted, there might be cause for a search. However, the behaviour of belligerent vessels and the outcome of subsequent proceedings in courts of law and the costs involved were hardly such as to allow neutral vessels to submit with confidence.[19]

A total absence of papers was also grounds for condemnation, as was discrepancy between papers and reality:

> The captor of the Swedish vessel *Isle de Hano* sought condemnation on the ground that the master, claiming to be a Swedish subject, was discovered at examination not to speak Swedish and the interrogatories had to be administered to him in Dutch.[20]

Any legal relationship with Holland, impossible during the mid-seventeenth century, was eased by the accession of William and Mary in 1688. On 22 October 1689, Sir Charles Hedges, newly appointed Judge of the High Court of Admiralty, wrote to the second Earl of Nottingham, a member of the Admiralty Board, in regard to an order in Council which demanded the confiscation by the Admiralty of some neutral Hamburg ships and their cargoes, on account of their trading with France, then at war with England:

> The court of Admiralty is a court of justice, and the judge sworn to administer it to the best of his judgment, and is as much obliged to observe the laws of nations, with respect to the municipall laws of the realm as the judges of the court of Westminster are bound to proceed according to statutes and the common law; and if the method prescribed for condemnation be not consonant to the laws of nations, as there is reason to doubt, they being the goods of subjects of allyes, I humbly beg your lordship will be pleased to consider the difficulty that I shall subject myself unto by such proceeding ...[21]

In 1696 the Act for preventing Frauds and Regulating Abuses in the Plantation Trade tightened the restrictions on foreign shipping in the colonial trade. No goods were to be carried to or from the colonies unless in English built ships. The only exceptions were ships which had become English after having been captured and condemned as prizes.[22]

The ancient usage and customs of the sea were under the jurisdiction of the Lord High Admiral's Lieutenant, Deputy General or Judge of the High Court

19 Davies, 'The Development of Prize Law', 149–60.

20 Deák and Jessup, 'Early Prize Court Procedure' Part 2, 833.

21 Deák and Jessup, 'Early Prize Court Procedure' Part 1, 685.

22 Thomas C. Barrow, *Trade and Empire: The British Customs Service in Colonial America 1660–1775* (Harvard University Press, 1967), 53. This provision became even more important in the eighteenth century.

of Admiralty. Under William and Mary and then Queen Anne the principles of protection of trade were reaffirmed, together with the regulation of traffic and escort and the keeping of records.

Neutral ships carrying goods to the enemy could well be Dutch. In the eighteenth century the Anglo-Dutch Treaty provided Dutch ships with a powerful benefit as the Dutch were usually non-combatants, while Britain was usually belligerent. As the century progressed, British merchants watched indignantly as Dutch vessels continued to carry cargoes to France or Spain, enriching all three countries. Nicolas Magens, the great German financier of London, asked in 1755:

> Might not those who fought the battles ask, what signifies our being masters at sea, if we shall not have liberty to stop ships from serving our enemy? And when we examine to the bottom of the thing, it appears very evident, that sea battles are fought not so much to kill people, as to be masters of trade whereby people live; and by stopping their supplies, to compel our enemies in the end to live in friendship with us.[23]

When asked if a ship with a Dutch pass, with fictitious bills of lading on board pretending they were bound for Holland instead of France, could be taken as a prize, Sir George Lee's response was:

> It has been several times determined in the Admiralty Court that a Dutch ship carrying a cargo of enemy's goods from one port to another of the enemy is not privileged by the said Treaty of 1674 and cannot protect the enemy's goods, and the goods have accordingly in such cases been condemned as lawful prize, but the ships have been restored.[24]

The emergence of a separate court of prize law administered by the Admiralty did not take place until late in the seventeenth century, until which there were conflicts of jurisdiction between common law courts and the Admiralty. Under the Commonwealth, special Commissioners were authorised to review and re-examine 'all sentences and proceedings whatsoever in any cause in our Courts of Admiralty concerning all such prizes as have been or shall be taken'.

23 Richard Pares, *Colonial Blockade and Neutral Rights 1739–1763* (Philadelphia, 1975), 181.

24 Reginald G. Marsden, ed., *Reports of Cases Determined by the High Court of Admiralty and upon appeal therefrom together with Extracts from the Books and Records of the High Court of Admiralty and the Court of the Judges Delegates* (William Clowes, 1885), 402.

The exclusive jurisdiction of the Admiralty Courts as to prize nevertheless survived, and the common law courts never encroached on them.[25]

In 1708 Queen Anne brought in what has since been known as the Prize Act. This Act transferred the whole benefit of prize from the Crown to the captor and effectively laid down the behaviour at sea of the navy throughout the eighteenth century. The justification for this is made clear in the title: 'An Act for the better securing the Trade of this Kingdom by Cruisers and Convoys, and for the encouragement of Cruisers'.[26] Queen Anne's advisors confirmed that in addition to the number of ships of war needed to protect home waters and accompany convoys to remote parts, at least 'forty-three ships of war be employed as cruisers in proper stations' in other words, to annoy the enemy. The Act went further into the detail of the deployment of her navy: 'the aforesaid men of war to be careened at least three times a year, or oftner if there shall be occasion'. The Act even laid down how the seamen were to be treated: 'the seamen onboard such cruisers shall not be turned over into any other ships but such only as are appointed for cruising'.[27] The treatment of the seamen will be returned to.

As far as this book is concerned, the kernel is the sixth element, an abridged version of which begins:

> For the better and more effectual encouragement of the sea-service ... if any ship or ships of war, privateer, merchant-ship or other vessel, shall be taken as prize by any of her Majesties ships of war or privateers, and adjudged as lawful prize in any of her Majesties Court of Admiralty, the flag-officer or officers, commander or commanders and other officers, seamen and others, *who shall be actually on board such ship or ships of war, or privateers*, which shall so take such prize or prizes, shall after such condemnation have the sole interest, and property in such prize or prizes, so taken and adjudged, to their own use ... and the whole produce thereof to be divided or distributed among the said officers, seamen and others, according to their respective shares.[28]

Section 8 of this Act, providing Head Money in the form of '£5 for every man which was living on board', will be returned to below.[29]

Every commission issued to commanders of his Majesty's ships contained the words, 'protect the trade and annoy the enemy'. This double injunction underlines the role of the navy as both protector of the trade which was the

25 Edward Stanley Roscoe, *A History of the English Prize Court* (Lloyds, 1924), 87.
26 Robinson, *Collectanea Maritima*, 188.
27 Robinson, *Collectanea Maritima*, 195.
28 Robinson, *Collectanea Maritima*, 198–201.
29 Robinson, *Collectanea Maritima*, 205.

life-blood of the country, and scourge of the enemy. In times of war the navy was inadequate to fulfil both roles, and private ships or 'privateers' were permitted and indeed encouraged to 'annoy the enemy'. The practice of authorising subjects to fit out private vessels for the purpose of annoying the trade of hostile nations was ancient. Privateers are not the subject of this study, but they occur often enough to make this point important.[30]

At the commencement of war, there had to be a proclamation or commission to put the jurisdiction of the Admiralty Court into effect. It directed:

> That the neat proceeds of all prizes, and bounty money for prisoners taken, be divided into eight equal parts; whereof the captain of the man of war who shall be actually on board at the taking of the prize, shall be allowed three eighths. *But in case any prize should be taken by any ship or ships under the command of a flag, the flag officer or officers being actually on board or directing or assisting in the capture, shall have one of the three eighths.*[31]

The result of this proclamation was bitter in-fighting between flag officers. When the War of Austrian Succession broke out in 1740 there was an additional section restricting the rights of flag officers in Jamaica or elsewhere, repeated in the proclamation of 1756. Admiral Boscawen in 1756 commented that 'his quota was an 8th of the whole, the other Admirals get half of that 8th when two, if but one, a third'.[32]

Once a prize had been taken, the rules and regulations followed and every detail of the behaviour of the captors towards the prize, its people and stores was laid down.[33] If a prize was taken into any port, at home or in one of his Majesty's foreign dominions, it had to remain there, without 'breaking bulk' or being unloaded, under the joint care of the collector and controller of customs, or the naval officer of the port, until the final sentence was given in the High Court of Admiralty. Any offender against this regulation risked his share being forfeited to the Royal Hospital at Greenwich.

The Statutes, which are examined later, dictated every move made by the captor:

> After the captor has conducted his prize into port, he, or one of his chief officers, must send as early as possible three or four of the

[30] Thomas Hartwell Horne, ed., *Compendium of the Statute Laws and Regulations of the Court of Admiralty relating to Ships of War, Privateers, Prizes, Re-captures and Prize Money* (London, 1803), 4.

[31] The remaining five eighths went to the officers and men on board. Robinson, *Collectanea Maritima*, 200–1.

[32] Christopher Lloyd, ed., *Naval Miscellany IV* (Navy Records Society, 1952), 224.

[33] 13 Geo.2, c.4 §5. Horne, ed., *Compendium of the Statute Laws*, 25.

> principal officers, including always the master and mate, before the judge to be sworn and examined upon such interrogatories, together with all such papers, passes, sea-briefs, charter-parties, bills of lading, cocketts, letters and other documents and writing as shall be found on board ship.[34]

The captor had to pay one guinea to the person assigned to moor the captured vessel safely, and also pay lights and post charges incurred on account of the prize, these costs also detailed later. The prize was examined and hatches and chests sealed, to ensure bulk was not broken.[35] Books, papers and all writings had to be secured and delivered to the Court of Admiralty with copies of the examinations, translated if necessary.

A prize retaken from the enemy was a recapture, and the recaptured ship and goods had to be restored to the former owner who paid salvage instead of prize, one-eighth part of the value of the ship, vessel, boats and goods. However, if the recaptor was a privateer, one-sixth of the value, without any deduction, was paid to and divided amongst the owner or owners, officers and seamen. If the recapture had been fitted out for war by the enemy it was not restored to previous owners, but was a lawful prize to the captors.[36]

Customs dues had to be paid on any goods or merchandise taken in captured ships.[37] Once costs of capture had also been paid, the 'neat' or net proceeds were divided into eight parts, of which the captain was allowed three eighths, one of which went to the flag officer, if he was entitled to it, as mentioned above. One eighth went to each of the next three divisions: senior officers, warrant officers, petty officers; the final two eighths were divided between everyone else.[38] These details are exemplified in Appendix 12 and the legal framework is discussed further in the following chapters.

Queen Anne's Act of 1708 effectively laid down the behaviour of the navy throughout the eighteenth century, and both the Crown and the Treasury abdicated their rights to share prize money.[39] Once war had been declared, any ship was entitled to capture property *of enemy character.* As this captured property was 'in legal terms a Droit of the Crown', a positive act of the Crown was necessary to grant the proceeds to the captor.[40]

34 22 Geo.2, c.33 stat 2§7.

35 Horne, ed., *Compendium of the Statute Laws*, 27.

36 Horne, ed., *Compendium of the Statute Laws*, 34.

37 Queen Anne specified that the goods thus brought for safe keeping into warehouses on shore had to be locked up with three keys: one kept by the keeper of customs at that port, one by the collector of customs, one by the agent, until the goods were appraised and sold. Robinson, *Collectanea Maritima*, 207.

38 Robinson, *Collectanea Maritima*, 202.

39 Gwyn, *Enterprising Admiral,* 15; 6 Anne, c.13 (1709) and 13 George II, c.4 (1740).

40 Hill, *Prizes of War*, 6.

Head and Gun Money

At the beginning of the century 'Gun Money' had been paid to captors at the rate of £10 per gun, so a fully crewed 74-gun ship brought in £740 to the captors. But this incentive was deemed insufficient. In 1740 'Head Money' introduced a major additional inducement for the navy, so that the 600 members of the enemy's crew – alive at the start of the engagement – each brought in £5 or £3,000 in total. Head Money and how it was established is discussed in more detail in later chapters. In an age when a captain was paid only £100 a year, at least a year in arrears, and an ordinary seaman less than £1 a month, often a year in arrears, the possibility of 'cash in hand', literally brought out to the captor by the agent within weeks of the capture, was a powerful motivating force when opportunity beckoned.[41]

The Treaty of Aix-la-Chapelle, signed on 18 October 1748, brought the War of Austrian Succession to an unconvincing conclusion. The European war had been bitterly fought between Britain, France, the Dutch Republic and Austria, Spain, Modena, Sardinia and Genoa. The preliminary treaty signed between the first three combatants on 30 April 1748 was later signed by the others, who could not afford to continue the war on their own. French finances were as compromised during this war as they were later in the century. By 1755 both the British and the French navies were engaging in hostile and provocative acts, each hoping that the other would overstep the mark. They moved from unconcealed hostility to undeclared and finally to open war. Greedy eyes watched the trade routes which criss-crossed the oceans and made the owners of merchant ships rich, and benefited their governments through customs and taxes.

41 Using the CPI inflation calculator, £100 in 1750 would today be worth £28,000 or £1 would be worth £280. This bounty was paid until the First World War, when it was paid to British submarine crew. Clapham, 'Booty, Bounty, Blockade and Prize', 1214.

2

The Years of Preparation and the Declaration of War 1756

The Bank of England, established on the Dutch pattern in 1694, made possible the loans to the government which financed the war. Millions of pounds were instantly subscribed whenever the bank needed it, at 3½ per cent for a fifteen-year loan.[1] There was no such financial security in France, where the *Marine* suffered from the lack of finance available to the King, who was the ultimate arbiter in the case of Prize appeals. The Admiralty remained averse to spending money to the last, but despite their caution, government funds kept being supported by the public, and the Treasury never ran out of resources. The huge sums dispersed by the Treasury as Head Money were testament to the vigour with which both private and Royal Navy vessels obeyed the injunction to 'protect the trade and annoy the enemy'. Testament, too, to the incentive 'the service' had been given.

Trade between nations created wealth, on which the stability of the government depended. As we have seen, the question as to whether the vigorous activities of protection and annoyance on the ocean were legal or not was addressed by the leading law lords of the day. Insurance was expensive but essential and brokers at Lloyd's were informed of merchant vessels which took themselves out of convoys, and therefore into the hands of French privateers.

The 1753 Report

The Seven Years' War was fought on land as well as at sea. Britain lent money to the King's nephew, Frederick the Great, King of Prussia, to support him during the War of Austrian Succession and the Silesian wars. Frederick withheld payment of interest on this Silesian loan, in reprisal for losses alleged to have been suffered by his subjects at the hands of English privateers.

A report was prepared in 1753 for the King by the solicitor general William Murray, later Earl of Mansfield, on the action of Frederick in withholding payment. It was signed, in addition, by three other eminent law lords: Sir George Lee, Dean of Arches, Judge of the prerogative court of Canterbury and

1 Daniel Baugh, *The Global Seven Years' War 1754–1763* (Pearson, 2011), 273.

the King's advocate; Sir Dudley Ryder, the attorney general; and Dr George Paul, the Admiralty advocate. This document was subsequently circulated amongst the courts of Europe. Murray's *1753 Report of the Law Officers* provided the legal basis which determined the decisions of the Seven Years' War, and referred to cases dating back to the seventeenth century between England and Holland (1668), England and Spain (1667), France and Holland (1697). The report was quoted in every textbook on international law. As late as 1833 it was said to be 'the most celebrated state paper of modern times', and Montesquieu characterised it as 'réponse sans réplique'.[2]

Legal Elements of the 1753 Report

The legal points made were unambiguous. When two powers are at war, they have the right, at sea, to take as prize the ships, goods and effects belonging to each other. The property of an enemy may be taken, but not that of a friend, provided that the friend is not acting on behalf of the enemy. If a friend is carrying the enemy's goods these may be taken as prize, but not the friend's goods. If the enemy is carrying the goods of a friend, these must be restored. Contraband goods which allow the enemy to carry on the war may be taken as prize, as the friend has departed from his neutrality by carrying the contraband goods.

To establish this point, Murray went back to the 1696 Act for preventing Frauds and Regulating Abuses in the Plantation Trade, which tightened the restrictions on foreign shipping in the colonial trade. No goods were to be carried to or from the colonies unless in English built ships. The only exceptions were English ships which had been captured and condemned as prizes.[3]

Judicial proceeding

The old-established laws of the sea provided a means whereby a capture could be declared a lawful prize: there had to be a regular judicial proceeding in a Court of Admiralty, in which the case for both parties was heard, before the prize was declared lawful and could then be disposed of. In court, the law of nations required good faith; therefore every ship must be provided with complete and genuine papers, and the master, at least, should be privy to the truth of the transaction. Murray expected sufficient evidence to acquit or condemn to come from the ship's papers and the preparatory examinations. If the claimant needed more time to send affidavits he must be granted it, but if these couldn't be produced, the ship was presumed to belong to the enemy.

2 Marsden, *Reports of Cases*, Vol. II, 348–74. The document was signed by Geo Lee, G. Paul, D. Ryder, W. Murray, 18 January 1753.

3 Barrow, *Trade and Empire*, 53.

Murray made clear that any ship's papers which were concealed, destroyed, missing or defective could only be considered as part of the neutral's claim to costs and damages if the court were induced to decree restitution on other grounds. The ship's papers alone were enough for the High Court of Admiralty, without intervention by the captor. This made the preliminary scrutiny of the papers the core of the proceedings in court.

Importance of papers

His report also confirmed that if there were contradictions between the testimony of those on board and the papers found in the ship, the judges in the prize court had to decide through their questions where the probability of truth lay. The throwing of papers overboard was already an unquestionable ground of prize. If the ship had been provided with no papers at all for an element of the lading – a rare occurrence – there were clear grounds for condemnation.

The further element of the rule concerned the use of fraudulent papers. Prize courts dealt rigorously with the use of such papers, where 'colouring' was the most frequent device. One neutral was permitted to carry goods to another neutral; if the cargo was contraband, duplicate papers might pretend the destination was neutral. According to the report of 1753, the presumption arising from concealed or destroyed (as also from missing or defective) papers was conclusive only upon the neutral's claim to costs and damages, provided other evidence induced the court to decree restitution.[4]

The Rule of '56

Murray's report was of fundamental importance when the Rule of '56 was being laid down. He appreciated that in time of war belligerents tried to cut off from the enemy the trade with its colonies which provided the national wealth which paid for armies and fleets.[5] The French attempted to maintain their colonial trade by allowing neutrals to carry French colonial goods, bolstering the financial benefits of that trade. This was frustrated by the Rule of '56, an economic weapon which reinforced the interdependence of the navy and commerce as elements of sea power.[6]

Neutral ships

Murray's thinking re-interpreted the seventeenth-century Dutch Treaty, the essence of which had been 'that if a neutral ship traded to a French colony, with all the privileges of a French ship, and is thus adopted and naturalised,

4 Deák and Jessup, 'Early Prize Court Procedure', 821.

5 Bourguignon, *Sir William Scott*, 224; Marsden, *Reports of Cases*, Vol. II, 350; Richard Pares, *War and Trade in the West Indies 1739–1763* (London, 1963), 175–80.

6 Admiral Sir Herbert Richmond, *Statesmen and Sea Power* (Oxford, 1946), 133.

Figure 1. William Murray, Lord Mansfield, by Jean Baptiste van Loo, oil on canvas, circa 1737.

it must be looked upon as a French ship, and is liable to be taken'.[7] It was forbidden for French goods to be transferred to a neutral ship to avoid the Rule, as merely loading cargo onto a neutral vessel for part of the voyage did not create a second, legal voyage.[8] Neutrals could not carry cargo between French colonies and France, and could not carry such cargo to a neutral port, as they had not done so in the past, nor could they indulge in cabotage or coastal trade. But despite this an increasing share of French trade was carried in neutral bottoms.

The Rule could be circumvented by the Dutch by trading with their own West Indian colonies, St Eustatius and Curaçao. If French goods were transhipped in the colonies' ports without going ashore, they were considered to be part of a continuous voyage, and therefore could be condemned.[9] If the presumed neutral vessel had changed its customary route, and had begun to trade with ports which would enable transhipment to an enemy, this broke the rule of continuous voyage. The Rule of '56 could be applied or not as the government required, and if it would suit its interests. Much time was occupied in court establishing if this had taken place.

It was illegal for a neutral in time of war to carry the trade of a belligerent which was closed to the neutral in time of peace. According to the great jurist Sir William Scott, writing at the end of the century, the most important addition to the doctrines of prize law was the Rule of War of 1756 which meant firstly that the enemy cargo aboard a neutral ship was subject to capture, and secondly the doctrine of continuous voyage. This imposed a partial blockade on the enemy's colonial ports, without having to maintain a naval force on station. Trading *with* the enemy was a fair neutral trade of long standing, but trading *for* the enemy meant engaging in newly created avenues.[10]

Because Britain was at war, trading *for* the enemy gave the Dutch an opportunity to benefit. The Dutch alliance had been strongest under William III, but over the years the tendency had been towards the English half of the alliance being the stronger. The Seven Years' War put a great strain on the alliance, as Dutch ships, all nominally neutral, carried naval goods from the Baltic to France. The ships were constantly stopped and searched, and if they were carrying naval goods these were confiscated. The harsh wartime measures were not enough to break the allegiance as both countries exerted themselves to avoid a real rupture. The treaty which had been formed in 1674 was 'quite badly in need both of revision and explanation' but this was something that neither side renegotiated formally. The Dutch convoys did not attempt to force British blockades, and the British devoted real efforts to stop British privateers'

7 Bourguignon, *Sir William Scott*, 226.

8 Bourguignon, *Sir William Scott*, 229.

9 Bourguignon, *Sir William Scott*, 229.

10 Hill, *Prizes of War*, 22.

predations in the Channel. Instead of seizing naval goods from Dutch ships, their cargoes were bought for British use, a solution which was tolerable for all parties except of course for the French. After the Seven Years' War the alliance was no longer anything more than a shell.[11]

Domicile of principals

Murray also made clear that the domicile of the principals of the prize would determine whether it was treated as an enemy or a friend. True domicile meant personal and familial domicile, and could only be established in one place.

Resisting visit and search

In previous centuries a *bona fide* neutral ship with neutral cargo on an innocent voyage had nothing to fear from visit and search. Murray did not include this in his Report of 1753. He did not anticipate that there would be any innocent voyages.

State of war even before declaration

Murray went further. In his view, it was not necessary for war to have been declared to constitute the state of war. However, ships which were in port at the declaration of war were to be exempted from capture. He reaffirmed the three-mile limit of territorial waters.[12] The international nature of prize law procedure was reinforced by the protests which accompanied violations, and over the centuries the legal rules were constantly applied. When war was declared, the protests were from those who wanted to return to the seventeenth-century interpretations, not the new Rule of '56.

International law of belligerent and neutral rights was accepted throughout the seventeenth and eighteenth centuries. Different courts applied the laws of prize court procedure differently, but all followed the same ancient body of law. The differences introduced by William Murray were widely discussed throughout Europe, commented upon by jurists in every country, most agreeing that they were consistent even if not acceptable to the Dutch and the French.[13] In the eyes of the Dutch they enforced harsh wartime measures.[14]

11 G.J.A. Raven and N.A.M. Rodger, eds, *Navies and Armies: The Anglo-Dutch Relationship in War and Peace 1688–1988* (Edinburgh, 1990), 24.

12 Three miles was the limit of artillery, so defined what could be protected from the land.

13 Bourguignon, *Sir William Scott*, 244.

14 Raven and Rodger, *Navies and Armies*, 24.

In September 1756, Lord Hardwicke wrote:

> All the European nations exclude foreigners from their American colonies ... the question is whether England shall suffer [the Dutch and the Danes] to trade thither in time of war, without seizure, when the French themselves will not suffer them to trade thither, in time of peace, on that very account.[15]

This amounted to a statement of international law.

This book will not enter into the vast hinterland of the trade between New York and the French in the Caribbean islands during the war. The Irish traders, a powerful group amongst the New York merchants, who 'displayed a vigorous contempt for British navigation laws', freighted cargoes to the French at the same time as they were outfitting British and colonial troops, as well as victualling the warships of the Royal Navy.[16]

Preparations for war began some time before 1756. Tension between France and Britain broke out into hostilities in the Ohio Valley, where the French built Fort Duquesnes. General Braddock failed to capture it in 1755. This signalled the beginning of reprisal, a limited act of violence where similar or equivalent had already taken place. The threat of the French possession of Louisburg sent Admiral Boscawen to the St Lawrence waterway to interrupt the restocking of the fort. Boscawen waited for the French, but missed the fleet in the prevailing fog. On 8 June 1755 Richard Howe, *Dunkirk* (60), captured the French warship *Alcide* after her captain had called across, asking if the two nations were at war. Despite the red pennant flying from Boscawen's flagship, not far away, Howe twice answered 'At peace, at peace', before unleashing a full broadside which dismasted the ship. The *Lys* was taken a few minutes later.[17] Boscawen confided to his wife Fanny that, 'To begin a war between two great powerful nations without an absolute order or declaration for it now and then gives me some serious thought. Some will abuse me but as it is on the fighting side, more will commend me.' He added, 'Unless we do make prizes of these ships I shall be ruined, and if we do at the old rate I shall get £5,000 and something more.[18] Boscawen failed, took only two ships, and the result was the utmost amount of harm with the least possible good.[19] It was a

15 Pares, *Colonial Blockade*, 197.

16 Thomas M. Truxes, *Defying Empire: Trading with the Enemy in Colonial New York* (Yale University Press, 2008), 7–8.

17 David Syrett, *Admiral Lord Howe a Biography* (Spellmount, 2006), 12; Baugh, *Global Seven Years' War*, 114. *L'Alcide* and *Lys* were both *en flute*: James Pritchard, *Louis XV's Navy 1748–1762* (McGill-Queen's University Press, 2009), 131.

18 Lloyd, ed., *Naval Miscellany IV*, 166 and 189.

19 Julian S. Corbett, *England in the Seven Years' War*, Vol. 1 (Greenhill, 1992), 58.

bitter disappointment to Boscawen and to the Admiralty that he was not able to capture enough to provoke the French into declaring war.

Admiral Thomas Smith was appointed as commander-in-chief to the Downs station, and sixty-four vessels were brought in by his squadron, as detailed below. Hawke was cruising between Ushant and Cape Finisterre, prepared to take everything he saw, when orders went out to the Channel Fleet to capture every French ship.[20] On 23 August 1755 Hawke received additional secret instructions that he was to divide his squadron to enable him to seize all French vessels entering the Channel or the Bay of Biscay.[21] In response to 'farther hostile preparations of the French, particularly against these kingdoms', orders went out to English ships of war on 27 September 1755 that all French ships encountered were to be taken.[22] In six months about 350 vessels and 7,500 seamen were seized.[23] Despite this provocation, the formal declaration of war was not made for another six months.

On the same day that he opened his secret instructions, Hawke drew up and signed an agreement with the captains in his squadron that they would share the profits from their capture of French vessels, the text of which is shown in Chapter 5. The order from the Admiralty was recorded in Augustus Hervey's journal in 1755:

> by these ships I received orders dated 27 August from the Admiralty to seize all French ships and send them to some British port. (This is a bold but very wrong, injudicious and impudent step of Lord Holland's, and will one day or other be a precedent for a stroke that will cost us very dear).[24]

His comment was typical of the man, who always knew better, but was in this event proved wrong.

Falmouth and *Colchester* of Boscawen's Western squadron were also active. James Kirk, *Lynn* (40), was on convoy duty to North America when he captured *L'Adryade* off Newfoundland. This capture was of interest as the first leg of her voyage had been to the coast of Guinea, where 280 slaves were bought. She was laden with the usual cargo of sugar, coffee and indigo from Cape François when intercepted *en route* to Nantes.

20 Ruddock Mackay, *The Hawke Papers: A Selection 1743–1771* (Navy Records Society, 1990), 123–4.

21 Mackay, *Hawke Papers*, 125.

22 TNA ADM 1/2009 Captains' Letters K 1751–56 Thomas Knackston 9 October 1755.

23 Hugh Boscawen, *The Capture of Louisbourg 1758* (University of Oklahoma Press, 2011), 10.

24 David Erskine, *Augustus Hervey's Journal* (Chatham, 2002), 185.

Two of the early captures were reported in the *London Gazette*:

> *Orford* arrived at Plymouth 16 April being sent in by Sir Edward Hawke with two French ships taken off Cape Ortegal by the *Newcastle*, one of them of 14 guns and 57 men and having 183 soldiers on board bound to Cape Breton; the other a schooner bound to Quebec with wine, musket balls and flower.[25]

> *Chichester* Captain Brett, is arrived at Plymouth and brought in with him a French ship for Mississippi with a quantity of arms and ordnance stores, 140 soldiers and 30 women, which was taken by *Harwich*, Capt. Rowley.[26]

The Cranbrook Commission

On 14 August George II set up a commission of fourteen experienced men to oversee the sale of the French prizes taken before the declaration of war: George Aufrère, Robert Featherstonhaugh, George Wombwell, John Barker, Timothy Brett, Robert Wilson, Henry Saxby, Albert Nesbitt, John Clevland the younger, John Eames and John Gwilt, together with Bartholomew Burton, Nicholas Linwood and Samuel Touchet Esq, were appointed as the King's Commissioners. To reward them for their trouble, care and expenses:

> … and for the service and expenses of any person employed under them and for the whole charge of executing the said Commission, an allowance after the rate of two pounds and ten shillings for every one hundred pounds of the net produce of such sales, to be equally divided and distributed amongst them.

The document listed the various expenses likely to be incurred by the members of the Commission, from brokerage, lighterage, wharfage, cooperage, storehouse room and incidental expenses. It made the point that no 'merchant of credit' would undertake such a commission on less than 2½ per cent of the net proceeds. The members of the Commission waived any demand for their own expenses. All goods, wares and merchandises were liable to the normal customs, duties and impositions as if they had been legally brought into the country. If commissioners were forced to travel widely to attend sales, the necessary number of attendant commissioners was reduced to three.[27]

25 *London Gazette* (LG) issue no. 9575 17 April 1756.

26 LG issue no. 9584 18 May 1756.

27 T/54 Treasury warrant 35–8. The Commission was updated by the King's grandson George III on 12 March 1762, but the final accounting of this Commission was not completed until 15 December 1764, accepted by the Treasury 4 August 1768, and on 7 January 1769, the beautifully scribed documents were presented to the Treasury.

The Commission was appointed for the express purpose of legitimising, securing and selling the prizes taken in this period, and receiving and accounting for the proceeds, which were Droits of the Crown (because they were taken before the declaration of war). The Commission had to work fast to legalise the seizure of so many French vessels. Once war had been declared, the proceeds went to the captors, so the business of the Commission was brief but controversial, causing numerous problems for the Treasury to which the Commission was responsible.[28] In 1761 the Commission was able to lend the public £630,000 from the prize revenue, and at the conclusion of the war the King transferred all proceeds to the public.[29]

The prisoners who had been captured before the outbreak of war were confined to the manor house of Sissinghurst. Leased in 1756, the building housed 1,000 prisoners until 1763, when it was evacuated at the Peace of Paris. The site of Sissinghurst explains why the committee that met to make decisions about the prisoners and their vessels was called the Cranbrook Commission, Sissinghurst being alongside the village of that name.

The first sixty-four captures from the French were made in September and October 1755, most off the coast of Normandy, some only a few miles off Dungeness, and brought in by *Roebuck*, *Centaur*, *Cruiser* or *Oxford* amongst others of Vice Admiral Thomas Smith's Downs squadron. The records of these captures and the interrogations of the French prisoners of war can be seen in the National Archives.[30] Of these vessels, forty were French coasting vessels, nine were bringing goods to or from Newfoundland, part of the fishing fleet there. Two vessels came from each of Russia and the West Indies, one was a fishing boat and was trading with England. One ship, *Les Deux Soeurs*, was of interest in that she was one-third owned in Holland, and when her contents were sold, one third was returned to Holland. I will return to the prisoners of war and the work of the Commission in the Conclusion.

The enemy could be weakened by capturing his vessels, and neutral ones, at sea anywhere. Denying the French *Marine* the seamen who were now prisoners of war was deliberate. In total this attack on French shipping, during 1755, resulting in 'terrible losses', brought in some 7,500 sailors and apprentices, more than half of them trained seamen.[31] On board the ships captured by Vice Admiral Smith's squadron were 655 men together with 115 passengers from Newfoundland on board *La Louise*, presumably workers in the fish processing station there. The cargoes carried by the other ships were almost immaterial: many of the ships were very small fishing vessels, and their cargoes of fish

28 Dora Mae Clark, *The Rise of the British Treasury: Colonial Administration of the Eighteenth Century* (Yale University Press, 1960), 104.

29 Clark, *British Treasury*, 105.

30 TNA HCA 32/259/1–64.

31 Jonathan R. Dull, *The French Navy and the Seven Years' War* (Nebraska, 2005), 38.

were not crucial. Ten however carried fish from Newfoundland, and this would have resulted in empty larders in Brittany. The salt carried by a further five small vessels would have made preserving more food possible, but in very small quantities.

The situation in North America where the French supported their Indian allies against the English was paralleled in the East Indies where the East India Company required more and more support against the trading forces of the French. Louisburg was a touchstone in North America: as part of the Treaty of Aix-la-Chapelle, France exchanged Louisburg for evacuation of the Low Countries. France also returned the trading post of Madras, which left the colonists feeling indignant and betrayed.[32]

By the end of the year more than three hundred trading vessels had been captured, together with over seven thousand seamen, fifteen per cent of those registered for naval service – enough to man nearly ten ships of the line.[33] The captures were taken into Gibraltar, Barbados, the Leeward Islands, Jamaica and South Carolina, for none of which are records easily available. A corresponding number of English vessels were lost, all reported in the *London Gazette* or *Lloyds List*. However, both sides recognised that war was only a matter of time, and the Admiralty set about preparing as many vessels as possible for war. Every commission carried the same message: 'protect the trade and annoy the enemy', although war had still not been declared. These early captures did not open the floodgates to indiscriminate piracy at sea, however.

The Diplomatic Revolution of 1756 rearranged European allegiances, but did not solve the situations in North America or the East Indies. Political tensions were high, and the European re-alignment which saw Maria Theresa of Austria sign the Treaty of Versailles with Louis XV also saw Russia and Sweden enter the war against Prussia. As these were important sources of naval goods, this was a blow to the English navy which relied on the Baltic states for timber for masts.

Declaration of War 1756

The declaration of war which took place in May 1756 opened the global war which was concluded in 1763 with the negotiation of peace in the Treaty of Paris. Although there had been a period of undeclared war for at least a year, the French attacks on English territory in America brought closer the official declaration of war, activated the force of law and advised British subjects and neutrals about their conduct at sea, thus making it subject to international

32 Boscawen, *Capture of Louisburg*, 7

33 Boscawen, *Capture of Louisburg*, 10.

law.[34] The French made noisy demonstrations that an attack on England was being planned, resulting in English forces being concentrated in the Channel. The Mediterranean was left uncontested against the French who used their naval resources in Toulon to capture Minorca, despite the poorly resourced Admiral Byng's efforts to protect the island.[35]

The Act of Parliament which determined the activities of the High Court of Admiralty was entitled '*An Act for the encouragement of seamen, and the more speedy and effectual manning of his Majesty's navy*', and begins:

> Whereas the unwarrantable hostilities begun by the French have necessarily engaged his Majesty in actual war with the French King in defence of his subjects and the rights and possession of his crown; and whereas his Majesty has been pleased to notify the same by proclamation, and a public declaration thereof, on the seventeenth day of May in the year of our lord one thousand seven hundred and fifty six ...[36]

The Act was intended to encourage not just every person at sea in the navy, but also those interested in private enterprise. British seamen employed abroad were encouraged to return to service in the English merchant service. Once it had been declared lawful prize, the property of the French king became a benefit to the naval personnel who had captured it. They had the right to shares, in carefully laid down proportions. Letters of marque were to be issued to privateers, in return for ten per cent of their takings. As usual, the Act was published in the *London Gazette*, which carried the announcement on 8 June 1756. The text lays the blame squarely on the shoulders of the French, whose 'unwarrantable proceedings ... usurpations ... and encroachments ... have been so notorious and so frequent' that war had to be declared. All persons 'of what nation soever' were warned not to transport contraband goods to any French territory as the ships doing so 'shall be condemned as good and lawful prize'.[37]

Taking prizes was not piracy if it was legitimised by Parliament, and if the strictly detailed provisions were adhered to. The lengthy text which follows was intended as the legal framework for the navy during the years of warfare, and repays careful reading. It was published in the *London Gazette* on 6 July 1756 and would have been closely scrutinised by anyone with an interest in the navy. It is reproduced as Appendix 1.

34 Pares, *Colonial Blockade*, 92.

35 Mahan, *Influence of Sea Power*, 284–5.

36 29 Geo.2. Naval Prizes Act c.34.

37 LG issue no. 9583 15 May 1756.

Privateers

This announcement was immediately followed by a notice from the Admiralty which opened the naval war to private enterprise as well. Private individuals who were prepared to fit out vessels could be issued with letters of marque entitling them to undertake 'reprizals' against the ships, goods and subjects of France.[38] This study does not examine the role of privateers in the war, but they were an important adjunct to the ships of the Royal Navy, and on one or two occasions there were joint actions. The privateers played their part in harassing the French, but were constrained by financial penalties if they stepped over the line into piracy. The securities they had to hand over in return for a letter of marque were substantial, amounting to £1,500 as surety for good behaviour. Queen Anne's innovation saw all captors receiving the entire value of their prizes. One result was to encourage privateering – there were more Bristol privateers in this war than in any earlier.

Proclamation of Prize Act

Repeating the words used earlier 'for the encouragement of seamen', the Prize Act reaffirmed that the benefits of taking prizes were to go directly to those who carried out the capture. Once this had been declared lawful prize, the captors were the sole beneficiaries of 'interest and property of and in all and every ship, vessel, goods and merchandise' taken from the French. As a further encouragement, the Treasury would pay Head Money, five pounds for every man alive on board a French vessel taken from the enemy at the start of the engagement. The Act went on to give the procedure by which this was to be established. Finally, the distribution of 'neat produce' from prizes and Head Money was stipulated, with every category of those on board included in the distribution of eight equal parts, as already described.

The captains were responsible for ensuring that accurate lists of the men and their 'qualities' were transmitted to the Commissioners of the Navy so that the bonuses could be distributed appropriately. There was also further instruction on the shares due to flag officers if there were more than one, and the right of commodores with captains under them, to one eighth of a share.

The other official publication which received wide distribution was the Articles of War. These were regularly read on board every naval ship to the assembled company, so were familiar to every man employed at sea. They were first used in the 1650s and amended by Act of Parliament in 1749. An amendment had been intended to apply naval discipline to officers on half pay, but furious opposition took this clause out. The court martial of Admiral Byng was under the twelfth Article, whereby he was convicted of 'failing to

38 LG issue no. 9590 8 June 1756.

do his utmost' to destroy the enemy.[39] The full text can be read at Appendix 2, and again repays close attention.

For the purposes of this study three Articles are directly concerned with prize taking or 'annoying the enemy'; Article 7 requires the sending on shore all papers found aboard prize ships; Article 8 forbids taking effects out of any prize before it is condemned; Article 9 forbids stripping or ill-using persons taken onboard a prize.

Five Articles are concerned with 'protecting the trade': Article 10 demands proper preparation for fight and the encouragement of the men in action; Article 11 warns everyone in the fleet to obey orders in time of battle; Article 12 warns against disobeying orders in time of action; Article 13 warns against not pursuing the enemy and not helping friends; Article 17 instructs the navy to take care of the merchant ships in convoys.

As Daniel Baugh put it, naval officers still carried something of the zest for plunder and prize money which made their Elizabethan forebears so formidable at sea. By the eighteenth century the control of the authorities was such that strategic requirements, or naval warfare, could – just – be contained alongside a natural ambition to found an estate.[40] Officers in the course of their duties had to be aware constantly of the need to stay on the right side of the law. Keeping the merchants protected was vitally important, as the merchants paid the taxes without which the war could not be fought. It was the merchants of Bristol who paid for the building of the *Milford* (28) in which Robert Man was killed in action, protecting the trade from the Bristol Channel from the French privateers lurking in the Atlantic.

As mentioned earlier, on 2 July 1755 Admiral Hawke had been sent secret instructions by Lord Anson. After listing the French attacks on British possessions in North America and elsewhere which formed the background to the decision, Hawke was directed to seize all French vessels entering the Channel or the Bay of Biscay as 'our Channel will be full of their privateers'. He was particularly asked to keep Anson aware of where he was, 'that I may send you the earliest notice if we have any accounts at the Admiralty of the French having begun the war with us'.[41]

Once war was declared, every captain received a directive from the Admiralty:

> Herewith you will receive a copy of His Majesty's Declaration of War against France, and you are hereby required and directed to publish the same by causing it to be read to your ships company and in consequence of the said declaration, you are to act in a hostile manner

39 N.A.M. Rodger, *Articles of War 1661, 1749 and 1866* (Mason, 1982), 22–8.

40 Baugh, *Naval Administration*, 112.

41 Mackay, *Hawke Papers*, 125.

> against the French King and his subjects by taking, sinking burning or otherwise destroying all ships of war or vessels belonging to the said French King or his subjects and by annoying or destroying them in the best manner you are able.[42]

Having prepared as carefully as possible for the war with France, the active captains of the Royal Navy went into action.

42 TNA AO ADM Admiralty out letters.

3

The Appointment of Prize Agents

Members of the eighteenth-century navy were accustomed to using agents. Officers were paid a year or more in arrears, and their crews were also often kept waiting even longer for their wages. There had to be a mechanism, at every level within the vessel, for keeping families, households or estates solvent. Mariners at all levels appointed agents to work for them on shore, whether or not they were in the additional capacity of prize agent. Acting for another in business was a profession in its own right. Naval agents collected wages or half-pay; bought for ready cash the 'tickets' which entitled the possessor to collect pay in the future; lent money to the wives of crew members and kept track of where the ships and their crews were. The captains' agents communicated to their clients if a problem had occurred with passing accounts through the Navy Board, for instance.[1] The young captain John Elliot explained to his family that he needed to have credit advanced him when he was sent to the Mediterranean:

> … I have some time ago appointed Innes and Clerk my agents in the city so if you think it proper to give me a credit on them or Messrs Campbell and Coutts the bankers in the Strand or in what other manner you propose … they have had a great deal of trouble about my wages etc when I was in the India Service and since I've been in the Navy and have served me well.[2]

In this case Innes and Clerk had financed the young man in expectation of his receiving the pay due to him from the Navy Board: they were acting as unofficial bankers, and providing an essential service to the navy while doing so. These agents were useful in wartime as well, when prize money might be anticipated. On many occasions when prize money was to be distributed the recipients were no longer close at hand, and the naval agent had to act as advocate or deputy, as explained in Chapter 10. Such agents were not, however, the prize agents, whose roles were complex and specifically tuned to making money out of captured vessels.

1 TNA ADM 1/2113 Captains' Letters M 1761 Man 10 June 1761.

2 NMM E/400 Elliot's letter to his father 6 January 1757 and to his aunt Mrs Murray 5 February 1757.

The Appointment of a Prize Agent

Taking an enemy's ships necessitated the appointment of a prize agent or agents to act for the captors once the vessel had been secured, and the process of claiming a prize started. At every level, officers and their crews had to have help in collecting their prize money, as they were often at sea when the agents had money to distribute. A licensed navy agent had to secure two other bondsmen, usually local tradesmen, for £200, before he could accept Prize Orders from seamen as a means of deferring payment for goods.[3] The formal Power of Attorney drawn up by the captain and signed by him and his entire crew either anticipated future captures or gave the name of the captured ship and its master. In the eighteenth century tax was paid on every legal document in the form of stamp duty. The stamp was not a separate piece of paper, the document itself was embossed with its value, a press having been applied to a corner of the paper showing the value of tax paid. The authorities stipulated that the stamp duty on this legal document was not more than one shilling – usually shown by two imprints of VI pence – and there was a form of words used when the agreement was drawn up in Guernsey, for example, where stamped paper was not used: 'signed, sealed and delivered in the presence of us where no stampt paper is to be had'.[4] The successful ship would continue with its commission, but not before the all-important document had been drawn up and signed by the entire company of the vessel which took the prize. There was always provision for members of the crew to add their names later, if they had been detached for some reason, such as taking the prize in to a safe port. An example of the text of this vital form can be read in Appendix 3.

The form of words which made it possible for the prize agent to operate on behalf of a captain and his crew varied slightly, but the originals of this formal document were ornamented with dozens of tiny blobs of red sealing wax, each next to the signature or the mark of the officers and men in the crew. The vital documents appointing prize agents are in the National Archives (TNA) in HCA 30. Looking at the original documents covers the researcher in tiny fragments of sealing wax, and brings home the circumstances in which each man on board would have approached a table covered in one of the huge sheets of parchment, with a candle burning to melt the wax. There were always a few men on board who could not sign their own names, whose presence is recorded with a 'John Smith his mark' entry. This happened most frequently on the first or second rate vessels which were most likely to have a large proportion of pressed landmen on board.

3 Geoffrey L. Green, *The Royal Navy and Anglo-Jewry 1740–1820* (Geoffrey Green, 1989), 181.

4 TNA HCA 30/16 70.

The Responsibilities of Prize Agents

It was very unusual for a prize agent to work on his own, as there was so much to do, most of it some distance from London. The prize agents carried enormous responsibility. As soon as the captured vessel was safely in Plymouth or Portsmouth, for instance, the sequence of duties began. The French officers and men were transferred to secure accommodation in the hands of the civilian authorities, and the three most senior officials interrogated, following the specified set list of questions, exemplified in Appendix 5. The vessel had to be secured and battened down against pilfering, and moored safely, with a team of watchmen. Local Customs officials had to be alerted if the vessel was a merchant ship carrying goods on which customs could be charged. Nothing could be done until the ship was declared a prize, so one of the team of agents became the captor's legal representative, called a proctor or advocate, and took on the responsibility of an appearance in court. Once the prize declaration had been made, then another of the team of prize agents could sell the ship, its cargo, furniture and fittings, for the financial advantage of the captor. The money which accrued from the various sales had to be banked for safe keeping (and to earn interest) until it was distributed. The agents had to be available to pay delayed distributions to individuals for three years after condemnation before the final reckoning to Greenwich Hospital. These stages are exemplified below.

Once the Crown gave up its interest in prize money in 1708 there was no longer any official supervision of prize agents. These were individuals occupied in a range of employments, who took on the role of agent in addition to other enterprises. They were usually part of a widespread naval web, so all had administrative and financial skills in common. Flag officers expected their secretaries to collect their share of prize money from the squadron's prize taking, as they would have known all the squadron's captains. Checking agents was impossible for the High Court of Admiralty or Greenwich Hospital to take on. Overcharging was easy and impossible to check. Captains had to keep an eye on what agents were doing, while ordinary seamen would have little opportunity of doing so.[5]

The Power of Attorney appointed the prize agent or agents responsible for all the work entailed in bringing about a successful distribution of prize money to the officers and crew. The prize money was the net or 'neat' result after paying out the many disbursements from the total income including the Head Money, bounty money, salvage money, sale of the ship and her 'tackle guns, apparel and furniture'. The first disbursement specified was the five per cent retained by the agent, but the costs, charges and expenses went on and on.

5 Tony Gutridge, 'Aspects of Naval Prize Agency 1793–1815', *Mariner's Mirror* (Society for Nautical Research, 1994), 46.

The prize agents came from a wide range of backgrounds, and were all accustomed to handling money. Of the hundreds listed in the surviving Power of Attorney documents, many had links with the navy in that fathers or brothers were commissioned officers. Admiral Henry Harrison and his son Captain Thomas Harrison used John Harrison, son and brother respectively. John Adcock was the purser of *Juno* (32), St Alban Roy purser of *Unicorn* (28) and Charles Hay purser of *Royal George* (100), which meant the appointment of a deputy who would go to sea instead. Earlier in the century Richard Drakeford had been purser in several ships before abandoning the sea and becoming a prize agent.

John Elliot always referred to his agents Innes and Clerk as his 'trusty friends'.[6] Admiral Charles Knowles appointed 'my friend' Samuel Touchet of London.[7] It was unexceptional that the men so appointed were merchants like Innes and Clerk of London, watchmakers like John Elliot of Plymouth and his son Walter 'of the same place', presumably also a businessman. John Bayne acted for Captain William Bayne, from Messrs Bayne and Adam's house, in York Street, St James's Square – then and now, a very prestigious address. Henry Casamajor of Bristol was a leading businessman. Mrs Sarah Nicholson was a merchant in Bush Lane, Cannon Street, London. Orlando Manley was a goldsmith in Plymouth, and was also used as an interpreter when French prisoners were being interrogated there.

Notifications in the *London Gazette* which had to accompany all distributions of prize money not carried out on board always included the address at which this would take place. Francis Baxter operated from Bond Court, Walbrook; James Dickson lived in Golden Square; John Hay lived in Chelsea; William Innes, Thomas Clerk and Co. operated in Lime Street Square; John Mackey worked from Princes Street; Alexander Macpherson lived in Craven Street; Edmund Mason operated from Crutched Friars; Tyringham Stephens was first the Naval Officer at Deal, and then Commissioner for Victualling from 17 March 1761, his London address being Tower Hill; John Warren was 'of Water Lane, London'.

Navy Board Officials as Prize Agents

Officials employed in various capacities in the Navy Board were also prize agents and would have fitted their work as prize agents around their official roles, or have employed their own agent to do the leg-work. The most prestigious was Timothy Brett, who was appointed by the Navy Board as an

6 TNA ADM 43/15 'Received the 31st July 1758 No 2611 Extra Clarke & Innes Bounty to the Hussar for taking the La Vengeance a French Privateer £1405'.

7 Samuel Touchet began as a cotton trader, but diversified into shipping and insurance broking. Oxford Dictionary of National Biography.

extra Commissioner from June 1756 to February 1761, then spending a month as Clerk of the Acts before final promotion to Controller of Treasurers' Accounts in March 1761 until his retirement in 1782. Edmund Mason was Clerk in the Bills and Accounts department until July 1750, then Chief Clerk responsible for seamen's wages until February 1761, when he succeeded Timothy Brett as Clerk of the Acts from 1761 until he died in 1773. George Marsh's career began in 1745 as Clerk in the Bills and Accounts department, and continued with constant promotion until his death as Commissioner in 1800.[8]

There were other prize agents familiar with the administration of the Navy Office. One was Charles Burley, who was nominated by William Brown, *Centaur* (20). Burley was Assistant Clerk of Acts from July 1743 until his retirement in May 1758.[9] The second was Henry Gunter, nominated by William Tucker, *Otter* (14). Gunter was Chief Clerk in the Victualling Accounts from December 1755 to February 1768, an important official.[10] A third was Alexander Chorley, nominated by Vincent Pearce, *Lizard* (28). Chorley was the clerk in the Ticket Office from 1741 to 1767, when he was appointed Commissioner of Victualling until 1794. John Lloyd was Clerk of the Survey at Portsmouth. Jonas Benjamin was the Naval Officer at Deal.

Philip Stephens

The name which cropped up most often during the analysis of the Letters of Attorney for Prize (TNA HCA 30/16) was that of Philip Stephens, who succeeded John Clevland as Secretary to the Admiralty on 18 June 1763. Stephens was Clerk to the Comptroller of Storekeepers Accounts from 1739–40 in the Victualling Office, then Clerk in the Ticket Office from 1740–51.[11] In this office, he caught the eye of George Anson, just back from his circumnavigation, and helped to sort out the complex pay problems of his crew. Stephens became Anson's agent and handled the huge sums of prize money due to both Anson and Sir Peter Warren.[12] He was appointed First Clerk in the Admiralty Office on 6 April 1751, an unprecedented promotion, and would

8 J.M. Collinge, *Navy Board Officials 1660–1832* (IHR, 1978), Brett 88, Marsh 121, Mason 121. https://jjhc.info/marshgeorge1800diary.

9 Collinge, *Navy Board*, 89.

10 Collinge, *Navy Board*, 106.

11 The clerks of the Ticket Office checked the paybooks of each vessel against the tickets issued to each seaman, on which he could claim his wages.

12 Anson would certainly have been instrumental in having Stephens transferred into the Admiralty.

then have moved into his tied accommodation in Spring Gardens, across the corner of Horse Guards Parade from the Admiralty Office.[13]

Stephens's competence, and the fact that the elderly Clevland relied on him more and more, was recognised by his appointment as Second Secretary on 16 October 1759, at a salary of £600 a year, raised to £800 in 1761. Shortly before Clevland's death in 1763 Stephens took over the role of Secretary to the Admiralty, but by then his name had stopped appearing in the appointments of prize agents.[14] He became a Member of Parliament first for Liskeard in 1759 until 1768, then for Sandwich from 1768 until 1806 when he retired with a pension of £1,500 a year. Stephens was created a baronet in 1795, with a seat on the Admiralty Board.

Given the importance of Stephens within the Admiralty administration, it is not surprising that so many naval officers entrusted their prize business to him. Between May 1756 and August 1758, out of the 217 appointments of prize agents in the Monitions file HCA 31/34, Philip Stephens was nominated seventy-four times, 34 per cent of the total. By far the most common was his appointment as one of a team of agents: Philip Stephens, Charles Brett, Edmund Mason and Alexander Macpherson, the team featuring in thirty-two appointments, 17 per cent of the total. On their own or in combination with other names, the team appear in ninety-five entries out of 217, 44 per cent. Team work was undoubtedly essential if one was to be successful as an agent, as the next chapter will demonstrate. The rest of the team were not quite as prestigious, but just as experienced: Charles Brett of Portsmouth had been Boscawen's flag lieutenant in the East Indies in 1747, Clerk of the Cheque in Portsmouth (1755–63), Paymaster to the Navy (1766–79) and eventually a Lord of the Admiralty (1782–88), apart from seven months in 1783. One brother was Captain John Brett, and his other brother was Timothy, mentioned above. Theirs was a very prestigious family. Edmund Mason was another official of the Navy Board, whose career is outlined above.[15] Alexander Macpherson had been admiral's secretary and purser in succession in *Russell*, *Montagu*, *Sandwich* and *Namur*, although he had lost money on all four, and was able

13 Collinge, *Navy Board*, 141; J.C. Sainty, *Admiralty Officials 1660–1870* (IHR, 1975), 153; Oxford Dictionary of National Biography. https://doi.org/10.1093/ref:odnb/26391 Portrait of Stephens by Sir William Beechey. NMM Art Collection.

14 Collinge, *Navy Board*, 141; Sainty, *Admiralty Officials*, 152.

15 It is likely that Mason was also Admiral Boscawen's agent. His wife wrote that 'Mr Mason has been here to tell me that there is soon to be a division of the prizes; that your share would be about £1,200 and that he wanted my order as to how to dispose of it.' Cecil Aspinall-Oglander, *Admiral's Wife: The Life and Letters of Mrs Edward Boscawen 1719–1761* (Longman, 1940), 91.

Figure 2. Philip Stephens, Secretary to the Admiralty, by unknown artist.

to draw his pay as a special concession, on giving large sureties.[16] These agents had the opportunity to benefit by at least five per cent of every prize taken by thirty-two of the most prestigious captains during the war. There is detail in Chapter 9 showing the enormous business managed by this team. Evidence of their professional status is the Power of Attorney drawn up by Thomas Taylor, *Seahorse* (24), in anticipation of future prizes. Naming McPherson, Mason and Tyringham Stephens, the document is a printed pro forma, with spaces left for the names of the vessel, agents and date to be entered by hand.[17]

These four men were also connected in a related official capacity, as overseers of the payment of customs dues and prize agent behaviour in the major ports. On the outbreak of war, the Admiralty appointed agents at each of the major ports to take care of the French prizes which were anticipated. Warrants were sent to Charles Brett for Portsmouth, William Hambly for Plymouth, Edmund Mason for Chatham and Tyringham Stephens for Deal and Dover, all signed by Philip Stephens, Second Secretary at the Admiralty.[18] The name of William Hambly is the only anomaly: he is not named as an agent anywhere else. Were these appointments sinecures? The societal separation between fees and salaries existed, and without further research it is impossible to say.

Admiral Boscawen commented to his wife:

> I told you in my last the captains had chosen the old set of agents, and yesterday they paid me a very handsome compliment by adding McPherson to them without my asking it. Mr. Mostyn proposed it, this will take something from the others. I wish their agency may enrich them. I was the first that cruised here last French war, I think I shall make more of it this war than the last. Mr. McPherson in this first instance will get £500 by it … I could not consent to a peace till I have got some more prize money.[19]

Captains as Agents

It cannot have been very convenient for the captains who nominated themselves as agents, although several of them did so. Edward Vernon, *Lyme* (28), nominated himself with John Vining Heron of Portsmouth, although he once used John Morshead of Plymouth. Edward Wheeler, *Isis* (50), appointed himself agent, without an alternative. Francis Wyatt, master and commander

[16] N.A.M. Rodger, *The Wooden World: An Anatomy of the Georgian Navy* (Collins, 1986), 97.

[17] TNA HCA 30/15.

[18] TNA ADM 6/18 Warrants and Commissions 1756. I am indebted to Chris Donnithorne for bringing this to my attention.

[19] Lloyd, ed., *Naval Miscellany IV*, 220, 222.

of the sloop *Lively* (20), did so as well, this time with William Armiger of Ely as his co-agent, and his lieutenant, Nathaniel Davis, heading the list of officers and crew who were to share the prize money.[20] Christopher Hill, *Dover* (44), nominated himself, and remained as agent when he was superseded in *Dover* by Bladen Tinker. James Hackman, master and commander of the sloop *Hazard* (8), appointed himself as one of the agents, nominating also Tyringham Stephens of Deal. A careful note was added to the usual copy that it was 'Sealed and delivered by the sixty five persons hereunder subscribed in the presence of us John Trehearne and William Wellard beginning with James Hackman and ending with Joseph Beeching.' As James Hackman was captain it must be supposed that the document was punctiliously drawn up.[21] When James Gilchrist, *Southampton* (32), took *L'Emeraude* he nominated himself as agent, with John Hay and George Marsh of the Navy Office, and again the letter of nomination is carefully worded: 'the lieutenant master warrant officers petty officers mariners and others or the major part of them now belonging to his Majesty's ship Southampton have nominated constituted authorised and appointed …'.[22]

Agents Abroad

The agents who worked abroad were of vital importance. It was logical that the vessels operating in the Mediterranean used John Dick, Consul in Leghorn, together with Messrs Le Froy and Sharron of Leghorn. He acted for all the prizes taken by captains such as Baillie, Bassett, Clements and Gwynn. While there, Richard Gwynn, *Ambuscade* (40), also named Clark Gayton, flag captain of *Prince* (90), as his agent.[23]

Captures in the East Indies were dealt with there. Henry Doige Esq. of Farham and John Michie Esq. of Buckingham Street, York Buildings, Strand, also paid out for captures in the East Indies, as did William Mackett of Channel Row, Westminster. There was no question of bringing prizes back to Europe for sale. George Papley of Kingston in Jamaica and William Warner of Antigua were responsible for a great deal of the West Indies business.[24]

Agents not based in England usually appointed a London-based agent to act on their behalf. The Guernsey-based Saumarez and Bell, appointed by Robert

20 TNA HCA 30/16 180–1, 269, 16, 184. (The figures 180–1 etc. refer to the pages in the HCA 30/16 file into which the Appointments of Agents were copied.)

21 TNA HCA 30/16 10.

22 TNA HCA 30/16 282.

23 TNA HCA 30/16 266–7. Leghorn is now Livorno, the Italian port city on the Tuscany coast.

24 Green, *Royal Navy*, 109.

Duff when he was operating off the Channel Islands, authorised Nicholas Le Marchant of London to act for them.[25]

In a slightly earlier period, Admiral Sir Peter Warren had done more than bring about prize captures for his squadron. He lent money to the officers and men of his own ship in anticipation of prize money due to them, as well as to crews of several ships in the squadron. His own prize fortune of £36,000 was put out as loans at five per cent, occasionally at four per cent.[26]

However, there was always an exception to this cooperation. The very successful captain Augustus Hervey, always his own man, did not approve. After the taking of the *Foudroyant* and *Orphée* on 8 April 1758 he commented that the captains had a meeting to choose their prize agent 'but I would not go as I thought only the three ships that were at the taking had the right of naming agents. However, Mr Brett, Mr Stephens, Mr Bately and Rudjard were named, the whole was very irregular.'[27] In fact, despite the captains' meeting to determine the agents to be used, only the captains and crews of *Monmouth* (70) and *Swiftsure* (70) shared the £4,400 Head Money paid for this capture. This will be mentioned again in Chapter 10.

The ten-year-old sloop *Dispatch* (10), under her master and commander John Hodges, had a successful career, taking privateers *Le Bigot* in 1756, *Le Frère Pierre* in 1757, *Le Vénérable* in January 1758, *Le Dieppoise* in February 1758 and *Le Nanon* in 1760. It was her taking of *Le Dieppoise* from her French commander, Charles Foliot, that resulted in the declaration of appointment of Francis Magnus as prize agent on a huge sheet, reproduced as Appendix 3. A few pages later in the legal clerk's copy book is a similar Power of Attorney drawn up for the same sloop *Dispatch* by Hodges and his officers and men, this time for their capture of *Vénérable*. On this form James Bucknall of Portsmouth is named as an agent in addition to Francis Magnus, and on both there is careful mention of the fact that the armed cutter *Hazard* was instrumental in the captures. These captures will be mentioned again in Chapter 10.

James Henshaw

The form used by the agent James Henshaw 'of the Liberty of the Tower of London' shows that after a long career in business he was extremely good at public relations, and had gone to the trouble of having a printed form prepared, the text of which is shown in Appendix 3, into which he simply inserted the name of the current client and the prize-taking ship, as appropriate.[28] As well

25 TNA HCA 30/16 333.

26 Gwyn, *Enterprising Admiral*, 75.

27 Erskine, *Augustus Hervey*, 279. The fourth agent in fact was Richard Rudyer, ADM 43/16/761. Bately the purser was mentioned several times in George Marsh's diary, 123.

28 TNA HCA 30/17.

as acting as a banker to his clients, lending money at five per cent, Henshaw was also a naval victualling agent.[29]

When *La Marie Rose* was taken by *Greyhound* (20) and *Antelope* (50) on 1 September 1756, the letter appointing Henshaw was dated 4 February 1757, adjudged 7 March 1757, and exhibited 3 March 1758. On it is the note: 'Received 27.5.1758 from out the Registry of this Court the original letter of attorney whereof the foregoing is a true copy pursuant to an order of Court of the 3.3.1758 for the use of Mr Henshaw'.[30]

Used as prize agent by the captains Augustus Hervey, Nicholas Vincent, Edward Jekyll and Thomas Gordon, Henshaw was also Hervey's man of business who paid his debts, and acted as his banker: 'The 6th I sent a bill of £200 to Mr Henshaw to pay off Mrs Voll's bill, my former tailor, in full.'[31] Henshaw must have been used to Hervey's disregard for personal wealth after many years of successful prize taking. When he took a little tartan in the Mediterranean Hervey agreed with his officers and people that it was not worth keeping, and sold it back to her master.[32]

When Henshaw died, Hervey nominated George Marsh as agent for his capture on 21 September 1762 of the *François Louis*, a French warship. The outcome, which Marsh described in his diary, is detailed in Chapter 6.[33]

There are several instances of a change of agent. Written into the agreement made by the bomb-ketch *Fire Drake* when *Le Postillon* was taken was a *caveat* in the form alongside the text: 'hereby revoking all former letters of attorney or agency given by us or any of us to any person or persons whatsoever in any manner relating the premises'.[34] James Webb 'revoked all previous attorneys' when he took *Prince de Conti* in *St Albans* (60) – which might have been as he took it in a joint capture with *Sheerness* (20).[35]

William Pettigrew of the *Queenborough* (24) died on 24 November 1756, and his wife Ann acted as his executrix, with Walter Harris of Croydon and Tyringham Stephens as agents.

29 The Liberty of the Tower of London was a small administrative area just outside the bounds of the Tower. Baugh refers to 'the ubiquitous Henshaw': *Naval Administration*, 400 n 103; Erskine, *Augustus Hervey*, 118.

30 TNA HCA 30/16 157. There is no mention within the form that the capture was awarded jointly to *Greyhound* and *Antelope*.

31 Erskine, *Augustus Hervey*, 146, 262.

32 Rodger, *Wooden World*, 137.

33 TNA ADM 43/20. Marsh diary, 95.

34 TNA HCA 30/16 169.

35 TNA HCA 30/16 174.

Joint Agreements within a Squadron

Cooperation between ships within squadrons was a necessary fact of naval life. Prize agents were appointed by flag officers so that they could take advantage of prizes taken by their squadron.[36] Sir Edward Hawke, a very experienced officer, organised a cooperative agreement with his squadron in the Channel on 23 August 1755, well before war was declared officially. It was 'signed sealed and delivered the day above mentioned in the presence of us Edward Hawke, George Hay'.[37]

This agreement confirmed that any prize taken by the squadron would be shared equally amongst them whether or not they were in sight. Any ship detached to be sent in with prizes, with dispatches or to be cleaned remained part of his fleet for two weeks after they arrived in port. The agreement was broken only if a ship was ordered away on other service or delayed beyond two weeks. Vice Admiral of the White Squadron, Hawke commanded some of the most powerful and successful players in the eighteenth-century navy. John Lockhart was the most junior of Hawke's team, merely a commander of the tiny *Savage* (8) sloop at the time he signed. Hawke contested vigorously allocation of prize money to any member of his squadron without deduction of the 'flag-eighth'.[38]

Admiral Harrison's Flag Share

Admiral Henry Harrison, having learned from Hawke, was quick to assert his right to the flag share of all prizes taken under his command. Needing to

[36] Horne, ed., *Compendium of the Statute Laws*, 54.

[37] George Hay was made Advocate General 'for all matters ecclesiastical and maritime relating to the crown'. LG issue no. 9636 16 November 1756. He was a most interesting man, a close friend of William Hogarth, whose portrait of Hay has unfortunately disappeared.

[38] The navy was organised into three squadrons, the Blue, the White, and, the most senior, the Red. Admirals were appointed first as Rear of the Blue, then as Vice before promotion to full Admiral. If their eventual ranks in the navy are added, the professional weight of this list is made clear: Henry Harrison, Vice Admiral of the Red; Harry Powlett, Admiral of the White; John Hamilton, died in post; Henry Ward, superannuated Rear Admiral; George Cockburn, Captain and Controller of the Navy; Charles Saunders, Admiral of the Blue; Charles Steevens, Rear Admiral of the Red; George Bridges Rodney, Admiral of the White; Charles Catford, died in post; Thomas Hanway, Commissioner of Victualling; John Montague, Admiral of the White; Peter Denis, Vice Admiral of the Red; Hugh Pigot, Admiral of the White; John Lloyd, Vice Admiral of the Blue; Robert Harland, Admiral of the Blue; Michael Everitt, Captain; John Storr, Rear Admiral of the Red; John Lockhart, Vice Admiral of the Blue; Joshua Rowley, Vice Admiral of the White; John Byron, Vice Admiral of the White.

appoint a temporary captain while John Lockhart was recovering from injuries he sustained on shore while separating sailors fighting with local soldiers, he ordered Thomas Baillie, recently made a post captain, to take *Tartar* (28) out for a cruise. In doing so he was exerting his authority as the admiral responsible for Plymouth, and became a beneficiary of any prizes Baillie took while on that cruise. On this occasion, Harrison appointed John Hullock of Saltash to take care of the proceeds of the sale of *Marie Victoire*, captured by Baillie.[39] As Harrison's prize agent, Hullock would have worked hard for his five per cent of the net proceeds 'for his care pains and troubles'.[40]

In a second legal statement more than 800 words long, Admiral Harrison consolidated his right to shares in all the prizes already taken by vessels cruising under his orders, as well as in the future, with his son John Harrison to receive five per cent of the proceeds. The captors and prizes were listed: Robert Haldane, *Shoreham* (24), in company with *Trident* (64) and *Hind* (24), had brought in the *Difficulty*, the *Black Prince* and the *Hardingcourt*; Lockhart had brought in *Penelope*; Graves, *Sheerness* (24), in company with *Falmouth* (50) *Seaford* (24) and *Swan* (14) had brought in *Automne* as well as the *Portmahon* privateer.[41]

The only captures made without the 'flag-eighth' were those where the commission was initiated by the Admiralty, and not at the direction of a flag officer, to which I return in Chapter 9.

Documentary Evidence of the Letters Appointing Agents

Fortunately for the researcher, the original documents appointing agents were copied into large folders, with numbered pages, the series HCA 30/16-19 covering this war. There is confirmation that the details of the original have been copied accurately, accompanied by more signatures. Photographing these folders was a great deal easier than trying to handle the originals safely. Unfortunately, the series is not complete, but data from those that survive has allowed an analysis of the occasions on which particular men or groups of men were used as agents.

The basic document did not vary. Most of those from the beginning of the series were appointing agents in the expectation of needing their services in the future. Others were drawn up once a prize had been taken, so the name of the prize and its master were included. If the prize was a ship of war or privateer, also included would be the number of men alive on board at the

[39] The *ingenue* had to be reminded what to do next: The Navy Board: '22 April Write to Capt. Baillie to desire he will give directions to the agent for capture of the *Tartar's Prize* to attend us in order to treat for her.' TNA ADM 106/2566.

[40] TNA HCA30/16 234.

[41] TNA HCA30/16 237.

time of taking the prize, to establish the amount of Head Money due from the Treasury. Following the text of the document was a list of the officers and men, always beginning with the name of the captain and usually including the ranks of the lesser officers, and the seaman's name and indication that he had not signed for himself. If this document did not include the ranks of officers, petty officers, etc. a copy of the pay book would have to be made available to the agent, as the shares of prize money depended on his knowing it. For the large ships, with crews of hundreds of men, these lists filled pages and one has compassion for the clerks who had to check every name before signing that the list was accurate. It was undoubtedly easier for the clerks to handle these folders than the original documents. In many cases where the file records the appointment of an agent for future prizes, in the space at the top of the first page is an entry recording the later capture of a prize, the master and the stages through which the claim had passed.

In the copying of these documents, it is possible to see the clerks at work behind the scenes, as the batching of documents is clear. Within the volume HCA 30/16, pages 36 to 128 record the choices made in favour of the team of Stephens, Brett, Mason and Macpherson by the captains of twenty-seven vessels. These ranged from Admirals Boscawen, Harrison, Holburne and Smith to Sir Piercy Brett, Lord Alexander Colville, Augustus Keppel, John Moore and Edward Vernon. Although the names of Stephens, Brett and Mason appear over and over again elsewhere, singly or together with other partners, that single block of documentation reinforces their position as the pre-eminent agents to the navy. The only other block which appears is that of John Elliot's 'trusty friends', who occupy pages 461 to 478 following his captures in *Hussar.*

Typical of these documents is that recording the taking of the French privateer *L'Infernal* on 10 March 1757, by Thomas Burnett's tiny sloop *Happy* (8) off Guernsey, and the next document in the folder, his retaking on 10 November 1756 of the *Baltimore* from the French privateer *Le Favourite*, in company with *Lynn* (44) and *Ferret* (14).[42] The privateer *Le Favourite* did not survive long. She was taken on 17 February 1757 by *Scorpion* (14), *Badger* (14) *Bonetta* (10) and the armed cutters *Shad Thames* and *St Michael.*[43]

Burnett and his crew appointed Charles Brett and Philip Stephens, with the Guernsey attorney Henry Budd, to be their agents in the matter of *L'Infernal.* Budd wasn't needed on the retaking of *Baltimore*, captured by the French privateer *Le Favourite*, in sight of *Lynn* and *Ferret*. *Happy* was so small that being in sight of other naval vessels enhanced her ability to prevail. The text of the appointment of agents is followed by fifty-seven names, headed by Thomas Burnett and including his son John Burnett. The copy was 'signed sealed and delivered being duly first stamped in the presence' of Thomas Bradshaw, Burnett's lieutenant, and John Pamphlett, Burnett's clerk.

42 Burnett retaking *Baltimore*. TNA HCA 30/16 362.

43 TNA HCA 30/16 360 and 362, signed 16 March 1756 and 4 February 1757.

Finally, in his own time and to carry out his personal responsibility, the agent had to make out the lists of men again, ranking them into 'divisions', the members of each division receiving a reducing proportion of the prize money. An example of this will be seen in Appendix 12.

William Innes and Thomas Clerk of Lime Street Square, as we have already seen, took their responsibilities as agents very seriously, and were always fully cognisant of their client's situation.[44] They wrote to John Elliot twice to warn him of potential difficulties ahead:

> Sir, We wrote you last post, and this now to acquaint you that Mr. Harris writes us from Plimouth about the Hermione that the 2nd Lieut. of the Unicorn has been suspended for Embezzling Cash and Goods to the amount of (they say) £2000 and Mr Roy who is one of the agents for the Unicorn told Mr Harris he does not apprehend you can share with them, as you met by accident. It would seem the Unicorn's folks have intention to trick your ship. We hope you'll go to Plimouth as fast as you can to get the matter settled. There was two Irish maills yesterday, but no letter from you. We imagine you had not got the papers prepared so soon as you expected.
>
> We are with respect
> Your most obliged and obedient servants
> Innes and Clerk
>
> From Innes and Clerk:
> London 26th January 1758
>
> Sir,
>
> We had only this day the pleasure of your agreeable favour the 17th inst. with the account confirmed of your taking the Vengeance privateer of St Maloes, the news of it came nine days ago via Cork to Bristol, 36 guns, 400 men but we see she had only 24 mounted of 12 and 9 pounders which are heavier mettal than yours. You have great honour by it and we sincerely congratulate you, on that gallant stroke, and revenging poor Capt. Death's loss, it must have been pitiless work one hour and three quarters and to kill so many of her men. Its miraculous that you lost only 6 and 15 wounded and that you are unhurt yourself makes us very happy. We notice she is much shattered and that you think of selling her at Kinsale. We fear she will not sell anything near her worth there, and hopes you might get her slightly repaired, to bring her to Plimouth or this Port, where she would pay more than the expence and insurance if you chuse to order any. There is some reason to think there will be a Spanish War, if so, the demand for privateers will increase. If you put her up to a sale, you can let her

44 Metropolitan Archive, London CLC/B/227-100.

go or not, as they bid sufficient or not. It is essential you are to send the Certificate for the Head Money and please mind to send a Prize list of all on board, as there are others than what you had the former cruise. It would not be amiss to send a Power of Attorney by these fresh hands. In case you go to Cork, please call for Messrs Paul and James Benson there, our friends, who will shew you all civilitys and they will be proper people to remit your money if you sell the prize.

We find the Unicorn's (Capt. Moore) folks have taken no notice of your sharing in the Hermione prize at Doctors Commons which is not very gentlemanly of them but we have claimed for your ship. The Purser and somebody of the Dock are the Unicorn's agents. We have enquired and cannot find you should show them the generosity formerly mentioned by appointing them. We hope you will not do it. We would have wrote you last week, but expected you to come with prize to Plimouth. All friends here join in best compliments. We are with kind respects etc

We hope Inglis and Wilson are well.[45]

The letters above from Innes and Clerk reveal the potential for financial fraud which was exploited by a few individuals.

Comparing ship's paybooks with the completed 'Power of Attorney' form has so far shown that great efforts were made to ensure that the whole ship benefited from the perils of taking a French-owned vessel. This will be illustrated further in Chapter 9. In the Staffordshire Archives was found a little slip of paper which testifies to the attempts made to keep track of crew members:

These are to certify the honourable the principal offices and commissioners of his Majesties navy that Stephen Coggon voluntarily entered on board his Majesties sloop Jamaica under my command on 20 day of this instant September, being as he says sent from the Amazon in a prest mans room to London and left behind when that ship sailed and that he is now actually on board the said sloop given under my hand this 25 day of September 1746.

M. Arbuthnott.[46]

45 NMM E/400 Elliot 26 January 1758.

46 Staffordshire Archives D1798/HM Drakeford/13. The agent Richard Drakeford is introduced more fully later in this chapter.

Legal Duties of a Prize Agent

Agents had to register their respective letters of attorney so that they could receive the bounty for seamen. The allowance to agents was 2½ per cent on receiving prize money, and a further 2½ per cent on distributing prize money to captors. There were other extra centages which arose from particular circumstances and could amount to no more than 14 per cent.[47] On first registering, the agent had to give surety to the court of £5,000 for the due execution of his trust. The letters of attorney had to be listed in books which recorded the dates of delivery and entry, the dates of the letters of attorney, the names and residences of the agents, the names of the ships of war, privateers or other prizes taken together with the names of the respective ships of war or privateers by which they had been taken, burnt, sunk or otherwise destroyed and likewise the date of condemnation and of appeal if any was made. Copies of this register had to be handed to the Treasurer of the Greenwich Hospital twice a year, within forty days of 25 December and 25 June. These registers were legal evidence in his Majesty's courts of law.[48] Failure to register etc. incurred a penalty of £500.[49] A proforma of this register is shown in Chapter 9.

Once the capture had been made, and safely brought into port, the action then devolved upon the agents who took possession and were responsible for getting the preliminary examinations taken. These answers to the printed interrogatories were then delivered to Doctors Commons ready for the court hearing where they were presented by the Registrar of the Admiralty court to the King's Proctor, who followed the opinion of his Majesty's Advocate as to taking out a monition which was then published. The agent would complete his element of this as quickly as possible, and from the dates observed the average length of time between the appointment of the agent and the condemnation of the prize was twelve weeks. The penalty for not registering within twenty days of the monition being posted was a forfeit of £5.[50]

Appendix 5 gives evidence of further business in the hands of the agent. The testimony of the interrogations as to the number of men alive on board the captured vessel at the start of the action was passed to the Treasury who, after a period of fifteen days, ordered a Bill to be made out for the bounty or Head Money due to the captors. The delay of fifteen days allowed time for a counter-claim to be lodged.

The goods and merchandise taken from ships condemned as prizes had to be carefully locked up until they could be valued and sold. Customs duties were then payable, this responsibility resting with the prize agent appointed by the

47 Horne, ed., *Compendium of the Statute Laws*, 5.

48 Horne, ed., *Compendium of the Statute Laws*, 56.

49 Horne, ed., *Compendium of the Statute Laws*, 57.

50 Horne, ed., *Compendium of the Statute Laws*, 56.

prize taker. After the sale or sales of the prize goods, a day was nominated by the prize agent for the distribution of the prize money. This was followed by further distributions over a period of time until, after three years, the residue went to Greenwich Hospital, as discussed in Chapter 9. This was usually about ten per cent of the total income.

The responsibility of prize agents relating to customs dues to be paid had expensive financial implications. Having been acquainted with the difficulties of surveying privateers, the Navy Board instructed the Master Attendant and Clerk of the Survey at Portsmouth to 'let the agents know the difficulties, and desire them to pay the £5 per cent demanded by the Customs on all prizes as soon as possible that no interruption may be given to the surveying measuring and reporting them as they have been directed'.[51] Chapter 10 gives evidence of the proportion of prize money which went to the Customs.

George Marsh

None of the books containing the financial affairs of any of the agents listed have been found, as these were personal items and not stored nationally. The diary of George Marsh has survived, and although he wrote this towards the end of his life, it provides a unique insight into the conditions of life and the work of a prize agent.

Marsh's diary entry for 23 October 1757 included: 'As I found I had wonderfully increased my private business as an Agent, I continued to carry that on in London'. The next day James Gilchrist of *Sutherland* (60) and his company appointed Marsh their agent for *L'Emerode* and *St Denis.* He dealt with the business expeditiously, and on 16 March 1758 had made up his accounts and paid the prize money for both prizes. Following this success, Gilchrist appointed Marsh agent for *Danae*, taken in sight of other ships.[52] By June 1760 Marsh's diary records his working double shifts to get both his official work in the Navy Office and his private agency business completed:

> Finding my agency business encreased very fast and have constantly great confinement and public business at the Navy Office from 10 o'clock in the morning 'till 3 and from 6 o'clock in the evening 'till 9 I was obliged to be up early and late and take every opportunity to carry on my Agency business, so as to finish that dayly, otherwise I should soon have been in great confusion therewith.[53]

51 TNA ADM 106/2566 19 May 1757.

52 George Marsh diary, Heath-Caldwell Family Archive, www.jjhc.info, 92, 93.

53 Marsh diary, 94

On the next page is even more agency business. On 30 September 1762 Augustus Hervey was returning from Havanna with the news of their success there and had reached the 'chops of the Channel' when he came across a French frigate of 10 guns, 'commanded by a Lieutenant of the French Navy whose pennant was flying aboard her' and took her. Named by Marsh the 'Francis Lewis', the vessel was claimed in Doctors Commons to be a private vessel, the property of an English merchant, despite the fact that she had 156 men on board. Marsh's diary does not have an explanation for this anomaly. It may have been that the merchant was involved in the French vessel's cargo of cloth, linen, buckles and buttons. The 'Francis Lewis' was bound for Newfoundland, and also carried brass guns, presumably to reinforce the fishing grounds there. The outcome of the case, heard in Doctors Commons, is described in Chapter 6.[54]

It was a coup for Marsh that he won the case in Doctors Commons, resulting in his client being awarded half instead of an eighth of the value of *Francis Lewis* (the French *François Louis*). As she was a French warship the Head Money awarded was considerable – £780 for the 156 men on board. It was a tribute to his energy as an agent that the prize money was awarded so swiftly. Sadly for the researcher, this is the only instance of Marsh's name being given as the recipient of Head Money, so providing evidence to corroborate his diary.

The result of his energy and efforts can be measured by the figures he gave the Earl of Egmont, first Lord of the Admiralty, comparing his annual income as a pay clerk of £160 with his private business as an agent which had brought him £1,500 the previous year.[55]

Eventually Marsh was appointed Clerk of the Acts, taking the place of Edmund Mason: 'who was supposed with many other gentlemen to have been poisoned, by something in their wine or food they drank and eat unfortunately, at a dinner at Salt Hill'.[56]

Richard Drakeford

The accounts and ledger book of Richard Drakeford have survived the vicissitudes of time and were made available through the Staffordshire Archives.[57] Drakeford was a naval purser and agent. He was agent for *Lenox* (70), one of the captors of *Princessa* which was worth over £19,000. He worked as an agent from 1737 to 1753 and his experience so nearly corresponds with the

54 Marsh diary, 95. TNA ADM 43-20.

55 Marsh diary, 98.

56 Marsh diary, 137.

57 J.S. Bromley, 'Prize Office and Prize Agency at Portsmouth 1689–1748', in *Hampshire Studies*, ed. J. Webb, N. Yates and S. Peacock (Portsmouth, 1981), 169–99. This article deals with Richard Drakeford, and led me to the Staffordshire Archives.

dates of the Seven Years' War, these accounts have been used as exemplars of the work any agent would have carried out on behalf of their clients.

The first letter makes clear that the appointment of an agent was not always a simple affair. The prize-taking captain's brother having been appointed from Newfoundland, the prize's temporary captain and the others involved were being warned off.[58]

> Dock near Plymouth Aug 12 1744
> Mr Drakeford
>
> Sir
>
> This day I rec'd a Letter of Attorney from my brother, Capt. Robert Young in the Kinsale from St Johns in Newfoundland, the 6th of June last that authorises & impowers me to take possession of the St Pierre, the Kinsale's prize; Lieut. Foley brought into your harbour and as his directions are that nothing is to be landed or sold till his further orders, Desire you will not land any of the goods till I see you which will be in a weeks time. I acquainted Mr Trevanion with this affair and doubtless he has wrote you on the subject. I am
>
> Sir your very humble servant
> Hasden Young.

There are many other letters containing the same message – that nothing was to be done by anyone outside the Young family. The matter was settled eventually, with the responsibility all in the Drakeford team's hands.

A further document in the Drakeford file explains the responsibility of the agent respecting customs duties on the cargo of a prize:[59]

> Gentlemen,
>
> Application having been made to us by Messrs W&B Jasper desiring liberty to export the whole or any part of the cargo of the St Pierre, a French prize consisting of sugar, coffee and other goods (landed at your port by Bill of Sight under a deposit of £1000) without entry inwards, or outwards, or paying any duties for the same, we have consulted the Patent Officers thereon, who have reported that the duties for these French prize sugars, coffee and other goods, are payable at your port. You are therefore to take care that all the said goods be regularly entered, and the duties paid agreeable to the practice here, and as to the tares, they are to be adjusted by the discharging officers

58 Staffordshire Archives D1798/HM Drakeford 13.

59 Staffordshire Archives D1798/HM Drakeford 13.

agreeable to their duties, and if any difficulties arise, the Collector, Controller and Surveyor must adjust the same.

We are your loving friends W Westby Jn Hill, S Mead, B Fairfax
Customs House, London 11 Sept 1744

The law laid down that there should be a minimum of delay between capturing the ship and the distribution of prize money and occasionally there was no delay at all. But there was a formidable list of activities to be carried out by the prize agents outside the court room. In addition to the pages of legal terminology that the clerks had to copy out over and over again, cases were often referred from one court to another, helping to explain why there were delays between capturing the ship and the distribution of prize money.

The Many and Varied Additional Responsibilities of the Prize Agent

Once there was a capture, the agent had to be active in getting the formal processes underway, as discussed in the next chapter. The agent was responsible for an enormous range of activities including protecting a prize from damage or theft. Each one of these actions resulted in a cost which was deducted from the proceeds before the 'neat' result could be distributed. As detailed in the Drakeford accounts, the agent had to: hire a pilot to bring the ship to a safe mooring and hire men to do this safely; hire men to watch over the prize while she was waiting to be sold; collect her papers together and ensure the examinations of her master and two others of her crew; hire an interpreter to translate the papers of the prize; hire clerks to take the depositions and buy stamped paper as well as plain paper for the notaries to use; hire a warehouse in which to store the assorted cargo and fixtures and fittings of the prize; hire a cart to carry the cargo to the storehouses; hire surveyors from the Customs department to oversee the establishment of customs due; pay the duties on the cargo; arrange to have the prize prepared for the sale; arrange the sale once condemnation was complete, then distribute the proceeds and arrange for 'call backs' for three years until the final lodging in Greenwich Hospital of the remainder.

One piece of evidence of the kind of endless deductions comes from the Drakeford accounts and is too special to be summarised in a line. The little slip of paper, with its idiosyncratic spelling but perfect accounting, records just one element of the duties of a prize agent.[60] This is typical of the endless 'deductions' so mourned by the captains, and represents one of the hundreds of cash disbursements which the agent had to make before the prize could be

60 Staffordshire Archives D1798/HM Drakeford 13.

sold. Here Wal Thomas is being reimbursed for the expenses he incurred in repairing *Kinsale*'s prize *St Pierre* while she was in the Scillies.

Table 1. Wal Thomas's expenses in Scillies.

Scilly 27th June 1744

Acct of a Bote & men that gave attendance to the Prize belonging to the Kinsale man of warr Leitenant Fowley Commander ye first

	£	s	d
June ye 10th 4 men & bote at 2s per day	0	10	0
ye 11th ditto 4 men & bote	0	10	0
ye 12th ditto 2 men & bote	0	6	0
ye 13th ditto 2 men & bote	0	6	0
ye 14th 3 men & bote	0	8	0
ye 15th 4 men & bote	0	10	0
	2	10	0
Extrey for carring Mr Skiner on board Twice	0	6	0
	2	16	0
To repearing ye bote 3 dayes	0	7	6
Rossin pitch 12 pounds at 2d per pound	0	2	0
Traine oaile one Gallon	0	2	0
Furze for Breiming ye Bote	0	1	2
Nailes & Brooms	0	1	10
Expence Keariening her on ye wayes	0	1	0
	0	15	6
	2	16	0
	3	11	6

Rc'd the contents of the above
by me Wal Thomas

What is clear from the Drakeford papers is that the agent earned his five per cent even without a problem such as that of contested agency. The papers also make clear that a substantial amount of money had to be available to the agent to make possible the deposits required by government agencies such as Customs before business could be done. The *St Pierre* which occupied Richard Drakeford in 1744 required a deposit of £1,000 to the Customs House in London before the cargo could be cleared for entry inwards, in addition to the duties liable on the goods which had to be paid. The complexity of clearing a prize through Customs will be dealt with in Chapter 8.

Amongst the papers for *Kinsale*'s capture of *St Pierre* was evidence of another strand of the agent's responsibilities. Lt. John Faulknor of the *Kinsale* died in 1747, and Drakeford, as his agent, dealt with the subsequent administration:

Table 2. Lt. Faulknor's funeral expenses.

	£	s	d
Mr John Faceys Bill	10	16	9
Dr Martyn's ditto	12	1	6
Mr Philips ditto the apothecary	8	11	4
John Scotts ditto for his coffin	2	12	6
Mr Rhodes ditto for burying him in the church yard	2	2	6
The 2 nurses bills	2	10	2
To paid a mans attendance on the funeral and going ?		6	6
Mr Kings bill for a pair of boots	1	3	0
Lieut. Shaws bill being money he paid for him at dock		10	5
Jonas Morgans 2 bills drawn on Mr Hawes for 16 guineas			
but returned for non payment	16	16	0
Mrs Rebecca Wilsons bills for board and lodging	27	11	2
	85	1	9
To wine at funeral		18	0
	85	19	9

Lieut. John Faulknor paid Mrs Wilson	9	9	0
Total sum	76	10	9
David Herbert says he owes him		5	6
	76	16	3
To paid the washerwomans bill		9	2
	77	5	5

What is also clear from the Drakeford papers is that distributing the prize money to the crew involved the use of naval agents who collected on behalf of other agents, each one presumably taking his five per cent, as demonstrated in Appendix 11.

4

The Capture of Prizes

The Admiralty's standing exhortation to its captains, incorporated in every commission, was to 'protect the trade and annoy the enemy', and with a little help from private enterprise, they did succeed in annoying the enemy. This book is not about privateering activities. These were a way of employing private enterprise to assist in the reduction of the enemy's trade, as every prize taken by a privateer weakened the trading wealth of the enemy and reduced the number of men available to the French navy, at no cost to the naval administration.[1] Instead the focus has been on the activities of the young men who were captains of sloops and frigates, and so involved in individual captures, rather than those in the larger ships, highly enough rated to fight in the line of battle as 'ships of the line'. There were fleet actions during the war, and they play their part in the story, but John Elliot was not the only captain content to stay in a sixth rate frigate rather than receive the higher pay due to a captain in a larger ship. He was much more likely to win prize money.

In the time of Queen Anne there had been restrictions on the behaviour of the captors, and these restrictions still applied. Furthermore, British ships of war or privateers were expressly forbidden to ransom any ship taken as prize, in order to reduce the men available to the French. The commander of a privateer who did so 'shall forfeit his commission to all intents and purposes and shall, together with his bail, be proceeded against according to the Law, and be condemned in costs and damages'.[2]

Head Money

First granted in 1708 and then in 1740, Head Money was a new inducement for the navy to reward captains and their crews if they fought to a conclusion against 'Ships of Force' and not just merchantmen.[3] Five pounds were paid:

> … for every man which was living on board such ship or ships so taken, sunk, burnt, or otherwise destroyed, at the beginning of the

[1] Gary M. Anderson and Adam Gifford Jn., 'Privateering and the Private Production of Naval Power', *Cato Journal* (Vol. 11 no. 1 1991).

[2] Marsden, *Reports of Cases*, 430.

[3] Baugh, *Naval Administration*, 141–2.

> engagement between them, the numbers of such men to be proved by the oaths of three or more of the chief officers or men which were belonging to the said ship or ships of war or privateers of the enemy at the time of her or their being taken as prize.[4]

It was Head Money which dictated the interest of the newspapers in numbers. The law which required agents to publish lists of captures for which prize money was due is invaluable to researchers. In June 1757 a list was published of the French vessels captured since 6 April 1756. It features the number of men on board for whom the £5 bounty was due, totalling 2,417, worth £12,085.[5] This subject is returned to in Chapter 9.

There are hundreds of accounts of capture during the war. Behind every one of these captures there is a story of heroism, bravery or just luck. The brief letters to the Admiralty in which the captains informed their Lordships of their successes are stripped of all emotion, as befits their formality. But their Lordships were aware that the public was desperate for news of the victories at sea, and perhaps of the wealth which would flow in due course, and in many cases the captains' letters have the notation from the Secretary on the turn back: 'send the marked passage to the papers'. Every captain was aware that if his letter to the Admiralty was published in the *London Gazette* and the other publications used by the Admiralty it would be read by his family and more widely. Other letters published in other papers were less constrained by formality, and many have been included here to give readers a flavour of the period.

Thomas Burnett, master and commander in the tiny ketch-rigged sloop *Happy* (8), was part of the squadron protecting the Channel Islands, where there were always opportunities for demonstrating courage and leadership. Burnett was in company with John Lockhart, *Tartar* (28), a very effective fighting team. As reported in Scotland, Lockhart and *Tartar* took the French privateer *Rose of St Malo* off the Start, which had the day before taken *Phoenix* of Dundee. *Phoenix* was still in sight after the engagement, and Lockhart went after her to effect a recapture, leaving Burnett in the tiny *Happy* to escort the French privateer into Plymouth:

> The Happy sloop of war has brought into Plymouth the Rose of St Malo, a French privateer of ten carriage guns and 90 men taken the 16th inst. by the Tartar off the Start. She had the day before taken the Phoenix of Dundee from Lisbon, which was in sight, and the Tartar went in chase of her.[6]

4 LG issue no. 7921 21 June 1740.

5 LG issue no. 9696 14 June 1757.

6 *Caledonian Mercury* 28 September 1756.

Lockhart and Burnett operated together again to take *L'Heureux*. Lockhart's letter to the Admiralty stated:

> I chased two snows who immediately separated and in about two hours afterwards his Majesty's sloop the Happy stood athwart the one that I was in chase of, and on the snow hoisting French colours the Happy fired at her but she outsailed the Happy greatly and in about an hour afterwards I came up with the chase who struck her French colours and prove to be L'Heureux, a snow privateer of St Maloes, ten guns six pounders and seventy-six men.[7]

Burnett's letter to the Admiralty when he took the much larger French privateer *L'Infernal* was typical of those formal reports: 'Be pleased to acquaint their Lordships that on the tenth instant we met with, engaged and took a French privateer called the Infernal, of Havre de Grace.'[8] Burnett's capture was reported in the national papers, which published a letter from 'an officer' on board the *Happy* sloop dated Guernsey 13 March 1757. Further details emerge from this letter: after a chase of five hours, the engagement lasted only seven minutes; the twenty soldiers being carried by *Happy* covered the crew when they boarded; the masts and rigging were shattered 'by their stern chase'; Burnett 'escaped a six-pounder that cut away the shroud just above his head'.[9] His success was even reported in Scotland, as *Infernal* had taken the *Adventure* tender in the Firth of Forth.[10] *L'Infernal* reappears in Chapter 10.

Happy's log next records a successful interception of a smuggler 'laden with brandy, tea and tobacco' which was brought back to the Customs House in Plymouth to be dealt with. The smuggler had 2,625 lb of tea, 1,665 gallons of rum and brandy, in two large boats and a sloop. Burnett seized the vessels, and sent the smugglers on board the *Duke* man of war.[11] Later a French privateer (unnamed in Burnett's letter, but identified by later developments as *L'Heureuse* of 12 guns) surrendered without a fight, as *Happy* was in company

7 TNA ADM 1/2044 Captains' Letters L Lockhart 21 September 1756

8 TNA ADM 1/1488 Captains' Letters B 1757 Burnett 10 March 1757. Burnett's reward was to be 'made post', commissioned as flag captain in *Cambridge* (80), his pay enhanced from 6s a day to 13s 6d. He disappears from the narrative as he no longer initiated correspondence, as *Cambridge* was Commodore John Moore's flag ship in the West Indies.

9 *Derby Mercury* Friday 18 March 1757.

10 *The Scots Magazine* Monday 7 March 1757. (I have queried the date of this report, as it appears to predate the capture!)

11 *London Evening Post* 17 August 1756.

with the other sloop on the station.[12] A French snow which had been taken by *Bideford* (20) and recaptured by a French privateer was retaken, as was another snow, this time an English one. *Happy* this time was in company with *Lynn* (44) and *Ferret* (14).

John Lockhart became a legend. Having served as first lieutenant to Sir Peter Warren (from whom he would have learned how to make money from prizes) and Lord Anson, he was made master and commander in the fireship *Vulcan* under Hawke, and in their cruise off Finisterre in 1747 captured six ships from the French. In 1755 Lockhart was 'made post', i.e. commissioned as a captain, first in *Savage* (8) and then promoted into *Tartar* (28). They became 'the terror of every French Frigate or privateer that issued from their ports', capturing in all nine vessels of force, carrying collectively 2,048 men, and 224 guns. The memoir of his life describes the engagement between *Mélampe*, of 36 guns and 320 chosen men, which had been specially commissioned to overpower *Tartar*:

> A very hot and obstinate engagement immediately ensued, but the enemy's colours were at length struck to the superior courage and discipline of the British commander and his gallant crew. The perfidious Frenchmen, stung with the disgraceful event of a conquest so unequal on the part of the British ship, after having hailed the Tartar acknowledged his surrender and submissively sued for quarter, made a desperate attempt to surprise and overpower her crew, whom he vainly supposed to be thrown off their guard, elated with victory. He boarded the Tartar, but in penetration, vigilance and courage he was more than overmatched by the British commander. The Frenchmen were vigorously repulsed, and more than fifty of them were killed or drowned in their unwarrantable effort.[13]

Lockhart's reputation reached the other side of the Atlantic:

> The Mermaid man of war, which arrived at Plymouth last Saturday, to the Westward of Scilly fell in with a French privateer off Granville of 22 guns and 190 Men, who was in chace of a brigantine bound for Gibraltar. The Tartar Man of War soon came in sight, and gave Chace also to the privateer, and being a clean ship soon came up with her, and after a broadside or two, the French Captain's head being struck off, the Privateer struck. Forty of the prisoners are on board the Mermaid.

12 The capture of *L'Heureuse* brought £380 to be shared with John Lockhart and the crew of *Tartar*. TNA ADM 43/15.

13 *Scots Magazine* 1 July 1790.

> The Tartar man of War is arrived at Plymouth, with the French Privateer above mentioned, which is called the Grand Jewedon, [Guidon] from Granville, mounting fourteen Four Pounders, six Six Pounders and 195 men.[14]

An extract of a letter from Dartmouth, 7 April:

> Yesterday came in here the privateer ship Phoenix of Bristol of 16 four pounders, Capt. Read, who has brought in the Bellona Privateer of St Malo's, of 20 six pounders besides swivels, and 120 men, she is more than 100 tons larger than the Phoenix. On the 3rd instant, after chasing, about 11 at night the Phoenix came up with the Bellona, fired a gun and hailed her. The Frenchman asked, 'What ship?' The Phoenix answered, 'The Tartar, Capt. Lockhart, and if you don't strike immediately, I will sink you.' The name of Tartar or Lockhart struck the Frenchmen with such a panic that the whole crew ran down to bundle up their cloaths, as we are told by a master of a ship who was a prisoner on board. The lieutenant and four or five men went on board and took possession of her.
>
> It is to be hoped that the name only of some other of our captains will strike terror into Frenchmen.[15]

Such a list of successes and such a reputation was rewarded. Merchants insured at Lloyd's presented a cup and salver to Lockhart in 1757:

> It is curiously chased and embossed, with the 7 French Privateers, his own ship, and arms. The salver is 26 inches diameter, with the following inscription:
>
> The gift of the two public companies the Underwriters and Merchants of the City of London, to Capt. Lockhart, Commander of the Tartar, for his signal service in supporting the trade, by distressing the French privateers in the year 1757.[16]

The Bristol merchants were not long behind their peers in London, and presented Lockhart with a gold cup worth £100 'for his great vigilance in taking so many French privateers'.[17] In Scotland the freedom of Dumfries 'was presented to him, as a mark of the high esteem they have for that gallant

14 *Annapolis Maryland Gazette* 10 February 1757.

15 *London Owen Weekly Chronicle or Universal Journal* 15 April 1758.

16 *Lloyds Evening Post and British Chronicle* 13 January 1758.

17 *Universal Chronicle and Weekly Gazette* 22 April 1758.

defender of the commercial interest of his country'.[18] On the other side of the Channel, 'French privateer taken by Orford … is one of five fitted out by Madame Pompadour, to look out for Capt. Lockhart'.[19]

Tartar was beloved by the English press as well as the public and her peers, and she again confounded French privateers unwilling to become prisoners:

> Friday arrived the Mount Osier, a French privateer of 20 carriage guns, nine-pounders, taken by the Tartar after two hours engagement. She had the assurance to board the Tartar, sword in hand, after she had struck her colours; but, according to the old saying, caught a Tartar, having 36 men killed in the attempt, besides many wounded.[20]

And from Portsmouth on 18 April:

> Yesterday arrived here the Tartar, Capt. Lockhart, who being on her passage to Plymouth with 15000l to pay the Dockyard there, on Friday met at the back of the Isle of Wight with a large French privateer, of 24 ten pounders and 240 men, engaged her an hour and a half, took her and brought her in here. Her name is the Duc d'Aiguillon, of St Maloes; had taken four small prizes and had ports for 20 guns more. The Tartar has suffered much and was forced this morning to go into harbour to dock and refit.

Later on the same page: 'There was a great number of spectators, from the Isle of Wight, of the engagement between the Tartar and the French privateer, crying out all the time, Well done, brave English boys etc.'[21]

Early in 1757 John Lockhart had attempted to separate warring factions of soldiers and seamen on the dockside and was too injured to take *Tartar* on her next commission. The local paper knew all about it:

> Letters from Plymouth bring the agreeable news that Capt. Lockhart is out of danger from the wounds he received in the late skirmish between some soldiers and sailors there, as he was endeavouring to part them, but that he will not be able to go the ensuing cruise in the Tartar, who now only waits another captain. We learn further that a great number of

[18] *Lloyds Evening Post and British Chronicle* 1 September 1758.

[19] *London Evening Post* 19 May 1757.

[20] Extract of a letter from Portsmouth 28 February. *London Read Weekly Journal or British Gazetteer*, 5 March 1757. The *Tartar*'s exploits were such that a chapter on *Tartar* was included in W.H. Long, *Naval Yarns* (Gibbings and Co., 1899), 49–52.

[21] *Schofields Middlewich Journal* 19 April 1757.

> the Tartar's men having resolved to go ashore and revenge their noble captain's cause, it coming to the captain's ear he very prudently sent orders to his first lieutenant to keep them all on board.[22]

An ambitious young lieutenant, Thomas Baillie was extremely fortunate to be poised for promotion and was 'made post' so that he could take *Tartar* out after a privateer which had been lurking off the shore. Despite their captain's inexperience, *Tartar*'s crew knew exactly what to do, and after a two-hour engagement *Marie Victoire* (24) was captured and brought in. Baillie commended John Lindsay, then lieutenant in *Tartar*, for 'having executed his duty during the action with great spirit and diligence'.[23] A newspaper reported that although the *Tartar* had only one man mortally wounded, *Marie Victoire* had a great number killed, and had nine killed at once by one shot from *Tartar* splitting one of the privateer's guns.[24] I return to *Marie Victoire* in Chapter 9.

Morale

By 1756 Admiral Boscawen was able to reassure his wife:

> To be sure, the whole French foreign trade is quite discontinued, either by order from their court or by their losses which, to be sure, last year and this have been very great ... at this time we have more than half their trading ships in our possession and if they should be reduced to trade entirely in neutral bottoms, it will ruin their marine, for from their own trade they must have their seamen. In deed, this scheme will not enrich us, but that we must suffer till we squabble with the Dutch, which I am apt to think will happen at last.[25]

Augustus Hervey had commented earlier on the boost to public morale when prize ships came in, as 'they drew conquests of people down and great fun was had here'.[26]

William Hotham, *Fortune* (10), another young aspirant in the Mediterranean, was fortunate enough to meet up with and overcome a much more powerful adversary. Admiral Charles Saunders informed their Lordships:

> As the Chesterfield and Fortune sloop were going to Barcelona for the trade, they fell in with a French ship from Marseille bound for Domingo of 26 guns, and one hundred and forty five men. Captain

22 *Evening Advertiser* 26 March 1757.
23 TNA ADM 1/1488 Captains' Letters B 1757 Baillie 28 March 1757.
24 *London Evening Post* 29 March 1757.
25 Lloyd, ed., *Naval Miscellany IV*, 237.
26 Bromley, 'Prize Office', 169.

> Hotham in the Fortune sloop engaged her an hour and a half, and took her before the Chesterfield got up. She had twelve men killed and thirteen wounded, the Fortune sloop had one killed and six wounded.[27]

Thanks to Admiral Saunders's return to the Admiralty, we have a list of the prizes taken by the nine ships under his command. During the four months from 16 June 1757, for example, Augustus Hervey, *Hampton Court* (64), took eleven vessels, James Webb, *St Albans* (60), took five, as did Thomas Stanhope, *Swiftsure* (70), while Richard Gwynn, *Ambuscade* (40), took three. Only one (Hervey's captured *Nymphe*) was a ship of war, but capturing thirty-two vessels took 1,380 men out of the French *marine* and made a significant difference. I will return to these prisoners of war in Chapter 10.

Not all attacks resulted in capture. As John Elliot reported about the unhappy vessel later identified as *L'Alcyon*:

> In company with his Majesty's ship Dolphin we chased a large French ship which I got alongside of at about 8 of the clock at night. We had not exchanged above two or three broadsides when the Dolphin came up about 10 or a little after the enemy lost all his masts and sank with his colours flying. I judged him to be a two deck ship with one tier of guns mounted, I could not possibly get a boat out to save one of his men, my lifts braces and tackles having been all shot away. The Dolphin sent her boat but could find no body.[28]

Unicorn (28) was another active ship. Lt. Michael Clements took over as captain when Captain John Rawlings was killed in the action against *Invincible*, and went out again after bringing her into Kinsale to capture her consort, which he did. Her purser was St Alban Roy, already mentioned as her agent. Lt. Michael Clements was not immediately rewarded for taking over from his mortally wounded captain, but he didn't have to wait long:

Extract of a letter from Dublin, 10 May:

> His Majesty's ship the Unicorn, of 20 guns, has taken and carried into Crookhaven, the Invincible privateer of St Malo's, 24 guns, Nine-Pounders, Nicholas Mitter Commander. Capt. Rawling of the Unicorn, the Boatswain, Armourer and six men were killed in the engagement. Lieut. Clements, who now commands the Unicorn, has sent 286 prisoners taken in the Invincible, to Kinsale.[29]

John Elliot did not take *Hermione*. But his letter to the Admiralty made clear that he had been involved in her capture:

[27] TNA ADM 1/384 Saunders 23 April 1757.

[28] TNA ADM 1/1759 1757–58 Captains' Letters E John Elliot 28 November 1757.

[29] *British Spy or New Universal London Weekly Journal* 21 May 1757.

> 28 November Plymouth Sound … On 19th I joined company with his Majesty's ship Unicorn and on 21st we chased two French ships of war; about 10 at night, being the headmost ship, I passed the sternmost of the enemy (which the Unicorn has taken) but lost sight of the ship I followed about midnight … The ship of war taken by his Majesty's ship Unicorn is from Louisbourg and mounts 26 12 pounders she engaged five hours and struck with the loss of her main and mizzen masts.[30]

Robert Craig in *Solebay* took a desperate privateer off Leith:

> On 23rd at 9am … we saw a French snow … in the evening we were within two gun shots on which we gained so much that lasted till we got up with her, which was not before eleven at night. Then found that she had sawed her gunnells thrown six of ten carriage guns she mounted and her boat overboard, and called the Chevallier Bart belonging to Dunkirk, with seventy eight men and three ransomers on board, one for a brig belonging to Dunbar and the other two cod smacks belonging to Harwich, the only prizes since she left Dunkirk, which was 5th instant, and this his first cruise since fitted as a privateer. We brought her in here and anchor'd last night after sunset.[31]

Archibald Kennedy's reports to the Admiralty convey the enthusiasm of a captain permitted to operate off the Lisbon coast, where his chance of prizes was high. Having safely delivered his convoy to Lisbon, Kennedy, *Flamborough* (20), set to work, and captured *Le Vermeulen*:

> Fell in with the noted French brigantine of Vigo and gave chace to her till 10 o'clock at night when I came up with her and took her. She mounted 16 carriage and 16 swivel guns and had onboard 111 very stout men. She was commanded by M. Jean Joseph Gassen and belongs to Marseilles she is the vessel that has done all the damage to the Oporto and Lisbon trades and has taken within this three years 32 English vessels and is accounted one of the best sailors out of France.[32]

His success was rewarded with a letter from the British Consul in Lisbon:

> The great service you have done your country in general and this factory in particular in taking the privateer that has, notwithstanding your vigilance, so long infested this coast, highly deserves applause and as British Consul give me leave for the Factory to return you their hearty thanks. I beg the favour that you would let me know the

30 TNA ADM 1/1759 1757–58 Captains' Letters E John Elliot 28 November 1757.

31 TNA ADM 2/1606 Captains' Letters C 1757–58 Craig 28 April 1757.

32 TNA ADM 2/2010 Captains' Letters K 1757–59 Kennedy 24 November 1759.

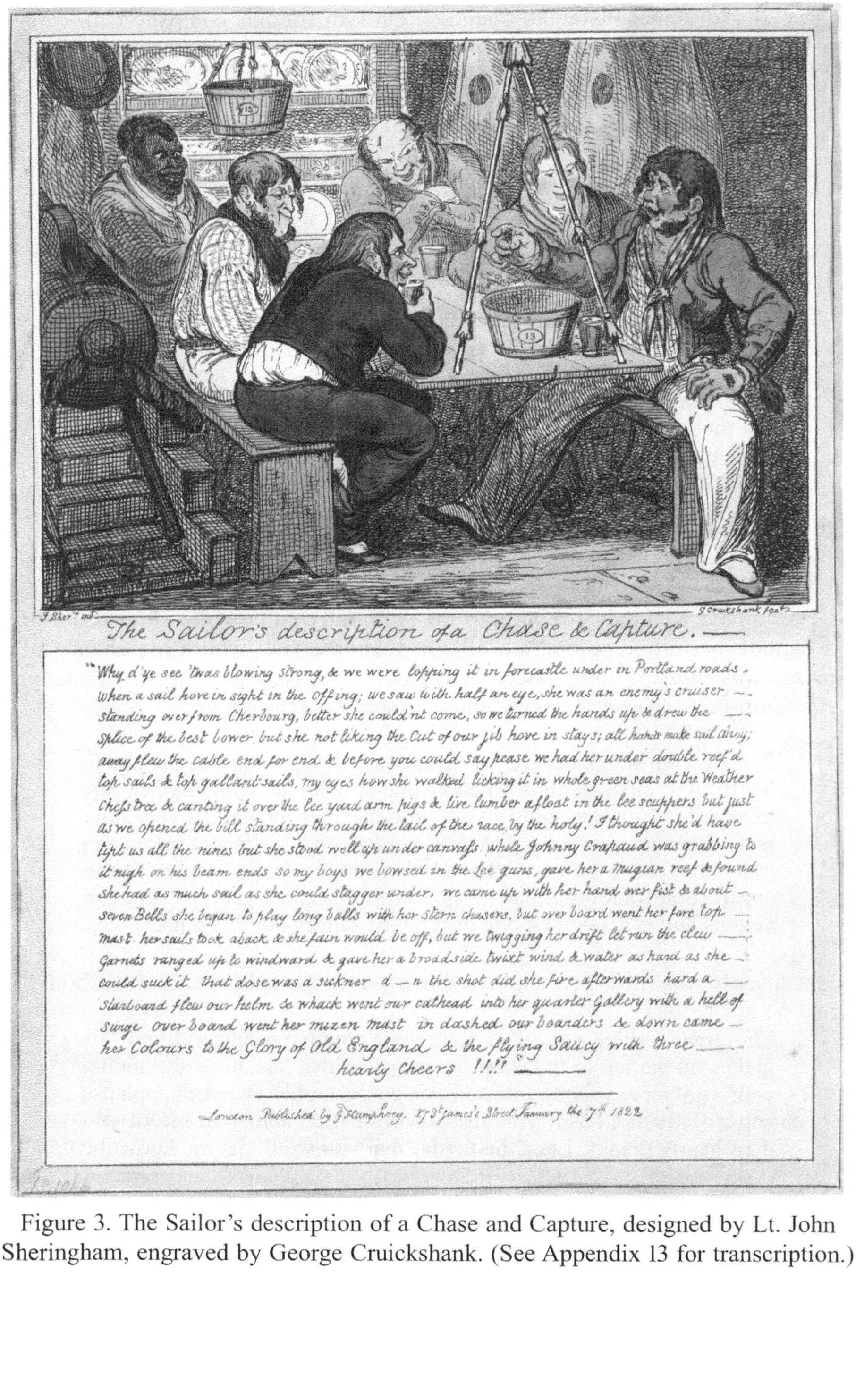

Figure 3. The Sailor's description of a Chase and Capture, designed by Lt. John Sheringham, engraved by George Cruickshank. (See Appendix 13 for transcription.)

> name of the privateer and Captain with some particular that you think ought to be communicated to Mr Pitt to whom I shall write by the next pacquet – pray learn if possible how many prizes she has taken and number of privateers that now rendezvous at Vigo. A Frankland.[33]

A few months later in company with *Bideford* (20), Kennedy found four enemy vessels, two of which made off. He pursued 'and I came up with the sternmost ship who poured a broadside into me, I thought I could do no less than return the compliment at the same time keeping after the headmost'. His efforts and those of *Bideford* were unavailing, and eventually the two French frigates were able to escape. Lancelot Skynner of *Bideford* was killed, with his first lieutenant, and it was Thomas Stace, the master, who reported the action:

> … everyone was sensible of the very superior forces of the two ships now standing towards us, besides that several other ships were coming in view, to whom the enemy was seen to make signals. No questions passed, shall we engage, the word was Now for Honour. We saluted each other with three cheers and stood in a line for the enemy who upon seeing this hauled up and obliged us to make the attack, which the Flamborough began (by our glasses) … before 7 pm and the Biddeford got close with the sternmost and commodores ship … [Signed]: Thomas Stace.[34]

In this case there were no prizes, but the encounter between the two sixth rates and the much larger French frigates *Malicieuse* (32) and *Opale* (32) was widely reported, commemorated on canvas and a beautiful engraving of the engagement on silver was made and presented to Kennedy.[35] Moreover, the trade was protected: '… the brave action has done great service, as it saved our convoy, which is since arrived and were so near as to hear the engagement'.[36]

Kennedy's attack on *Malicieuse* and *Opale* was reported in *Derby Mercury*, 9 May 1760, following a letter from Lisbon, 8 April. The French had taken *Penguin*, Captain Harris, and after sinking his ship put Harris and his crew on board a Swedish ship which carried them to Vigo. By this chain of events Captain Harris was in Vigo to report the version given by *Malicieux* and *Opale* to explain their shattered state – that they had been attacked by two 36s.[37] Kennedy met Harris when he had been exchanged, and he was able to

33 TNA ADM 2/2010 Captains' Letters K 1757–59 Kennedy 24 November 1759.

34 TNA ADM 2/2011 Captains' Letters K 1760–62 Kennedy 14 April 1760. Kennedy's attack on *Malicieuse* was also reported in *Aberdeen Press and Journal* 26 May 1760; *Leeds Intelligencer* 13 May 1760; *Caledonian Mercury* 27 October 1760.

35 On view at Culzean Castle, home of the Earls of Kennedy.

36 *London Evening Post* 8 May 1760.

37 *Aberdeen Press and Journal* 19 May 1760.

confirm the disparity of the combatants, the two British of 20 guns, the two French of 32 guns. In addition, the gossip in Lisbon about *Malicieuse* was that:

> … sides appears to be full of shell holes and her stern very much mauled and it is said had 21 men killed and 32 wounded and reports that she engaged an English frigate of 40 guns and dismasted her but lost sight of her in the night, otherwise insinuates would have took the Englishman and that she left her partner engaged with one of our 36 gun frigates.[38]

Many captains were able to take advantage of the fact that their vessels were French built, and not therefore obviously a threat. Guernsey privateers carried out frauds as they could pass for Frenchmen.[39]

Lloyds List told the wonderful story of the *Arethusa* of Hull, taken on 17 November by a privateer from Bayonne:

> … who after taking out the captain and all his hands, except four, man'd her with French men and sent her to Bayonne; but the French for want of judgement and a hard gale coming on, gave the care of the ship to the four Englishmen, who have brought her into Cowes.[40]

Convoy or Capture – 'protect the trade or annoy the enemy'

The Admiralty instructed merchants that 'on its being made to appear to them that any commanders of men-of-war had been defective in their duty, of convoying or protecting their ships or pursuing privateers on notice being given they should be dealt with according to their deserts'.[41] Insurance rates for merchant ships reflected whether or not they were in convoy. The rate of six per cent without convoy or three per cent in convoy was paid by the wine importing house of James Gordon for shipments from Madeira to London.[42]

Edmund Affleck, *Launceston* (40), engaged in accompanying a convoy to Lisbon, paid heed to one of the official regulations addressed to captains protecting convoys:

38 TNA ADM 2/2011 Captains' Letters K 1760–62 Kennedy 3 May 1760.

39 Pares, *Colonial Blockade*, 63.

40 *Lloyds List* No. 2283 5 November 1757.

41 Gomer Williams, *History of the Liverpool Privateers and Letters of Marque 1744–1812* (Liverpool, 2004), 116.

42 Ralph Davis, *The Rise of the English Shipping Industry in the 17th and 18th Centuries* (David and Charles, 1962), 319.

> If a captain or commander has transports or merchantmen under convoy and deserts the convoy to take a prize he forfeits his share, and faces court martial unless the hostile ship or vessel was armed and fitted for war and was hovering about or bearing down on the convoy.[43]

Affleck reported that while he was sailing ahead of the convoy he sighted a French ship and chased her '… but had the mortification to see I did not gain on her and about 11pm lost sight of her'. Affleck returned to the convoy, 'which all joined'. On that occasion the Lords were pleased with his conduct: first that he chased the privateer, but more important, that he returned to safeguard his charges from other attentions.[44]

Recaptures

Many of the numerous privateer captures listed were retaken on both sides as prize crews were not strong enough to withstand recapture. The English *Prince Edward* was taken 30 January 1759 by a French privateer, *Providence*, then retaken in February by the *Mary*, whose captain put 469 raw hides on board her, his own property. A week later she was retaken by *Petit Guave*, and the mate of the *Prince Edward* agreed to ransom her to the *Petit Guave*. This complication had to be resolved on appeal, as described in Chapter 7.

Recaptures by his Majesty's ships were returned to the original owners on payment of one-eighth part of the value, this sum to be paid to the capturing vessel and shared in the usual way. If retaken by a privateer, one-sixth part of the value – without any deductions – would be paid to and divided amongst the owner or owners, officers and seamen as mutually agreed.[45] The taking back of vessels previously captured by the French was taken seriously, and blazoned in the press. The *London Gazette* carried details of wonderful recaptures which would perhaps have inspired other brave souls to attempt the same feat:

> Letters from Barcelona relate that an English vessel, richly laden … had been taken eight days before by a French privateer … the captain left on board no more than four mariners of her own crew, viz: the English mate Peter Murray, the boatswain and two sailors … the English mate observing the French commander to be fast asleep in the cabin, had found means to enter the same, to provide himself there with a pistol and three cutlasses, and then to attack and drive away from the quarterdeck to the forecastle eight French mariners who were on watch, after wounding one who refused to retire. That upon this the French commander being awakened by the noise, came to the

43 Horne, ed., *Compendium of the Statute Laws*, 71.

44 TNA ADM 2/1442 Captains' Letters A 1758–61 Affleck 24 May 1759.

45 Horne, ed., *Compendium of the Statute Laws*, 35. 13 Geo.2, c.4, §18.

> cabbin door with a pistol in his hand, which he endeavoured to fire on the English mate, but that his pistol's not going off, gave the later an opportunity of firing his own, with the good success of lodging two balls in the French commander's shoulder and forcing him thereby to retire. At this time the other three English mariners were come from below deck, from whence they forced the eight French ones before mentioned, to go down in the hold with their comrades, with menaces to kill the first who should appear again on the deck. That in the meanwhile the English mate had drawn out of the cabbin all the arms and laid them near him on the deck. After which he had taken command of the vessel, and ordered four of the French mariners to come out of the hold, and to be stationed between the forecastle and the main mast, with prohibition, on pain of death, of coming nearer the quarterdeck or not executing his commands for navigating the vessel. That with these precautions he had the good luck to bring the vessel that morning at an anchor in the port of Barcelona, where he had made immediately his declaration before the English consul of this whole transaction.[46]

The rescuing of a prize from the captors by the crew of such prize was, by the Court of Admiralty, considered as a meritorious act, and every person who assisted in a rescue had a lien on the property thus saved. Did the four intrepid English mariners receive one-eighth part of the value of their 'richly-laden' vessel to share between them?

Henry Phillips Towry, *Juno* (32), reported that he brought back into the service a vessel which had been taken:

> Please to acquaint their Lordships that since I parted company with the Venus on the 15th instant, I fell in with the Dutchess of Gramont a privateer of Saint Malo's of 12 guns which I took after a chace of three hours. This ship was formaly his Majestys sloop the Hawk.[47]

Recaptures and Salvage

Recaptures and salvage were an age-old custom under *Consolato del mare*, but in the sixteenth century the rule became that ownership was transferred to the recaptor if the vessel had been in enemy hands for more than twenty-four hours. Once twenty-four hours had passed, ownership could be transferred back, but only after ransom was paid. The level of salvage was set so low that proprietors almost always wanted to buy their property back. In general it

46 LG issue no. 9702 5 July 1757.

47 TNA ADM 1/2588 Captains' Letters T 1760–61 Towry 17 June 1761.

was one-eighth of the independently assessed value. Privateers got one-sixth.[48] In cases of recapture, a further set of questions were appended so that every witness was interrogated 'as to the time place and circumstances of capture and recapture so that it may appear with certainty the number of hours the prize was in the enemys custody and their treatment'.[49]

La Subtille, with thirty-eight men on board, was taken by Thomas Burnett in *Rochester* (50). She had been taken and retaken many times, under at least one previous name, *Le Messager de Bordeaux*. Two previous masters had been François Marin and then Jacques Lemarie, but the interrogated crew 'knew nothing'.[50]

Ransom

The Ransom Bill dated from 1711, in which ransomers were to be fed at the rate of 3s 4d per day until the time of their arrival in England.[51] Parliament had promoted the practice of ransom by the Prize Act of 1739 which insisted that prizes could only be condemned in London. This clause was not reintroduced in 1762 when war was declared against Spain.[52]

Many privateers preferred to ransom the vessel they captured, as a means of getting some money from the capture. The alternative involved carrying more men than were needed, to form a prize crew and sail back to the home port. This crew risked not sharing subsequent prize money. Taking 'ransomers' on board solved this problem. A hostage (usually the chief mate) was taken into the privateer. French privateers carried a large number of blank ransom bills in French and English, in anticipation of doing deals as the voyage proceeded.[53] The master signed a form undertaking to pay the specified sum of money on his arrival in port (perhaps no more than a quarter or fifth of the value of the ship and cargo) whereupon the ship was released, with protection valid for twenty-four hours against other French privateers. It is impossible for this reason to estimate how many English ships were taken – the figure quoted for captures includes a large number that were ransomed.[54] The presence of 'ransoms' on board captured privateers was accepted as normal. But if the captor in turn was captured with ransom notes on him, these went to the new captor, and the original captor got nothing.[55] Privateers were warned not to

48 Hill, *Prizes of War*, 126.
49 TNA HCA 32.
50 TNA HCA 32/243/10.
51 Marsden, *Reports of Cases*, 222.
52 Pares, *Colonial Blockade*, 24.
53 Pares, *Colonial Blockade*, 25.
54 Davis, *English Shipping Industry*, 69.
55 Pares, *Colonial Blockade*, 19.

take the master's word for the value of cargo.[56] In case of ransom, the interrogators were directed to ask

> into the reasons and conditions of the ransom and be very circumspect as to the number of prisoners which may have been released and the place where the ship was discharged the quality of her cargo and the time of her being released with the necessity for leaving the prisoners.

Ransomers are returned to in Chapter 10.

The Admiralty was at pains to reinforce the message that the enemy's vessels had to be taken off the sea. Typical is their letter to Michael Clements on 10 June 1760 that he would be provided with 'four months provisions except beer of which he is to have one month ... to range along the coast between Cape Finisterre and the Borlings to intercept the enemy's privateers which infest that coast'.[57] Imagine a French warship being commissioned to range along the English south coast!

François Thurot

One of the privateers infesting the entire coast was Captain François Thurot. He was a very interesting character, actually commissioned by the French who made use of his swashbuckling inclinations to attract attention elsewhere than along the French coast. They made use of Thurot's reputation to distract the British from their blockade of the French coast, and sent him to make a landing in Ireland. The French provided him with over a thousand soldiers and he set off to Denmark in the frigate *Maréchal de Belle-Isle* with *Bégon*, *Blonde*, *Terpsichore*, *Amaranthe* and the sloop *Faucon*. Thurot prowled along the eastern coast, as far north as Scotland, refitting when he needed to do so in Scandinavia. He met up with Robert Craig, *Solebay* (28), and Benjamin Marlow, *Dolphin* (24), north of Leith, and the unfortunate Craig was badly injured.[58] Thurot had by this time taken between thirty and forty prizes, although credited with many more. Reduced to *Maréchal de Belle-Isle*, *Blonde* and *Terpsichore* the French eventually landed at Carrickfergus and took the dilapidated fort with little difficulty. Letters were sent by the Lieutenant General of Ireland to ports on the south coast asking for help, and Elliot, *Æolus* (32), Clement, *Pallas* (36), and Loggie, *Brilliant* (36), happened to be in Kinsale refitting after the defeat of Conflans in Quiberon Bay. As the senior

56 Pares, *Colonial Blockade*, 21.

57 TNA ADM 2/85 to Captain Clements 10 June 1760.

58 *The Newcastle Courant* 17 June 1758 didn't have it quite right: 'It is currently reported that Capt Craig of the Solebay man of war, is dead of the wounds he received in the engagement with the above frigate.'

officer, Elliot took charge and the three frigates made their way up the Irish Sea towards the French, driven by strong winds. Thurot was determined to make a stand when they met off the Isle of Man, the other French frigates tried to stay at a distance but were pursued. *Maréchal de Belle-Isle* was reduced to a wreck before the crew admitted defeat, their captain dead.[59]

Trade in Liverpool had been brought to a standstill by the presence of Thurot in the Irish Sea. Insurance premiums on vessels from Liverpool to Jamaica rose to twelve guineas per cent and to North America to ten guineas. The response from Liverpool was to send out their own privateer.[60] The Liverpool merchants put up a guarantee fund of £700 to send out their privateer *Liverpool* against Thurot. But only twenty-eight out of the crew of 207 appeared, and the plan had to be dropped.[61]

After the defeat of François Thurot, the news was internationally reported:

> Belfast March 1. This morning arrived in our harbour, and came to anchor off Carrickfergus, his Majesty's ship Pallas, Captain Clements Commander. The Pallas brought with her about 500 prisoners, 100 of whom are officers, being almost all that were with the French squadron, who are now landed at Carrickfergus, and she is to return tomorrow to rejoin the Squadron. The Occasion of bringing the Prisoners here was to ease the ships, to prevent an infection from the number of Wounded.
>
> Lieutenant Sharpe, of the Pallas, says that three men were killed in attempting to strike the colours of the Belleisle; during which attempt M. Thurot was killed, ten minutes after his first order to strike.[62]

Following this engagement John Elliot wrote to his father: 'I have lost my voice giving orders in so much that I cannot speak above my breath.'[63] He was gratified by the public response to his success, as well as the £1,000 he received from the King. He summed up his affairs:

> You'll be surprised when I tell you that notwithstanding the many prizes I have taken my whole stake is £2,500, aside the profits of the last expedition come in which with the £1000 I am to expect of the King will be two more. In all you may set me down as between four and five thousand which is a great deal in three years but when

59 *Terpsichore* had been a privateer before being bought by the French navy. Pritchard, *Louis XV's Navy*, 135.

60 Williams, *Liverpool Privateers*, 87.

61 Pares, *Colonial Blockade*, 28.

62 *Annapolis Maryland Gazette* 15 May 1760.

63 NMM ELL/400 24 February 1758.

> the number of prizes is considered it hardly can be believed … for I share in five prizes of war besides two destroyed, two privateers, half a dozen merchantmen and two retaken English ships.[64]

Archibald Kennedy was rewarded by the Admiralty for his activities while protecting Lisbon with the captured *Blonde* (32), and returned to the Lisbon station:

> A gentleman in town has received a letter from his son, surgeon on board his Majesty's ship the le Blond, Capt. Kennedy, which brings a confirmation of the carrying a French East Indiaman valued at 130,000l into the port of Lisbon. He further adds that, for a fortnight preceding the day of his letter, he had done duty, though surgeon, and kept guard on quarter-deck, on account of the great number of French prisoners.[65]

The muster book of *Blonde* gives the name of this intrepid surgeon as Thomas Stevenson, and the prize brought in £23,000.[66] Kennedy's other captures were *Le Boutin*, *Le Grande Despoire*, *Hardi*, *St Gregory*, as well as several further privateers. She also recaptured *Industry*, *Orleans*, *Penelope* and *Diamond*, all taken into Lisbon.[67]

One French ship of war was captured with only one shot being fired. Thomas Saumarez, *Antelope* (50), was in Kings Road when he was told of a French ship lying in Lundy Road. He found her off Ilfracombe, and although she hoisted colours, they then came down again. *Antelope* fired a gun, which was not returned. Saumarez sent his first lieutenant to know if they had surrendered. When the boat didn't return, he bore down on her stern and asked if she had struck, and was answered that they had. The very confused French vessel was *Belliqueux* (64) with 417 men.[68]

Louisburg 1758

Taking enemy vessels off the sea was not restricted to single combat. A second fleet set off under Admiral Boscawen to capture Louisburg. His efforts this

64 NMM ELL/400 22 April 1758.

65 *London Chronicle* 25 March 1762.

66 TNA ADM 36/5119 Muster Book *Blonde* 1762.

67 'A large French ship, Name unknown, from Bordeaux for Martinico with Flour, Wine etc is carried into Lisbon by the Blonde Man of War, Capt. Kennedy.' *Lloyds List* No. 2636 17 April 1761; 'The St Gregory, a French ship from Martinico, is taken by the Blonde Man of War, and carried into Lisbon.' *Lloyds List* No. 2666 31 July 1761.

68 LG issue no. 9843 11 November 1758. Kings Road was a naval anchorage at the mouth of the Avon River where it flows into the Bristol Channel.

time achieved perfect success, and the list was published of the forty-one ships to benefit from the capture, with the accompanying list of prizes: the taking of *Bienfaisant* and *Echo*, and burning in the harbour of Louisburg of *Prudent*, *Entreprenant*, *Célèbre*, *Capricieux*, *L'Apollon* and *Fidelle*, as well as the recapture of *Muscliffe*, *Dolphin* sloop and the prize *Sellerie*. There was Head Money for *Bienfaisant*, *Prudent*, *Entreprenant*, *Le Célèbre*, *Capricieux*, *L'Apollon* and *Fidèle*. *Boreas*'s Power of Attorney form specifies 'prize or prizes taken or seized by us'.[69] *Echo*'s Head Money was paid only to *Juno* and *Scarborough*. The bounties were paid to each ship in turn as she returned to harbour, beginning on 8 January 1760.[70]

We are indebted to one of John Elliot's colleagues, Edward Wheeler, *Isis* (50), for information about a joint attack off Plymouth on 25 March 1758:

> On 20th inst. being cruising on the coast of France, about five in the afternoon in company with the Æolus frigate of 30 guns, Capt Elliot, we fell in with a French fleet of merchant ships of 35 sail (convoyed by four of the French King's frigates) off the Isle of Rhé. Capt Elliot in the Æolus who greatly outsailed the Isis, began the attack with one of the frigates, viz le Blond of 32 guns and about 300 men and the Minion [Mignonne] of 20 guns and 142 men and continued the attack with great bravery and intrepidity, within pistol shot before we could come up to his assistance, occasioned by our running to leeward in order to attack the Commodore; and before we came up the Minion had struck to the Æolus ...[71]

Elliot wrote to the Admiralty to warn them that the first officer of *Mignonne* told him that the privateer had sailed in through the Needles and out at St Helens to reconnoitre the fleet at Spithead and that it had been done since by a sloop.[72] Elliot also wrote graphically to his father from Kinsale about his capture of the privateer *Vengeance*:

> I could not get up with him before three in the evening and then he brought too, and he behaved extreamly well for the first half hour when we was hardly within musket shot, but when I got close alongside he hardly fired one gun for my 6 or 7 however he held out till he was almost sinking, two of his masts gone 8 guns dismounted and 52 men killed and lost with the masts and 87 wounded, I had 6

69 TNA ADM HCA 30/15.

70 LG issue no. 9957 15 December 1759.

71 *Sussex Advertiser* 2 April 1759.

72 TNA ADM 1/1759 Captains' Letters E 1757–58 Elliot 22 March 1759. 'A French Privateer of 6 guns, was taken off the Back of the Isle of Wight by the Alderney Sloop of War, and is brought into Portsmouth.' *Lloyds List* No. 2629 24 March 1761.

> men killed, the lieutenant of marines and 14 wounded the weather was so bad and a lee shore that we were very near loosing her on the coast of Ireland, I sent only my first lieutenant and 6 men on board her and left the French to pump or sink but the weather cleared up and we towed her into this port. She is a very fine ship and mounted 32 guns in summer but only 24 now and 329 men. She is fit for nothing but a privateer and as that spirit is almost over she'll prove but an indifferent prize however I have no reason to complain for if I share with the Unicorn I shall go near to get 2 thousand pounds by the Hussar these three months that I've been to the windward.[73]

Elliot also wrote to his brother Gilbert, a Commissioner on the Admiralty Board, who had ordered *Vengeance* to be surveyed and bought into the navy, and commented to him:

> Lord Anson's proposing an other ship for me dose one great honour but I find the Hussar so good that I have not the smalest desire of changing and privateer fighting us is the best thing in the World for now the people is a little accustomed to it we shall allways get the better for I find they were much more expert in her than the last … the privateer has 37 wounded but I can not learn the exact number killed the French say only 36 or 8 but my people say they through 40 odd overboard besides 18 lost with the masts, so I've called it 82 to the Board.[74]

Elliot was not alone in refusing the offer of a larger vessel, which would give him a slightly higher salary, but would restrict his prize-taking activities. Many successful frigate captains resisted promotion to larger vessels, and evidence of reasoning behind this reluctance can be seen in the table of captures of the tranche studied, whose fruitful years of money-making were all in the frigates into which they were first made post.

Joint captures were not always harmoniously resolved. For small privateers seeking to benefit, 'being in sight only will not be sufficient … if, by the mere act of hanging on to his Majesty's ships to pick up the crumbs of the captors'.[75] When *Arc en Ciel* was taken as she was going into Louisburg on 12 June 1756 her immediate assailants were *Lichfield* (50) and *Norwich* (50). Also in sight were *Centurion* (60) and *Fourgeux* (64), other members of a group of ships cruising in company. Separated by fog, *Success* (20) knew nothing of the capture until informed of it subsequently, but together with *Baltimore* (14), the other vessel in the group, claimed a share. It took four years, but

73 NMM E/400 January 1758.

74 NMM E/400 January 1758.

75 Hill, *Prizes of War*, 74.

there was an appeal, discussed in Chapter 8 along with other captures where the appeal was the focus of interest.[76]

Thomas Harrison, *Venus* (36), was a very successful captain whose letters convey his professional ability. Released from Admiral Boscawen's fleet in Quiberon Bay in 1761, Harrison began by taking *Brune*, of 32 guns and 316 men:

> After a chace of four hours began to fire her stern chaser at me but as it was inclinable to calm I did not return any fire till I got within pistol shot of him which was about an hour after. At ten he began to engage and continued till past twelve, when the Juno coming up and firing a few guns he struck. She sailed from Brest on 29 Dec. … I had the good fortune to have four men killed and eighteen wounded, of which last is myself, slightly, my first lieutenant and the master, the former of which was at his quarters the whole time, but the latter was so much hurt as to be disabled. The rest of my wounded (except one) I hope will recover … mainmast had five shot through it, which I had much trouble to save, all the shrouds rigging being shot away and sails and rigging very much damaged … On 14th having then a jury main yard and top mast rigged discovered a sail to leeward and gave chase and at half past one she struck to me. She is the Saint Mark belonging to St Malo. She had taken two prizes, both of which were ransomed, one for £300 the other for £75. The ransom I found on board. The prizes are both arrived in Plymouth.[77]

On 3 April Harrison reported that while in company with William Fortescue, *Hero* (74), they captured *Bertin*, a *Cie des Indes* ship carrying $24,000 in cash or 'specie'. On 6 April his prize was *Lyon*, a privateer from Bayonne. This was reprinted for the public:

> His Majesty's ships the Hero, commanded by Capt. William Fortescue and the Venus, commanded by Capt. Thomas Harrison, on the 2nd instant … fell in with and took a French East India Ship called the Bertin, pierced for 64 guns, mounting 28 and manned with 353 men, 93 of them soldiers, belonging to the French East India Company, from Port L'Orient, bound to the Isle de France and Pondicherry, laded with ordnance and naval stores and merchandize, and 24,000 dollars. She sailed in company with the Valiant East India ship, of the same size and force, and the Fidelle frigate of 24 guns, belonging to the

76 Marsden, *Reports of Cases*, 71–2.

77 TNA ADM 1/1896 Captains' Letters H 1761 Harrison 16 January 1761; reported in *London Annual Register*, 1 January 1761. 'The la Brune Frigate of 32 Guns and 350 Men, from Brest, and a Privateer of 8 Guns and 50 Men, are brought into Plymouth by the Venus Frigate of War, Capt. Harrison.' *Lloyds List* No. 2611 20 January 1761.

> company, on the 28th past. Capt. Fortescue sent the Venus with the prize to Portsmouth, where they are arrived, and went in quest of the other India ship and frigate.
>
> The Venus also brought to Plymouth the Lion privateer of Bayonne, of 6 carriage guns and 12 swivels and 85 men, which she fell in with and took the 6th instant.[78]

Harrison continued his captures, and reported on 27 December:

> … engaged and took Le Boullogne, French East India Company ship bound to L'Orient laden with coffee and pepper. Action took about an hour, in which I had one man killed and 8 wounded, the Boullogne 8 killed and 17 wounded, among the latter was the Captain and another officer. She had 20 guns mounted and 192 men. She is with me in Plymouth.[79]

Not all attempts at capture were successful, even though this one resulted in the destruction of the target. William Hotham described chasing two vessels which took refuge in Aviles Bay. He followed them in, and received some fire from them and from a small battery on the headland. He anchored with a spring on his anchor so that he could fire both at the vessels and the battery. The battery and the vessels were both abandoned, and Lt Thomas Pasley was sent on shore to take possession of the larger vessel, which grounded in the night and was found to be bulged before the tide could rise enough to re-float her, so she was burned instead.[80]

Another prize that got away was described by Rear Admiral Rodney who gave an account:

> Capt. Ourry of the Acteon gave chace on the 16th to a French privateer of 16 guns and near 200 men, and drove her on shore between the Cape Barfleur and La Hogue. The enemy threw their guns and carriages overboard during the chace; and as it blew hard at N.E. and a great sea, the moment she struck, the masts went over her side, and the sea made a breach over her and she was effectively destroyed.[81]

78 *London Evening Post* 21 April 1761.

79 TNA ADM 1/1897 Captains' Letters H 1762 Harrison 1 January 1762.

80 TNA ADM 1/1897 Letters H 1762 Hotham 21 September 1762. Thomas Pasley's promotion to master and commander was backdated to this enterprise. The ship they destroyed at Aviles was the 32-gun *San Josef.* Pasley was John Elliot's cousin, on board with him at the defeat of Thurot.

81 *Public Advertiser* 26 November 1760.

On another occasion the prize did not escape, although the captain did not survive to receive his reward. Lt. Nash of the *Milford* wrote to the Admiralty:

> On Sunday the 7th, at ten in the morning, we saw a sail, which we came up with at ten at night, and engaged in Lat 34.15N and Long15.7W from the meridian of London. We had the misfortune to have Capt. Man shot through the right thigh at the beginning of the engagement, with a six-pound ball: he expired about three on Monday morning. Mr Day, first lieutenant, received a musket ball in the middle of his forehead, about half past eleven, which he died of on Wednesday morning, being most of the time delirious. I received some slight wounds, about half past two on Monday morning, thwart my eyes, face and hands, by a wad and splinters. Half an hour later the enemy struck, with the loss of her main and mizen masts and fore-top mast. She proved to be the Glory, a letter of marque … loaded with wine, flour, brandy, bale goods etc and had been a privateer of Bayonne.[82]

Neutral waters were not to be used for prize taking. In general, thanks to Bynkershoek, 'the dominion of the land ends where the force of arms ends' – water within cannon shot of shore was under jurisdiction of shore, i.e. one league or three miles.[83] However, if the land was French, this did not apply. Moreover, ports which were blockaded were not accessible to neutral trade. An interesting joint capture was made when four Swedish vessels were cut out from Conquet Road. The close blockade of Brest was maintained by constant surveillance, and Admiral Hawke sent Augustus Hervey, *Monmouth* (70), and Michael Clements, *Pallas* (36), 'to annoy and distress the enemy' every way they could.[84] Having spotted four Swedish vessels sheltering behind Conquet castle, Hervey, supported by Clements, by this time captain in his own right in *Pallas*, sent men in the boats of both ships to cut the four vessels out, which they achieved. He was suspicious about their being there in the first place, as Sweden was a source of naval supplies much needed in the French arsenals, and normal trade was denied during a blockade. In typical fashion, Hervey reported his taking the four ships and concluded:

> … and in about two hours and a half the boats (being covered by the fire of our two ships) brought those four vessels out (who hoisted Swede's colours) from the fire of four forts and a battery and other detached pieces of cannon on points of rocks. I cannot help, Sir, commending to you the bravery of the officers and seamen on this occasion.[85]

82 *The Scots Magazine* 5 April 1762.

83 Hill, *Prizes of War*, 118.

84 Erskine, *Augustus Hervey*, 304.

85 Mackay, ed., *Hawke Papers*, 243, 245.

A letter from Admiral Hawke to the Admiralty described the action, and his conclusion that the four Swedish vessels were harbouring contraband:

> The four he has now sent to me are furnished with cargoes according to their own account, which appear to be but too necessary to the enemy in their present equipment. Besides from their manner of stowage and some other circumstances, there is ground to suspect they have guns and other contraband goods underneath all. As the weather will not permit me to search with them here, I have sent them into Plymouth under care of the Pallas, there to be detained till their Lordships pleasure be known.

Hawke sent Clements specific orders about the treatment of the vessels:

> You are hereby required and directed to proceed forthwith with the four Swedish vessels cut out of Conquet Road to the port of Plymouth and there see them laid up in safety, either in the Hamoaze or Catwater, till the determination of the Lords Commissioners of the Admiralty shall be known, leaving you all and singular concerned as captors to take what steps you shall think necessary for your own interest.[86]

When Hawke reported the capture to the Admiralty, the Secretary minuted that the Commissioner at Plymouth was to cause the ships to be thoroughly rummaged in the presence of the Customs House officers and some person on behalf of the captors and to send if there is any contraband goods on board and report what he finds to the Lords.[87]

Information about one of the most extraordinary captures came from the deposition of James Haleren, a quartermaster on board *Lowestoffe* (28). It seemed very unusual for one of the captor's crew to be interrogated, but his deposition explained the circumstances. Haleren was a Shetlander, and had sailed for years in the merchant service before, at a guess, being pressed into the navy. When *Lowestoffe* came up with the prize *La Bonté* after a three-hour chase off Cape Ortegal, there was no resistance. He was sent across in a boat to take her as a prize, but before they reached her side the crew on board had left her in their boats, leaving nobody on board. Haleren was then joined by Mr Barber, one of the lieutenants of the *Lowestoffe*, who took possession of her. She was loaded with sugar, coffee, cacao, indigo and some hides.[88]

86 Mackay, ed., *Hawke Papers*, 242.

87 Clevland's minute on Hawke's letter 16 July 1759. Mackay, ed., *Hawke Papers*, 242.

88 TNA HCA 32/170/12. Contains full details of the vessel, her cargo, master, etc.

West Indies

Throughout the war British vessels were busy in the West Indies. Under the command of Admiral Cotes at Jamaica, Arthur Forrest's *Augusta* (60) was one of three vessels tasked to find and capture eight French merchantmen which they had been advised were ready to leave Port au Prince. The three vessels did not operate together, *Augusta* being ordered to cruise off the Guanarve for three days, the others cruising off Cape Nicholas. Forrest's description of his capture of eight French vessels off Hispaniola is a classic. Having spotted the merchant vessels close under the land he crept up on them from behind, and took the first, *St Pierre*, without firing a shot and therefore without warning the others. He shifted the prisoners, armed *St Pierre* and dispatched her to cut off any of the enemy that attempted to enter the port of Petit Guave. At daybreak he came up with the fleet, and attacked immediately, dropping boats to board them as soon as each struck. The whole fleet except for *Mars* was taken, with 190 men and most of the officers on board the prizes, and 300 prisoners on board. With only 212 men still on board to guard the prisoners, work the ship and fight her, they followed *Mars* and only when she ran into a shoal did she strike. This feat is returned to in Chapter 8.

Captures on Land

After exploring so many naval captures, it might seem irrelevant to mention captures on land. However, the events which follow were only made possible as a result of naval strategy, and some of the most substantial prizes of this war were not taken at sea.

Capture of Guadaloupe

To gain a prize which could be traded for Minorca, an amphibious force was sent to capture Martinique. An unexpectedly strong French resistance caused the emphasis to shift to Guadaloupe, which was successfully taken instead, without the horrendous death toll from disease which was Martinique's legacy. Guadaloupe was a very impressive prize, and within a year had sent more than ten thousand tons of sugar to Britain. It was the opposite of the smuggling centre, the Dutch St Eustatius, producing nothing of its own, but providing cover for clandestine traffic of all kinds. The contemporary Richard Gardiner described the island of St Eustatius as:

> … the barest and least fertile, notwithstanding the Dutch carry on a very powerful trade in the West Indies from it and it has been for some years the market of Europe. Being poor and naked in itself and in all appearance like a ragged rock, it thrives by borrowed commodities and a clandestine traffic with the powers at war; transporting the produce of one enemy to another under the pretence of neutral bottoms …

> it is an island of smugglers and the common receptacle of all the thieves in Europe.[89]

Captures from Spain at Manila and Havana

Once Spain was incautious enough to declare war, plans were immediately made to take Manila, the centre of Spanish trade in the East Indies, and Havana, the capital of Spanish Cuba. The spoils of these enterprises will be discussed in Chapter 10.

The capture of Havana was a brilliant amphibious exercise. The huge fleet of ships of war and transports was organised, provisioned and collected within two months. The transports had to be guided and protected as the attacking fleet made landfall a few miles away from Havana, having approached from the 'wrong' side, to avoid detection by the Spanish navy, inside the harbour. The invading forces were decimated by disease but eventually a mine under the walls of the defending Morro Castle was detonated on 30 July and the city of Havana and the Spanish naval vessels sheltering there capitulated on 14 August. Three million pounds in gold and silver and a large proportion of the Spanish fleet were seized.[90]

A similar attack on Manila, on the other side of the world, caught the Spanish completely wrong-footed, as the attacking force, collected in India from the East India Company, arrived before the news that Spain was at war with Britain. The *Santissima Trinidad* was captured with a cargo of Chinese goods worth $1.5 million, not easily converted into cash. The galleon *Filipina*, carrying American silver from Acapulco on board and the returns on the previous year's investment, was not captured. When she was found, her cargo had already been taken off by boat and hidden.[91] The value of *Filipina*'s cargo was to have been counted in the ransom, but the arrangement was never carried out. The contents of the Cavite arsenal were declared prize despite the fact that the arsenal was on shore: they were Spanish naval stores

89 Richard Gardiner, *An account of the expedition to the West Indies, against Martinico, Guadalupe and other the Leeward Islands* (London, 1759), 88. Gardiner was Captain of Marines on *Rippon* during the campaign.

90 Admiral Pocock, writing from Havana harbour on 9 October 1762, reported to the Admiralty Secretary John Clevland that the French frigates *Diadème*, *Brilliant* and *L'Opale* were making the passage of transports hazardous. However, after convoying merchant vessels through the windward passage, *L'Opale* struck some rocks and was lost with two British transports. *Diadème* also struck twice but got off. British prisoners on board reported their experience to Pocock who passed it on: 'At this very time the French seamen behaved in so disorderly and mutinous manner that their officers put arms into the hands of the English prisoners to keep the Frenchmen in obedience. I mention this fact as an extraordinary instance seldom to be met with.' David Syrett, ed., *The Siege and Capture of Havana 1762* (Navy Records Society, 1970), 301.

91 Nicholas Tracy, *Manila Ransomed* (Exeter, 1995), 87.

at a Spanish naval station, taken by a British naval force as the result of an amphibious engagement, just as the taking of Havana resulted in most of the Spanish navy being declared prize. The soldiers, sailors and irregulars sacked the city, seizing at least a million dollars' worth of plunder.[92]

Once war with Spain had been declared, her ships were legitimate targets. In February 1762 Thomas Harrison brought in more intelligence:

> On 11 Jan fell in with the Night of Creole French privateer belonging to Bayonne of 8 four pounders and 84 men … there were on board three Dutch men and an English prisoner who says that there are twelve Spanish men of war in Ferol four of which are almost ready for sea also two Venetian ships.

On 19 March Harrison had more success and more intelligence to impart:

> At one the same day I discovered a sail bearing down which I found to be an enemy. After four hours chace I came up with her when she struck. She proved to be the Ana Celeste Marca from Bordeaux bound to St Domingo who sailed from hence 28 February in company with seven other ships all bound to the West Indies. The … had 800 000 pds on board … being in company with the three ships I was chased in the afternoon by a ship who I soon found to be a privateer as he lay to look at me at about 2 miles distance some time. And not liking my appearance made sail from me to whom I gave chace of … in which I ran 60 leagues his maintopmast going over the side I came up with her. It proved to be the Amabel Josepha, a Spanish privateer belonging to St Sebastian of 14 guns and 103 men being the first privateer that has been out of Spain. She sailed from the Groyne the 12 Jan.[93]

On 1 May:

> … at eight in the morning discovered two sail to whom I gave chace and found them to be both privateers one a brigg the other a ship but soon after they divided, the one steering NW the other SE I followed the ship and after a chase of eight hours came up with her after exchanging a broadside at each other she struck proved to be the Miquellet of Bayonne Capt. Culhound of 14 guns and 136 men had been out about three weeks and taken the Fair American Minshall from South Carolina for London out of which ship he had taken nine tons of indigo. The privateer had two men killed. As soon as I shifted the prisoners I endeavoured to find the other privateer but the weather proving foggy for several days we could see nothing of her.

92 Fred Anderson, *Crucible of War: The Seven Years' War and the Fate of the Empire in British North America 1754–1766* (Faber and Faber, 2000), 805 n 11.

93 Reported in the *Caledonian Mercury* 29 March 1762.

> On the 13 May … I retook the Cornwall brig belonging to Guernsey from Barbados who had been taken the day before by the Casket of Bevonia privateer of Marseilles of 12 guns and 106 men who had been out two months and taken no other prize. I went in immediate pursuit but the weather being thick saw nothing of her. She sailed in company with another privateer of 28 guns and 240 men who is gone to cruise off the Western Islands. On the 2nd June I took up a boat with two French prisoners deserters from Kingsale who had been three days at sea without any subsistence. On the 3rd I gave chase to a ship who I discovered to be a privateer but proving calm he got his oars out and rowed. I did the same with oars and boats for 12 hours in which he gained but little of me. The next day a breeze springing up after a chace of eight hours I came up with her and after exchanging two broadsides at each other she struck and proved to be the Signora de Begonia a Spanish privateer belonging to Bilboa commanded by Martin Sopagna of 16 six pounders 20 swivels and 195 men had been out 11 days had taken a Dutch ship bound to Lisbon with 800 barrels of powder and a Portuguese schooner with 200 pipes of wine for our fleet at ports and he informed me that war was declared against the Portuguese before he sailed and that the Spaniards had entered Portugal and taken the towns of Tame and Braganza.[94]

The tranche of captains whose exploits were detailed above did themselves proud. There are hundreds of similar stories which could be told about captures, and these letters show something of the range of their experiences.

94 Reported in *London Chronicle* 12 June 1762.

5

Monitions Issued by the High Court of Admiralty

High Court of Admiralty

A monition was a warning, usually issued by an ecclesiastical court, advising an individual not to commit an offence. However, as issued by the High Court of Admiralty, the warning was that the interested parties should attend the court hearing about to be held. The decision to be made was whether the capture was a legitimate prize and could be condemned, or not and should be returned.

There was a concentration of ecclesiastical lawyers in the City of London, and in the fifteenth century these became loosely associated into a Society which fulfilled the functions of an Inn of Court. Referred to as 'Doctors of the Arches' in 1496, the advocates together with a few proctors specialised in canon and civil law.[1] Their ancient home was the church of St Mary-le-Bow, or in Latin, Sancta Maria de Arcubus – the Arches. After the great fire of London in 1666 the premises in which Doctors Commons were based were rapidly rebuilt around two quadrangles, one entered from Great Knightrider Street, the other from St Benet's Hill, with a covered passage connecting them. The new court room was used for the sittings of the Court of Admiralty and of the prerogative Court of Canterbury and the Bishop of London's Consistory Court.

Doctors Commons

No trace of Doctors Commons survives, although the space where the building once stood is just below St Paul's Cathedral.

Sir Thomas Salusbury

Sir Thomas Salusbury, Knight and Doctor of Laws, was appointed Judge of the Admiralty Court in 1752 'so long as he shall behave himself, with a salary of £400 *per annum*', in effect having been appointed for life. He inherited the

1 G.D. Squibb, *Doctors' Commons: A History of the College of Advocates and Doctors of Law* (Clarendon Press, 1977), 16. Charles Dickens described Doctors Commons in *David Copperfield*, ed. N. Burgis (Oxford, 1981), 292.

post from his father-in-law Sir Henry Penrice, who had held the post from 1715 to 1751, and therefore kept in the family the fortune of £150,000 which Penrice had amassed during his tenure. The Letters Patent appointing Sir Thomas take more than 2,400 words to explain the complexity and gravity of his appointment, encompassing as it did:

> … any business or injury whatsoever done to or to be done as well in upon or by the sea or public streams or fresh waters ports rivers creeks and places overflown whatsoever within the ebbing and flowing of the sea and high water mark or upon any of the shores or banks to them or either of them adjacent from any of the first bridges towards the sea through England and Ireland and the dominions thereof or elsewhere beyond the seas …[2]

Salusbury remained in the post for twenty-two years. His epitaph was merely that 'he was a respectable judge'.[3] As early as October 1758 Lord Hardwicke suggested it would be a very good thing if Sir Thomas Salusbury could be induced to resign his office, as his administration of justice was said to be very strange. Having been appointed for life, he could only be turned out with his consent.[4] Judges were not usually appointed for their legal qualifications: not only was he Sir Henry Penrice's son-in-law, he had also been Hardwicke's protégé.[5] The government afterwards wished it could get rid of 'this passionate old fool'.[6] It is not possible to know from this distance in time, with the resources at our disposal, which of Salusbury's decisions were 'foolish'. The written records are copybook evidence only that the rulings were intended to be a simple condemnation or release. The cases which were called into question and appealed are dealt with in Chapter 7.

In 1756 Sir Thomas Salusbury asked the Lords of the Admiralty 'as to the character of certain ships, whether they were of war or private; the answer is that he not they is the judge'.[7]

Responsible for the High Court of Admiralty during the Seven Years' War, the judgements Sir Thomas passed down are central to our understanding of the processes by which prize money was allocated. It must be remembered that prize money was only one of his responsibilities: maintaining discipline

2 Marsden, *Reports of Cases*, 345.

3 W. Senior, 'Sir Henry Penrice and Sir Thomas Salusbury', *Mariner's Mirror* (Society for Nautical Research, February 1927), 38–44.

4 Pares, *Colonial Blockade*, 85.

5 Sir Lewis Namier and John Brooks, *The House of Commons 1754–1790* (HMSO, 1964), 599–600.

6 Pares, *Colonial Blockade*, 132.

7 Reginald G. Marsden, 'Prize Law', *Journal of the Society of Comparative Legislation* (Cambridge University Press, 1915), 91.

within the navy; murder on the high seas; the wearing of illegal colours; failure by merchantmen to salute the King's Navy when they met it, all fell within the general criminal jurisdiction of the Court of Admiralty over offences committed at sea.

Members of the College

The lawyers who practised in Doctors Commons were civilians, all with doctorates in civil law from Oxbridge. The necessity of holding a doctor's degree before being admitted as an advocate meant the average age was about thirty, and the need for an initial 'year of silence' meant that membership was restricted to those whose fathers could support them for a year. The law they dispensed developed during the seventeenth and eighteenth centuries, particularly after the crucial Convoys and Cruisers Act of 1708 which laid down the guidelines intended to protect the trade, and defined the records to be kept.[8]

The senior lawyers who made up the High Court of Admiralty signed official documents with their titles: usually Sir Thomas Salusbury himself, together with the Register. The Register was the principal official not just of the Admiralty Court, but of the Court of Delegates. The Register was required to be of great experience and ability, as his position was one of trust and consequence. Not only did he have to enrol or enter among the rolls all the acts of the court, he also gave the parties copies of the court proceedings if they asked for them, and also preserved all records of the court.[9] In 1758 Godfrey Lee Farrant became Register, and appointed George Bellas the deputy Register. In 1759 Farrant replaced Bellas with Nathaniel Bishop. Dr Andrew Ducarel was a doctor of civil law from 1742, admitted as a member of Doctors Commons in 1743, and served as Librarian from 1754–57 and as Treasurer from 1757–61. He acted as Salusbury's surrogate when necessary. Dr John Bettesworth had been a Dean of the Arches from 1710 to 1751. The Admiralty Procurator was a go-between between the Admiralty and the court. He intervened if the captor became liable for costs if the ship was restored, when the Droits fund might be used to pay any compensation due. The Register and Marshall were there for administrative support. The Marshall also scrutinised applications for letters of marque.

Dr George Hay

The most interesting member of the Court was Dr George Hay, whose signature can be seen whenever and wherever maritime affairs were debated. As one of the Lords of the Admiralty from November 1756 to April 1757 and July 1757 to July 1765, Dr Hay would have been familiar with the lovely room in

8 Hill, *Prizes of War*, 8.

9 G.I.O. Duncan, *The High Court of Delegates* (Cambridge, 1971), 191.

Figure 4. Doctors Commons, 1805, showing the dining room to the right.

Admiralty House where the Lords of the Admiralty and the Secretary met to conduct the business of the Royal Navy, and as such, was one of the signatories of Protections, intended to save individuals from the rigours of impressment. Working at the same time in the parallel world of the Court of Admiralty, Hay was also one of the Deans of the Arches from 1764 to 1778, appointed by the Archbishop of Canterbury to hear appeals from consistory courts. He took over from Salusbury as Judge of the Admiralty Court in 1773, was followed by Sir James Marriot in 1778, before Sir William Scott (Lord Stowell) in 1798. Sir Christopher Robinson, who succeeded Lord Stowell in 1828, spent several years of his tenure in Doctors Commons in writing the book *Collectanea Maritima* which is often cited as a reference in this work.[10]

Most officials had no salary. Until the reforms of 1840, they subsisted entirely on fees, which could vary according to whether or not conditions of peace or war prevailed. The reality is that fees amounted to about 3.4 per cent of the whole.[11] This is discussed in more detail in Chapter 10. The lawyers who made up the High Court of Admiralty were professionals in their own right, and were only called on to do duty in the court of prize jurisdiction when necessary. This was infrequent at the outset of the war, but as the pace intensified, so would their attendance, as shown by the dates of Salusbury's decisions.

The Work of the High Court of Admiralty

There were two aspects to the work of the Admiralty Court. The first was called its Instance jurisdiction which involved ordinary civil disputes between private litigants. Claims for salvage, or wages, or damages for collision were determined in this jurisdiction. It was so called because suits were brought at the instance of a party.[12]

The second part was called the Prize jurisdiction. This was the aspect that laid the foundation for this book. Its name comes, of course, from the fact that ships captured during hostilities, whether merchantmen or warships, were known as 'prizes'. Every captured prize had to be the subject of adjudication

10 Sir George Hay, Chancellor of the diocese of Worcester, was the King's Advocate General from March 1755 to May 1756 and November 1756 to July 1764, the brief periods out of office due to the change in government. Hay was a Member of Parliament from 1754 until his death in 1778.

11 Hill, *Prizes of War*, 163–9.

12 TNA HCA 5/. These hard-backed books are a diary of the cases heard in the Instance court, from disputed wages of sailors to the King's right to the whale which was found in the Thames and brought to Deptford. Fascinating though they are, with the familiar names of Judges, they are not part of the prize law and regretfully have to be laid aside.

by the High Court of Admiralty. Prizes and their cargoes, if condemned by the decree of the Court, were sold and the proceeds divided in varying proportions between the captors and, in some cases, the Crown. But the arrest of shipping was not meant to be out-and-out piracy. Not all seizures were lawful and it was the role of the Admiralty Judge to determine whether the prizes should be returned to their owners or condemned and sold.

The dining room

Once the decision had been taken in the common hall of the Doctors Commons, the Court adjourned for the final legal action of condemning a prize to the peace and quiet of the dining room, seen through the open door on the right of the little print shown in Figure 4. Every sentence was followed by this rubric, only the date changing:

> This sentence was read signed promulged by the Judge aforesaid upon Friday the twenty eighth day of January in the year of our Lord one thousand seven hundred and fifty seven in the Dining Room near the Common Hall of Doctors Commons London (the Court being adjourned from the said Hall) in presence of the two credible witnesses named in the Act of Court. Which I attest Geo. Bellas Notary Publick Deputy Register.[13]

Lodging a monition and the essential documentation

As soon as the captured vessel was safely in port, two processes were set in motion. The first was the securing of the vessel and its contents. To this end the Admiralty had provided warrants for named officials in each major port, as discussed in Chapter 4: William Hambly in Plymouth, Charles Brett in Portsmouth, Tyringham Stephens in Deal and Dover and Edmund Mason in Chatham. These men worked with the Customs officials to ensure that dues were paid on French goods. In addition to the Admiralty responsibilities of these officials, as prize agents they also had duties on behalf of their clients. The many captors who had already appointed the team of Mason, Brett, Macpherson or Stephens were confident they were highly experienced professionals. As they were already on the spot, already with authority to act, difficulties were being minimised.

The second process was the requirement for a responsible official to undertake the questioning of the captain, master and at least one other senior member of the crew, each undertaken separately and afterwards compared. There were printed sheets of questions, so that every prize would be handled in the same way. The list of questions which made up the interrogation is

13 TNA HCA 32/204.

provided at Appendix 5. Major ports had French-speaking notaries who could translate the questions into French and the answers into English. The written answers usually dispensed with the questions, listing simply its number. Hundreds of sets of these questions and their answers are to be found in the boxes containing the series HCA 32, the Prize Court papers relating to cases concerning ships captured as prizes in time of war.

Sir James Marriott, King's Advocate from 1767, used the phrase 'out of her own mouth' to describe the methods of the Admiralty Courts, which he claimed:

> … decide by Evidence out of the Mouth of the Captured Party, and not of the Captor whose evidence, as well as the Evidence of Third Persons, is never admitted, but where no other proof can be had; as when the Captured abscond, or have destroyed all the papers.[14]

The questions began by establishing where the individual lived, and then his responsibility as far as the ship and its cargo were concerned at the time of the capture. Details of the ship's history, ownership and cargo were established, together providing information which would prove whether the ship and its cargo were in reality neutral and innocent, or involved in carrying contraband.

The interrogation of the senior officers of *St Amand* is an exemplar of the hundreds of documents stored in the National Archives, as it contains most of the features of these wonderful pieces of evidence:[15]

- The clerks who prepared the texts for signature were careful not to deface the stamps impressed into the top margin, and left gaps in the text of the top line on the cover page and the following page for the stamps to be clearly visible.
- The name of the captured ship could change: on the cover the ship is *St Amand*; inside she is recorded as being the *St Aman*.
- The ship changed hands several times: first taken by *Bedford* on 5 October and sent to England under a prize crew of ten English sailors and one Frenchman, she was retaken on 26 October by the French privateer *Port Mahoon*, and on 4 November finally taken by Thomas Burnett, *Happy* (8), in company with James Kirk, *Lynn* (44). It is impossible to say how many ships were taken during the war as the separate occasions of each capture are not necessarily recorded.

14 Deák and Jessup, 'Early Prize Court Procedure', 692 n 60. Marriott was made Judge of the High Court of Admiralty in 1778.

15 TNA HCA 32/168/18.

- No matter how willing the witnesses were, there were questions they were in no position to answer, not having been in the original crew but part of a temporary prize crew.
- The formal interrogations followed precisely the sequence laid down, designed to elicit the facts, corroborated if possible by the second and third sets of answers.
- Thomas Oldfield, one of the *Bedford*'s prize crew, must have been relieved to be taken back to England, with the possibility of rejoining his ship instead of being incarcerated in a French prison. Would he have shared in the prize money claimed by *Happy* and *Lynn*?
- Included in the packet is the printed *Commission en Guerre* issued to Louis Guyot du Clos, master of *Le St Aman* in 1756, which entitled him to take prizes. Also included is the list of merchandise she was carrying.
- Interrogations taken in Guernsey were recorded on paper which was not stamped, that is not legally binding, but were always accompanied by an attestation to the fact.

The Treasury charged a fee for every legal document, and in the Prize Court every document is impressed with two five shilling stamps, thus costing the prize agents ten shillings before the costs of endless copies were added in to the deductions.

Proctors

Proctors were the individuals who managed causes in a court, a cause being a legal claim that allowed a party to seek judicial relief. They prepared the cases, drawing on the evidence from the prize agents who arranged for the standing interrogatories to be carried out, and provided the ship's papers. Proctors then prepared monitions or warnings to be posted on the pillars of the Royal Exchange (see below). If the case resulted in condemnation, the proctor would inform the prize agent who arranged the sale of the vessel and its tackle and furniture and the goods on board. The prize agent would prepare the final accounts, then submit them to the proctor, who would 'bring them in' to court for formal finalising; the distribution would take place very soon after. The average time between 'bringing in' and the appearance of the notice in the *London Gazette* was about a week.

An exemplar of a monition

When John Elliot captured *La Marie Madelaine*, master Jean le Febure, he sent his second lieutenant Samuel Burford to attest to the handing over of the papers etc. to his prize agent, in the presence of Orlando Manley, Commissioner, and John Kerly, Notary Public, on 10 June 1758. The prize agent's application to Sir Thomas Salusbury to have the prize sentenced is couched in suitably formal language. It was passed to Thomas Tyndall, the proctor, who presented it in court at the hearing:

> That all and singular the premises were and are true publick and notorious and thereof there was and is a publick voice fame and report of which legal proof being made the party proponent prays you the Right Worshipful Sir Thomas Salusbury Knight Doctor of Laws Lieutenant President and Judge of the High Court of Admiralty of England that right and justice may be truly administered to him and his party in the premises and that the said ship her tackle apparel and furniture and the goods taken therein be pronounced to belong at the time of capture of the same to the French king his vassals subjects or others inhabiting within his countries territories or dominions and subject to confiscation and to be adjudged and condemned as and for good and lawful prize by you and your definitive sentence to be given in this behalf.

The allegation was given by Tyndall and admitted on 27 July 1758.[16]

The combination of Thomas Tyndall being the proctor who accepted the monition, which was then signed in addition by George Hay, was repeated over and over again, as George Hay was the King's Advocate General 'for all matters ecclesiastical and maritime relating to the crown'.[17]

Of the sample taken of HCA 32, only two monitions were handled by the pair Andrew Coltee Ducarel and William Gostling: Thomas Harrison's retaking on 7 May 1761 of the *Lowell Pacquet* fighting as the privateer *Le Lyon*; and the privateer *Terrible* captained by William Death which took the Spanish merchantman *Nostra Senora del Rosario* when she anchored in the Hope on her way to offload her cargo in London, 18 November 1756.

The National Archives holds hundreds of monitions in the series HCA 31. Each pile of about 250 sheets of parchment covers the business of approximately six months of work by the Register. An example of the text can be read at Appendix 4. This gives the wording for a capture by a ship of war. A capture by a privateer has additional wording to take account of the fact that the privateer is operating under the licence of a letter of marque. There are two stacks of sheets for each of the years from 1757 onwards. The heading of each sheet is identical, being the titles of the officials of the High Court of Admiralty, doing their duty in the name of the King. Only once all the formalities have been observed does the specific identity of that document emerge, with the name of the prize, the captor and the port into which it was taken. Once this has been entered, legal formalities return, and the owners of the prize and those with an interest in her are warned that in twenty days'

16 TNA HCA 32/219/6.

17 LG issue no. 9636 16 November 1756.

time there will be an opportunity to state why the ship and her contents should not be declared a prize. The Court was not assuming that the captured vessel was a prize, until the evidence 'out of her mouth' had been heard. The owners of a French privateer would not bother to contest the fact, but the Court was not taking anything for granted. In the case of Thomas Lynn, captor of the Spanish *San Juan Baptista*, there was an appeal by the Spanish owners, and he was monished to appear in court:

> Thomas Lynn the captor and respondent had been diligently sought for at Lloyds, the Jamaica, Antigua and Edinburgh Coffee Houses and other places near the Royal Exchange with an intent to have served him personally therewith, but that he could not be found.[18]

The method of alerting the proctors of prize takers to the date of the hearing might seem a little bizarre to modern readers:

> This Monition was duly executed by affixing the same for some time on one of the Pillars of the Royal Exchange London at the usual time of Merchants resorting there and leaving thereon a true copy thereof and also by citing at the Premises all Persons in general having or pretending to have any Right Title or Interest to appear as therein directed ...[19]

This text was written on the reverse of every 'monition' and a copy was fixed to one of the pillars of the Royal Exchange so that it could be read there during the working hours of the lawyers and prize agents representing the captors, giving them notice of the date on which the hearing would be held. The pillars must have been plastered with papers in various stages of disintegration. A further copy of the monition would be given to the chosen advocate; an example of such an instruction is shown below.

Pinned inside the heavy sheets of the Monitions documents was a small piece of paper, properly impressed with two sixpence stamps, which testified:

> Nicholas King of Plymouth in the County of Devon, gentleman, maketh oath that on the thirtieth day of March last he personally served William Trelawny Esq with the original monition hereunto annexed by showing him the same monition and leaving with him a true copy thereof and at the same time acquainting him with the contents thereof by monishing and citing the said William Trelawny to appear agreeable to the directions of the said monition.

18 TNA HCA 47/5. There was a Scarlet Pimpernel-like quality in the search for Thomas Lynn or his proctors.

19 TNA HCA 31/35.

The above named Nicholas King
was duely sworne to the truth of
the above at Plymouth aforesaid [signed] Nicholas King
the first day of April one thousand
seven hundred and fifty seven
before me
John Kerly a master extraordinary in Chancery[20]

Nicholas King, a prize agent based in Plymouth, had testified that William Trelawny, the advocate or professional pleader in the Court of Justice in London, had thereby been instructed to appear at Doctors Commons. John Kerly took in the affidavits relating to the case so that they were ready to be studied by the Court. The usual preparatory examination had to take place within five days of a request being made, followed by twenty days' notice being given of a monition. The Judge would, within ten days if possible, give sentence respecting the capture.[21]

The Royal Exchange

Behind the Royal Exchange was a large courtyard, surrounded by those useful pillars. The offices of the insurance firm 'The Society of Lloyd's' occupied two rooms here from 1713. The Royal Exchange was destroyed by fire in 1838, and many of Lloyd's early records were lost in the blaze.

The process of issuing the monition

The stack of paper lodged at HCA 31/39, dating from January to the end of June 1758, contains 234 monitions. One hundred and ninety-one of these were captures by privateers, meaning only one-fifth were by ships of war. Some of the captures were not, strictly speaking, by ships of war. One wonders what blandishments were used by the pilot boat which brought *Imperatrice* into Ilfracombe. The *Tartar* armed cutter was usually used to pursue smugglers, but together with *Merlin* and *Esther* under Andrew Dishington, they brought into Hastings three Dutch vessels.

The increasing rate at which the vessels were being brought in is also evident from the dates at which the monitions were issued. At the end of this tranche, between 13 and 30 June 1758, forty-nine monitions were issued. At the beginning of the year, only ten were issued in January (perhaps because fewer vessels operated in winter).

Only one out of this tranche of monitions was rejected. Richard Taylor in the privateer *Loyal Pitt* brought in *St Jaen* on 14 December 1757. She was

20 TNA HCA 31/35.

21 Horne, ed., *Compendium of the Statute Laws*, 39.

Danish, and on 15 March 1758 her proctor appeared and explained that at the time of the capture of *St Jaen*, her master and the other crew were subjects of the Danish king, and the clapboards and staves she carried had been consigned for Bordeaux by the widow of Frederick Schroder, a subject of the king of Prussia. The cargo, none of it contraband, was provided with the proper passport or sea-brief. In this case it was the proctor of *Loyal Pitt* who was monished to appear and explain his behaviour. On 6 May 1758 the Court of Admiralty heard the evidence, and established that *St Jaen*, her master, crew and goods were neutral:

> … and thereupon our beloved Sir Thomas Salusbury … hath decreed the said ship St Jaen and her tackle apparel and furniture and all and singular the goods wares and merchandizes laden therein to be released from the capture and seizure made in this behalf and restored and delivered to the said Pieter Jaensen the master for the use of himself and others the said owners and proprietors thereof with costs and damages (justice so requiring).[22]

Sadly, the legal documents do not explain how the owners of the *Loyal Pitt* paid the costs and damages they had inflicted on the neutral vessel.

Porrected

The word 'porrected' appears on the cover of many of the little files of documents. According to the Oxford Dictionary, porrected means (in this context) that the file was put forward to be submitted for examination or correction at a later date. In the dictionary, the comment is that this usage is obsolete except in ecclesiastic law. It certainly wasn't obsolete in eighteenth-century London, where files were often 'porrected'.

It seems likely that the major players in the prize agent business would have had agents of their own, based in London, to whom would be delegated the responsibility for visiting the pillars at the Royal Exchange regularly and reporting back when the papers had to be defended.

The labour of the lawyers is the most remarkable witness to the 'deductions' which so bothered John Elliot and his peers. The books of accounts consist of pages and pages of carefully entered details justifying each of the deductions. Featured is the charge for producing copies of documents – each one would be copied many times so that at each stage Sir Thomas Salusbury, the Judge who made the ultimate decisions, had in front of him neat, clean versions of the various attested documents.

22 TNA HCA 32/39.

Figure 5. The Courtyard inside the Royal Exchange, anon.

6

The Condemnation of a Prize

When Reginald Marsden prepared for the Navy Records Society the two volumes of *Law and Custom of the Sea* printed in 1915–16, he commented:

> … the prize records are in a fair state of preservation, and the prize sentences, in particular, appear to have been carefully filed and preserved. They exist in vast numbers and were at an early date bound in volumes and indexed. They are, however, disappointing as regards the light which it might have been expected they would throw on the growth of prize law. Framed as they are in the same bare and technical terms, they contain little more than a bald statement of the condemnation or order for restitution of the ship or goods in dispute.[1]

Over one hundred years later, exactly the same comment can be made. They are evidence of the huge amount of work done behind the scenes by the clerks who copied and recopied the documents, and prepared the indices to the volumes. If you know the name of the capture, you are taken to the page on which the condemnation is recorded. But we learn very little of the thinking of the law lord who passed down the condemnation or release of the vessel.

The law of nations required good faith, therefore every ship had to be provided with complete and genuine papers, and the master at least ought to be privy to the truth of the transaction (although the French contended that the master could not be expected to have such knowledge). During the trial, evidence was consulted to determine the ownership of the vessel and cargo, with the caveat that the doctrine of 'free ship, free goods' had to be established. Enemy goods on a neutral ship might or might not be free. Once neutral ownership had been established, the destination of the ship and cargo was determined. A neutral destination was sufficient to release the ship and its cargo. But if the destination was to an enemy and there was a blockade, that was sufficient to condemn the ship. If there was no blockade, then the nature of the cargo determined whether or not it was contraband.

[1] Marsden, ed., *Law and Custom of the Sea*, Vol. 1, viii.

Prize agents sought answers to the statutory questions of the interrogations immediately, while the crew was still intact and available to give testimony. The primary evidence was always the ship's papers. Letters or documents of lading were also part of the case, and combined with testimony from the crew if there was conflict or variance. If papers were missing this was always cause for concern and perhaps condemnation. In order to secure documentary evidence, the captured vessel became the object of the law at the moment of capture. From earliest times the law of the sea required the captured vessel to be brought into port without being despoiled in any way.

The three most senior members of the crew were interrogated separately under oath by legal officials, usually common law magistrates. The lengthy list of questions, shown in Appendix 5, was adhered to in every case, and gave detailed information on the nationality, ownership and destination of the vessel; the status of the master and the crew; the time and place of lading of any part of the cargo and the circumstances of the capture. One of the intentions was to establish whether there was any 'colouring' of the goods. The evidence to acquit or condemn came from the ship, taken 'out of her mouth'. If there was doubt resulting from the ship's papers and preparatory examinations, and the property did not sufficiently appear to be neutral, the owner was afforded time to send affidavits to supply the defect. The Court was not judging the case in advance of possible further evidence being produced. If the owner could not show the property to be neutral, it was assumed that it belonged to the enemy. French jurists who analysed Murray's Memorandum of 1753 line by line, objected to the idea that judgement could be rendered against the ship if the papers were in order, on the basis of the captor's suspicions.[2] However there was a long list of captures where the hidden documents were found only after a search.[3] The interrogations, together with their translations, are a constant presence in the papers stored in TNA in HCA 32.

On 5 July 1757 Sir Thomas Salusbury condemned twenty-seven vessels 'as presumed to be French property or otherwise confiscable'.[4] The Rule of War of 1756 was based on presumptions.[5] If the captured ship could be shown

2 Deák and Jessup, 'Early Court Procedure', 693.

3 An item in the Drakeford papers was interesting. Amongst the boatswain's stores itemised for the sale of the condemned *St Pierre* was a Dutch ensign and pendant. D 1798/HM Drakeford/13.

4 TNA HCA 34/39. There are 205 decisions in HCA 34/37, between 30.7.1756 and 28.1.1757; 196 decisions in HCA 34/38, between 5.2.1757 and 29.6.1757; 204 decisions in HCA 34/39, between 5.7.1757 and 31.5.1758; 204 decisions in HCA 34/40, between 7.5.1758 and 17.5.1760; 190 decisions in HCA 34/4, between 3.6.1758 and 7.1.1762; 176 decisions in HCA 34/42, between 16.2.1762 and 9.12.1768.

5 Pares, *Colonial Blockade*, 121. The *annus mirabilis* for prize taking was between July 1756 and July 1757.

to be concealing the true purpose of her voyage, this gave Salusbury the evidence he needed. The kind of concealment being practised was reported in the newspaper:

> Not long ago, one of our cruisers ranging along the Spanish shore, in the Bay of Biscay, met with a small vessel which hoisted Spanish colours, on which the Commander of the English ship was satisfied without examination. But one of the lieutenants desiring she might be brought to, in order to purchase some lemons, as she was a supposed Spaniard; on boarding, found her, to his amazement, a French privateer of one carriage gun and 8 men, whose practice it had been to lie close to shore, and surprise such defenceless ships as fell in her way. This might serve as a caution to our cruisers, not to take things too readily for granted, as instances of this kind often happen.[6]

In June 1758 a search of the Dutch snow *Prince William* found a large packet of French letters to French merchants describing how to conceal merchandise in Dutch bottoms.[7]

Archibald Kennedy, *Flamborough* (20), had an interesting encounter with a Spanish vessel with two captains in 1759 on its way to Quebec. Her cargo was French, as were one captain and the greater part of her crew. 'As this is carrying commerce contrary to the Treaties embinding between the Government of Great Britain and Spain besides the intention of assisting … his Majestys enemy with provisions', Kennedy took her in to Gibraltar where she was declared prize.[8]

The Working of the High Court of Admiralty

It is clear from a study of the bound books of HCA 34 that when the High Court of Admiralty met to make their decisions, they worked on batches of prizes on any one day. On 28 August 1756 decisions were made on eight captures: *Le Saint Onge* by John Rawling, *Seaford* (20), taken into Plymouth; then seven prizes taken by Arthur Gardiner, *Colchester* (50), taken into Portsmouth: *L'Actif, La Subtille, La Flore de Havre, La Ville de Rouen, La Roze Blanche, Le Vainqueur* and *Le Victorieux*. On 9 September, the next time the Court met, only two decisions were made: one was on the capture of *Promethe* by the privateer *Anson* out of Bristol, under Robert Wapshutt, the other on the capture of *Le Solide* by Augustus Keppel's *Torbay* (74).

6 *Caledonian Mercury*, 13 April 1761.

7 Williams, *Liverpool Privateers*, 152.

8 TNA ADM 1/2010 Captains' Letters K Kennedy 8 August 1759. John Clevland, Secretary of the Admiralty, ordered his clerks to 'send a copy of the letters for Mr Pitts information'.

When the Court met again on 27 September, seven further decisions were made. This time the privateer captain Wapshutt was in business again, bringing in two further prizes; four other privateers were involved, taking their prizes into Topsham, Pool, Lisbon and Plymouth. Only one of his Majesty's ships was involved on this day, the *Antelope* (50) under Clark Gayton, who took *St Helene* into Plymouth. And so the decisions go on, usually taken at the rate of about five a day, rising to forty-three on 23 November 1756, when the orgy of prize taking which resulted from the declaration of war seems to have reached a climax.

To the dismay of the court clerk on 10 August 1757, Sir Thomas Salusbury did not appear. The condemnation was ready for him to sign, but his surrogate had to step in and take his place. The clerk had to squeeze in the alteration: 'We Andrew Coltee Ducarel Doctor of Laws Surrogate to the Right Worshipful' before Sir Thomas's name in the document. As always, it had been carefully prepared in the beautiful clerkly hand, leaving gaps for a different clerk to fill in the names of the ships dealt with that day. Salusbury did not reappear until September.[9]

The condemnation of *L'Heureux* followed the usual pattern. It begins in characters twice as tall as the rest of the text: 'In the name of God Amen! We Sir Thomas Salusbury', before continuing with a different smaller script. The first part of a monition was always the legal preamble to the decision, repeating the assertion that Salusbury had 'heard seen and understood and fully and maturely discussed the merits and circumstances of a certain business' before the court finally got down to the business of that condemnation. In a third script which is dashed off, cramped, with corrections roughly inserted, the details of this capture are provided. *L'Heureux*'s commander had been Pierre Crespin, but at the time of capture Richard Thomas Bell was in charge. The names of John Lockhart and Thomas Burnett and their ships of war are entered in the same quick scribble, before sixty-nine lines in the lawyer's italic hand take us to the condemnation. As usual, it was the absence of anyone to speak for *L'Heureux* which provoked the sentence. Despite being 'monished and cited' thereby proving contumacious, there was no one to speak against the King's proctor who put the case that the ship and her 'tackle apparel and furniture' were all goods belonging to the French king. Therefore, Salusbury could 'call on the name of Christ', having heard legal council's opinion, and 'pronounce, decree and declare' that the ship had been lawfully taken and was subject to being condemned as good and lawful prize. He also stated that seventy-six men had been alive on board her at the start of the engagement. This would have entitled the captors to £380 Head Money.[10] In the Treasury

9 TNA HCA 34/39 26.
10 TNA HCA 34/37 55.

list this is recorded as £375 of Head Money.[11] The reason for the discrepancy has not been established.

If the capture was a ship of war, or without doubt the property of the enemy, condemnation generally took place within the course of six weeks from the arrival of the prize in port. If the capture was a ship claimed to be neutral property, the proceedings were slower. During this time a perishable cargo might be sold by court order. If the case, contested or not, resulted in condemnation, then the agents proceeded to sell the prize, as discussed in Chapter 8. The Court was slow at the beginning of the war, but got through cases in an average of two months by the end.

George Marsh, mentioned above, was the agent for an interesting capture by Augustus Hervey, as recounted in his diary:

> The Hon. Augustus Hervey … in coming into the chops of the Channel in His Majesty's ship Dragon with the news of our having taken Havanna, took a French Frigate of War of 10 Guns named the Francis Lewis, to which he appointed me this day sole agent, and tho' she was claimed by an English Merchant as his private property, and not a ship of War, and he prosecuted me for her as such in Doctors Commons, I cast him there by proving to the Court that she was commanded by a Lieutenant of the French Navy whose pennant was flying on board her and as such she was so condemned accordingly, by which I got a moiety [half] of her, instead of one eighth and all lading consisting of Brass Guns, cloth, linen, buckles, buttons etc etc etc bound to Newfoundland, which was at this time in possession of the French, and notwithstanding the Law suit, the prize money was paid in less than four months after she was taken which amounted [not] to about 6,000.[12]

The clerks didn't always get it right. There are many examples where it is clear that someone didn't approve of the text he was supposed to sign, and had it re-written.[13] The complaint was made against Salusbury that there was never evidence of the judicial reasons for his decisions. Re-written texts are evidence that the complaint was justified: if the clerk wrote out the condemnations in advance, was it the clerk making the decisions or the Judge?

After the condemnation, the next legal stage was the application to the Treasury for Head Money, approved in this case only five weeks later by the

11 TNA ADM 43/14. TNA HCA 32/199/19.

12 https://jjhc.info/marshgeorge1800diary 95. TNA ADM 43/20: the Head Money of £780 was part of this prize money. It must be assumed that Marsh had not intended to add the word 'not'.

13 HCA 34/39 64.

Admiralty's solicitor, Samuel Seddon. With the papers in the file is a list of the stages through which the proceedings have passed. The text reads as follows:

> The state of the case of Messrs Benjamin Bond junior, William Baillie and John Lloyd claiming payment of Bounty Money at £5 p head for 236 men taken in the La Marie Victoire a French privateer by his Majestys ship the Tartar Captain Thomas Baillie Commander on 27 March 1757
>
> They have produced
> The Proof Condemnation dated the 20th July 1757
> A certificate from the Deputy mayor of Portsmouth for 236 men
> A letter of Attorney from the captain officers and ships company of the Tartar appointing them agents
> A list of the ships company certified as usual.
>
> I humbly certify that I have perused the state of the case, with the proofs of Messrs Benjamin Bond junior, William Baillie and John Lloyd claiming bounty money for two hundred and thirty six men taken in the La Marie Victoire, a French privateer, by his Majestys ship the Tartar, Captain Thomas Baillie Commander, and that I have no objection to any of the said proofs, nor to the making out a Bill to the said Messrs Benjamin Bond junior, William Baillie and John Lloyd for the Bounty money claimed as aforesaid. I am with great respect, Gentlemen, your Honour's most humble and obedient servant, Samuel Seddon
>
> Pickadilly
> 2 September 1757[14]

A longer exemplar, for *L'Heureux* captured by Lockhart and Burnett, is included as Appendix 7.

Condemnation of a ransom

The judgement in the case of a ransom held by the French privateer *Le Singe* took over 800 words. The merchant vessel *Guardogue* had been taken by *Le Singe*, and a ransom of £300 taken. When *Le Singe* in turn was taken by the English privateer *Deptford* the ransom bill was passed on, and Salusbury eventually pronounced in favour of the *Deptford*, awarding her the £300.[15]

Condemnations of ransoms were not very frequent, but four occur in the period covered by HCA 34/40: 11 June 1758 to 17 May 1760. The other three

14 TNA ADM 43/15.
15 TNA HCA 34/40 29.

examples were all dealt with on one day, 6 November 1759, when the captured ships were *Le St Jean Baptiste*, *Le St Jacques* and a second *Le St Jean Baptiste*. The wording is exactly the same, the only differences being the names of the holder of the ransom, and the ship which made the capture. An easy job for the clerk, who simply copied out the earlier version.

Dutch neutrality

The Dutch had been defensive allies of England since the accession of William III, and at the same time deeply involved in trade with and for France. After the previous century of naval warfare, the Dutch succeeded in keeping out of major engagements in the eighteenth century, despite trade being so vital to their interests. The progress of the war at sea was affected by the events taking place on land. Holland was particularly vulnerable to French attacks by land. The mutual treaty between Britain and Holland contained clauses binding both countries to provide military support. Faced with the certainty of war, Britain withdrew her troops, and Holland refused to send 6,000 troops to England. On 25 May 1756, a week after the British declaration of war, the Dutch declared their neutrality.

As the 'wagonners of Europe' the Dutch depended on trade. The question of neutral status concerned neutral trading rights, the maintenance of neutral security, '*les lois de la sociabilité*' (the laws governing associations) and whether a neutral should impartially serve all belligerents, or refuse assistance to them. Many of the cases dealt with during the war hinged on the question of neutrality, and the international implications of this concept. Books were published during and after the war arguing both sides of the question: the Swiss Emer de Vattel, influenced by Grotius's thinking on international law, wrote *The law of nations* in 1758; the Dane Martin Hübner, whose *De la saisie des bâtiments neutres* was published in 1759, set out the case that cargo in neutral ships was not a legitimate prize in warfare. Later in the century Sir James Marriott, whose *Formulare instrumentarum* on admiralty law had some influence on American maritime law, was appointed Judge of the High Court of Admiralty in 1778. His successor was Sir William Scott, the much more able man. It is a great pity that the Court of Admiralty in the middle of the century did not have a Judge as lucid as Lord Stowell was at the end. Hill quotes from him to give a masterly summation of a difficult case:

> … it is the rule of this court, which I shall ever hold, till I am better instructed by a superior Court, that if a neutral shall weave a web of fraud of this sort, this Court will not take the trouble of picking out the threads for him, in order to distinguish between the sound and the unsound; if he is detected in fraud he will be involved in toto.[16]

[16] Hill, *Prizes of War*, 30.

The crucial element of the Dutch neutral status however was the fact that it did not stop them from carrying naval stores from the Baltic to France, and this caused some alarm in England. Later in the year when an examination was made of a convoy of Dutch ships, and it was discovered that they were carrying naval stores to France, this caused an international incident. Lord Chancellor Hardwicke discussed the outcome with his son Joseph Yorke, the British diplomatic representative to the Dutch republic, who was in a crucial position and able, if anyone was, to explain Britain's position to the Dutch. The discussion point he outlined was that Dutch trade with France had customarily fallen into five categories: trade in contraband, specifically naval stores to be used by the French; the import of Dutch goods into France in Dutch ships also characterised as coastwise trade or 'cabotage'; the over-shipping from Iberian to French ports of French goods which had begun their journeys in French ships; and trade to and from the Caribbean settlements.[17] Hardwicke knew that smuggling between the Dutch and French settlements would be almost impossible to stop, as in many cases the trade was between the republic and its own colonies, and having been a long-established trade was 'customary'. He saw no problem relating to the customary trade of neutral goods being carried in Dutch bottoms if they did not include contraband or naval goods. Moreover, the treaty of 1674 which established 'free ships' meant 'free goods' existed in Atlantic waters as well as European.

As a result, exports by the Dutch of French goods were sanctioned if they were on a Dutch account. If on a French account, Hardwicke believed this constituted hiring the Dutch ship by the French exporter, and the customary trade to France of neutral goods should be disregarded. If the freight was of naval stores which would prejudice the war if they were carried on French account, these goods would be liable to seizure, and the Dutch shipowner could be compensated by receiving the value of the goods seized. If Dutch ships carrying masts were stopped and searched, the masts were bought by the Navy Board for use in the British navy. If goods were brought in French ships and transferred to Dutch vessels to avoid capture, they were not protected in any way. The Dutch believed in documents witnessed in front of notaries, but these were not respected in English Admiralty courts.[18]

Joseph Yorke's conclusion on the position of the Dutch traders was:

> … the proper bounds that ought and must be set between interrupting the real fair trade of the Dutch, and suffering them to carry on the trade of the enemy in a manner that passes the bounds of the neutrality they

[17] Alice Clare Carter, 'The Dutch as Neutrals in the Seven Years' War', *The International and Comparative Law Quarterly* (Vol. 12 no. 3 1963), 818–34.

[18] Carter, 'Dutch as Neutrals', 824.

> profess … carrying on for them a trade which they cannot support of themselves in time of war, and to which the Dutch are not admitted in time of peace.[19]

When Dutch vessels transporting cannon from Sweden to France were captured by the English, this affected all three countries. England was determined to render impossible the imminent French attack on British soil, and it was vital that the cannon should be denied to France. Eventually the Dutch were placated when the cannon were bought by the Ordnance.

Pares quotes a Prussian lawyer who admitted that a neutral nation has the right to trade to all places not blockaded in all goods not contraband, 'provided it only carries its own trade without engaging in what might be justly called doing the enemy's trade for him'. Neutrals were prevented from trading *for* the enemy while they might lawfully continue to trade *with* him.[20]

The Duke of Newcastle recognised the problems when he wrote in March 1756, proposing to justify his self-interested action by what international jurists called *Droit de Necessité*:

> The article in the treaty of 1674 'free ships – free goods', you know lays us under the greatest difficulties here, and indeed were it to be complied with, it would be impossible to carry on a war with France. And, therefore, I will own freely to you that whatsoever had happened we must some way or other have broken thro' that engagement.[21]

Other possibly suspicious behaviour

Thomas Harrison, *Venus* (36), twice came upon merchant ships which had been abandoned at sea. Part of an English convoy bound for Jamaica, the first ship had a distress flag flying, but when he came up to it there was not a person on board. The nine feet of water in the hold was soon pumped out, the leak found and stopped. Later the same day he approached a second ship flying a distress signal. Again, the ship was deserted, and the hold soon cleared of water. Harrison had a suspicion that there 'may not be some trick in the intended loss of these ships, or at least the latter, as she did not seem well found for a West Indian voyage'.[22] Insurance scams were practised a long time ago.

19 Marsden, *Reports of Cases*, 382.
20 Pares, *Colonial Blockade*, 183.
21 Carter, 'Dutch as Neutrals', 825.
22 TNA ADM 1/1897 Captains' Letters H 1762 Harrison 19 March 1762.

Colonial Vice Admiralty Courts

Vice Admiralty Courts abroad were set up in same way as the Court in London, with a Judge, Register, Marshal and proctors, but without the independent and experienced personnel. Charges in overseas cases were not simply court fees, but fees charged by advocates and agents and were on occasion 'enormous'. In some such courts the man responsible for administering prize cases was the same man as represented the case in court. Court fees paid in Malta were a principal abuse. A commission was set up to establish the scales of fees for Vice Admiralty Courts.[23]

West Indies

In the West Indies Admiral Hardy became increasingly frustrated. He gathered evidence that North American vessels regularly flew Spanish flags, carried Spanish crew and carried Spanish passports, to allow them to bring provisions and other articles in short supply into Cape François (on the north coast of St Domingo, now Haiti), in return for French sugar, molasses, indigo, coffee and cotton. The American vessels called first at Monte Christi to transfer some goods into Spanish coasting vessels, before travelling on to French West Indian ports such as Cape François or Fort Dauphin and others. When Hardy returned to England in 1757 he brought with him Lord Loudoun, commander of the British expedition against Louisburg. Loudoun wrote about his exasperation: 'The truth is no rule or law has any force in this country, and all of them … have carried on a trade with the enemy the whole time.'[24]

It was not until the British presence in the West Indies became much stronger and more experienced that the flow of unlawful trade was reduced. Hardy's replacement, Admiral Holmes, wrote that: 'it has been lately reported here that … Monte Christi is admitted, by the government and courts at home, to be a free port'. But Holmes's little squadron succeeded in their efforts, and a North American businessman complained that: 'The place is well guarded by seven of his Majesty's ships of war who seem determined to destroy the trade.'[25]

Admiral Holmes was attempting to close down the forbidden trade carried out between merchants from America, Ireland, Scotland and England and the French islands of the West Indies. In 1761 the tiny port of Monte Christi in the West Indies had sixty-nine vessels in port, none daring to put to sea while Holmes's frigates waited to secure them. Eventually the American-owned *Recovery* put to sea, having planned a collusive capture by *Harlequin*, an American privateer. *Harlequin* 'captured' *Recovery*, and put a prize crew

23 Hill, *Prizes of War*, 97–114.
24 Truxes, *Defying Empire*, 72–3.
25 Truxes, *Defying Empire*, 127.

aboard her with the intention of sending her back to America. Two days into this journey, *Recovery* was taken by the frigate *Hussar*, and brought to Port Royal in Jamaica to be condemned. The second lieutenant of *Hussar* had discovered sixteen incriminating documents in the sea chest of *Recovery*'s boatswain, so the case for condemnation included the facts that *Recovery*'s trade with Spain had been fictitious, the capture by *Harlequin* had been collusive, and that the captain had perjured himself. Admiral Holmes prosecuted North American vessels trading with the enemy, pursuing prize money which he and his squadron stood to gain from the Jamaican Vice Admiralty Court.[26] Collusion between vessels which pretended to have captured a prize was not uncommon. Papers hidden, not in the boatswain's locker but by being 'sowed in the hinder part of his breeches', were part of the case against Captain William Carlisle who was arrested on a charge of treason.[27]

During the Seven Years' War neutral ships suspected of carrying enemy goods took up twenty per cent of prize cases. For some time after the start of the war Dutch neutral carriers were undisturbed, but once it was demonstrated that they could be prosecuted, the cases multiplied, with the poor quality of forged papers often revealed. By 1760 ships were dispatched from contiguous Dutch islands to French settlements, with goods being shipped as Dutch produce.

New York

New York became the destination of choice for British privateers seeking condemnation of their prizes. The Judge sitting in a Vice Admiralty Court was the sole arbiter of any dispute, as he sat without a jury, and Judge Lewis Morris appreciated the multiple benefits to his community of successful privateering.[28] It was estimated that the prize courts brought over £2 million to New York during the wars of the mid-eighteenth century. The New York *Mercury* reported that fifty-nine of the eighty-five prizes taken by local privateers had been returned to New York to be condemned. In 1758 Morris condemned seventy-one prizes, and only five of those judgements in neutral prize cases were reversed on appeal in London. Whereas a weak judge could ruin a case by not focusing on evidence of changes in handwriting in the Dutch papers, of false dates and contradictory facts, Morris was scathing about such practices, in one case dismissing the case with 'the owners appear to be novices in the art of colouring, which that nation is famed for'.[29] Other evidence he quoted

26 Truxes, *Defying Empire*, 129–203.

27 Truxes, *Defying Empire*, 148.

28 Michael Watson, 'Judge Lewis Morris, the New York Vice-Admiralty Court, and Colonial Privateering, 1739–1762', *New York History* (Vol. 78 no. 2 1997), 117–46.

29 Watson, 'Judge Lewis Morris', 141.

of the clear 'colouring' in the Dutch papers was: a French supercargo on board pretending to be a passenger; the 'captain' not appearing to be aware of the cargo he was carrying; the cargo ostensibly destined to French merchants at Hispaniola; essential papers concealed.[30]

The snow *Johnson* was given false cover by pretending the vessel had already been taken by the privateer *Mars*, so when stopped by Lancelot Holmes, *Bonetta* (10), on course to guide the British navy through Old Bahama Channel off Cuba at the taking of Havana, he was duped and let them go. But they were caught again on entering New York, and despite throwing papers over the side, Attorney General Kempe achieved his aim, and the two chief defendants were each fined £1,568.[31]

In contrast, between December 1759 and June 1760, South Carolina Vice Admiralty judges released or refused to proceed against a number of flag-of-truce vessels which had been taken for trading with the enemy.

Ireland

Ireland had had a longstanding commercial relationship with France, a traditional clandestine exchange of Irish wool for French wine. By the mid-eighteenth century the French took fifty per cent of Irish beef exports. This trade however was made illegal by the declaration of war which expressly wiped out the longstanding principle of 'free ships, free goods'.

Ireland had always been a special case. In 1745 a petition had been sent to the Admiralty commissioners by Dr Baillie who wanted the Irish Admiralty Court to be independent. He claimed:

> … a strong demand amongst the merchant class for a grant of prize commission, and that the concession of this entitlement would act as an incentive to Irish ship owners to seek letters of marque and assist in the war effort against France … a very great hardship and discouragement to the fitters out of privateers, not to be allowed to have such prizes as they bring into Ireland, tried there, if they desire it, considering the expense and delay attending their transmitting the necessary papers and evidence over to England.[32]

30 C.M. Hough, ed., *Reports of Cases in the Vice Admiralty of the Provinces of New York and in the Court of Admiralty in the State of New York 1715–1788* (New Haven, 1925), 94–9.

31 Truxes, *Defying Empire*, 167.

32 Kevin Costello, 'The Court of Admiralty of Ireland 1745–1756', *The American Journal of Legal History* (Vol. 50 no. 1 2008), 44.

Irish independence was confirmed on this occasion. However, the Court of Admiralty in Ireland was reduced to the subordinate status of a Vice Admiralty Court in 1752, and this judgement was specifically repeated in 1756.[33]

The legal basis of condemnation ensured that taking enemy vessels off the sea conformed to 'proper' behaviour. This was not piracy, but a systematic reduction of the enemy's ability to fight at sea. The lawyers in Doctors Commons were not interested in the engagement itself, only in the results. Their conclusions provide a clear understanding of the benefit of the Prize Act to the Royal Navy in the monetary value of their endeavours.

33 Costello, 'Court of Admiralty of Ireland', 40.

7

Appeal against Condemnation

The Appeal Court consisted of at least three Lords Commissioners from the following list: Lord President of Council; John Carteret 2nd Earl Granville; Earl Cholmondeley; Earl of Kinnoul; Lord Berkeley of Strathclyde; Lord Sandys; Lord Mansfield; Robert Nugent Esq.; and Welbore Ellis Esq.[1]

The Lords Commissioners were advised by two experienced Council, men of the standing of Dr George Hay, of Doctors Commons, or William Murray when he was Attorney General. Between 1751 and 1766 the Lords Commissioners heard and determined 234 Prize appeals. Of these, 44 came from the English High Court of Admiralty, 88 came from Jamaica, 23 from New York, 19 from Antigua, and the remaining 19 from the other nine Vice Admiralty Courts.[2]

A shared capture took place before war was declared, when William Gordon, *St Albans* (60), Hugh Palliser, *Eagle* (60), and Mark Milbank, *Romney* (50), were detached in May 1756 by Admiral Boscawen to cruise off Cape Ortegal. They took *La Fidelle* and jointly took *Thisbe* before they separated to chase three other French vessels, *Triton*, *St Mark* and *Venus*, successfully capturing them all while the British ships were in company although not always in sight. There was no contesting the fact that the Admiral was entitled to his eighth share. At the appeal before the Court, the first question was whether the crew of Admiral Boscawen's vessel and the other ships under his command were also entitled to a share of the prizes. William Murray, the Attorney General, responded that 'no part of the squadron which remained with the Admiral is entitled to any share of these prizes'. Dr George Hay's addition to this was that 'the officers and men remaining with Admiral Boscawen are not entitled to any share of the prizes taken by St Albans, Eagle and Romney'. When asked how the prizes should be distributed between the three British vessels, Murray's conclusion was that the ships had aided each other, despite not being in sight at all times, and were entitled as joint captures. And Dr George Hay's response was that the three British ships were cruising together, and equally

1 TNA HCA 38/7 Lords Minutes, Friday 19 December 1760.

2 The Vice Admiralty Courts were in: Jamaica, New York, Antigua, St Christophers, Newfoundland, Rhode Island, Pennsylvania, Virginia, Gibraltar, Maryland, Montserrat, North Carolina. Bourguignon, *Sir William Scott*, 28–9.

entitled to the prizes, while being in sight or not was immaterial.[3] This is one of the Appeal cases chosen by Marsden as exemplars of the guidance given to the Court by the experienced Council. It is to be regretted that he gave so few of this period relating to Prize appeals, as opposed to Instance (employment, ownership, wages, etc.).

The papers recording these Appeal cases in the National Archives are lodged in HCA 47. There are dozens of little parcels of papers, literally notes made at the time of the sitting of the Appeal Court, a mixture of 'clerkly hand' inscribed headings which give the date, followed by 'Present Lord President' and under that a number, usually 3, 4 or 5, which suggests that once whoever the Lord President for that day was seated, it didn't matter who else was at the table provided there were at least two other members of the Appeal Court. The beautifully inscribed name of the vessel and the names of the two Law Lords acting as proctors or advisors were then followed in another hand by the outcome, such as one passed on 27 November 1760 on *The Snow Rotterdam*: 'The Lords having heard the proofs and Council on the libels by their final decree or sentence affirmed the sentence of the Judges below condemning ship and cargo.'[4] The 'Judges below' were the Vice Admiralty Court which in this case were not challenged, *The Snow Rotterdam* being confirmed as a prize by the Appeal Court.

It is very rare that there is an explanation of the thinking behind a decision of the Appeal Judges. They did not have to explain themselves. Most of the cases in Reginald Marsden's edition of 1885 of the High Court of Admiralty are simply accompanied by the names of other similar cases. In 1760, under the heading 'neutral ships coming with cargoes from French ports in West Indies' are listed on 10 July *Gerigtigheit*, *Petronella and Elizabeth*, *Speedwell* (reversing that part of the sentence which condemned claimant in double costs); on 14 July *St Marcus*, *St Fernando* (reversing that part of the sentence which condemned claimant in double costs), *Zeelandia*, *Rouingsber*, *Esther*; on 15 July *Nassau* (reversing condemnation of claimant in double costs), *Spa Galley* (reversing condemnation of claimant in double costs), and reversing costs *Stadt Rotterdam* and *Johannes*. The *Snow Rotterdam* followed on 27 November 1760.[5]

In each of the cases 'condemning the claimant in double costs', if a plaintiff is awarded more at trial than the sum they offered to settle for before trial, the Court could award them double costs. The next day, the judgement on *Amsterdam* was:

3 Marsden, *Reports of Cases*, 370–1.

4 TNA HCA 48/7.

5 Marsden, *Reports of Cases*, 219–20.

> The Lords having heard the proofs and Council on both sides by their final decree or sentence reversed that part of the sentence which condemned the claimants in costs but affirmed that part of the sentence of the Judge below which condemned ship and cargo.

Also on Thursday, the sentence on *Petronella and Elizabeth* (mentioned above) was to reverse that part of the original sentence which imposed double costs, but affirm the condemnation of ship and cargo.

On Wednesday 9 July 1760 the Lord President Earl Granville, with Lord Berkeley and Lord Mansfield, having Altham and Farrar as Council, gave identical judgements on three cases from the Jamaican Vice Admiralty Court, 'the court below': *Juffrow Alida*, *Isaac Galley* and *Vrou Anna*, namely that:

> The Lords having heard the proofs and Council on both sides by their final decree or sentence reversed that part of the sentence which condemned the claimant in double costs but affirmed that part of the sentence of the judges below which condemned ship and cargo.

More was to come that day. With Gostling and Farrar as Council, the Lords, having heard the proofs and Council on both sides of the appeal against *Pieter and David*, reversed the previous judgement of the Vice Admiralty Court which condemned only part of the cargo, pronounced the whole ship and cargo to be restored, and condemned the captor to pay costs and damages to the time of restitution to the agent within a month. In the next case, that of *Juffrow Johanna*, heard with Smith and Farrar as Council, the note taker had to scratch out his first summary and then his second, before the final decision: to reverse the part of the original sentence which condemned the cargo, and restore the value of it.[6]

The Appeal Lords were exasperated by delay. *St Antonio de Padua*, taken by *Sheerness* into Gibraltar on 14 January 1759, was restored on 12 March as Spanish property. The captor, John Clark, appealed but his agent did not prosecute the appeal, and did not confirm this until 8 August 1760. The final note on the file is: 'It is above 21 months.'[7]

William Saltern Willet, *Chichester* (70), and Edward Wheeler, *Isis* (50), cruising in company on 4 January 1758, chased the privateer *L'Actif*, which was actually seized by *Isis* while *Chichester*, despite splitting her main top-sail, pursued another vessel, *Touraine*. *Isis* then took up that chase, leaving

6 TNA HCA 38/7; Marsden, *Reports of Cases*, 212. This is one of the sequence of cases used by Marsden to illustrate the work of the Appeal Court. Marsden simply gives the name of the prize, the date of the decision, and 'to the same purpose' – rattling off a series of identical judgements may have been the result of batching similar cases, or of the temperature in the court room.

7 TNA HCA 48/7.

Chichester to secure the first prize. *Isis* was successful, capturing *Touraine* the next morning. The initial hearing gave both captures to *Isis* but this was appealed against by *Chichester*. A monition was issued from the Court of Admiralty to establish why *Touraine* should not be condemned to *Isis*, to which Willet, commander of *Chichester*, as well as the French captain of *Touraine*, confirmed the sequence of the chase outlined above. On 11 December 1758 the Judge of the second hearing shared both captures with *Chichester*. Wheeler appealed, but the Appeal Court on 14 March 1760 confirmed the judgement – both ships shared both prizes.[8]

In July 1760 an interesting capture was made in the West Indies when an English brigantine *John and William* was taken as she was leaving the French port of Cape François with a cargo of sugar and rum, although pretending to be exchanging prisoners under a 'flag of truce'. This led to a unique appeal. James Innes, the Advocate General of Jamaica, had initially acted for the captors, then changed the charge to that of exporting flour (providing flour to the French islands was prohibited under the Flour Act of 1757).[9] The Judge of the Vice Admiralty Court accepted this change of charge, and in August 1760 condemned the ship and cargo with half the value of the ship and cargo going to the King, the other half to the captors. On appeal on 9 July 1763 the sentence was reversed, the ship and cargo declared a lawful prize of the captors, 'and on account of the misbehaviour of the respondent, James Innes Esq … pronounced that he should personally pay the costs occasioned …'. On the same day the cases of five other vessels, all pretending to be exchanging prisoners but actually carrying sugar and rum to Philadelphia, were given the same decision by the Appeal Court.[10]

Samuel Faulkner, *Windsor* (60), took *La Pacifique* off Finisterre on 13 March 1758, which involved him in a conflict of interest with Sir Edward Hawke who became his commanding officer when he arrived in Plymouth. Faulkner had been commissioned by the Admiralty to undertake the cruise, and only found out that he had been placed under the command of Sir Edward Hawke when he returned to Plymouth with his prize. Hawke appealed for his one-eighth of the prize money, and was initially awarded the 'flag-eighth' in May 1761 by Sir Thomas Salusbury. However, Faulkner appealed, and in July 1764 this decision was reversed by the Appeal Court, as Faulkner had not been commissioned by Hawke but by the Admiralty to take the cruise. Faulkner had to wait six years to receive the disputed eighth share.[11]

8 Marsden, *Reports of Cases*, 169–70.

9 Pares, *War and Trade*, 437.

10 Marsden, *Reports of Cases*, 193–4.

11 TNA HCA 34/39/187; Edward Stanley Roscoe, ed., *Reports of Prize Cases* (London, 1905), 3–4; Sir William Burrell, ed., *Reports of Cases determined by the High Court of Admiralty and upon appeal therefrom* (London, 1885), 158–9.

The Danish *St Jacob* was taken with a cargo of oil and lemons on her way to Havre de Grace. Initially the Judge of the Admiralty condemned the oil to be contraband, but the ship belonged to Danish subjects and had to be returned. The money obtained by selling the lemons was to be returned to the master, whose lemons they had been. On 29 June 1759 this judgement was reversed by the Appeal Court on the grounds that no part of the cargo could be claimed as contraband, and the net produce of the sale should be returned to the proctor for the master of the *St Jacob*, the owner of the lemons.[12]

For the first years of the war, there was a delicate balancing act designed to keep Spain neutral. The Court of Appeal consisted of allies of William Pitt or the Duke of Newcastle, and attempted to demonstrate that Spanish shipowners would be treated with respect in the Court of Prize Appeal. A Spanish ship, the *Jesus Maria y Joseph*, was taken by a privateer, *Britannia*, between Corunna and St Sebastian, with a cargo of coffee, saltpetre, dye-wood, pepper and Indian bale goods which had been brought by a French *Cie des Indes* ship to Corunna. The master, on examination, revealed that he believed the voyage was to have ended in France, and the Spanish vessel had been made use of to avoid the English cruisers which might have taken the French vessel. On 27 December 1756 the cargo of saltpetre was condemned as contraband, although the ship and its other cargo were to be restored. This decision was appealed, and on 15 July 1759 the Lords of the Court of Appeal, their Council on this occasion being Rushworth and Tyndall, ordered the claimant to make proof that the ship and cargo were Spanish and not bound elsewhere than St Sebastian, within two months. The questions they asked were: whether there was proof that the ship was bound to a French port; whether saltpetre was a contraband; whether a Spanish vessel was entitled to complete a voyage for a French East Indiaman. An allegation was examined on 17 December 1760, with the Lords postponing a decision until after the Christmas break. In September 1761 the respondents' proctor petitioned to be allowed to withdraw the appeal, and five years after the first decision, the Lords confirmed the decree of the Judge in Gibraltar.[13]

John Lindsay, the young lieutenant in *Tartar* who was commended by Thomas Baillie for his efforts in the taking of *Marie Victoire*, became a prize taker in his own right in the West Indies. Lindsay, *Trent* (28), took *The Betsey* on 31 October 1760, and by December she was declared a prize, sold and the proceeds secured by Lindsay's agent. There was an appeal, and Lindsay's agent deferred handing over the proceeds until the appeal had been settled. It was three years before the Appeal Court determined that the Vice Admiralty Court had to pursue the rightful payment of the proceeds to Lindsay.[14] On 5 March

12 Roscoe, *Reports of Prize Cases*, 6.

13 Roscoe, *Reports of Prize Cases*, 6–7.

14 Marsden, *Reports of Cases*, 194–5

1762, in company this time with Richard Carteret, *Glasgow* (20), Lindsay took *The Francis*, laden with sugar, indigo and coffee, and travelling between Cape François and St Eustatia, with the same result. Despite the original decree by the Vice Admiralty Court in Jamaica, the subsequent appeal by the master of *The Francis* held up the distribution of their prize money. Again, the Appeal Court 'pronounced that the appeal was deserted and gave power to the Judge below to proceed and execute his sentence notwithstanding the appeal'.

Collusion

Lindsay had two other cases initiated against him in the Vice Admiralty Court in Jamaica, both of which were characterised by long delays. After Lindsay had taken *Pompey*, Cornelius Tucker, her master, initiated an appeal against Lindsay and against James Innes, the Attorney General of the local Vice Admiralty Court. The appeal was postponed to the first day of the third session, then to the first session of the next term, then to the last session, and again to the first day of the next term.[15] When Lindsay took *La Belle Savage*, her master used the same legal team to appeal, to the same purpose. The dates of the five sessions were noted in the margin of the court papers.

Lindsay appealed against this Jamaican judgement. *Pompey* had apparently already been taken by the *Charming Sally* privateer when Lindsay intercepted her on 22 December 1761 and brought her back to Jamaica. The court ruled in Lindsay's favour on 19 March 1762, having found that the owners of *Pompey* and *Charming Sally* had colluded by pretending that the privateer had taken her. This was confirmed on appeal on 9 July 1763. Lindsay received half of the value of the prize, the other half going to the King as a Droit. Lindsay had another appeal upheld that day: the identical decision was given in the case of *La Belle Savage*.[16]

A further judgement was made in Lindsay's favour over *Beaver*, a vessel which had flag-of-truce status issued by the Governor of Philadelphia.[17] *Beaver* had sailed from Pennsylvania with some dry goods and empty barrels, but no French prisoners. She then sailed from Port au Prince on 14 January 1760 with 500 hogsheads of sugar, but no British prisoners. A few hours later *Beaver* had been taken by the *Eagle* privateer, who put a prize master on

15 TNA HCA 5/140.

16 Burrell, *Reports of Cases*, 194–5.

17 The commission as 'flag of truce' from the Governor of Pennsylvania read: 'Whereas in pursuance of the rules and practice of war I have despatched the ship *Beaver* under the protection and security of a flag of truce to carry to Port-au-Prince in the island of Hispaniola the French prisoners specified in a list hereto annexed, and to bring from thence such of the subjects of his Britannic Majesty as may be delivered in exchange for said prisoners'. Marsden, *Reports of Cases*, 165–6.

board with a copy of the privateer's commission. Several other flag-of-truce vessels sailed at the same time, all taken by *Eagle*. On 15 January Lindsay seized *Beaver*, despite her having the privateer's commission on board, and took her to Jamaica where on 14 May the Vice Admiralty Court decreed that she had to be restored. Lindsay appealed, and two years later, on 13 July 1762, the Lords reversed the sentence, awarding the ship and its cargo to Lindsay as lawful prize.[18] Twenty-one other cases where merchant ships had been given 'flag-of-truce' status by the Governors of American states were also condemned on appeal between 1762 and 1765. It may have helped Lindsay's case that his aunt had married William Murray, now Lord Mansfield.[19]

Many of the appeals against the judgements of the High Court of Admiralty involved privateers, one asking whether a privateer could be justified in seizing a ship as a prize, lying at anchor in the River Thames with Customs officials on board. In this case, the privateer *Terrible* had to restore the ship and goods.[20] Another appeal focused on whether, the true papers being concealed, the ship trading with a French port ought not to be considered a French ship. In this case, Hyde Parker, *Squirrel* (20), was awarded the *America* and her cargo of coffee, captured on a voyage between Port au Prince and Amsterdam. The grounds for condemnation were that the *America* was hired by a French colony with a cargo admitted to be of French property, and for the purposes of the court therefore a French vessel and justly condemned.[21]

One of the appeals successfully upheld by the captor was that of Broderick Hartwell, *Lizard* (28), who took *De Juffrow Titia*, bound from Port Louis to Brest with a cargo of timber. His proctor, Tyndall, argued that the vessel was carrying naval stores to a port being blockaded, and therefore although the vessel was released, her cargo was condemned.[22]

Richard Faulkner, *Marlborough* (80), twice took vessels with interesting histories, both determined on 27 November 1760. The *Charming Elizabeth* had been taken by the enemy and condemned before he recaptured her. The original owners claimed her back, offering to pay one-eighth of her value in salvage. Their claim was upheld, and they paid the salvage value as promised. The *Florence* had also been taken by the French and condemned before Faulkner recaptured her. In both cases the argument was whether an English ship, captured by the enemy and subsequently recaptured by a man-of-war, should

18 Marsden, *Reports of Cases*, 166.

19 Lindsay brought back from the West Indies his illegitimate daughter Belle, who was brought up by Lord Mansfield with his own daughters. Her story was the subject of a film in 2013.

20 TNA HCA IND 1_18989. No 1

21 TNA HCA IND 1_18989. No 4.

22 TNA HCA IND 1_18989. No 26.

be restored to the first owners, paying one-eighth salvage. The judgement was that the ship and goods were restored, with interest from the sale.[23]

Penhallow Cuming, *Blandford* (20), also had two decisions in his favour made on 5 March 1761. He had taken two ships claiming to be Dutch: *Vreede*, trading in provisions between Amsterdam and Curaçao, and *Vryhyd*, trading in dry goods between Port au Prince and Amsterdam. Both were condemned with their cargoes on the grounds that the papers were fictitious and colourable, and both were in fact adopted French ships.[24]

Then decisions began to be reversed. In July 1761 the Lords Commissioners of Prize Causes reversed the condemnations of the Vice Admiralty Court in Gibraltar, ordering the restitution of six ships and cargoes to the appellants, or full value. On 4 July 1761 it was reported that the Lords of Appeals had affirmed the status of Monte Christi as a neutral port, open to Dutch and Danish as well as British merchantmen. This decision was lauded in North America, where the suggestion that the trade benefited the French was dismissed in favour of accusations of severe and cruel hardships laid by the British on the American colonies. The *New York Gazette* claimed that his Majesty's loyal subjects in America had been unjustly deprived of the privilege of trade to Monte Christi and the other neutral ports of Europe and America which fellow subjects in Britain and Ireland had enjoyed.[25] Were the Lords of the Appeal Court bowing to the pressure from British merchants?

As shown above, not all the decisions were in the captors' favour. The port of Dunkirk being blockaded in 1759, an English privateer took *Die Vier Gebroeders*, at anchor under Dungeness. The Dutch owners had accepted a charter party from Rochelle to take a full lading of brandy and salt to Dunkirk. The first judgement in November 1759 was that the ship should be returned to the owners, but that the cargo was a lawful prize as Dunkirk was blockaded. The owners appealed, and in July 1760 the Lords decided that although it was generally known that Dunkirk was blockaded, the parties were given three months in which to plead and prove their cases.[26]

There was another appeal against the captor, this time against a decision by the Vice Admiralty Court in Halifax. Thomas Burnett, *Rochester* (50), now patrolling in the St Lawrence waterway, took into Halifax the Guernsey snow *The Two Brothers*. She was carrying wine and brandy, and Burnett recognised her master, Nicholas le Mesurier, from his spell in the Channel Islands, and suspected him of being a smuggler. She was condemned in September 1761, and sold. Five months later, however, there was an appeal against this decision, instigated by Lloyd's of London, who had insured the ship and her cargo.

23 HCA IND 1_18989. Nos. 74 and 77.
24 HCA IND 1_18989. Nos. 95 and 96.
25 Truxes, *Defying Empire*, 134–5.
26 Roscoe, *Reports of Prize Cases*, 5.

Evidence against Burnett's case was powerful: *The Two Brothers* had joined a fleet in Plymouth and had paid customs dues there on the wine; Burnett had 'broken bulk', had 'scuttled the deck to remove some dozens of wine'. Burnett did not contest the decision at the appeal that the ship and cargo had to be restored, being involved at the time in attacking Havana. How did he pay for this to be done? Was this another occasion on which the Droits fund was involved? The appeal is detailed in Appendix 10.

Many of the Vice Admiralty Courts' decisions resulted in appeals. An account has already been given in Chapter 4 of the capture on 24 December 1757 by Arthur Forrest, *Augusta* (60), of a series of eight French merchantmen off Hispaniola, and the *Mars* which should have protected them. With great exertion, they were taken into Jamaica. The Vice Admiralty Court in Jamaica having separated the nine captures into separate cases, the entire judgement was reversed on appeal, the Lords making the point that by so doing the court was 'tending only to vexation and accumulation of expense'.[27] This was a clear case of local corruption corrected by the Lords.

A claim was made against Forrest by the captains and crew of the *Marlborough* (80) and *Princess Mary* (60), also part of Admiral Cotes's squadron, that as they had all been based at Jamaica, they insisted on their right to share the prizes, despite their logs showing that they had not been within eighteen leagues of the activities of *Augusta*. Five reasons were given for refusing the claim for compensation: the *Marlborough* and *Princess Mary* had never seen the eight merchantmen, having chosen to cruise elsewhere; none of the merchantmen would have been persuaded to submit as a result of their potential threat; the claimants had not exerted any effort in the initial capture, nor in the subsequent ones, which became more and more difficult as the numbers of prisoners on board increased, and the numbers of *Augusta*'s officers reduced, being engaged as they were in sailing the succession of prizes to safety; on leaving Admiral Cotes, the claimants had refused to make a joint arrangement to share captures and were never closer than eighteen leagues to the activities of the *Augusta*, and therefore were of no material benefit during the captures; none of the officers or prisoners on board *Augusta* testified that any other ship had been in sight during the whole engagement. It was established that the string of submissions had been the result only of the exertions of the *Augusta*'s much reduced crew. Finally, the clinching argument was repeated by Dr George Hay, that 'those who shall be actually on board at the taking' were the only ones to benefit.[28]

[27] TNA HCA 48/7; Burrell, *Reports of Cases*, 167–9. There is an unusual error in this report: it states Forrest took eighty merchantmen, not eight.

[28] HCA 45/2/1. By the time of the claim Forrest was a national hero, having in November taken on a much stronger French force protecting a French convoy at the

The Vice Admiralty Court in Jamaica was not the only one guilty of malpractice. On 12 May 1761 Commodore James Douglas wrote to Jonathan Blehnman, Judge of the Vice Admiralty Court of Barbados:

> … and since the article of fees is on the carpet … must beg leave to acquaint you that the charges of condemnation are greater here than in any other island … have enclosed you the charges of the Advocate and Proctor on each prize; whether it is necessary to have either when a prize is not disputed, and how much, I leave to your determination as you are Judge of the Admiralty and the only person who can tax their bills.[29]

While Spain was neutral the British navy had to treat her vessels with caution, and captains were at pains to inform Mr Pitt (the leader of the government party in the Commons) of their courtesies. However, Thomas Lynn, *Roebuck* (44), captured a Spanish vessel *St Jean Baptista* and took her in to Madeira for the interrogations, then on to Antigua, his destination. The cargo, of cloth and bale goods, was Spanish property although the Spanish pass had expired. The Spanish master refused to claim his vessel in Antigua, and in April 1758 the Vice Admiralty Court declared the ship and cargo lawful prize, but as there had been doubts about the legality of the capture, Captain Lynn had to give security that he would be available to answer an appeal if it was made within a year. In March 1759 there was an appeal, and two years later the Appeal Lords reversed the decision of the Vice Admiralty Court, and decreed that the ship and cargo had to be restored, and the full value paid to the Spanish owner, condemning Lynn to pay all costs and damages, as he had 'unwarrantably' carried the prize to Antigua and proceeded in that court.[30] Did the Droits fund help him out?

In August 1760 the Spanish ambassador complained of the sentences being awarded in the prize courts. Pitt told the Lords of Admiralty immediately to do justice to Spanish ships, and followed up this advice with:

> Mr Pitt is of opinion that the Lords of Admiralty can very well give directions *consistent with law*, to the judges of the court of Admiralty, founded upon the King's pleasure, signified by the Secretary of State;

battle of Cape François, this time with the help of Maurice Suckling who had his young nephew Nelson on board.

29 N.A.M. Rodger, ed., 'The Douglas Papers', *The Naval Miscellany 5* (Navy Records Society, 1984), 263–4.

30 Burrell, *Reports of Cases*, 201–2.

> if the Lords are of that opinion, it would not be amiss to transmit the King's pleasure to the judge without any loss of time, quoting Mr Pitt for so doing, let the effect be what it will.[31]

The judgements were calculated to balance the demands of the privateering lobby and the need for the legal system to appear to be impartial. Once Pitt and Newcastle fell from power with the death of George II, Spain took the opportunity of signing a secret family compact with the Bourbons. It was a great relief when Spain declared war in 1762, and her vessels were legitimate targets, on the open sea as well as in Cuba and the Far East. England declared war on Spain, and everything changed.[32]

Spain's two trading centres of Manila and Havana were attacked. The seizure of ships and goods has already been dealt with, but a claim arose about the merchant ship *Constanza* at Havana. Loaded with sugar, snuff, cocoa, tobacco, hides and logwood at the time of the attack on Havana, she was taken along with the Spanish ships of war. As Sir George Pocock and the Duke of Albemarle had declared that all ships in the harbour would be delivered to the British, but that private property would be respected, a claim was made on behalf of the owner of *Constanza* that as she was not owned by the king of Spain she was not a prize. This claim was rejected by Sir Thomas Salusbury on 4 May 1763, and when the claim was repeated, the Lords confirmed on 16 July 1765 that the *Constanza* had been one of the Spanish ships in the harbour and as such was a legitimate prize.[33]

On the other side of the world, when Manila was taken, the first article of capitulation specified that the effects and possessions of the inhabitants were secure. The *Santissima Trinidad*, having sailed before the capture on 1 August 1762, had to return to port after suffering damage in a storm, and was taken by *Argo* (28) and *Panther* (60). She was condemned to *Argo* and *Panther* as lawful prize on 14 November 1763, a decision immediately appealed against. On 14 August 1765 the Lords confirmed that the prize was lawful, as she had been taken at sea.[34]

The capture of *Arc en Ciel* as she was going into Louisburg by *Litchfield* (50) and *Norwich* (50) in sight of *Centurion* and *Fourgeux* gave rise to an appeal. Initially the Judge in the Vice Admiralty Court of Nova Scotia accepted the claim, not just of the four ships in sight, but the two others which, having

31 Pares, *Colonial Blockade*, 100. Pitt to the Lords of the Admiralty, 1 August 1760, ADM 1/4124, no. 10.

32 Anna Brinkman, 'Spain and Neutrality', in *Co-Dependent Empires during the Seven Years' War: Strategy, Spanish Neutrality and the Law* (Imperial Entanglements, 2017).

33 Burrell, *Reports of Cases*, 161.

34 Burrell, *Reports of Cases*, 163.

been separated by heavy fog, had not been in sight at the time of the capture. This judgement was on the grounds that the vessels were all of the one squadron, and on the same cruise. On appeal in London on 14 March 1761, the Lords reversed this decision. The squadron had been sailing together on 10 June 1756, but in the afternoon *Success* and *Baltimore* were separated from the others by fog, and didn't see them again until 17 June when *Litchfield* informed them of having taken the prize on 12 June. The Lords gave the capture of *Arc en Ciel* only to the commanders etc. of the four ships in sight at the time of the capture.[35]

The complicated capture and re-capture of *Prince Edward* mentioned in Chapter 4 took some sorting out at appeal. The English *Prince Edward*, captured by the French privateer *Providence*, recaptured by the English *Mary*, was taken again by the French *Petit Guave* and ransomed, with Charles Batten, the original French mate, as ransom. Wood, the prize master of *Mary*, carried the *Prince Edward* into Jamaica where she arrived in April. It was not until October 1759 that the judgement was given in the Vice Admiralty Court, that the ship and her cargo should be restored to the claimant, paying one-half, free of all deductions, for salvage to the owners of *Mary*. In 1763 the Appeal Court reversed this sentence, and ordered the ship to be restored without paying any salvage to the respondent, and ordered the 469 hides to be restored to the captain of the *Mary*.[36]

The eight Appeal decisions taken on 9 July 1763, all reversing the decisions taken by James Innes, Advocate General of Jamaica, suggest there was a strong probability that the Vice Admiralty Courts overseas were biased in favour of local business, and needed the oversight of the Court in London. Local interests were, at times, being too forcefully supported. The long delays involved in some appeals would also have made the financial complications even more difficult.

35 Marsden, *Reports of Cases*, 171–2; Burrell, *Reports of Cases*, 171–2.

36 TNA HCA 47/5.

8

The Processes Involved in the Sale of a Prize

In the National Archives there is a huge roll of stiff cream paper which contains the accounts of the Cranbrook Commissioners appointed to be responsible for the sales of French prizes before the declaration of war. The Treasury was determined that everything was done by the book, although it took until 1769 before finalising their accounts from the war.[1]

Disposing of the captures made before war was declared took place without delay, the announcement taking place in November 1756 that Commissioners had sent 'proper persons' to Gibraltar, Barbados, the Leeward Islands, Jamaica and South Carolina to begin the sales in January, so that 'all merchants inclined to become purchasers, may have time to give orders to their correspondents accordingly'.[2]

First refusal of the prize ship together with its tackle was given to his Majesty's Navy, and guns, arms and ordnance stores were offered to the Board of Ordnance. If accepted at a fair and reasonable valuation, these were paid for by bills or debentures. If rejected, the certificate of the refusal was given to the agent of the captor within six weeks, this certificate entitled the vessel to be considered as British built. The importance of this was that British trade could only be carried in British vessels, so these vessels could cheaply become part of the merchant fleet. The Navy or Victualling Boards were entitled to buy any naval stores without waiting for the condemnation of the vessel.[3]

Ambitious captains offered their captures to the Admiralty as a means of getting more vessels into 'the service' as they called it. Many of them were proud of the achievement of having captured a fine ship, and this was an occasion on which the Lords of the Admiralty could show their appreciation of their captains' behaviour. The Admiralty asked the Navy Board to survey captured vessels, but if their survey showed defects which would be expensive to put right, the Board would not recommend purchase.

In January 1761 Harrison, *Venus* (36), and Fortescue, *Juno* (32), took *Brune*, a French privateer. Harrison wrote to the Admiralty accordingly:

1 TNA AO 1/1820/482.

2 LG issue no. 9639 27 November 1756.

3 Horne, ed., *Compendium of the Statute Laws*, 321.

> As the Brune frigate is now safe in Hamoze, I beg leave to offer her to their Lordships for his Majesty's service, for which I believe she will be found extremely fit, if their Lordships will be so good as to order her to be surveyed, which will much oblige …[4]

Brune was indeed fit to be purchased, for £4,327, made up of £3,734 for her hull and £593 for her stores.[5] Harrison shared a second capture with Fortescue. This was *Bertin*, the *Cie des Indes* ship built at L'Orient in 1760. Harrison wrote:

> Bertin is extream fine ship and sails well. If their Lordships are in want of men of war and will be pleased to order her to be surveyed, I make no doubt of her being found fit for the service, as it is the first time she was ever at sea.[6]

Harrison was right to be optimistic. *Bertin* was taken into the navy as *Belleisle*, having been bought by the Navy Board for £19,074, made up of £16,919 for her hull, £1,020 for her masts and yards and £1,134 for her furniture and stores. Very little damage had to be put right, as she was taken *en flute* on her maiden voyage, carrying troops.[7] The Admiralty liked to flaunt their French captures and gave them appropriate names. Renaming the captured vessel *Belleisle* was a reminder that the French minister of war was the duc de Belle-Isle. Harrison's capture *Boullogne*, taken on 27 December 1761, was taken into the navy as *Boulogne*, the name of the French town, rather than leaving it as the name of a nobleman connected with the French *Cie des Indes*. She was purchased for £3,362, of which £3,288 was for her hull, £74 for her stores.[8]

The Navy Board were not in business to be generous to captors: the officials existed to save the Royal Navy as much money as they could, and the prices they offered for vessels bought in would have been keen. Thomas Baillie wrote to the Admiralty in May 1757:

> I am already like to have an action brought against me by the Tartar's ships company for suffering the ship to be sold to the Government, the captors being offered near one thousand pounds more by the merchants in which case I hope their lordships will indemnify me.[9]

4 TNA ADM 1/1896 Captains' Letters H 1761 Harrison 16 January1761.

5 Rif Winfield, *British Warships in the Age of Sail* (Seaforth, 2007), 202.

6 TNA ADM 1/1896 Captains' Letters H 1761 Harrison 4 April 1761.

7 Winfield, *British Warships*, 96. *En flute* meant she was not being used as a warship. Her lower-deck guns had been stowed, and the empty gunports made her look like a flute.

8 Winfield, *British Warships*, 202.

9 TNA ADM 1/1488 Captains' Letters B 1757 Baillie May 1757.

They did not, of course. The crew of *Tartar* became used to receiving prize money, as John Lockhart was one of the most prolific frigate commanders. His crew would have calculated the number of shillings by which each man would have benefited if the extra thousand pounds had come their way. Admiral Harrison might also have had a word with the inexperienced young man, as his share was also reduced by Baillie's having accepted less than the price the merchants might have paid for *Marie Victoire.* The Navy Board had paid £4,258 for *La Marie Victoire* and spent another £1,107 refitting her before she was commissioned as *Tartar's Prize* under her captor.[10] *Tartar's Prize* had the usual defects of a French-built ship. Baillie included a letter from the ship's cook, which described the difficulty of cooking on board:

> … on account of the smoakyness of the gally which in truth is so great that no man living can stand it, especially as the fireplace is fore and aft and the kettles only hanging ones, which have more than once fell over on the deck, scalded the people and always burning the cables and stoppers.[11]

Also dissatisfied by the Navy Board's decisions, Lockhart wrote to the Admiralty after the capture of *Cerf*:

> The Navy Board surveyed the Cerf privateer and by their report I am afraid though her frame is sound yet her decks are otherwise and some of her timbers rotten, she will be rejected to the great loss of the captures, for when once she is found unfit for his Majesty's service, she will be blown upon, and in all probability the captures will entirely lose the sale of her. I therefore hope their Lordships will be so good as to take it into consideration.[12]

They did not, even for Lockhart.

A letter from the Navy Board, dated 11 January 1747, relates to the earlier war, but so neatly encapsulates the tension between the captors and the Navy Board it is worth quoting in full:

> Having Directed the Officers of Plymouth yard (as we acquainted you by our letter of 26 past) to join with such persons as should be appointed by the captors of the Renommée, and survey and appraise the hull of the said ship, and receive from the said officers a report concerning the same wherein they have stated the manner by which

10 Winfield, *British Warships*, 265.

11 TNA ADM 1/1488 Captains' Letters B 1757 Baillie 4 September 1757. French vessels were not designed to stay at sea for any length of time.

12 TNA ADM 1/2045 Captains' Letters L 1756 Lockhart 1 November 1756.

> they formed their appraisement, also an account of the value as insisted on by the agents to the captors; and the said agents having transmitted to us the appraisement made by two masters of ships and one shipwright, and sent us a letter on this subject, we send you copys of the whole for the information of the Right Honorable the Lords Commissioners of the Admiralty, and must pray leave to observe to their Lordships that as Captain Shirley in the course of his dispute in order to obtain five pounds a tun for his prize, has asserted that as much or more was given for the Amazon and Inverness (in both which instances he has been misinformed) so now the persons employed by the ship up to that price, have affirmed that the said prize is worth above twenty shillings a tun, more than the ship Two Crowns (having discovered that she was sold for four pounds a tun) which is an arbitrary and unreasonable way of judging of the value. But as our officers may be supposed to have as good judgement as those on the part of the captors, and to be wholly unbiased, and so more likely to give an impartial account, we intirely agree with them on their valuation. And we must further pray leave to observe to their Lordships, that it has been the constant and invariable rule of this Board, in matters of this nature, to have the opinion of the officers of his Majesty's yards for their consideration, and as a guide for them, whereby to form their judgement in the purchasing stores and particularly prizes of the service of the Crown, therefore if the captors do not think fit to take four pounds a tun for the Renommée, we submit it to their Lordships whether it would not be for the advantage of the Government, that they should be permitted to dispose of her to the merchants, as we mentioned in our letter of the 26th past.[13]

The question of where and when to sell prizes was the captain's own. Burnett sold *L'Infernal* in Jersey where he knew there was a keen market for such craft. Innes and Clerk suggested to Elliot that he should have repairs done in England rather than Ireland as they would be done more cheaply and bring in a better return.

Purchases by the Navy Board

A key member of the team associated with Philip Stephens of the Admiralty was Alexander Macpherson of Craven Street, the Strand, who was their liaison with the Navy Board. He was also the nominated agent used by the Navy Board for their disbursements, and paid out for the reduction of Louisburg and destroying the fleet in the harbour on 8 January 1760.[14] Macpherson's meeting with the Navy Board on 5 January 1759 established the value of *Echo*'s

13 NMM ADM 354.

14 LG issue no. 10063 20 December 1760.

hull at £3,777, with her furniture and stores worth a further £293. However, to put her hull into service would cost £400, and Macpherson agreed to this deduction.[15] A few days later, on 19 January 1759, he met with the Navy Board at which the value of *Bienfaisant* was determined. The system of valuation used by the Navy Board was arcane, but the figure they came up with for the hull was £15,301, from which £2,500 would be 'abated' to cover the costs of putting her into condition for service.[16] A further £834 would be paid for her masts, furniture and stores, giving the total to be entered on the bill of sale of £13,363.[17]

Not every prize was bought by the Navy Board, but the following are typical of the range of valuations given to purchased prizes: the privateer *La Subtile* was taken on 28 August 1756 by *Hazard* (8) in the North Sea and purchased on 20 November 1756 for £350 as *Hazard's Prize*; already mentioned was the privateer *La Marie Victoire* purchased 29 April 1757 for £4,258 as *Tartar's Prize*; the privateer *Le General Lally* taken 14 April 1757 by *Flamborough* (20) was purchased on 20 May 1757 for £1,154 as *Flamboroughs Prize*; the privateer *La Glaneur* taken 10 December 1757 by *Gibraltar* (20) was purchased for £795 as *Gibraltar's Prize*; the privateer *Le Rostan*, taken 3 February 1758 by *Torbay* (74) and *Chichester* (70), was purchased on 13 March 1758 for £4,865 as *Crescent*; *La Bellone*, taken 21 February 1759 by *Vestal* (32), was purchased on 14 June 1759 for £4,100 as *Repulse*. The privateer *La Mélampe* taken 2 November 1757 by *Tartar* (28) and purchased for £5,398 kept her name, *Melampe*, without the accent, to remind the French where she had come from. The privateer *Le Comte de Saint-Florentine* taken 4 April 1759 by *Achilles* (60) was purchased for £7,061 as *Saint Florentine*. *L'Arethuse* was taken on 18 May 1759 by *Chatham* (50), *Venus* (36) and *Thames* (32) and purchased for £4,656 as *Arethusa*. The corvette *Terpsichore* was taken on 28 February 1760 by *Æolus* (32), *Pallas* (36) and *Brilliant* (36) in their action against François Thurot and purchased for £2,888 together with the frigate *Blonde* purchased for £3,855. *Danae* (French *La Danae*), taken on 28 March 1759 by *Southampton* (32) and *Melampe* (36), was purchased for £7,472 (£6,930 hull, £541 furniture and stores). *Flora* (French *La Vestale*) was taken on 8 January

15 TNA ADM 106/2569.

16 The calculation was based on the figure of 1360 9/94 at £11 5s a ton. Mungo Murray's *Treatise on ship building and navigation: in three parts wherein the theory, practice and application of the necessary instruments are perspicuously handled* will enlighten any interested reader on the use of the number 94 in calculating a ship's tonnage from her dimensions, and vice versa. Printed by D. Henry and R. Cave for the author, and sold by A. Millar in the Strand; J. Scott in Exchange Alley; T. Jefferys at the corner of St Martin's Lane, Charing Cross; Messrs Greig and Campbell at Union-Stairs; and by the Author at his House at Deptford. MDCCLIV p 104.

17 TNA ADM 106/2569.

1761 by *Unicorn* (28) and purchased for £4,402. *Baleine* (*Cie des Indes La Baleine*) was taken at Pondicherry in October 1760 by the boats of *Southsea Castle* of Admiral Stevens's squadron, and purchased by him.[18]

A big prize, such as *Arc en Ciel*, attracted a lot of attention. She had been taken on 12 June 1756, in a combined action by *Norwich* (50), *Litchfield* (50), *Fougueux* (64) and *Centurion* (60) but was not offered for sale until 1759. Henry Martin, who brought her back from Louisburg in 1758, had a list of complaints about the ship, the most telling of which was that 'most of the brickwork about our fireplace and copper had fallen down by the working of the ship in the almost continual gales of wind'.[19] There were many discussions with the Navy Board, which was determined to get the best possible price for her even if she had proved to be too wet to keep and her repair having been estimated to cost £13,812. The Navy Board hoped that publicity about the forthcoming sale would attract attention from merchant owners:

> The principal officers and Commissioners of his Majesty's Navy give notice that on Thursday the sixth day of next month at 11 o'clock in the morning precisely they will expose to sale at this office the hull of his Majesty's ship Arc en Ciel burthen 1100 tonnes with six hand pumps, now lying at his Majesty's yard at Chatham; also eight Greenland boats, lying at his Majesty's yard at Deptford; where such persons as are willing to be purchasers may have the liberty of viewing them at any time in the proper working hours of the said yards to the day of sale: and as a deposit of £25 per cent or in proportion thereto is to be made by the persons who shall purchase the said ship and boats, all persons who shall attend the said sale, to take notice thereof, and come prepared for that purpose; and unless the ship and boats so purchased shall be paid for, and taken away the end of 40 days after the date of sale, the deposit shall be forfeited and become property of the Crown.

In the event her hull and stores were purchased on 20 February 1758 for £5,330, the hull being worth £606. The combined nominal crews of 1,500 men, or their agents, received an advance payment on account of their respective shares of the prize's hull and stores on 15 September 1759, at the King's Head Tavern in Fenchurch Street. They were recalled for three years to the same place on the last Saturday in every month until the law suits were determined and the final distribution made.[20]

When the Admiralty, under the direction of Philip Stephens, appointed agents at each of the major ports, they (or their deputies) were there to ensure that the prize agents had carefully locked up the goods and merchandise from

18 Winfield, *British Warships*, 200, 265, 31.

19 TNA ADM 1/2110 Captains' Letters M 1758 Martin 23 October 1758.

20 LG issue no. 9927 1 September 1759.

ships taken as prizes until they could be condemned, valued and sold. Customs dues were then payable, all this responsibility resting with the prize agent appointed by the prize taker. After the sale or sales of the prize goods, a day was nominated by the prize agent for the distribution of the prize money. This was followed by further distributions over a period of time until, after three years, the residue went to Greenwich Hospital, as described in Chapter 9.

To illustrate the negotiations required by the Customs House, the following letter directed to the prize agents relating to the *St Pierre* lying at Portsmouth is an exemplar:

> Gentlemen,
>
> Application having been made to us by Messrs W&B Jasper desiring liberty to export the whole or any part of the cargo of the St Pierre, a French prize consisting of sugar, coffee and other goods (landed at your port by Bill of Sight under a deposit of £1000) without entry inwards, or outwards, or paying any duties for the same, we have consulted the Patent Officers thereon, who have reported that the duties for these French prize sugars, coffee and other goods, are payable at your port. You are therefore to take care that all the said goods be regularly entered, and the duties paid agreeable to the practice here, and as to the tares, they are to be adjusted by the discharging officers agreeable to their duties, and if any difficulties arise, the Collector, Controller and Surveyor must adjust the same.
>
> We are your loving friends W Westby Jn Hill, S Mead, B Fairfax
> Customs House, London 11 Sept 1744[21]

The sums of money payable as the customs due were not inconsiderable. The cargo of *St Pierre* was sold for £15,273 9s 9d and on this customs dues of £8,051 7s 10d were paid.

Publicity in the *London Gazette*

Three copies of the *London Gazette* had to be given to the collector of customs or chief officer of the port or place where the condemnation took place: one for the treasurer of Greenwich Hospital, one for the treasurer or paymaster of the navy in London, one to be preserved by the chief officer.

21 Staffordshire Archives D1798/HM Drakeford/13.

Private Sale of Prizes

If the prize was not bought by the Navy Board, the agent would arrange the sale of prize vessels and goods, which historically took place 'by the candle'. Bidders could make an offer as long as a small piece of candle burned, the bid made just before the flame went out being successful.

Michael Clements's prize *Robuste* and her contents were advertised in the national press. It was in the agent's interest to whip up as much interest in the sales as possible, as his five per cent would be enhanced if there was brisk bidding before the candle flame flickered and died.

> For sale by the candle at Lloyd's Coffee House in Lombard Street, on Thursday 22nd February, at twelve o'clock at noon
>
> The Good Ship ROBUSTE
>
> A French ship of War, burthen 600 tons more or less, a prime sailor and extremely well found. Length upon the main deck 119, breadth upon the main deck 19 feet 2 inches, length of the quarter deck 55 feet 8 inches, heighth betwixt decks 5 feet 3 inches, extreme breadth on the lower deck 33 feet 5 inches, depth in the hold 14 feet 3 inches, mounted when taken 22 nine-pounders, and two twelve pounders on her main deck, three ports of a side between decks for guns, taken by his Majesty's ships Alcide and Acteon, James Douglas and Michael Clements, Esqrs, Commanders, now lying at Plymouth and there to be delivered. Inventories to be had on board at the place of sale, and of BENJ. VAUGHAN and Son, and FRANCIS FANNNG, Brokers.
>
> The cargo of that valuable prize the Robuste, taken by the Acteon Capt. Clements, consists of 100 tons of bomb shells and shot, 1750 barrels flour, 250 hogsheads wine, 100 casks and cases soldiers cloathing, 60 bales sailcloth, 16 bales linen, 1 bale handkerchiefs, 25 tons cordage, 30 barrels pitch, 30 barrels tar, 5 barrels tallow, 3 ditto brimstone, 50 casks of musket balls and small shot, 5 tons and 90 boxes candles, 10 bales of kersey bunting, 1500c.match 1500c.oakham.
>
> For SALE by the CANDLE
> At the Star Tavern Great Room, Southside Street, Plymouth
>
> The following goods, viz:
>
> For home consumption,
>
> 19 coils of rope, 13 hawsers of different sizes, a quantity of spun yarn, ditto of oakum, ditto of match, ditto new blocks, 82 pieces sailcloth, 7 ditto damaged, 347 bomb shells, 6 large beds and mortars,

6 twenty-four pounders and 18 eighteen ditto new and very good, a quantity of Crow and Iron Work, ditto of gun carriages, 10 kegs of musket balls.

Being part of the cargo landed out of the Robust, a French ship of War, taken by his Majesty's ships Alcide and Acteon, James Douglas and Michael Clements, Esqrs, Commanders.

The goods to be seen by applying to Francis Fanning, or George Winne in Plymouth, where catalogues may be had, at the place of sale, and of BENJ. VAUGHAN and Son, and FRANCIS FANNING, Brokers.[22]

An example of the meticulous accounting required by the prize agent after one of these sessions of sales is to be seen in Appendix 11. The following is a summary of the voluminous accounts relating to the prize *St Pierre*:

Table 3. Proceeds of the sale of *St Pierre*.

	£	s	d
Sale of ship, tackle, apparel, furniture, etc.	800	0	0
Sugar	12056	10	5
Coffee	1520	5	10
Cocoa	45	9	0
Indigo	951	4	11
Cotton	296	13	8
Bread, firewood	3	5	12
	16073	9	10
Deductions			
Customs	8051	7	10
Charges	968	1	1
Agents commission at 5%	803	13	6
Balance due to captors	6250	7	5
	16073	9	10

22 *Whitehall Evening Post* 14 October 1758; *Gazetteer and London Daily Advertiser* 11 April 1759.

Out of a prize worth £16,000 it would have seemed very hard to the captors that they shared only £6,250. The reality was that the state, in the shape of the Customs officials, had to have their portion first, and nothing would have been achieved without the efforts of all the agents. The 2½ per cent they took on every item sold was hard earned. That their commission was one-tenth of the customs fee puts it into perspective.[23]

23 Staffordshire Archives D1798/HM Drakeford.

9

The Distribution of the Proceeds of Taking a Prize

After the sale or sales of the prize the agent had to make two public notifications of the distribution of shares in the *London Gazette* or, if in a Vice Admiralty Court, in the newspaper of most authority in the island or place where the condemnation had taken place. The notification had to be made at least three days before the initial distribution and contain the address of the agent, and the precise day of the month and year in which the further distributions would take place. If these conditions of advertisement were not met, there was a penalty of £500 payable to Greenwich Hospital.

The prize agent had further responsibilities: if the captured ship was thought fit to be brought into the navy once it had been condemned as a prize, a bill for her value, together with that of her 'stores, apparel, guns, and furniture', had to be made out within fifteen days 'according to the course of the navy' to be distributed and divided as laid down. 'And for the further encouragement of such officers, seamen and others who shall actually serve on board' the distribution was made without fee or reward.[1] The amazing number of deductions for legal fees and charges had of course already been made, but the morale of the men concerned was maintained.

Admiralty and Parliament were anxious that the Prize Acts after 1739 achieved their goal of encouraging seamen, and that payments of prize and bounty money were made promptly, accurately and publicly in order to do so. The very detailed paper work was intended to defeat fraud. There is one example of very slow distribution given later in this chapter, but on the whole, after a slow start, Admiralty cases took on average two months from capture to distribution.[2]

Cranbrook Commission

The Cranbrook Commissioners worked fast to get their papers in order as soon as possible. Eventually the final announcement on their efforts was made:

1 LG issue no. 9598 6 July 1756.

2 Pares, *Colonial Blockade*, 142.

> Prize Office London April 2 1761
>
> The Commissioners for the sale of French Prizes, taken before the Declaration of War, do hereby give Notice to all Persons who have disbursed Money on Account of the said Prizes, that they deliver their Accounts into this office, with proper vouchers, on or before the 2nd day of July next, otherwise they will be excluded.
>
> By order of the Commissioners, Samuel Gardner, Secretary[3]

It was not their fault that the final accounting after this announcement took so long and that it was another seven years before that figure was established.

As already detailed above, the goods and merchandise taken from ships condemned as prizes had to be carefully locked up until they could be valued and sold. Customs and other duties were then payable, this responsibility resting with the prize agent appointed by the prize taker. There would probably be several sales: of the ship's hull, its tackle and its contents.

As outlined in Chapter 3, the agent prepared a schedule for the disbursement to the ship's company of the net proceeds, in accordance with the scales of distribution laid down by Proclamation and drawing on the list supplied to him by the capturing ship showing the name and status of every man on board at the time of capture. The next time the captor returned to port the agent would take his books there, carefully drawn up to make distribution on board easier. The *London Gazette* notices about payment on board could usually not be specific as to time: for the crew of *Terrible* which had taken *L'Heureux* 'for those who did not receive their prize money before the departure of the said ship from England'.[4] '*Tartar*, for taking *Le Grand Gideon* the next time she returns to Plymouth.'[5] Lockhart took *Duc d'Aguillon* on 14 April 1757, and was paid out nine months later:

> Notice is hereby given to the officers and company of his Majesty's ship Tartar who were actually on board at the taking of Le Duc d'Aguillon French Privateer, that they will be paid their respective shares of the said privateer, and Head Money, on Friday 27 January instant, on board the said ship at Plymouth.[6]

There were occasions when the payments were made on board a different vessel – presumably one with a larger deck on which the disbursement could take place. The men of *Prince Edward* were warned: 'the commission and

3 LG issue no. 10091 28 March 1761.
4 LG issue no. 9924 21 August 1759.
5 LG issue no. 9700 28 June 1757.
6 LG issue no. 9760 24 January 1758.

warrant officers will be paid on Tuesday 21 August 1759 at the French Horn in Crutched Friars and the petty offices and men on board the *Mars* on her arrival at Spithead'.[7]

Burnett's log of September 1756 does not name the snow, but eight months later the questions of the insurance and ownership of *Baltimore* had been resolved, and the *London Gazette* reported that *Happy*'s crew were to be paid immediately in Portsmouth.[8] For Thomas Burnett and the small group of men he took with him into his next command, *Cambridge* (80), their attorneys could have received the money on the first Tuesday in every month at the French Horn Tavern at Crutched Friars, close to the Navy Board.

Recalls

The *London Gazette* published the days on which a prize agent would return to his office, with the all-important books, to pay out recalls. For one reason or another, there were always crew members who were not on board for the initial payment of prize money. Their nominated agents would have opportunity to obtain the money later, on one of the advertised days for the following three years. The prize agent could retain the money left after the first distribution and make up any late payments as 'recalls' or a recall agent could be used, who would also have a scale of charges. Prize agents could put this un-reclaimed money out to interest, and could collude with other agents to raise charges. The residue, usually about ten per cent of the whole, went to Greenwich Hospital as detailed below. It was considered that after three years of 'recalls' any individual who had not yet collected his entitlement, or directed an agent to do so on his behalf, was probably dead or indifferent. Greenwich Hospital made use of every source of income to benefit naval pensioners, widows and orphans.

Group action by agents was not uncommon:

> To the *Hussar*, for the *Heureux Malouin*, on the 11th of April; for the *Alexander*, *Legere* and *Mary Magdalene*, on the 13th of July 1759; To the *Isis*, Edward Wheeler Esq Commander on the 21st April; and for the *Hermione* Frigate on the 26th of April 1760: on the 21st of April; and to the *Aeolus*, John Elliot Esq Commander, on the 26th of same month 1760, for the *Mignone* Frigate.
>
> Philip Stephens, Esq of Spring Gardens)
> John Lloyd Esq of Plymouth) Agents
> William Innes and Thomas Clerk, of Lime Street Square)

7 LG issue no. 9924 21 August 1759.

8 LG issue no. 9758 17 January 1758.

> N.B. The Recalls continue to be made at Mr Innes's, the first Wednesday in every month, for three years, from the above dates of payment; and those shares not demanded within that time, become forfeited to Greenwich Hospital.[9]

The agent Lt. St Alban Roy was teamed with John Lloyd to pay *Unicorn* for the *Hermione*'s hull money on 8 July 1758 and the Head Money on 28 December 1758.[10]

The team of Benjamin Bond jun. Esq. of London, Capt. Richard Baillie, of his Majesty's Land Service, and John Lloyd of Plymouth paid out to *Tartar* for the capture of *Marie Victoire* on 13 March 1758. It seems likely that Capt. Richard Baillie was a relation of the young Thomas Baillie whose actions resulted in her capture.[11] Head Money for *Marie Victoire*'s crew of 236 (alive on board at the start of the engagement) came to £1,180. Admiral Henry Harrison, who had drawn up so carefully the appointment of advocates on *Tartar*'s behalf, would have ensured that his son John was on hand to receive his share.

Baillie took several prizes in *Tartar's Prize* in the Mediterranean: *La Marquis de Chetenoise*, *St Antony de Padua*, a tartane *St Peter* and a polacre *St Peter*. These prizes were all dealt with by John Dick, Consul in Leghorn. Eventually in 1761 *Tartar's Prize* sprang a plank in a gale and Baillie and his crew were lucky to be rescued by a passing Danish ship and taken to Malta.[12]

Fleet Actions

Fleet actions resulted in hard and very complicated work by the agents. As mentioned in Chapter 4, after the capture of Louisburg in 1758, *Echo*'s Head Money was paid only to *Juno* and *Scarborough*, not to the rest of Boscawen's fleet. The whole fleet benefited from Head Money paid for the burning in the harbour of *Bienfaisant*, *Prudent*, *Entreprenant*, *Le Célèbre*, *Capricieux*, *L'Appollon* and *Fidelle* as well as the recapture of *Muscliffe*, *Dolphin* sloop and the prize *Sellerie*.[13] Alexander Macpherson paid out to each of Boscawen's fleet in turn as the ships returned to harbour, beginning on 8 January 1760.[14]

The action in the Mediterranean on 28 February 1758 which resulted in the capture of *Foudroyant* and *Orphée* led to a complicated series of distributions. *Monmouth* and *Swiftsure*, the actual captors of the French vessels,

9 LG issue no. 10056 25 November 1760.
10 LG issue no. 10062 16 December 1760.
11 LG issue no. 10062 16 December 1760.
12 *Lloyds List* No. 2534 25 April 1760.
13 LG issue no. 9957 15 December 1759.
14 LG issue no. 9957 15 December 1759.

received their 'bounties' or Head Money from Mr Rudyard at Gibraltar. The produce of the hulls, stores and fittings of *Foudroyant* and *Orphée* was paid by Rudyard to the officers and companies of *Prince*, *Culloden*, *Jersey*, *St Albans* and *Thetis* hospital ship when they arrived in Gibraltar. The further vessels, *Monmouth*, *Hampton Court*, *Revenge*, *Montagu*, *Preston*, *Swiftsure*, *Princess Louisa*, *Berwick*, *St George* and *Fowey*, were paid when they subsequently arrived in Gibraltar. Any men missing from the companies of *Montagu* and *Hampton Court*, both having been paid off and the bulk of whose men had been 'turned over' into ships still abroad, were paid at the French Horn in Crutched Friars, viz. *Montagu* 4 October, and *Hampton Court* 11 October 1759. Once all the other ships' prize lists had been sent on from Gibraltar to London, the remaining men were also recalled on the last Tuesday in every month for three years after the respective shares had been paid on board.[15] There was always the problem of men 'turned over' into other vessels without returning to England. Their agents had, somehow, to keep track of them.

Just before Christmas in 1760 the *London Gazette* published a list of prizes for which follow-up distribution was still taking place on one day a month, evidence of the number of prizes taken. The team of Stephens, Brett, Mason and Macpherson was foremost amongst the agents, as evidenced by the total of 223 listed in the one issue illustrated below, their distributor being Edmund Mason of Crutched Friars, for which the first payment dates are given for the first nine examples:

> … for the Sauterelle, Lowestoffe, 2.2.58; for the St Jacques, Mareschal de Belleisle, Le Jeanette, Medway, 1.4.58; Marlborough 26.4.58; Windsor 6.5.58; Sheerness 19.6.58; Newcastle 4.7.58; Prince Frederick 4.7.58; Bedford 16.11.58; for the St Jacques, Prince Edward 28.9.58; …[16]

In 1762 Philip Stevens officially dropped out as he became Secretary to the Admiralty, although it seems very unlikely that he stopped receiving a share of the income derived from the original team. Messrs Mason, Brett and Macpherson went on being responsible for dozens of payments.

For her two captures mentioned in Chapter 4, John Hodges, *Dispatch* (8), received her rewards later the same year, as recorded in successive entries in ADM 43/15 for Head Money in 1758, namely *Le Vénérable* for which she

15 LG issue no. 9931 15 September 1759.

16 Fanny Boscawen wrote to her husband in 1748: 'Lord Anson's secretary, Mr Stephens, was with Mason, and he told me that Lord Anson and Sir P. Warren had determined to receive all their share in Navy bills, which were at 2 per cent discount, and bore 5 per cent interest.' Aspinal-Oglander, *Admiral's Wife*, 92.

received £255 and *Le Dieppoise*, for which she received £245, both dated 31 July 1758.

As mentioned above, when prize money was distributed, a distinction was frequently made between the officers, petty officers and foremast men who were paid separately from the rest of 'the people'. Presumably these more senior officers could be relied on to return to their ship after picking up their prize money from the prize agent on shore, whereas the much more numerous 'people' were paid on board. 'The people' would do much better in a small ship with fewer to share the proceeds.[17] It is rare for the exact amount of prize money to be distributed to be published, but the officers and foremast men of *Captain* and *Rye* were rewarded for their capture of the *Felicité* with substantial rewards. The agents, John and William Maynes, of Austin Friars near the Royal Exchange, distributed to each commissioned officer £7 12s; each warrant officer received £3 6s 6d; each petty officer received 17s 8d and the foremast men 3s 7d.[18] As usual, the 'people' were paid on board.

When the *St Martha* was taken by vessels from the Downs squadron, the officers from *Ambuscade* were paid at the French Horn, Crutched Friars on 10 February 1757. *Merlin* was paid on board at Sheerness on the same day. The petty officers and foremast men of *Brilliant* were paid their prize money on board *Stork* in Portsmouth, the petty officers and foremast men of the armed vessel *Maryland Planter* were paid on board the *Enterprise* at Sheerness on 15 February. *Portmahon* had to wait until her return to England.[19] When the company of *Dover* (44) were warned to collect their prize money for taking *Bastienne* on 15 November 1756, the captain and commission and warrant officers were to report to the Navy Coffee House in Crutched Friars on Thursday 4 April 1758, while the company under the rank of warrant officer or mate were to be paid their respective shares of the prize at the Kings Arms, Portsmouth on Tuesday 11 April.[20] The *Prince Edward* (44) took the *Chevreuil* from San Domingo on 14 February 1759. The commission and warrant officers were paid on Tuesday 21 August 1759 at the French Horn in Crutched Friars and the petty officers and men received their prize money on board the *Mars* on her arrival at Spithead, the recalls at the said French Horn the third Tuesday in every month.[21] It must have been a nightmare for their agents.

[17] Tim Clayton, *Tars: The Men Who Made Britain Rule the Waves* (Hodder, 2008), 298.

[18] LG issue no. 9706 19 July 1757.

[19] LG issue no. 9696 14 June 1757.

[20] LG issue no. 9776 21 March 1758.

[21] LG issue no. 9924 21 August 1759.

In 1758 the *London Gazette* gave notice that:

> Notice is hereby given that there is money in hand to pay for the oxen sheep and some stores taken in French vessels off Minorca by a squadron of his Majesty's ships under the command of Sir Edward Hawke, cruising there from 19 July 1756 to the latter end of September following; also for the produce of the St John and St James polacre: the commanders thereof of the respective ships and vessels entitled to share in these captures are desired to send their prize lists without loss of time to Mr Chorley of the Navy office in order to prevent delays in the distribution.[22]

Ordinary seamen had to have help in collecting their prize money, as they were often at sea when the agents had money to distribute. A licensed navy agent had to secure two other bondsmen, usually local tradesmen, for £200, before he could accept Prize Orders from seamen as a means of deferring payment for goods.[23] Details of these additional agents are revealed in the analysis which follows.

Analysis of Drakeford Distribution of Prize Money from *St Pierre*

Thanks to Richard Drakeford, an almost complete list of a distribution has survived, to be seen in Appendix 11. A complicated picture of agency is revealed by an analysis of the 242 individuals listed in the agent's book. Forty-two men received nothing: six were marked 'DD', without any money alongside their names, presumably having died before taking the prize so not entitled to any share; twenty-one men had deserted, marked 'R' or 'ran' in the paybook, with one man marked 'D' deserted; two were discharged 'DSQ' to sick quarters; a further twelve men have nothing against their names. For nearly one-fifth of the complement to receive nothing was unexpected.

The busiest agents collected money for more than one member of the crew: John Vincent collected for seventy crew; Edward Jasper for twenty-four crew; J. Malraven for fourteen members, all but one of whom had specified Hugh Dixey; B. Bechinoe collected on behalf of seventeen family members. The ubiquitous J. Henshaw here collected on behalf of only one member of the crew. Hasden Young, brother of the captain, was his agent as well as for a further three members of the crew. Twenty-five wives benefited, ten of those without attorneys, as did three fathers, two mothers, two sisters and one brother. Almost all of the prize money was distributed on 21 January 1745,

[22] LG issue no. 9774 31 January 1758.

[23] Green, *Royal Navy*, 181.

with fifteen further on 7 February and two on 14 February. When the money actually reached the named recipients is of course something we cannot tell.

Legal Fees HCA 2

Court costs were only part of the expenses paid out before distribution. There was also demurrage, wages, wastage of cargo and losses by too low valuations on appraisement.[24] In the legal department there were fixed rates for each stage, although the way the courts worked seemed to guarantee as many repetitions of small fees as possible. The Judges for instance charged a flat fee of £1 for each sentence or interlocutory order. This interlocutory order was merely a provisional decision, to postpone the hearing to a later date. Tracking the appeal hearings through the court papers shows that many of them are postponed or 'porrected' to a hearing date only two weeks later, but with the potential perhaps of double the charges thereby. There were complaints about the costs of the court, but it appears that it was the recurrence of the small costs which led to the disproportionate totals.

The ledgers in which legal fees are recorded were painstakingly maintained, although the arithmetic has been shown to be suspect. The charges so far identified are for monitions, copying, interrogatories, appraisement, translations, bail, announcement of sale, of which by far the most common are copies, revealing the meticulous accounting for every penny which could be charged to the expense of taking prizes. The columns are headed with the persons who received the payments, the first column being the total of the subsequent ones, i.e. Judge, Register, Deputy, Marshal, Deputy, Cryer.

When one reaches the final pages in each ledger where the totals are listed, the charges for each element of the work of the High Court of Admiralty are listed. Each letter of marque was worth 14s 10d to the Register; a warrant was worth 1s 6d to the Register; a bail was worth 3s 6d; a bail with a release was worth 9s 2d.

The books of charges by the lawyers would have made discouraging reading for the officers and men of the prize taker: their dozens of pages list the charges for every conceivable deduction from the sale of the vessel and its 'cargoes, tackle, guns, apparel and furniture'. It does not seem that charges of 2s 2d or 8s 6d are very high, but when added together they become a considerable proportion of the whole, especially when so many of the charges are simply for the endless copies. Every step in every cause had its price, irrespective of its importance, and the proctor's bill of costs represented his entire recoverable reward. Costs were taxed between counsel and client. The pages and pages of these files reveal the accounting for every penny which could be charged

24 Pares, *Colonial Blockade*, 142.

to the expense of taking prizes, and are invaluable to the researcher. Below is one page from one of the books of accounting records, showing the enormous task of the clerks who did nothing else but make copies:

Table 4. Legal charges within Doctors Commons.

An Account of what hath been received in the Admiralty Office for the Judge Register Deputy Marshal Deputy and Cryer from the 1st January 1757 to the 1st of July following

		£ s d **total**	**Judge**	**Register**	**Deputy**	**Marshall**
Smith	For Monn.in de Giljaume	0 3 2		0 2 2	0 1 0	
Tyndall	For copy & ? in le Fidelle & Com	0 8 6		0 8 6		
	For ditto in la Colombe	0 8 6		0 8 6		
	For ditto in la Jean Louis	0 8 6		0 8 6		
	For ditto in the Yser Pott	0 8 6		0 8 6		
	For ditto in Le St Joseph	0 8 6		0 8 6		
	For ditto in L'Aigle	0 6 6		0 6 6		
	For copy & ditto in L'Esprit & C	0 6 6		0 6 6		
	For ditto in La Vigilante Magdaleine	0 6 6		0 6 6		
	For copy &? In Le Bon Amy &Com	0 4 6		0 4 6		
Farrar	For copy Interr. In Le St Paul	0 6 0		0 4 0	0 2 0	

Crespigny	For Comm. Appraisement & sale of brandy	0 15 4		0 13 4	0 2 0
Tyndall	For copy Sentence in Le Duc de Bourgoigne	0 6 0		0 4 0	0 2 0
	For copy ditto in Le Viarme	0 6 0			
	For copy ditto in La Victoire	0 6 0			
	For copy ditto in L'Aimable Marg.	0 6 0			
	For copy ditto in l'Aimable Rose	0 6 0			
	For copy ditto in Les Tres Venerable	0 6 0			
	For copy ditto in La Belle Heleine	0 6 0			
	For bail	0 3 6	0 1 0	0 1 6	0 1 0
	For decree of sale	0 7 9		0 6 9	0 1 0
Tyndall	For copy sentence in Le Mareshal de Belisle	0 6 0		0 4 0	0 2 0

Cases Where Vessels Were Restored to Owners

The situation of a captain who brought in a prize only to have it returned to the owner created a problem, for which a solution was proposed in Parliament: 'If officers have detained vessels improperly should have such heavy costs awarded against them by the Courts of Admiralty as almost to ruin them, is it fit they should be remunerated in any other manner than by Parliament?' It was not surprising that at the end of the century, George Rose, the Treasurer of the Navy, kept a 'slush fund' to reimburse captors who had brought in prizes *bona fide*.[25] Claude de Crespigny administered the fund, and a proportion went to reimburse the costs of the captors whose prizes had been restored.[26]

Vice Admiralty Courts

Agents who had to deal with condemnations made by the Vice Admiralty Courts in the West Indies were always at a disadvantage when their disbursements had to be made. They were under the same legal obligation as were agents based in England to complete a timely payment of prize money. The advertisement below represents the agents' frustration at the slow take up by nominated members of all the crews in Admiral Moore's fleet in the West Indies. Despite the best intentions of the crew members, many of them would have been taken from Antigua long before the condemnation took place, and might not even have returned to England at all. The situation would have been even more difficult for the widows or family members of the large numbers killed by disease or in action.[27]

> Portsmouth December 14 1763
>
> Whereas sundry Prizes were put into the Hands of Robert Browne and William Warner of Antigua, during the Command of Admiral Moore on the Leeward Island Station; and afterwards the Subscriber of this Advertisement was concerned for sundry other prizes taken by some of the Men of War under the command of Sir James Douglas, on the said station. And whereas there are sundry Shares of said Prizes still unpaid, although the said William Warner attended several Days for four Months last Winter, at the Castle Tavern in Lombard Street, London, to recall the said Lists, and to pay off the said Prize Money: he therefore gives this public Notice (as his Affairs require his Return to and Residence in Antigua) that the said Lists will be recalled the first Tuesday and Wednesday in every month, at the said Robert Brown's Counting House, or at the Subscriber's office in Antigua till the 1st of January 1765, in order to pay off all legal Demands; after which, such Prize Monies as have lain Three Years and upwards in the said Agents hands, and not legally demanded in Person or by proper Powers, as well the Monies for R. and D.D. men, will be paid into the Hands of the Treasurer of Greenwich Hospital, agreeable to Act of Parliament. William Warner, Agent.

25 Hill, *Prizes of War*, 92.

26 Hill, *Prizes of War*, 91.

27 Capt. Burnett, *Marlborough* (68), and his crew were providentially rescued when their vessel foundered mid-Atlantic after taking part in the capture of Havana. They had to leave all personal possessions behind. Did they manage to save their bounty money from Havana? A.B. McLeod, *British Naval Captains of the Seven Years' War* (Boydell and Brewer, 2012), 176.

Ransoms

Merchant ships captured by the French were not taken as prizes. Instead, they took a 'ransom bill' from the commander of the captured vessel, which bound him and the owners of the vessel and its cargo to pay a certain amount of money at a future date, entered in the bill. The duplicate of this bill was kept by the captor, together with a hostage, usually a mate of the captured vessel, who would be released when the ransom was paid. The released ship was then supposed to proceed to a designated port within a limited time.[28] The back pages of *Lloyds List* would have been scanned eagerly for news of merchant ships taken by the French and ransomed. Captured privateers often had ransomers on board.[29] If the ransom was not paid it was difficult for the individual who had effectively been made responsible for the payment to put pressure on the owners of his vessel to secure his release. His only hope was to be re-captured from his captors before being taken ashore.

The British government was against ransoms as they wanted captive seamen who could be returned in exchange for captured English seamen. Eventually the Privateers Act of 1759 made it a capital offence to agree to ransom with neutrals.[30]

Capture of Louisburg

Hugh Boscawen provided the sum of money which was distributed after the capture of Louisburg.[31] The total was £33,989 5s 7d, distributed amongst those present in the age-old system, whereby Admiral Boscawen received a one-sixteenth share, amounting to £2,129 1s 7d. His two flag officers received a similar share, £1,064 10s 9d each. The forty-one captains shared one-quarter between them, £201 1s. There were 176 lieutenants sharing one-eighth of the total, receiving £23 17s 8d. The 407 warrant officers shared a similar eighth, receiving £10 6s 4d each. There were 1,288 petty officers sharing one-eighth so each received £3 5s 3d. The 13,388 seamen shared one-quarter of the whole, each receiving 13s 0d. This doesn't sound much, but it represented a good proportion of a month's wages. Proceeds from the merchantmen and their cargoes were part of the prize money shared amongst the fleet. The Navy Board also bought *Bienfaisant* for £13,636 6s.

28 W. Senior, 'Ransom Bills', *Law Quarterly Review 34* (1918), 49, 50.

29 *Lloyds List* No. 26632 12 July 1761: 'The Aurora Privateer from Rochelle with the ransomer from the Betty, Cathcart, on board, is taken by the Aquilon Man of War Capt. Ogle.'

30 Pares, *Colonial Blockade*, 20, 23.

31 Boscawen, *Capture of Louisburg*, 353.

Head Money

The inducement of Head Money inspired the captains and their crews to court danger and fight well. The National Archives in ADM 43 provide evidence for the way in which this reward was accounted for. Each little bundle of documents was numbered, so that it is possible to draw up a list and watch the system in action. Not every bundle has been found, so there are gaps in the file below. But the system was robust. Once the prize had been condemned, the legal document giving the number of men on board was established. The document was then passed to the Treasury for the Head Money to be paid out to the agent, who did not have to exert himself as he did when the prize had to be sold.

The table below is the list of thirty-one payments of Head Money recorded between March and December 1757. The original documents contained only the name of the agents, through whom the money was distributed.[32]

Table 5. Record of Head Money paid March–December 1757.

No.	Date	Agents used	Prize	Captor	Bounty
290	28 March	Henry Gunter and John Lloyd	Comtesse de la Mark	Otter	250
375	19 April	William Butter and Henry Budd	L'Emanuel	Lynn	120
395	22 April	Redstone, Bensley, Brett and Stephens	L'Heureux	Tartar and Happy	380
550	31 May	Richard Kee and Messrs Devonshire and Reeves	Le Glorieux	Prince Edward	360
551	31 May	Edward Vernon and John Morstead	Le Lys	Lyme	290
552	31 May	James Dickson	Le Duc de Penthiere	Aldborough	510
553	31 May	Henry Douglas, Philip Stephens and John Lloyd	Le Montroziere	Tartar	845

32 TNA ADM 43/14 for 1757. (P) signifies that the captor was a privateer.

792	21 July	Edward Vernon and John Vining	L'Entreprenant	Lyme and Deal Castle	630
793	21 July	Charles Burley and Francis Magnus	Le Dange	Centuar and Dispatch	280
820	28 July	James Hickman, Tyringham Stephens	Le Subtile	Hazard	430
822	28 July	James Bensley and John Lloyd	Le Grand Gideon	Tartar	955
823	28 July	Edmund Mason	Le Bretagne	Lowestoff	500
825	28 July	Oliver Toulmin and Thomas Foreworthy	La Cigale	Unicorn	510
939	26 Aug.	Thomas Maude, Thomas Bellet, Thomas Harrison	La Genevieve	Porcupine	540
941	26 Aug.	Charles Brett, Philip Stephens and Henry Budd	L'Infernal	Happy	375
1162	30 Sept.	William Renstone and James Bensley	Le Cerf	Tartar	1055
1237	13 Oct.	Christopher Joliffe	Le Barnard	Jamaica	495
1238	13 Oct.	Thomas Oakley	L'Hardy Mendiant	Scorpion	225
1359	31 Oct.	Norman Durward	Le Menon	Ranger (P)	210
1387	9 Oct.	Benjamin Bond Jn, William Baillie and John Lloyd	La Marie Victoire	Tartar	1180

1502	9 Dec.	Stephens, Brett, Mason and Macpherson	Le Puisieulx	Essex	1095
1503	9 Dec.	Stephens, Brett, Mason, Macpherson, James Dickson and Edward Wheeler	Le Comte de Heronville	Essex and Isis	845
1504	9 Dec.	James Dickson and Edward Wheeler	Le Prince de Turenne	Isis	335
1505	9 Dec.	Edmund Mason, Alexander Macpherson and John Lloyd	L'Ardencourt	Lowestoff	385
1506	9 Dec.	Edmund Mason, Alexander Macpherson and John Lloyd	Le Difficulté	Lowestoff	245
1508	9 Dec.	Manbey, Bennet, Huddy, Brander, Hore	L'Union	St George (P)	475
1509	9 Dec.	Manbey, Bennet, Huddy, Brander, Hore	Le Marquise de L'Amon	St George (P)	680
1609	27 Oct.	Murry, Loving, Dudman, Snell, Weatherall, Healy, West, Bird and Hotham	Le Comte de Gisors	Deptford (P)	375
1643	31 Dec.	William Graves and Thomas Brent	Le Port Mahan	Sheerness	420

1644	31 Dec.	Stephens, Brett, Mason, Macpherson and John Lloyd	La Santarelle	Lowestoff	765
1645	31 Dec.	James Dickson and Edward Wheeler	L'Escarboucle	Isis	585
				Total paid	16,345

These vouchers, providing details behind the £16,345 paid out as Head Money between March and December 1757, are only part of the financial burden carried by the Treasury. Using the Navy Board documents gave an even more positive perspective on Head Money. These figures represent all the vessels, not just those for which the vouchers were found.[33]

Table 6. Total Head Money paid out 1757–65.

Year	No. of men	Total paid out
1757	5,475	27,375
1758	10,334	51,670
1759	10,601	53,110
1760	11,221	56,105
1761	10,351	51,755
1762	8,093	40,465
1763	9,750	48,750
1764	2,969	14,845
1765	332	1,660
TOTAL	69,126	345,630

The payments by the Admiralty represent a substantial return to those naval vessels (and some privateers) who took it upon themselves to capture their French counterparts. This is evidence of the willingness of the government to reward the captors. It is not surprising that an embargo was placed on French privateers, crews of which were removed for service in naval vessels.

[33] The *London Gazette* reported that no Head Money was to be paid to the officers and men of *Roebuck*, following their capture of *La Portmahone*. LG issue no. 9769 28 February 1758.

John Lockhart's Agents

The staff in the archive section of the Royal Bank of Scotland made available the details of an account John Lockhart held in Drummonds Bank for some years while he was an active captain. Lockhart three times received money into his bank account from Joshua Thomas. As Thomas was not Lockhart's designated agent a reason for these payments was not obvious, until on scanning the list of agents in ADM 43 (payments of Head Money) emerged the name Joshua Thomas, agent to Captain John Rushworth, *Alarm* (32), when he captured *La Lutine* in 1761. (*Garland* is also credited with capture.) The reason why Joshua Thomas paid John Lockhart three fairly small sums of money, £26, £26 and £6, could well be the fact that the hull, cargo, fittings, etc. would be sold off separately, so the money would come in to the agent, and therefore to the captor, in small amounts.[34]

A second source of money for John Lockhart, again not from his nominated agent, was from Captain Edward Wheeler. On 24 January (year not stated on bank document) £46 was paid in cash by James Unwin on behalf of Captain Edward Wheeler. As Wheeler was an active captain, and responsible for captures in his own right as commander of *Isis* (50), a check in the ADM 43 vouchers showed that yes, Edward Wheeler named himself as one of his agents.[35] This is unusual, as the captain would normally have been expected to be at sea, capturing more prizes, rather than attending Doctors Commons. As they shared the capture of *Mignone* this may have been the reason for this pay out, corroborated by the announcement in the *London Gazette*:

> To the Hussar for the Heureux Malouin, on the 11th of April; for the Alexander, Legere and Mary Magdalene, on 13th July 1759; and for the Hermione frigate on 26th April 1760; to the Isis, Edward Wheeler, Esq Commander, on the 21st of April; and to the Æolus, John Elliot Esq Commander, on 26th of the same month 1760 for the Mignone Frigate.
>
> Philip Stephens Esq of Spring Gardens,
> John Lloyd, Esq of Plymouth
> William Innes and Thomas Clerk of Lime Street Square, Agents.
>
> N.B. The Recalls continue to be made at Mr Innes's, the first Wednesday in every month, for three years, from the above dates of payment; and those shares not demanded within that time, become forfeited to Greenwich Hospital.[36]

34 NatWest Group Archives SE/11306 John Lockhart Ross Account March 1760: DR/427/28 f.171; Sept 1763: DR/427/47 f.748.

35 TNA ADM 43/1503 and 1504.

36 LG issue no. 10056 25 November 1760.

Once Spain entered the war, she was no longer an ally to whom courtesies had to be maintained. New Yorkers, who had been trading with Spain as well as France, made it almost impossible for troops, supplies and armaments to be gathered for the attack on Havana.[37]

Capture of *Hermione*

The capture of *Hermione*, the Spanish treasure ship which had sailed from Lima before Spain's declaration of war was known there, is the most famous prize of all. She was only a day's sail from the Algarve coast when she was captured by Herbert Sawyer, *Active* (28), and Philemon Pownal, *Favorite* (18), of Admiral Saunders's squadron. So enormously rich did she prove that after deducting all expenses, more than half a million pounds was distributed in prize money. Beatson, the contemporary historian, described the triumph:

> The treasure was conveyed from Portsmouth to London in twenty wagons, escorted by a party of sailors. The waggons were decorated with the British colours flying, having those of Spain underneath them … on their coming to London they were joined by a troop of light dragoons, with a band of music … and in this manner did they march on through the City to the Tower, amid the acclamations of a prodigious concourse of people.[38]

Saunders and his two fortunate captains each received £65,000, commissioned officers £13,000 and every seaman nearly £500.[39]

Capture of Havana

The amount of money to be distributed after the Havana campaign was huge, more than £737,000. The brothers Albemarle were able to divide the treasure evenly between the army and the navy, acting on precedents going back to William III, Anne 1702 and George II 1740.[40] The Earl of Albemarle as commander-in-chief of the land and Vice Admiral Sir George Pocock as commander-in-chief of the naval forces had between them one-third (five-fifteenths) of the whole. Lt. General George Augustus Elliot Esq., and the Honourable Augustus Keppel, second in command respectively of the land

[37] Truxes, *Defying Empire*, 143.

[38] Robert Beatson, *Naval and Military Memoirs of Great Britain from the year 1727 to the present time* (Edinburgh, 1790), II 588.

[39] Corbet, *Seven Years' War*, Vol. II, 321, 354.

[40] Corbet, *Seven Years' War*, Vol. II, 283.

and sea forces, received between them over £122,000, one-fifteenth share.[41] The remaining nine-fifteenths share was equally divided between the army and navy, with each receiving £367,981 15s 6d. The army's share was divided as the Earl of Albemarle thought fit: every private receiving £4 1s 8d. The navy's share was divided into eight equal parts and divided in the same manner and proportion as prize money was usually distributed: the forty-two captains receiving three eighths or £4,385 each; the 183 lieutenants one eighth or £251; the 363 warrant officers an eighth or £126; the 1,302 petty officers an eighth or £35; and the 12,607 seamen one quarter or £7. For this distribution, captains of ships-of-the-line were counted as equivalent to captains of frigates, bomb-ketches or armed vessels.

The prize money was distributed to the navy over some time, the first distribution of £209,995 and second of £42,472 taking place at Havana. A third distribution in April 1767 was the result of goods brought back to England and sold there, which amounted to £62,504, agents' fees being £5,066. Finally, it was not until 1770 that the produce of ships-of-war, stores and Head Money was distributed, valued at £36,882, the agents' fees being £2,526. The 'cut money' as it was called was paid to the army in specie at Havana, whereas the expense of exchanging local currency into sterling cost the navy £2,800.[42]

As a footnote to the campaign at Havana, there is an entry in the Navy Board accounts: 'expense of medicines and necessaries for sick seamen supplied by the surgeons of his Majesty's Ships employed at the reduction of the Havanna £9,238.10.10'.[43]

Capture of Manila

The British occupied Manila and Cavite from October 1762 until April 1764. The Peace of Paris was concluded on 10 February 1763, so the conquest of Manila had served no strategic purpose in the war. The terms of occupation had been based on: the disarming of Spanish troops; the surrender intact of the stores in Manila and Cavite; a ransom of $4 million, half to be paid immediately, for the property of the residents of Manila. Once the East Indies squadron returned to Madras there were not sufficient men or ships to achieve control. More valuable was the dockyard at Cavite, well stocked with naval stores of all kinds, as all the vessels involved were decayed and weakened by the years they had been away from docks.

41 The Keppels received over £150,000 between them: a commander-in-chief's share, a second-in-command's share and a major-general's share – probably the only men satisfied with the division of the prize money. The family's fortune was made by the campaign. Syrett, ed., *Siege and Capture of Havana*, xxxiv.

42 Syrett, ed., *Siege and Capture of Havana*, 144, 305–13.

43 ADM 49/38 Estimate of the debt of the Navy Board.

There were three distributions of the Manila prize money. The first, of \$526,306, was for the specie, jewels, gold and silver plate and merchandise received in part payment of the ransom. The second, of \$92,561, was from naval victualling and ordnance stores, and from secreted effects seized. The third included \$13,319 for the sale of goods captured in the galley taken in the siege.[44]

Spain never paid the ransom. The political difficulties at the end of the war ensured this was not enforced. The East India Company took one third of the prize money. The remaining £112,960 was divided as usual, down to the sailors and soldiers who received £5 3d. Admiral Cornish made a small fortune from the ransom and his share of the capture of the *Santissima Trinidad*.[45] Tracy quotes the East India Company Captain Horne who concluded:

> So much for the Manilla expedition, which … has been attended with numberless fatall Consequences without being attended with any One good … Except the Admiral and General and a few Captains of men of war, I don't know a person but what are Considerable Sufferers, indeed chiefly oweing to the misconduct of our chiefs (who if they have their deserts all deserve the gallows).[46]

Distribution of Other Prize Money Won Abroad

Some figures are difficult to establish, and without the agents' books remain unknown. It is tantalising that the captain's log for *Cambridge* 12 July 1759 recorded: 'Agent came on board and paid the ships company prize money for the Guadaloupe.'[47]

East Indies

Details of the actions of the navy in the East Indies are few and far between, but there was an announcement in the *London Gazette* about the further payment of shares due to the captors:

> Notice is hereby given that there will be paid to the officers and Companies of His Majesty's ships Kent, Tyger, Salisbury, Bridgewater, Kingfisher sloop and Thunder bomb that were actually on board the said ships at the reduction of the Forts of Budgia Budgia, Tanna and Hughleu, and who did receive their respective shares of the Produce given to the captors in the East Indies, that the shares due to the said captors will be paid at the King's Arms on Great Tower Hill

44 Tracy, *Manila Ransomed*, 113.

45 Baugh, *Global Seven Years' War*, 634–5.

46 Tracy, *Manila Ransomed*, 109.

47 TNA ADM 51 *Cambridge* log May–December 1759.

> on Tuesday 5th May by Mr Dickson, the corner of Gould Square Crutched Friars. Henry Doige of Farham William Mackett of Channel Row, Westminster, Agents.[48]

The formal pages of the Treasury accounts give a glimpse of other courageous deeds in the East Indies. Twenty-four English seamen and a Dutchman took advantage of a French vessel *Le Fatehay*, lying in the Portuguese settlement of Goa, despite their not having a commission as a privateer, and handed her to the British *Medway Prize*, complete with officers and men. The capture was therefore a Droit to the Crown, and the £3,100 from its sale went to the Crown. However, the *Medway Prize*'s agent asked that the twenty-five men be rewarded for their enterprise, and the sum of £1,000 was allocated to them, to 'recompense their service and to encourage the British sailors on future occasions to follow their example in serving their King and Country and distressing their enemies at the hazard of their lives and liberties'.[49]

The Flag Share

The contentious issue of the share claimed by the flag officer was longstanding. In 1747 Admiral Sir Peter Warren shared the flag's prize money with the future Lord Anson, and in 1748 the flag's eighth share was further divided not only with the future Sir Edward Hawke, second in command, but also with Vice Admiral Schryver, who commanded a Dutch squadron attached to the Western squadron.[50] The division was not always amicable, and there was considerable feeling about the share which went to the flag officer. When Rodney captured the French Indiaman *Montmartel* with 200,000 pounds of coffee from the Isle de Bourbon, he was sailing under Admiralty orders, so no admiral could claim an eighth share. This did not prevent Boscawen from putting in a claim from North America when he heard of the capture.[51] Admiral Boscawen wrote to his wife in June 1756:

> I shall not omit carrying a prize to him [Mostyn] if we can meet one on our way. It must be a good one to be worth taking when I have two admirals to share with me. My quota is but an 8th of the whole, the other admirals get half of that 8th from me when two, if but one, a third.[52]

48 LG issue no. 10098 21 April 1761.
49 TNA T52.
50 Gwyn, *Enterprising Admiral*, 17.
51 Spinney, *Rodney*, 141.
52 Lloyd, ed., *Naval Miscellany IV*, 224.

Credit

Credit was universally used, a contemporary judgement being that two-thirds of all transactions involved credit rather than cash. The flexibility of Britain's credit markets was both its greatest asset and its greatest drawback: it made possible investments and trade, but also made traders vulnerable in a trade crisis.[53] Prize money was of vital importance within a community of wives and widows. These women were used to living off credit given them by local traders or navy agents. They petitioned for the unpaid shares, showing that although the amounts due to their husbands were small, they were vitally needed. Agents passed on the commission to local men, who charged five per cent for picking up local business. This involved looking out for the wives or widows who were still dependent on the few coins they might receive to relieve them of the debts they would have accumulated.[54] The agents listed in the Drakeford distribution were doubtless part of this community.

Rodger comments that sailors usually spent their prize money on drink. He quotes the log from *Achilles* in 1762 which reports: 'the men in great confusion, having the day before received fourteen pounds prize money, and could not get their anchors up to save the tide'.[55]

The Quietus or Remainder

The records of the National Audit Office hold a series of entries, detailing the multitudinous fees paid, and exemplifying the extent to which various levels of the legal world benefited from the taking of prizes. 'Passing the Prize account through the several offices of the Exchequer' cost £258. The three auditors were paid the total of £539. A few pages later the following account appears.[56]

53 John Brewer, *The Sinews of Power: War, Money and the English State 1688–1783* (Harvard University Press, 1990), 186.

54 Bromley, 'Prize Office', 185.

55 Rodger, *Wooden World*, 74.

56 TNA AO 3/326.

Table 7. The National Audit Office summary of fees paid.

Fees paid in passing the account of David Wilson Esq late Commissary of Accounts at the Havana from 25 December 1762 to 9 July 1763

		£	s	d
1766 20 June	Paid at the Treasury for Warrants allowing the State and Paying the balance	12	12	0
	At the Chancellors on declaration	3	6	0
	At the Treasury	2	18	6
	At the King's Remembrancer	2	12	6
	At the Treasurer's Remembrancer	2	12	6
	At the Pipe Office for the Quietus	8	8	0
	Passing fee	5	5	0
		37	14	6
	Settled this account 30th September 1766			

Fees on passing the Account of the Commissioner for Prizes taken before the Declaration of War 1756

		£	s	d
1768	Received on account of fees	517	15	6
August 4th	Paid at the Treasury for Fees on allowing examining and declaring the account	337	17	6
1769 January 7th	Chancellors on Declaration	21	0	0
July 6th	Kings Remembrancer	10	10	0
October 31	Treasurers ditto	10	10	0
August 10th	Pipe Office	80	0	0
	Passing Fee	5	5	0
		465	2	6
	Delivered the Quietus to Mr Camps 7 Feb.1770			

Greenwich Hospital

The Greenwich Hospital, recipient of the many fines referred to in previous chapters, was established by the Royal Charter of William and Mary of 25 October 1694: for 'such seamen as by age, wounds or other accidents, are rendered incapable of further service and for the widows of such as happens to be slain in the sea service'. Designed by Sir Christopher Wren, the buildings provided a refuge for disabled seamen. Every sailor, merchant or naval, had sixpence deducted from his pay every month, although only naval sailors were admitted. In 1766 there were 1,800 in-pensioners and 1,400 out-pensioners who lived with their wives and families.[57] Orphans were looked after and widows supported.

The Drakeford papers very helpfully included a proforma of the form of words to be used by an agent on delivering the unclaimed money. A fine of £500 could be imposed if there was a delay of more than three months between the date of the first deposit with the Hospital and the final submission.

Table 8. Proforma for delivering undistributed prize money to the Greenwich Hospital.

Account showing what money is remaining unpaid of the produce of the prize _________

taken by his Majestys ship _______Capt. ______ Commander on the ______which money not having been paid per capacity demanded in the space of three years after the payment was advertised the ____day of _____in the year _____ by ______ agent to the captors is to be applied to the use of Greenwich Hospital according to the act of parliament made and provided in that regard.

Persons Names	Quality	Sum
Geo. Knowles	Mid	10
Wm Knott	Ab	3
Jn Sterne	Capt Servant	3

A.B. Agent to the captors of the ______taken by his Majestys ship, Captain ______Commander maketh oath that the gross produce of the said ship, goods, tackle, furniture bounty or head money amounted to the sum of ______ that all charges on the same including commission,

[57] E.C. Coleman, ed., *The Navy List March 1766* (Ancholme Publishing, 2001), 174–9.

> or agency, amounting to the sum of ______and the neat proceeds amount to the sum of ______which hath been paid to the persons intitled thereto (save some odd pence and fractions) except the sum of ______ as by the aforesaid account which sum hath not been legally demanded.[58]

The proceeds of a capture had to pass through many processes before the final distribution took place. Queen Anne's government and those which succeeded her did their best to ensure that the benefits of prize were enjoyed by the people who had earned them.

58 Stafford Archives D1798/HM Drakeford.

10

Prisoners of War

It was important for the navy that as many French mariners as possible could be taken off the sea. Head Money made ships of war very acceptable targets, but merchant vessels also carried sailors. Privateers carried many more men, as they needed to fight as well as to take possession of their captures. One way and another, a large number of French sailors landed up in England. By the end of 1758 the French admitted that the British had 20,000 prisoners to France's 3,000.[1] It was important that the equivalent captured English were exchanged as soon as possible, and cartels were organised as soon as it was feasible to do so, to bring English sailors back into service quickly. Few prisoner exchanges took place after 1757 when most British prisoners had been repatriated.[2] As described below, prisoner exchange in the West Indies, where 'flags of truce' were used as a device to trade with the enemy, was a law unto itself.

The status of French prisoners was of concern before war was declared, and the *London Gazette* carried a long article about it;

> There having been various and injurious reports relating to the State of the French sailors detained in England, it is thought proper to remove any prejudice that may be entertained to give the following account of their treatment.
>
> Upon general orders being given to seize French ships, the numbers immediately brought into our ports were so great, that for want of proper places to confine the men ashore, they were put on board HM ships in Harbour, where they were victualled in every respect as the English seamen, till places proper for their security and accommodation could be provided on land, when they were victualled in the same manner as during the late war with France, each person being allowed for every seven days the following proportion and specie of provision, viz: Bread ten pounds and a half, beef four pounds and a half, beer, seven quarts, cheese, six ounces.

1 Pritchard, *Louis XV's Navy*, 81.
2 Pritchard, *Louis XV's Navy*, 82.

The report goes on to say that when the sailors were sick, they were treated in hospitals and taken care of:

> Notwithstanding this precaution many of them have died, which may be attributed to their being come from foreign voyages before their confinement, by which they have contracted scorbutic and other disorders, but neither pains nor expense have been spared in providing for them, and everything possible hath been done for persons in their unfortunate condition.[3]

It is impossible to tell from this evidence whether the French sailors did get the victuals to which they were entitled. But at least the instruction was to treat them well, in the hope that reciprocal treatment would be afforded to the British prisoners in France. It is likely that the good intentions of the authorities were rendered meaningless by the actions of the guards on the ground. But the prisoners themselves were the ones who sold their clothes for money for tobacco. Prisoners also made money for themselves, by making items which could be sold. The number of French prisoners received by the Commission for Sick and Hurt Seamen between 14 October 1755 and 11 November 1762 was 64,373. Of these, 8,499 died in Britain – 13 per cent.[4]

Initially the French king provided the Royal Bounty from his private purse, intended to finance the relief and comfort of prisoners in confinement, the payment of their homeward passages when exchanged, and to pay the dues levied on them by the British government when entering and leaving the country. In 1759 this Bounty was withdrawn completely. A London committee opened a public subscription, and raised £7,000 from which 3,131 coats, 2,034 waistcoats, 3,185 pairs of shoes, 3,054 pairs of breeches, 6,146 shirts, 3,006 caps and 3,134 pairs of stockings were provided to the different prisons.[5]

The prisoners confined at Sissinghurst called it 'le Chateau', which became 'the Castle' to the locals. The officers from these vessels, always housed separately, were billeted in Wilsley House, in Cranbrook, a large Tudor building, and were permitted to move locally on parole. A public house on the outskirts of the village, to which the officers had access, was situated at the junction of three tracks, and had been known as 'Three Wents'. The French visitors called it instead 'Trois Chemins', and to this day it is known as 'The Three Chimneys'.

As the Admiralty explained in the letter below to the Commissioners for Exchanging Prisoners, when the officers were sent back to France, they were

3 LG issue no. 9553 7 February 1756.

4 Pritchard, *Louis XV's Navy*, 81, quoting TNA ADM 98/9, 222.

5 Francis Abell, *Prisoners of War in Britain 1756 to 1815* (Humphrey Milford, 1914), 8.

to depart from ports which were not naval dockyards, so that no intelligence could be obtained.

> Whereas you have acquainted us by your letter of 29th instant that Mons. Berryer the Minister of the Marine in France has desired that all the French King's Officers prisoner in England may be permitted to return to France on their parole; and whereas you represent you cannot conceive there is any objection (except with regard to those whose conduct may have rendered it proper to confine them for some little time by way of example) to comply with his request, as by that means they will cease to be an expense to the government and be equally incapable of serving; we do hereby signify our approval thereof and require and direct you forthwith to permit such as you shall think deserving the indulgence to return to France on their paroles accordingly … those in Hampshire to embark at Southampton, the rest at Dover, and to proceed from thence to vessels which you are to provide on the most reasonable terms you can, for this service.[6]

The expense of the huge numbers of naval prisoners was immense. The amount due for sick and wounded includes the expenses of prisoners of war. The Navy Board estimate of expenses under various heads at 31 December is shown in Table 9.[7]

6 TNA ADM 2/82 13 January 1759 to Commissioners for Exchanging Prisoners of War.

7 TNA ADM 49/38.

Table 9. Navy Board estimate of expenses of prisoners of war.

	1756	**1757**	**1758**	**1759**	**1760**	**1762**	**1764**	**1765**
Due for the quarters and cure of sick and wounded seamen, set on shore from his Majesty's ships at the several Ports, and for Prisoners of War and contingencies relating to the said service:	86,177	93,910	95,467	92,977	97,027	113,628	28,754	30,297
Subsisting Prisoners of War and French Neutrals	89,424	144,422	192,983	191,989	?	472	17,095	
Bounty of £5 per head for Men belonging to the Enemys ships of war or privateers which have been taken or destroyed in the late war		27,375	51,670	53,110	56,105	40,465	14,845	1,660

Subsisting prisoners of war and French neutrals increased the debt of the navy in the year ending 31 December 1757 by £89,424. In the following year the figure was £144,422. To the year ending 1759 subsisting prisoners of war and French neutrals cost £191,989.

French Prisoners Identified in Head Money Returns

In the previous chapter the Navy Board lists of the £5 Head Money paid out to the captors give a precise number for the French mariners taken off the sea. Between 1757 and 1765 a total of 69,126 men were alive at the start of the engagements in which they were captured. Many were killed during the captures, but the rest, as prisoners, were removed from service in French ships of war. Many will have been exchanged in cartels, but after a period as prisoners of war they might not have been healthy enough to go back to sea. The instructions were always to choose the least able to be returned, not the young and healthy.

From the point of view of a naval historian, the total amount of Head Money paid out as a result of the Seven Years' War, £373,010, would have added nine more *Bellona* class ships of the line to the navy, each one costing about £40,000.[8] This was serious money, but it seems that the benefit of taking French seamen off the sea was sufficient inducement for this huge total to be distributed to the officers and men of the King's Navy.

Prisoners of War in the Mediterranean

Rear Admiral Charles Saunders, commander-in-chief in the Mediterranean, was relieved to find the cartel system working to his advantage. He wrote from Gibraltar:

> When I came in I found a cartel ship here from Toulon, with one hundred and forty prisoners on board, eleven of which are foreigners, fifteen masters of vessels and twenty boys. The men I have distributed among the ships, which will complete their complements, and prevent any future asking for soldiers from the Garrison; the last time I sailed from hence I had one subaltern, four sergeants, four corporals, one drum and ninety-six private men.
>
> Copy of an agreement for the exchange of prisoners of War at Gibraltar
>
> Captain Claude Rouve Commander of the French polacre called the Superb (by virtue of a sufficient power and authority to him granted for

[8] TNA ADM 43/20.

that purpose) doth hereby promise and agree to, and with Leeds Booth Agent for Prisoners of War at this Port, that the said Claude Rouve shall as soon as wind and weather will permit, proceed with the said polacre to the port of Marseilles or Toulon, and from thence bring to this port, as many English prisoners as his polacre can contain, and on his arrival here, deliver them to the Admiral and Commander in Chief or in the absence of a Flag officer, to the honorable Charles Colby esq Superintendent of this port, and Commissioner of his Majesty's navy, to be exchanged for the like number of French prisoners to be released from hence. In consideration whereof the said Leeds Booth doth promise and engage to, and with the said Claude Rouve, that all French prisoners which shall be brought to this port by any of his Britannick Majesty's Ships shall be immediately released, and set at liberty by way of exchange for English to be delivered here by the said Claude Rouve, who is to be allowed five dollars per man for their passage which is to be paid by the said Agent on making a right and true delivery of all men received on board the said polacre at Marseilles or Toulon. In case of any inequality in the number of prisoners that shall be released on either side, in consequence of this agreement the overplus shall be allowed and made good at any future exchange of prisoners between the two Nations. Done interchangeably at Gibraltar this 19th day of June 1757.

[signed] Vera Copia Leeds Booth[9]

A letter written by Admiral Henry Osborne, who took over from Rear Admiral Saunders, gives an insight into a possible solution to the problem of prisoners of war at Gibraltar:

His Majesty's ships that have hitherto made any prisoners on the French in these seas, have had no other way of disposing them than by putting them ashore at Gibraltar, but there not being now sufficient room for their security in the Garrison, they no sooner are landed but they get into Spain, and from thence to France, by which means the French get their seamen again, and we have none of ours in return for them. Therefore to reap some advantage from this great inconveniency of not being able to keep what we take, it has been proposed to me to settle a cartel between us and France for the release of prisoners in these seas. And on my arrival at Gibraltar I found a cartel vessel that has brought prisoners from Toulon, treating with us on that subject, the master of which propose to bring us an equal number of English prisoners to Gibraltar, or to put them on board any Man of War he meets in his way thither, we paying five dollars a man towards the charge of the vessel, besides six pence a head per day for their

9 TNA Charles Saunders Gibraltar 29 May 1757.

> provisions, which I thought so reasonable I could not help accepting of the offer for the present, not doubting of their Lordships seeing (as I do) the advantage it will be to the Fleet to have their losses recruited in this manner. I gave no hopes to continue this for any time, as I had no authority from their Lordships, but if their Lordships approve if its being continued for the future, I desire they will please to give me their direction, and give orders to the Commissioners of the Sick and Hurt to pay the Bills their agent here shall draw on them for this service.
>
> [signed] Henry Osborne[10]

Released prisoners were desperately needed back at sea, and the Navy Board ordered Commissioner Hughes that these men should receive two months' pay in advance as soon as they were 'entered on board any of his Majesty's ships at Portsmouth'.[11]

After Elliot's capture of Thurot's squadron, he had to deal with a huge number of French prisoners. His response was swift and practical, and he was confident that his solution would be acceptable:

> I have likewise hired a snow and sent her to Whitehaven with 200 of them escorted by two Irish customhouse smacks for which I have agreed to pay the owner of her £25 sterling being the lowest I could possibly agree for. I have drawn a Bill of this date on the Commissioners for Sick and Hurt Seamen etc for that sum and acquainted them by letter with the above particulars. I hope their Lordships will give orders that the Bill may be honoured.[12]

Prisoners of War in the West Indies

Admirals tried to ensure that prisoners were exchanged in batches of at least forty, but some colonies placed a prisoner on each merchant ship to protect the ship from questioning about its trade.[13] Merchants who took back to the West Indies captured French prisoners for expatriation, bringing back liberated British subjects, did so at their own expense: nearly every British colony issued licences to ship's captains for this purpose. 'Flag of Truce' trade became very important as a means of circumventing the legislation against trading with the enemy. By the end of 1758, when the trade came into prominence, it had little to do with bringing back prisoners of war, and everything to do with providing a pretext for large-scale exchange of re-exported British manufactured goods.

10 TNA ADM 1/ 3 June 1757 (read in London 8 August).

11 TNA ADM 106/2566.

12 TNA ADM 1/1760 Captains' Letters E 1759–62 Elliot 29 February 1760.

13 Pares, *War and Trade*, 446, 449.

Colonial governments were reluctant to support prisoners of war, and instead of sending back ships full of prisoners under flags of truce as cartels, one or two men would be transported in each ship, otherwise loaded with sugar, sugar products, indigo, coffee and cotton.[14]

Flags of truce were issued in New York by Lewis Morris, the aged Judge of the Court of Vice Admiralty. On 10 March 1760 the brig *General Amherst* was issued with a commission to take French prisoners to Cape François, but sailed the next day without any on board. With her cargo sold and replaced with 158 hogsheads and 5 barrels of brown sugar she managed to find two British prisoners of war for her return voyage, still under flag of truce. By 1759 certificates were being traded without names of prisoners, let alone physical bodies on board. In mid-January 1760 John Lindsay, *Trent* (28), picked up eight flag-trucers coming out of Port au Prince with 1,600 hogsheads of sugar. Flag-trucing captains buried their contraband under other cargo, and were given instructions as to how the ships were to be loaded to conceal the truth. By the end of February *Trent* and her three fellow warships had brought in twenty-four flag-trucers to the Jamaican Vice Admiralty Court.[15]

Happy's paybook gives an interesting illustration of the movement of prisoners of war in small sloops. There is a list of the nineteen French prisoners taken out of the French privateer *Le Heureux* 16 September 1756, and victualled at 2/3s allowance.[16] When Burnett took *L'Infernal* in March 1757 he brought back to England from Jersey the eight French prisoners who had been the captain and officers of the privateer.[17]

Thomas Harrison's capture of *Boullogne* resulted in more than her 'fine hull'. He used his influence with the Admiralty to speak on behalf of the officers he captured, but without their names it has not been possible to trace the outcome.

> … she sails well, having chased her eight hours. The Captain and officers beg I would intercede with their Lordships for their exchange as they behaved so well hope their Lordships will indulge them with as soon as consented several of them having commissions from the French King. PS the Count de Estaign Marshall de Camp of the Kings Army is also a passenger on board.[18]

Thomas Harrison also mentioned the good behaviour of his prisoner towards their English prisoners from previous captures: 'Capt. Delahom of the Miscallot

14 Truxes, *Defying Empire*, 89.

15 Truxes, *Defying Empire*, 90, 92, 101.

16 TNA ADM 36/5758 *Happy* paybook.

17 TNA ADM 1/1488 Captains' Letters B 1757 Burnett 19 March 1757.

18 TNA ADM 1/1897 Captains' Letters H 1762 Harrison 1 January 1762.

has behaved extremely well to Lt Haynes of the Arethusa who he formerly took and many others when prisoners at Bayonne.'

When Robert Man, *Milford* (28), caught off Finisterre the *Fidelis* brig, a French privateer from Bayonne with four guns and sixty-three men when she first sailed, there were only forty-five men on board when he took her, a measure of how many prizes the brig had taken and the danger of reducing a crew beyond safety. There were thirteen English prisoners on board from two prizes, the *Edinburgh* from South Carolina and a schooner from Boston.[19]

Ransomers

Just as taking French seamen off the ocean reduced France's capacity for retaliation, it was very important to return to the service English officers and seamen who had been captured and ransomed. For this reason, the government did not encourage ransom – they wanted French prisoners who could be exchanged.

When Henry Martin, *Danae* (38), took *Colibry* of Dunkirk it was the fact that he had three ransoms on board that was of interest. *Colibry* had taken the *Britannia* of Rhode Island, the *Peggy* of Dundee and the *General Hodgson* packet from Belleisle.[20] Taylor Penny, *Looe* (40), wrote to the Admiralty with an account from William Franklin, a merchant captain bound for Topsham from Bristol who was ransomed. The privateer which took his vessel had seven ransomers on board, and the privateer captain boasted that he 'waited in that station in order to interrupt the Bristol trade'. Penny begged the Admiralty to warn the local trade, including that from Fishguard.[21]

The situation of a hostage, which is what the ransomers were, is exemplified by the case of the unfortunate Francis Burt and an unnamed member of the crew who were the ransomers when their ship, *Charming Nancy*, was taken. When the ship completed her voyage and sold her cargo, their ransoms were not paid. Burt's family appealed to the Court of Admiralty for guidance as to whether they could bring an action against the master of *Charming Nancy*. Dr George Hay's response was that the ship and her cargo could be proceeded against. If the owners could not produce sufficient to redeem the hostages, then an action could be taken against the master for having fraudulently ransomed both the hostages. Sadly, history does not relate what happened next.[22]

Concern about prisoners of the French would have been felt throughout the maritime world. Friends and family would have been relieved that Robert Faulkner's capture of *Courageux* was widely reported in the press, because of the number of ransomers on board:

19 TNA ADM 1/2113 Captains' Letters M 1761 Man 11 April 1761.

20 TNA ADM 1/2113 Captains' Letters M 1761 Martin 7 September 1761.

21 TNA ADM 1/2297 Captains' Letters P 1760 Penny August 1760.

22 Burrell, *Reports of Cases*, 399.

> … the Neptune, Capt. Redyard, from New London to Barbadoes with provisions and horses, one ransomer, William Bott, Mate, for £300. The Brotherhood, Coffin, from Piscataqua to Antigua with lumber, one ransomer Samuel Hartford, mate for £200, owner John Warner, in Piscataqua. The Endeavour, Anderson from Newport Rhode Island to Madeira with provisions, one ransomer Jona Chace, sailor, for £300 owner Henry Bower of Swansea in the Bay Government. The Granby Capt. Appower, from Philadelphia to Jamaica with provisions, two ransomers (John Story mate on board the Courageux and the second mate on board the Malicieuse) for £1500 owner Willing and Morris of Philadelphia. The Colonel Clive, Capt. Ronquest, from Jamaica to London with sugar and rum, for £5000 owners Messrs Tinder and Green in London; three ransomers, Wm Hooper, surgeon on board the Courageux, one on board the Malicieuse and one on board the Harmione. The Catherine, Capt. Archibald McMillan from Virginia to Glasgow, one ransomer John Duncan, mate, for £900 owners John Glasford and Co of Glasgow.[23]

This report is interesting as it confirms that prisoners were split between the French ships, and not permitted to sail together, to prevent collusion. A letter from Lisbon gave further details about the taking of *Courageux*:

> … 200 men were killed and 108 wounded in the engagement and 23 men were drowned the day after they were taken, by an alarm of fire on board the prize, which was soon extinguished. She has on board about 200 tons of goods, mostly indigo, and is reckoned worth about 80,000l. … the *Courageux* had a great number of ransomers on board, which were taken on the coast of North America.[24]

At the beginning of 1759 John Elliot was approached by William Fullerton who had been in the prize *L'Heureuse*, taken by Elliot in August 1758. The prize had been retaken by the French and Fullerton was returned from France on 1 January 1759. Elliot asked if his wages for the five months could be paid by bill.[25]

Shortage of French Seamen

A London paper reported in May 1759 that: 'the French are so greatly streightened for Seamen, that the Arethusa frigate, taken by the Thames, Capt.

23 *Aberdeen Press and Journal* 14 September 1761.

24 *Caledonian Mercury* 9 Sept. 1761.

25 TNA ADM 1/1760 Captains' Letters E 1759–62 Elliot January 1759.

Colby, was chiefly manned with landmen. An embargo is likewise laid on all their shipping, and 'tis said their Privateers are called in.'[26]

Charles Medows also reported the difficulty the French were having in gathering seamen for their ships. The intelligence he passed on to the Admiralty from the captain of the privateer *Duc de Broglie* he had just captured was that the embargo on their privateers had just been taken off, but that they stripped them of their men so frequently that he had raised 600 for his ship before they permitted him to keep the 116 men on board.[27]

The difficulties the French were having with manning their ships were also reported by Henry John Phillips:

> … had been an embargo on all privateers till the first of December. It was then taken off and all those of 20 guns and upwards were permitted to sail, but not to have above 50 seamen each, all the rest were landmen and the whole number from Brest, St Malo and Grandville will not exceed seven or eight.[28]

Detailed study of the French navy has revealed that it was unable to pay its crews. In response to the non-payment of their wages, sailors and workers deserted from the arsenals, and convicts were brought in instead, introducing dysentery and typhus.[29] Sailors attempted to enrol in privateers instead: most of the 9,000 men captured in 1761 were captured aboard privateers, despite the embargoes.[30] Because the *Marine* used conscription through registration, French seamen were driven to resist the levies, desert in large numbers and flee the country.[31]

Important though it was for Britain to take French seamen off their ships, the organisation on shore was not always ready to receive them, as the Commissioner for South and West had not been able to appoint anybody to receive prisoners at Portland when Edmund Affleck tried to land prisoners he had recently taken:

> … that no person here being appointed to take charge of prisoners, I am obliged to retain them on board and as much inconvenience may rise from their occasioning sickness in the ship as the warm weather is advancing should I be fortunate enough to add largely to

26 *Whitehall Evening Post or London Intelligencer* 29 May 1759.

27 TNA ADM 1/2109 Captains' Letters M 1757 Medows December 1757.

28 TNA ADM 1/2296 Captains' Letters P 1759 Phillips 28 January 1759.

29 Pritchard, *Louis XV's Navy*, 109.

30 Dull, *The French Navy*, 212.

31 Pritchard, *Louis XV's Navy*, 71.

> the present number I am to desire their Lordships will be pleased to give directions for their being landed here.[32]

It may seem unreasonable to judge the success or failure of the war in terms of men imprisoned. In a naval war, having sailors to crew the ships of war was essential. Not only were the French crucially short of materiel for new ships, and resorted to buying privateers for their *Marine*, they were also desperately short of trained men for their ships. Most of the 9,000 Frenchmen made prisoner in 1761 were captured aboard privateers, as sailors deserted to private enterprise instead of the *Marine* which did not pay or feed them.[33]

32 TNA ADM 1/1442 Captains' Letters A 1758–61 Affleck 7 April 1760.

33 Dull, *The French Navy*, 212.

Conclusion

Queen Anne would have been deeply gratified by the long-term benefits to the Royal Navy and to Britain as a whole of her ruling on legal prizes in 1708. The fact that all the profits of success at sea went to the men responsible, and not into her coffers, provided motivation for enterprise and daring during conflict at sea, and made morale the key word throughout the century. Admiral Boscawen's letters to his wife reveal the thinking in the fleet:

> The French will not be pleased at this cruise of mine. We have insulted their coasts, destroyed their home trade, and made some little impression on their foreign trade, whilst their squadron at Brest, (though ready for the sea) has not dared to stir out. By the letters I have seen their trading towns are in great distress, many of their merchants bankrupt, their manufacturers idle, and the wives and families of their seamen starving, whilst I believe our trade never was more flourishing. I don't yet hear they have any privateers at sea.[1]

The motivation provided by the money which accrued to those who had taken part in the engagement boosted morale, and in battle, morale is everything. Every man on board would know that victory could result in his sudden acquisition of wealth beyond the limits of his pay. The status of a man who had won prize money is graphically illustrated in Cruickshank's cartoon (see Figure 3).

The attraction of naval service in wartime was the chance of prize money, although reality rarely matched expectations. Most vessels took no prizes, and the distribution system favoured senior officers.[2] Despite that, the British fought expecting to win. The song 'Heart of Oak', words by David Garrick and music by William Boyce, was written to celebrate the naval achievements of the *annus mirabilis* of 1759.

> Come cheer up, my lads! 'tis to glory we steer,
> To add something more to this wonderful year;
> To honour we call you, as free men not slaves,
> For who are so free as the sons of the waves?
>
> *Chorus*:
> Heart of oak are our ships, heart of oak are our men;

1 Lloyd, ed., *Naval Miscellany IV*, 238.

2 Peter Earle, *Sailors: English Merchant Seamen 1650–1775* (Methuen, 1998), 185.

We always are ready, steady, boys, steady!
We'll fight and we'll conquer again and again.
We ne'er see our foes, but we wish them to stay;
They never see us, but they wish us away;
If they run, why we follow, and run them ashore
For, if they won't fight us, we cannot do more.[3]

Another song which has survived and come down to us celebrated the Gosport Ladies who benefited from the prize money won by their sailor rather than their soldier friends:

Don't you see the ships a-coming?
Don't you see them in full sail?
Don't you see the ships a-coming?
With the prizes at their tail?
Oh! my little rolling sailor,
Oh! my little rolling he;
I do love a jolly sailor
Blithe and merry might he be.
Sailors they get all the money,
Soldiers they get none but brass;
I do love a jolly sailor,
Soldiers they may kiss my arse
Oh! my little rolling sailor,
Oh! my little rolling he;
I do love a jolly sailor
Soldiers may be damned for me.[4]

The subject of naval prizes might not have seemed appropriate for female readers, but *The Royal Female Magazine or, the Ladies General Repository of Pleasure and Improvement for March 1760. Being a Collection of Essays, mostly original, on the most interesting and entertaining subjects. (Dedicated to her Royal Highness the Princess Dowager of Wales by Charles Honeycombe Esq.*) considered otherwise. This magazine had a long list of the contents, all considered suitable for female readers, such as:

> an affecting Anecdote from the History of the Marchioness of Pompadour; an interesting account of the History of Kissing; on Modesty, Beauty and the proper means of Pleasing; miscellaneous Poetry; … Events of the War, particularly a distinct account of M.

3 Marcus, *Heart of Oak*, 255.
4 Christopher C. Lloyd, ed., *Above and Under Hatches* (London, 1957), 10.

> Thurot's Invasion of Ireland, and of the battle in which he was killed and his Fleet all taken by Capt. Elliot. Universal History, Domestic Occurrences, Lists of Births, Marriages etc.[5]

The contrast with the *Marine* of the French king could not have been starker. The French fought bravely and suffered dreadful casualties before surrendering, but they were blockaded in their ports, not able to practise gunnery at sea as did the British. They fired into the rigging of their opponents, to prevent their assailants being able to chase them. The British fired into the 'charnel house', the centre of the enemy's hull, or into their stems and sterns if they could manoeuvre themselves into position there, and caused horrific casualties by so doing. A cannon ball fired at close quarters had the power to smash right through a ship's hull. The resulting showers of splinters caused dreadful wounds. Head Money was paid on the number of French alive at the start of the engagement, not at the end when blood was sometimes seen trickling from the scuppers of the shattered hull.

From the perspective of the French, Mahan quoted the French historian Henri Martin who said in his *Histoire de France*:

> From June 1756, to June 1760, French privateers captured from the English more than twenty-five hundred merchantmen. In 1761, though France had not, so to speak, a single ship-of-the-line at sea, and though the English had taken two hundred and forty of our privateers, their comrades still took eight hundred and twelve vessels. But … the prodigious growth of the English shipping explains the number of these prizes … While the commerce of France was nearly destroyed, the trading fleet of England covered the seas. Every year her commerce was increasing; the money which the war carried out was returned by the produce of her industry.[6]

Mahan also quoted de Lapeyrouse-Bonfils as saying in his *Histoire de la Marine Française*:

> The English fleets, having nothing to resist them, swept the seas. Our privateers and single cruisers, having no fleet to keep down the abundance of their enemies, ran short careers. Twenty thousand French seamen lay in English prisons.[7]

Another comment from the French perspective concluded that capture too often followed after under-manned warships with inexperienced, untrained

5 *Oxford Journal* 29 March 1760.
6 Mahan, *Sea Power*, 134.
7 Mahan, *Sea Power*, 135.

sailors put to sea with inept officers in command to confront an enemy honed to a fine edge of effectiveness by long periods spent at sea under a wide variety of conditions.[8]

The income generated by privateers never compensated the British merchants for the loss of international trade during wartime. As Gomer stated in his introduction, during the Seven Years' War the number of enemy vessels captured fell as foreign merchants simply stayed in port. Despite issuing 2,105 commissions between 1756 and 1762, the court adjudicated only 382 prizes of privateering.[9] It can be argued that privateering was a way of employing private enterprise to assist in the reduction of the enemy's trade. Every prize taken by a privateer weakened the trading wealth of the enemy, at no cost to the naval administration.[10]

Amongst the beneficiaries of war were the naval dockyard workers, whose wages rose during hostilities. When the end of the war came, Edward Gibbon remarked in 1762, 'This day the SUSPENSION OF ARMS was solemnly declared at Portsmouth and Gosport, to the great regret of their inhabitants, who find their account much better in war.'[11]

It might be assumed that dockyard workers were not the only beneficiaries of the war, as workers in the legal system at all levels were also paid for their labours. The law courts in the Seven Years' War were without a great juror such as Lord Stowell later in the century. He called one of his great principles 'the Rule of the War of 1756', for which he had to thank Lord Mansfield.[12]

The naval war was a considerable success for the law courts. Lord Mansfield said:

> Mutual convenience, eternal principles of justice, the wisest regulations of policy and the consent of nations have established a system of procedure, a code of law, and a court for the trial of prize. Every country sues in these courts of the others, which are all governed by one and the same law, equally known to each.[13]

The minutely detailed paper work, exemplified in the previous chapters, existed to show how every penny was spent. On the other hand, they also show meticulous accounting for every penny which could be charged to the expense of taking prizes. Agents had to trust each other, and were contemptuous of any colleague who let them down. The severe financial penalties for not handing

8 Pritchard, *Louis XV's Navy*, 208.
9 Williams, *Liverpool Privateers*, xxi.
10 Anderson and Gifford, 'Privateering', 1.
11 Brewer, *Sinews of Power*, 196.
12 Pares, *Colonial Blockade*, 309.
13 Pares, *Colonial Blockade*, 149.

over in timely manner any residue of prize money to the Greenwich Hospital were intended to ensure prompt and honest behaviour.

It could be argued that the courts deliberately boosted their income by porrecting cases. In their defence it must be suggested that the courts dealt with multiple facets of the law, Instance as well as Prize, and if the time allocated to prize ran out, they had no choice but to porrect cases.

As Richard Hill pointed out at the end of the century – practice not having changed throughout the century – court officials relied on fees rather than salaries, and those fees had to come from their business. The proceeds of the prizes themselves provided the fees, and it seems that they amounted to about the same level as the agents', that is five per cent. At no time did these fees discourage prize taking, despite the captains bemoaning 'the deductions'.[14] It was not until the beginning of the nineteenth century that 'a reputation for dishonesty and sharp practice' within the ranks of prize agents was addressed.[15] That development is outside the remit of this work.

What Has Been Learned from This Study?

If Henry Mayhew had lived fifty years earlier, had taken his one cruise in a naval vessel rather than a merchant one, and had asked his searching questions of 'the people' of the Seven Years' War, present-day scholars would have enjoyed a much better understanding of the lives they lived.[16] As it is, we have to rely on the few published accounts of the lives of ordinary sailors. The wonderful narrative of William Spavins, recounted many years after his experiences, concludes by explaining that the prize money to which he was entitled had not been collected by his agent, and that he was benefiting from the Chatham Chest to which he had contributed all his working life.[17] It is not surprising that it is the captains rather than their crews who have attracted attention. The captains who wrote the letters to the Admiralty on which this study was based were the men making the decisions and bearing the responsibility from which everyone else benefited. It was their desire to make their reputations, and thereby their fortunes, which spun the web of incidents and ultimately the victory of 'the service' against the French.

No evidence was found of the operation of a 'slush fund' as described by Richard Hill of the Napoleonic navy. In his words it was 'a means of adjusting anomalies in a complex and potentially unfair set of circumstances'. Droits of Admiralty, being the proceeds of enemies' ships seized in port or taken

14 Hill, *Prizes of War*, 169.

15 Gutridge, 'Naval Prize Agency', 45–53.

16 Stephen Fisher, ed., *Lisbon as a Port Town etc* (Exeter Maritime Studies, 1988), 116–23.

17 Spavins, *William Spavins*, 169.

by un-commissioned captors or from wrecks and derelicts, had historically belonged to the Court of Admiralty, but were now, in certain circumstances, allowed to the captor. The use of Droits of Admiralty to defray the legal costs of those who had brought in prizes *bona fide* was a sensible measure.[18] It is not surprising that there was little publicity surrounding its use.

This study has illustrated the legal world enacted in Doctors Commons and in the dining room beside it. To hold the captors to account, to lay down standards of behaviour on and off the seas, was an accomplishment of the system, despite the inadequacies of Sir Thomas Salusbury who signed his name thousands of times during the years of war.

Having been immersed in the documents which have brought this period so vividly alive, it is difficult to remember that in the middle of the eighteenth century any means of communication was as fragile as papers stuck to pillars in a courtyard in London. Despite the difficulties, the legal world of that time was robust. The full weight of government legislation demanded the quickest possible payments of rewards due to those who put their lives at risk to 'annoy the enemy'. The many responsibilities of the prize agents were acknowledged, but their reward was limited to five per cent of the net outcome of a prize.

This study has not examined the potential for fraud, as sufficient primary documents no longer exist. It has concentrated on the speed with which the prize agents completed the tasks with which they had been entrusted. It has also shone a light on the range of tasks for which there was a payment of a fee rather than the security of a wage. From the highest officials in the land sitting as the Appeal Court, to the clerk in Doctors Commons copying out the monition, the waterman in Plymouth dockyard securing a prize before sale, the agent distributing a few farthings to a widow off Portsmouth point, all were rewarded for their time and effort with a fee on which they lived. Despite these deductions, the motivation provided to the men of the navy was beyond calculation.

Queen Anne would have been proud and happy to know the long-term consequences of her wisdom and generosity in granting the proceeds of naval war to the captors not the Crown. The Royal Navy did indeed 'protect the trade and annoy the enemy' around the world. The establishment of the British Empire was the final result.

18 Hill, *Prizes of War*, 92.

APPENDIX 1

PROCLAMATION OF PRIZE ACT 1756

Once war had been declared against France, the King signed the Prize Act into law. It was then immediately proclaimed through the *London Gazette*, the usual official channel for dissemination of information. The Prize Act laid down the proportions into which any benefit from taking a prize would be divided.[1]

The elements were:

- Once any capture had been judged a lawful prize, all benefit went to those on board the captor
- Five pounds would be paid for every one of the enemy alive at the start of the engagement, without deductions
- The bounty would be divided into eight parts, the captain receiving three eighths unless he was under the command of a flag officer, who had one of his eighths
- One eighth to be divided amongst the lieutenants, the master and the captain of marines
- One eighth to be divided amongst the warrant officers
- One eighth to be divided amongst the inferior warrant officers
- Two eighths to be divided amongst the able and ordinary seamen and everyone else
- A list of everyone on board the captor had to be made, and checked for accuracy
- An agent had to be appointed to act for the ship's company
- The produce of the agent's labour was to be distributed in the same proportions

[1] Thomas Tegg published a marvellous cartoon, at the time of the Napoleonic War, in which a sailor, on his knees, is praying 'that the enemy's shot may be distributed in the same proportion as the prize money, the greatest part among the officers'. James Davey and Richard Johns, *Broadsides: Caricature and the Navy 1756–1815* (Seaforth, 2012), 35.

- The geographic location of a flag officer entitled to a one eighth portion was laid down

By the King a proclamation appointing the distribution of prizes taken, and the bounty for taking or destroying ships of war or privateers of the enemy from the time of his Majesty's declaration of war against France. George R.

Whereas by an act of Parliament made in the present session of Parliament entitled "An Act for the encouragement of seamen and the more speedy and effectual manning of his Majesty's Navy", it is amongst other things enacted that the flag officers commanders and other officers, seamen, marines, and soldiers, on-board every ship and vessel of war in our pay shall have the sole interest and property of and in all and every ship, vessel, goods, and merchandises, which they shall take from and after the seventeenth day of May, in the year of our Lord one thousand seven hundred and fifty six, during the continuance of this war against France (being first judged lawful prize in any of our courts of Admiralty in Great Britain, or in our plantations in America, or elsewhere) to be divided in such proportions, and after such manner, as we, our heirs and successors, shall think fit to order and direct by proclamation or proclamations to be issued for those purposes. And as a further encouragement to the officers, seamen, marines, soldiers, and others, on board our ships of war, as also of privateers to attack, take, and destroy, any ships of force belonging to the enemy, it is thereby also enacted, that there shall be paid by the treasurer of our Navy, upon bills to be made forth by the Commissioners of the Navy, to be paid according to the course thereof, without fee or reward, unto the officers, seamen, marines, soldiers, or others, that shall have been actually on board any of our ships or ships of war, or privateer or privateers, in any action where any ship or ships of war, or privateers, shall have been taken from the enemy, sunk, burnt, or otherwise destroyed, since our declaration of war against France, dated the said seventeenth day of May, one thousand seven hundred and fifty six, five pounds for every man which was living on board any ship or ships so taken, sunk, burnt, or otherwise destroyed, at the beginning of the engagement between them; the numbers of such men to be proved by the oaths of three or more of the chief officers or men which were belonging to the said ship or ships of war, or privateers, of the enemy, or belonging to any of them, at the time of her or their being taken as prize, sunk, burnt, or otherwise destroyed, before the Mayor, or other Chief Magistrate of the port, within any of our dominions, whereunto any prize, or officers, or men, of such ships as were sunk, burnt, or otherwise destroyed, shall be brought, or before the British Consul, or vice consul, residing at any neutral port to which such prize, or officers, or men, shall be brought; which oaths the said Mayor, or other chief magistrate of such port, or Consul, or vice consul, are thereby respectively empowered and required to administer, and shall forthwith grant a certificate thereof, without fee or reward, directed to the Commissioners of the Navy; upon producing which certificate to the

Commissioners of the Navy, together with an authentic copy of the condemnation of such ship so taken, or if such ship be sunk, burned, or otherwise destroyed, on producing only a certificate from the Mayor, or other chief magistrate, or Consul, or vice consul, as aforesaid, the said Commissioners of our Navy, or such person or persons as they shall appoint for that purpose shall, according to the course of the Navy, within fifteen days, make out bills for the amount of such bounty, directed to the treasurer of the Navy, payable to, and to be divided amongst the officers, seamen, marines and soldiers, on board our ships of war, in manner, form, and proportion, as by our proclamation, to be issued for that purpose, shall be directed and appointed; and amongst the owners, officers, and seamen of any private vessel or ship of war, in such manner and proportion, as by any agreement in writing they should have entered into for that purpose, shall be directed: but it is nevertheless provided by the said Act, that in all cases where such oath and certificate cannot be administered or granted, at the first port whereunto any prize, or officers, or men of such ships as shall be taken, sunk, burnt, or otherwise destroyed, shall be brought, such oath or oaths relating to any prize or prizes that shall be taken, or to any ships of our enemies, that shall be sunk, burnt, or otherwise destroyed as aforesaid, shall and may be administered, taken by and before the Mayor or other chief magistrate of any port within any of our dominions, or by or before the British Consul, or vice consul, residing at any neutral port whereunto any prize or prizes or officers, or men, of any ship belonging to our enemies as shall be taken, sunk, burnt, or otherwise destroyed, shall at the time afterwards be brought (proof being first made, by affidavit for such person or persons of the inability of making such oath or oaths, and obtaining such certificate at the said first port) and the Mayor, or other chief magistrate, Consul, or vice consul, shall thereupon grant such certificate and certificates as are therein before directed; which certificate and certificates shall be good and effectual, to all intents and purposes, as if the same were granted by the Mayor or other chief magistrate, Consul, or vice consul, of the port to which such prize or prizes, officers, or men, as aforesaid, shall be first brought; any thing in the said Act contained to the contrary thereof in any wise notwithstanding. We taking the premises into consideration, do pursuant to the said Act of Parliament (with the advice of our privy Council) by this our Proclamation, order, direct, and appoint, that the neat produce of all prizes taken by our ships of war, and bounty money for the taking, sinking, burning or otherwise destroying the enemy's ships of war, or privateers, be divided into eight equal parts, and be distributed in manner following; that is to say, to the captain or captains of any of our ships of war, who shall be actually on board the taking of any prize, or at the taking, sinking, burning, or destroying any of the enemy's ships of war, or privateers, three eighths parts; but in case any such prize shall be taken, or ship of war, or privateer, of the enemy be taken, sunk, burnt, or destroyed, by any of our ship or ships of war, under the command of a flag or flags, the flag officer or officers being actually on board, or directing and assisting in the capture, to have one of the said three eighths parts; the said one eighth part to be paid to such flag or flag officers, in such proportions, and subject to such regulations, as are hereinafter for that purpose mentioned: to the captains of marines and land forces, sea lieutenants and master, on board any such ships, one eighth part, to be equally divided amongst them: to the lieutenants and quartermasters of marines and lieutenants, ensigns, and quartermasters of land forces, boatswain, gunner, purser, carpenter, master's mate, chirurgeon, pilot and chaplain, on board any such ship, one eighth part, to be equally divided amongst them: to the midshipman, secretary to flag officers, captain's clerk, master sailmaker, carpenter's mates, boatswain's mates, gunner's mates, master at arms, corporals, yeomen of the sheets, coxswain, quartermasters, quartermaster's mates, chirurgeon's mates, yeoman of the powder room, and sergeant of marines, or land forces, on board any such ships, one eighth part to be equally divided amongst them: to the trumpeters, quarter gunners, carpenter's crew, steward, cook, armourer, steward's mate, cook's mate, gunsmith, cooper, swabber, ordinary trumpeter, barber, able seaman, ordinary seaman, and marine or other soldiers, and all other persons doing duty, or assisting on board any such ships, two eighths parts to be equally divided amongst them: and in case any sea captain, inferior commission or warrant sea offices, belonging to any ship of war, for whom any shares of prizes, or of the bounty money for ships taken, sunk, burnt, or destroyed, are hereby allowed, be absent at the time of the capture of any prize, or at the capture, burning, sinking, or destroying, any ships of war, or privateers, of the enemy, the share of such sea captain, inferior commission or warrant officer, shall be cast into the shares hereby allowed to the trumpeters, quarter gunners, carpenter's crew, steward, cook, steward's mate, cook's mate, gunsmith, cooper, swabber, ordinary trumpeter, barber, able seaman, ordinary seaman, and marine or other soldiers, and other persons doing duty, or assisting on board any such ships, to be equally divided amongst them. Provided, that if any officer or officers on board any of our ships of war, at the time of taking any such prizes, or at the taking, sinking, burning, or destroying, any ships of war, or privateers, of the enemy, shall have more commissions or offices than one, he or they shall be entitled only to the share or shares of the said prizes, and the bounty money for the enemy's ships of war, or privateers, taken, sunk, burned, or destroyed, which, according to the above mentioned distribution, shall belong to his or their respective superior commissions or offices.

And we do hereby strictly enjoin all and every commander and commanders of any ships of war taking any prize, or taking, sinking, burning, or destroying, any of the enemy's ships of war, or privateers, as soon as may be, to transmit to the Commissioners of our navy, a true list of the names of all the officers, seamen, marines, soldiers or others who were actually on board our ships of war under his command at the taking such prize, or at the taking, sinking, burning or destroying, any such ships of war or privateers of the enemy; which list shall contain the quality of the service of each person on board, and be subscribed by the captain or commanding officer, and three or more of the chief officers on board. And we do hereby require and direct the Commissioners of our Navy, or any three or more of them, to examine or cause to be examined, such lists by the muster books of such ships of war, and lists annexed thereto, to see that such lists doth agree with the said muster book and annexed lists, as to the names, qualities or ratings of the officers, seamen, marines, soldiers and others, belonging to such ship of war; and upon request, forthwith to grant a certificate of the truth of any list transmitted to them, to the agents nominated and appointed by the captors, pursuant to the said Act, to take care or dispose of such prize or of such bounty money for ships taken, sunk burnt or destroyed; and also to give or cause to be given, unto the agents who shall, at any time or times, be appointed as aforesaid by the captors, all such lists from the muster book of any such ships of war, and annexed lists, as the said agents shall find requisite for their direction in paying the produce of such prizes, or the bounty, in case any bounty shall be due for taking the same, and to be otherwise aiding and assisting to the said agents as shall be necessary. And as touching the one eighth part herein before mentioned to be granted to the flag or flag officers who shall be actually on board at the taking of any prize or at the taking, sinking, burning or destroying , any ships of war or privateers of the enemy, or shall be directing or assisting therein, We have thought fit, and do, by these presents, publish, order and declare, that the following regulations be observed; firstly, that a flag officer commanding in chief, where there is but one flag officer upon service, shall have to his own use the said one eighth part of the prizes taken, and bounty money for the enemies ships taken, sunk, burnt or otherwise destroyed by ships under his command; secondly, that a flag officer, sent to command at Jamaica or elsewhere, shall have no right to any share of the prizes taken, or bounty money for ships taken, sunk, burned, or destroyed, by ships employed there before he arrives at the place to which he is sent, and actually takes upon him the command: thirdly, that when an inferior flag officer or private ships are sent out to reinforce a superior flag officer at Jamaica or elsewhere, the said superior flag officer shall have no right to any share in the prizes taken or bounty money for ships sunk, taken, burnt, or destroyed, by them, before they arrived within the limits of his command, and actually receive some orders from him: fourthly, the chief flag officer on returning home from Jamaica, or elsewhere, shall have no share of the prizes taken, or bounty money for ships taken, sunk, burnt, or destroyed, by the ships left behind to act under another command; fifthly that if a flag officer is sent to command in the out ports of this kingdom, he shall have no share of the prizes taken or bounty money for ships taken, sunk, burnt or destroyed by ships that sailed from that port by order from the Admiralty; sixthly, that when more flag officers than one serve together, the eighth part of the prizes taken and bounty money for the taking, sinking, burning or destroying ships of war or privateers of the enemy, by any ships of the fleet or squadron, shall be divided in the following proportions; *videlicet*, if there be but two flag officers, the chief shall have two third parts of the said one eighth part, and the other shall have the remaining third part; but if the number of flag officers be more than two, the chief shall have only one half, and the other half should be divided equally among the other flag officers: seventhly, that Commodores, with captains under them, shall be esteemed as flag officers, with respect to their right to an eighth part of prizes taken, and bounty money for ships taken, sunk, burnt, or destroyed, whether commanding in chief, or serving under command.

Given at our court at Kensington the seventh day of July, one thousand seven hundred and fifty six, in the thirtieth year in our reign.

God save the King.[2]

[2] LG issue no. 9598 6 July 1756.

APPENDIX 2

ARTICLES OF WAR 1749[1]

Under the Test Act of 1673 the Georgian navy only employed officers who were members of the Church of England. Alexander Schomberg had to become a Christian before he could be commissioned as a lieutenant.[2] Chaplains were carried in ships of the line, and they would have taken the service on Sunday. If there was no chaplain, the captain took the service. After the service, it was expected that the captain would read the Articles of War to the crew, gathered below him on the deck. The rules which pertained to prizes were carefully worded to leave no ambiguity at all in the minds of the listening crew.

- Everyone on board was reminded of the standard of behaviour expected, and the punishment determined by court martial if not achieved
- Every member of the navy, from flag officers down, had to behave appropriately
- Spying for or consorting with the enemy was forbidden
- Every element of any prize taken had to be respected and secured
- No member of the enemy's crew was to be molested once taken
- Every effort would be made to achieve success
- Deserters would be court martialled
- Convoys would be protected against all dangers, and without charge
- Mutiny would be punished by death
- Complaints about food or anything else should be reported to officers
- Aggression against an officer or any other person in the fleet would be punished by court martial
- Powder, shot and other stores were not to be wasted or embezzled
- Damage to goods captured from the enemy would be punished by court martial
- Negligence in carrying out any office would be punished by court martial
- Murder, buggery or robbery by anyone in the fleet would be punished by death or otherwise by sentence of court martial
- Any person who falsified official records would be cashiered

1 Rodger, *Articles of War*, 21–34.

2 Green, *Royal Navy*, 16.

- Provost martials and all other officers would keep prisoners safely apprehended until trial
- Flag officers or other officers convicted of behaviour unbecoming to an officer would be dismissed the service
- Any person in service who committed a crime on shore would be tried by court martial as if the crime had taken place on board

***

1. All commanders, captains, and officers, in or belonging to any of His Majesty's ships or vessels of war, shall cause the public worship of Almighty God, according to the liturgy of the Church of England established by law, to be solemnly, orderly and reverently performed in their respective ships; and shall take care that prayers and preaching, by the chaplains in holy orders of the respective ships, be performed diligently; and that the Lord's day be observed according to law.
2. All flag officers, and all persons in or belonging to His Majesty's ships or vessels of war, being guilty of profane oaths, cursings, execrations, drunkenness, uncleanness, or other scandalous actions, in derogation of God's honour, and corruption of good manners, shall incur such punishment as a court-martial shall think fit to impose, and as the nature and degree of their offence shall deserve.
3. If any officer, mariner, soldier, or other person of the fleet, shall give, hold, or entertain intelligence to or with any enemy or rebel, without leave from the king's majesty, or the lord high admiral, or the commissioners for executing the office of lord high admiral, commander in chief, or his commanding officer, every such person so offending, and being thereof convicted by the sentence of a court-martial, shall be punished with death.
4. If any letter of message from any enemy or rebel, be conveyed to any officer, mariner, or soldier or other in the fleet, and the said officer, mariner, or soldier, or other as aforesaid, shall not, within twelve hours, having opportunity so to do, acquaint his superior or a commanding officer, or if any superior officer being acquainted therewith, shall not in convenient time reveal the same to the commander in chief of the squadron, every such person so offending, and being convicted thereof by the sentence of the court-martial, shall be punished with death, or such other punishment as the nature and degree of the offense shall deserve, and the court-martial shall impose.
5. All spies, and all persons whatsoever, who shall come, or be found, in the nature of spies, to bring or deliver any seducing letters or messages from any enemy or rebel, or endeavor to corrupt any captain, officer, mariner, or other in the fleet, to betray his trust, being convicted of any

such offense by the sentence of the court-martial, shall be punished with death, or such other punishment, as the nature and degree of the offence shall deserve, and the court-martial shall impose.

6. No person in the fleet shall receive an enemy or rebel with money, victuals, powder, shot, arms, ammunition, or any other supplies whatsoever, directly or indirectly, upon pain of death, or such other punishment as the court-martial shall think fit to impose, and as the nature and degree of the crime shall deserve.

7. All the papers, charter parties, bills of lading, passports, and other writings whatsoever, that shall be taken, seized, or found aboard any ship or ships which shall be surprized or taken as prize, shall be duly preserved, and the very originals shall by the commanding officer of the ship which shall take such prize, be sent entirely, and without fraud, to the court of the admiralty, or such other court of commissioners, as shall be authorized to determine whether such prize be lawful capture, there to be viewed, made use of, and proceeded upon according to law, upon pain that every person offending herein, shall forfeit and lose his share of the capture, and shall suffer such further punishment, as the nature and degree of his offense shall be found to deserve, and the court-martial shall impose.

8. No person in or belonging to the fleet shall take out of any prize, or ship seized for prize, any money, plate, or goods, unless it shall be necessary for the better securing thereof, or for the necessary use and service of any of His Majesty's ships or vessels of war, before the same be adjudged lawful prize in some admiralty court; but the full and entire account of the whole, without embezzlement, shall be brought in, and judgment passed entirely upon the whole without fraud, upon pain that every person offending herein shall forfeit and lose his share of the capture, and suffer such further punishment as shall be imposed by a court-martial, or such court of admiralty, according to the nature and degree of the offense.

9. If any ship or vessel be taken as prize, none of the officers, mariners, or other persons on board her, shall be stripped of their clothes, or in any sort pillaged, beaten, or evil-intreated, upon the pain that the person or persons so offending, shall be liable to such punishment as a court-martial shall think fit to inflict.

10. Every flag officer, captain and commander in the fleet, who, upon signal or order of fight, or sight of any ship or ships which it may be his duty to engage, or who, upon likelihood of engagement, shall not make the necessary preparations for fight, and shall not in his own person, and according to his place, encourage the inferior officers and men to fight courageously, shall suffer death, or such

other punishment, as from the nature and degree of the offence a court-martial shall deem him to deserve; and if any person in the fleet shall treacherously or cowardly yield or cry for quarter, every person so offending, and being convicted thereof by the sentence of a court-martial, shall suffer death.

11. Every person in the fleet, who shall not duly observe the orders of the admiral, flag officer, commander of any squadron or division, or other his superior officer, for assailing, joining battle with, or making defense against any fleet, squadron, or ship, or shall not obey the orders of his superior officer as aforesaid in the time of action, to the best of his power, or shall not use all possible endeavours to put the same effectually into execution, every person so offending, and being convicted thereof by the sentence of the court-martial, shall suffer death, or such other punishment, as from the nature and degree of the offence a court-martial shall deem him to deserve.

12. Every person in the fleet, who through cowardice, negligence, or disaffection, shall in time of action withdraw or keep back, or not come into the fight or engagement, or shall not do his utmost to take or destroy every ship which it shall be his duty to engage, and to assist and relieve all and every of His Majesty's ships, or those of his allies, which it shall be his duty to assist and relieve, every such person so offending, and being convicted thereof by the sentence of a court-martial, shall suffer death.

13. Every person in the fleet, who through cowardice, negligence, or disaffection, shall forbear to pursue the chase of any enemy, pirate or rebel, beaten or flying; or shall not relieve or assist a known friend in view to the utmost of his power; being convicted of any such offense by the sentence of a court-martial, shall suffer death.

14. If when action, or any service shall be commanded, any person in the fleet shall presume or to delay or discourage the said action or service, upon pretence of arrears of wages, or upon any pretence whatsoever, every person so offending, being convicted thereof by the sentence of the court-martial, shall suffer death, or such other punishment, as from the nature and degree of the offense a court-martial shall deem him to deserve.

15. Every person in or belonging to the fleet, who shall desert or entice others so to do, shall suffer death, or such other punishment as the circumstances of the offense shall deserve, and a court-martial shall judge fit: and if any commanding officer of any of His Majesty's ships or vessels of war shall receive or entertain a deserter from any other of His Majesty's ships or vessels, after discovering him to be such deserter, and shall not with all convenient speed give notice

to the captain of the ship or vessel to which such deserter belongs; or if the said ships or vessels are at any considerable distance from each other, to the secretary of the admiralty, or to the commander in chief; every person so offending, and being convicted thereof by the sentence of the court-martial, shall be cashiered.

16. The officers and seamen of all ships appointed for convoy and guard of merchant ships, or of any other, shall diligently attend upon that charge, without delay, according to their instructions in that behalf; and whosoever shall be faulty therein, and shall not faithfully perform their duty, and defend the ships and goods in their convoy, without either diverting to other parts or occasions, or refusing or neglecting to fight in their defence, if they be assailed, or running away cowardly, and submitting the ships in their convoy to peril and hazard; or shall demand or exact any money or other reward from any merchant or master for convoying any ships or vessels entrusted to their care, or shall misuse the masters or mariners thereof; shall be condemned to make reparation of the damage to the merchants, owners, and others, as the court of admiralty shall adjudge, and also be punished criminally according to the quality of their offences, be it by pains of death, or other punishment, according as shall be adjudged fit by the court-martial.

17. If any captain, commander, or other officer of any of His Majesty's ships or vessels, shall receive on board, or permit to be received on board such ship or vessel, any goods or merchandises whatsoever, other than for the sole use of the ship or vessel, except gold, silver, or jewels, and except the goods and merchandisers belonging to any merchant, or other ship or vessel which may be shipwrecked, or in imminent danger of being shipwrecked, either on the high seas, or in any port, creek, or harbour, in order to the preserving them for their proper owners, and except such goods or merchandisers as he shall at any time be ordered to take or receive on board by order of the lord high admiral of Great Britain, or the commissioners for executing the office of lord high admiral for the time being; every person so offending, being convicted thereof by the sentence of the court-martial shall be cashiered, and be for ever afterwards rendered incapable to serve in any place or office in the naval service of His Majesty, his heirs and successors.

18. If any person in or belonging to the fleet shall make or endeavor to make any mutinous assembly upon any pretence whatsoever, every person offending herein, and being convicted thereof by the sentence of the court-martial, shall suffer death: and if any person in or belonging to the fleet shall utter any words of sedition or mutiny, he shall suffer death, or such other punishment as a court-martial

shall deem him to deserve: and if any officer, mariner, or soldier on or belonging to the fleet, shall behave himself with contempt to his superior officer, being in the execution of his office, he shall be punished according to the nature of his offence by the judgment of a court-martial.

19. If any person in the fleet shall conceal any traitorous or mutinous practice or design, being convicted thereof by the sentence of a court-martial, he shall suffer death, or any other punishment as a court-martial shall think fit; and if any person, in or belonging to the fleet, shall conceal any traitorous or mutinous words spoken by any, to the prejudice of His Majesty or government, or any words, practice, or design, tending to the hindrance of the service, and shall not forthwith reveal the same to the commanding officer, or being present at any mutiny or sedition, shall not use his utmost endeavours to suppress the same, he shall be punished as a court-martial shall think he deserves.

20. If any person in the fleet shall find cause of complaint of the unwholesomeness of the victual, or upon other just ground, he shall quietly make the same known to his superior, or captain, or commander in chief, as the occasion may deserve, that such present remedy may be had as the matter may require; and the said superior, captain, or commander in chief, shall, as far as he

is able, cause the same to be presently remedied; and no person in the fleet, upon any such or other pretence, shall attempt to stir up any disturbance, upon pain of such punishment, as a court-martial shall think fit to inflict, according to the degree of the offence.

21. If any officer, mariner, soldier or other person in the fleet, shall strike any of his superior officers, or draw, or offer to draw, or lift up any weapon against him, being in the execution of his office, on any pretence whatsoever, every such person being convicted of any such offense, by the sentence of a court-martial, shall suffer death; and if any officer, mariner, soldier or other person in the fleet, shall presume to quarrel with any of his superior officers, being in the execution of his office, or shall disobey any lawful command of any of his superior officers; every such person being convicted of any such offence, by the sentence of a court-martial, shall suffer death, or such other punishment, as shall, according to the nature and degree of his offence, be inflicted upon him by the sentence of a court-martial.

22. If any person in the fleet shall quarrel or fight with any other person in the fleet, or use reproachful or provoking speeches or gestures, tending to make any quarrel or disturbance, he shall, upon being convicted thereof, suffer such punishment as the offence shall deserve, and a court-martial shall impose.

23. There shall be no wasteful expense of any powder, shot, ammunition, or other stores in the fleet, nor any embezzlement thereof, but the stores and provisions shall be careful preserved, upon pain of such punishment to be inflicted upon the offenders, abettors, buyers and receivers (being persons subject to naval discipline) as shall be by a court-martial found just in that behalf.

24. Every person in the fleet, who shall unlawfully burn or set fire to any magazine or store of powder, or ship, boat, ketch, hoy or vessel, or tackle or furniture thereunto belonging, not then appertaining to an enemy, pirate, or rebel, being convicted of any such offence, by the sentence of a court-martial, shall suffer death.

25. Care shall be taken in the conducting and steering of any of His Majesty's ships, that through willfulness, negligence, or other defaults, no ship be stranded, or run upon any rocks or sands, or split or hazarded, upon pain, that such as shall be found guilty therein, be punished by death, or such other punishment, as the offence by a court-martial shall be judged to deserve.

26. No person in or belonging to the fleet shall sleep upon his watch, or negligently perform the duty imposed on him, or forsake his station, upon pain of death, or such other punishment as a court-martial shall think fit to impose, and as the circumstances of the case shall require.

27. All murders committed by any person in the fleet, shall be punished with death by the sentence of a court-martial.

28. If any person in the fleet shall commit the unnatural and detestable sin of buggery and sodomy with man or beast, he shall be punished with death by the sentence of a court-martial.

29. All robbery committed by any person in the fleet, shall be punished with death, or otherwise, as a court-martial, upon consideration of the circumstances, shall find meet.

30. Every officer or other person in the fleet, who shall knowingly make or sign a false muster or muster book, or who shall command, counsel, or procure the making or signing thereof, or who shall aid or abet any other person in the making or signing thereof, shall, upon proof of any such offence being made before a court-martial, be cashiered, and rendered incapable of further employment in His Majesty's naval service.

31. No provost martial belonging to the fleet shall refuse to apprehend any criminal, whom he shall be authorized by legal warrant to apprehend, or to receive or keep any prisoner committed to his charge, or willfully suffer him to escape, being once in his custody, or dismiss him without lawful order, upon pain of such punishment as a court-martial shall deem him fit to deserve; and all captains, officers, and others in

the fleet, shall do their endeavour to detect, apprehend, and bring to punishment all offenders, and shall assist the officers appointed for that purpose therein, upon pain of being proceeded against, and punished by a court-martial, according to the nature and degree of the offence.

32. If any flag officer, captain, or commander, or lieutenant belonging to the fleet, shall be convicted before a court-martial of behaving in a scandalous, infamous, cruel, oppressive, or fraudulent manner, unbecoming the character of an officer, he shall be dismissed from His Majesty's service.

33. Every person being in actual service and full pay, and part of the crew in or belonging to any of His Majesty's ships or vessels of war, who shall be guilty of mutiny, desertion, or disobedience to any lawful command, in any part of His Majesty's dominions on shore, when in actual service relative to the fleet, shall be liable to be tried by a court-martial, and suffer the like punishment for every such offence, as if the same had been committed at sea on board any of His Majesty's ships or vessels of war.

34. If any person who shall be in the actual service and full pay of His Majesty' ships and vessels of war, shall commit upon the shore, in any place or places out of His Majesty's dominions, any of the crimes punishable by these articles and orders, the person so offending shall be liable to be tried and punished for the same, in like manner, to all intents and purposes, as if the same crimes had been committed at sea, on board any of His Majesty's ships or vessels of war.

35. All other crimes not capital committed by any person or persons in the fleet, which are not mentioned in this act, or for which no punishment is hereby directed to be inflicted, shall be punished by the laws and customs in such cases used at sea.

APPENDIX 3

APPOINTMENT OF POWER OF ATTORNEY[1]

The individuals entitled to bounty or prize money were not likely to be able to take their cases to court. It was essential that an agent be appointed to work on the behalf of men still at sea, turned over into another ship, or who had died since the capture. The appointment was probably the captain's decision alone, but every member of the crew had to signify his agreement for this to provide maximum benefit to all. The importance of this legal document can be seen in the meticulous copy made for the use of the court, carefully filed and indexed. These documents do not make clear the status of the individual. That happened later.

- The identity of the vessel and the date of the document is made clear
- The identity of the agent and his address is established
- The prize is named, together with any other vessels involved in the capture
- The agent is instructed to act on behalf of the captor to receive the bounty or Head Money, sell the prize and everything pertaining to her, before distributing the prize money to the officers and crew
- The agent is entitled to retain five per cent of the proceeds of the capture
- This Power of Attorney is dated 7 February 1758
- A note on the cover of the document adds the information that the prize was condemned on 18 March 1758

James Henshaw's form contains the same instructions but without the visual effect of the *Dispatch*'s brilliantly decorated legal document.

Power of Attorney of the Officers mariners
Sloop Dispatch

[1] *Dispatch* took *La Dieppoise* on 7 February 1758, and her appointment of agents is a particularly striking witness to the importance attached to this document, a huge sheet (approximately A0) of which each line of script has been represented separately.

Please to register this Power of Attorney
March 18 1758

Know all men by these presents that we who have hereunto set our hands and seals being the Officers Mariners and others or the major part of them now belonging to his Majesty's Sloop Dispatch

Have constituted authorised and appointed, and by these presents do constitute authorise and appoint Mr Francis Magnus Merchant in Broad Street near the Royal Exchange London to be our true

And Lawful attorney and Agent for us in our names and to our uses to Sollicit transact and take care of all our concern and interest in the French Privateer called the Dieppois of Dieppe Charles

Folliot late commander Seized and taken by us in company with his Majesty's armed cutter the Hazard together with her tackle guns apparel and furniture and also all the Head Money Gun

Money, Bounty Money, Salvage money or other money whatsoever arising from the said capture and interest giving and hereby granting to our said attorney and agent our full power and

Authority in the premises, for inventorizing appraising selling and condemning the said prize her tackle, guns apparel and furniture, and for receiving the money arising thereon, and also the

Said head money, gun money, bounty money, salvage money or any other money whatsoever to which we are or shall be intitled to as aforesaid and afterwards to make a distribution of the neat product

Thereof to us or to persons having lawful authority from us, allowing the said Mr Francis Magnus at the rate of five per cent of the neat produce thereof for all such money, as he shall receive for and

On account of the said prize, and on all head money, gun money, bounty money, salvage money or other money whatsoever and also allowing him to retain all the costs and charges and expenses

Which he shall be at in prosecuting and compleating our said interest concern or title therein and generally giving and hereby granting unto our said attorney and agent our full power and authority for recovering, compounding and discharging the same and generally to do and act in the aforesaid prize for us and for our use and safety and fully and effectively to all intents and purposes as

We ourselves might or could do collectively or separately being personally present, ratifying and confirming all and whatsoever our said attorney and agent shall lawfully do or cause to be

Done in the premises aforesaid by virtue of these presents in Witness whereof we have hereunto set our hands and seals seventh day of February in the year of our Lord One

Thousand seven hundred and fifty eight and in the thirty first year of the reign of our sovereign Lord George the Second, over Great Britain France and Ireland etc

John Hodges (master and commander)
James Mitchell (lieutenant)
John Major
etc, being the names of the officers and men on board

[On the outside of the form was the following inscription:]
Dispatch
Registered in the High Court of Admiralty
of England for the Prize Dieppois Charles
Foliot Commander a french privateer
condemned the eighteenth day of March
1758, as taken by his Majesty's sloop
of war the Dispatch John Hodges esq
Commander
Witness my hand this 13th day of August 1760

James Henshaw's Form[2]

Know all men by these presents, that we who have hereunto set out hands and seals, being the Captain, Officers, Seamen and others, now or late belonging to His Majesty's …….. the ………… have constituted and appointed, and do hereby constitute, authorise and appoint ………….. of the ………….. to be our true and lawful Attorney and Agent of us, in our Names and to our Uses, to solicit, transact, and take care of all our concerns and interest in

2 TNA HCA 30/17.

any Prize or Prizes, Seizures or Recaptures that have been or shall be taken, seized, retaken or destroyed by the said ship, or to which we are, or shall be intitled by any means whatsoever: And in all Head-Money, or other money arising from such Capture and Interest. Giving and hereby granting to our said Attorney and Agent our full power and authority in the Premises, for Inventorying, Appraising, Condemning and Selling the said Prize or Prizes, Seizure and Recaptures, their Cargoes, Tackle, Guns, Apparel and Furniture and for receiving the money arising thereon and also the said Head-money, and our several Shares of the whole, and for recovering, obtaining, compounding and discharging the same; and generally to do and to act for us and for our Use and Safety, as fully and effectively to all Intents and Purposes, as we ourselves might or could do, collectively or separately, being personally present; Acquaintances and Releases and other Discharges to make and grant, ratifying and confirming all and whatsoever our said Attorney and Agent or his Substitutes shall lawfully do or cause to be done, in the premises, by Virtue of these presents, in Witness whereof we have hereunto set our Hands and Seals the …….. day of ……. In the Year of our Lord 17 …. and in the …….. Year of the Reign of our Sovereign Lord King GEORGE the Second by the Grace of God over Great Britain etc

Sealed and Delivered
in the presence of us

APPENDIX 4

MONITION: TAKING OF *SAN JUAN BAPTISTA*[1]

A monition was a warning that an individual was expected to appear before the court at which the legality or otherwise of his actions would be determined. In this case Thomas Lynn, captain of *Roebuck*, having taken as prize the Spanish *San Juan Baptista*, is now being pursued to argue the case against the Spanish proctor.

***

San Juan Baptista Monition to set further proceedings against Thomas Lynn Esquire

George the Third by the Grace of God of Great Britain France and Ireland King Defender of the Faith To all and singular our officers and witnesses and other our liege subjects being literate persons whosoever in and throughout our Kingdom of Great Britain and to John Joplin Officer of our High Court of Delegates Greeting; Whereas our beloved Andrew Coltée Ducarel Doctor of Laws Surrogate of our right Trusty and right intirely beloved our Judges or Commissioners by us specially appointed by Virtue of our Letters Patent under our Great Seal of Great Britain for the hearing and final determination of all causes of Appeal and Complaint as to ships and goods seized and taken as Prize in a certain Business of Appeal and Complaint of Nullity promoted by Don Francisco Guerra de la Vega claimant of the ship San Juan Baptista (Don Juan Francisco Capan Master) and goods therein against Thomas Lynn Esquire the commander and the Officers, seamen and others of our ship Roebuck the captors of the said ship and goods rightly and duly and duly proceeding at the Petition of the Proctor of the said Don Francisco Guerra de la Vega alledging that by a certificate ?? the Monition to see further proceedings this day returned it appears that Thomas Lynn the captor and respondent had been diligently sought for at Lloyds, the Jamaica, Antigua and Edinburgh Coffee Houses and other places near the Royal Exchange with an intent to have served him

[1] TNA HCA 47/5. The search for Thomas Lynn's proctors made this the exemplar to choose.

personally therewith, but that he could not be found to be so served together with an affidavit of the truth of ? Certificate, also a Certificate endorsed on the said monition of the personal service thereof on James Dixon the agent of the said Captain Thomas Lynn as appeared by a letter annexed to an attestation of Thomas Murphy both which are exhibited and alledging that the personal service of the said monition is verified by the said attestation of the mandatory annexed to the said monition hath decreed the said Thomas Lynn Esq to be monished cited and called to judgement at the time and place underwritten and to the effect hereafter expressed (justice so requiring). We therefore strictly charge and command you jointly and severally that you omit not by reason of any Liberty or ? but that you monished and cited can so to be monished and cited peremptorily the said Thomas Lynn

personally if he can be so cited and you can have safe and free ? so to do, otherwise by affixing of these presents upon one of the Pillars of the Royal Exchange of our city of London at the usual time of the public resort of merchants thither and by all other ways means and methods whatsoever whereby you can or may more effectually so that this Monition by ways and means may most likely come to the knowledge of the said Thomas Lynn Esq that he appears before our said Commissioner or any three or more of them in the Privy Council Chamber at the York Pitt or before their Surrogate in the Dining Room near the Common Hall of Doctors Commons London the thirtieth day after service of these presents, if it be a Court day otherwise on the Court day the next following and on every Court day next afterward between the usual hours of hearing of causes there then and there to see a schedule of costs and damages given in and to attend the liquidation thereof and to see and hear further proceedings had and done in the said cause or business on behalf of the said Don Francisco Guerra de la Vega as may be necessary until the final liquidation of the said

costs and damages and until the Report or Decree made thereon shall be duly carried into Execution and the Execution thereof shall be finally compleated according to the Exigency of the Law and former proceedings and further to do and ? in this behalf as to justice shall appertain, and that you duly certify our aforesaid Commissioners or any three or more of them or their surrogate what you shall do in the premises together with these presents given at London under the seal of our High Court of Delegates the twenty sixth day of February in the year of our Lord 1763 and of our reign the third.

APPENDIX 5

THE QUESTIONS ASKED IN INTERROGATIONS[1]

To ensure that condemnations were based on evidence 'out of their mouths', a set of questions was devised and used universally. The questions established:

- The nationality of the individual being examined
- The circumstances of the capture
- The name and nationality of the master of the captured vessel
- The identity, cargo and destination of the vessel
- If the vessel had already been a prize
- If any personal loss had been sustained
- In what country the ship had been insured
- If the cargo was personally owned or destined for market

Separate questions were directed at individuals who might have been ransomed, to establish the conditions of their treatment.

***

To all commanders, masters, officers, mariners, and others of any ship, vessel, goods or merchandises, which have or shall be seized, or taken as prize, by any private ship of war, or any vessel acting without any commission, and to such other persons who shall be brought to be examined in preparatory,

First, let each witness be interrogated to every of the following questions, and their answers to each severally wrote down; as, where were you born? And where have you lived for these seven years last past? Where do you now live? And how long have you lived in that place? And to what prince or state are you, or have you ever been a subject? And of what cities or towns have you been admitted burgher, or freeman? And at what time you was so admitted?

[1] TNA HCA 32.

2. Was you present at the time of taking and seizing the ship and her lading, or any of the goods and merchandises concerning which you are now examined? If not, how and when was you first made acquainted therewith? and had the ship concerning which you are now examined, any commission for war from any, and what prince or state?
3. In what place, latitude or port, and in what year month and day was the ship and goods, concerning which you are now examined, taken and seized upon what pretence and for what reason were they seized? In what place or port were they carried and under the colours of what Kingdom or state did the said ship sail? Was any resistance made at the time when the said ship was taken? And if yea, how many guns were fired and by whom, and by what ship or ships were you taken? Was such vessel a ship of war, privateer or a vessel acting without any commission, as you believe.
4. What is the name of the master or commander of the ship or vessel taken? How long have you known the said master, and who appointed him to the command of the said ship? Where did such master take possession of her, and what was the name of the person who delivered the possession to the said master? Where doth he live? Where is the said masters fix'd place of abode? How long hath he lived there? Where was he born? And of what prince or state is he now a subject? Is he married? If yea, where doth his wife and family reside?
5. Of what tonnage or burthen is the ship which hath been taken? What was the number of mariners, and of what country where the said seamen or mariners? Did they all come on board at the same port or different ports, and who shipped or hired them, and when and where?
6. Had you, or any of the officers or mariners belonging to the ship or vessel concerning which you are now examined, any, and what part, share or interest in the said ship, or in any of her lading? If yea, set forth who, and what goods or interest you or they have? Did you belong to the said ship or vessel at the time she was seized and taken? In what capacity did you belong to her? How long have you known her? When and where did you first see her, and where was she built?
7. What is the name of the said ship? How long hath she been so called? Do you know of any other name or names by which she hath been called? If yea, what were they? Had she any passport or sea-brief on board, and from what prince or state? To what ports and places was the said ship or vessel bound in her voyage? To and from what ports and places did she sail during her said voyage before she was taken?

Where did her last voyage begin, and where was the said voyage to have ended? Set forth the quality of every cargo the ship hath carried from the date of her passport to the time of her capture, and what ports such cargoes have been delivered at.

8. What lading did the ship carry at the time of her first setting sail in her last voyage, and what particular sort of lading and goods had she on board at the time when she was taken? In what year and what month was the same put on board? Set forth the different species of the lading, and the quantities of each sort.

9. Who were the owners of the ship or vessel concerning which you are now examined, at the time when she was seized? How do you know that they were the owners of the said ship at that time? Of what nation or country are such owners by birth? Where do they reside, and where doth their wives or families reside? To what prince or state are they subjects?

10. Was any bill of sale made to the aforesaid owners of the said ship, and if any such was made, in what month and year where and in the presence of what witnesses was such bill of sale made, where did you last see it and what is become of it?

11. Was the lading put on board in one port and at one time, or at several ports and at several times, and at what ports by name? set forth what quantities of each sort of goods were shipped at each port.

12. What are the names of the respective laders or owners of the said goods? What countrymen are they? Where do they now live and carry on their business or trade, and where were the said goods to be delivered? Can you take upon yourself to answer that you believe, that at the time of the lading the cargo, and at the present time, and also if the goods shall be restored and unladen at the destined ports, the goods did, and will belong to the same persons and to none others.

13. How many bills of lading were signed for the goods seized on board the said ship? Were any of those bills colourable, or were any bills of lading signed which were of a different tenor from those which were on board the ship at the time when she was taken? What were the contents of such other bills of lading and what became of them?

14. Are there in Great Britain any bills of lading, invoices, letters or instruments relative to the ship or goods concerning which you are now examined? If yea, set forth where they are, and in whose possession, and what are the purports thereof, and when were they brought or sent to this Kingdom.

15. Was there any charterparty signed for the voyage in which the ship, concerning which you are now examined, was seized and taken? What became thereof? When, where and between whom, was such charter-party made, and what were the contents of it?
16. What papers, bills of lading, letters or other writings, were on board the ship at the time she took her departure from her last clearing port, before her being taken as prize? Were any of them afterwards burnt, torn, thrown overboard, destroyed or concealed, and when, and by whom, and who was then present?
17. Has the ship concerning which you are examined, been at any time, and when seized, as prize, and condemned as such? If yea, set forth into which port she was carried, and by whom, and by what authority, and on what account or reason she was condemned.
18. Have you sustained any loss by the seizing and taking the said ship concerning which you are examined? If yes, in what manner do you compute such your loss? Have you already received any indemnity, satisfaction or promise of satisfaction, for any part of the damage which you have or may sustain by this capture and detention, and when, and from whom?
19. Is the said ship or goods or any and what part insured and in what country? If yes, for what voyage is such insurance made, and at what premium, and when was such insurance made?
20. In case you had arrived at your destined port, would your cargo, or any part thereof, on being unladen, have immediately become the property of the consignee, or any other person, and whom; or was the lader to take the chance of the market for the sale of his goods?

[This was the end of the printed sheets. In cases of recapture, a further set of questions was appended.]

After having interrogated on the above interrogatories then interrogate every witness as to the time place and circumstances of capture and recapture that it may appear with certainty the number of hours the prize was in the enemies custody and their treatment

and in case of ransom

after having interrogated on the above interrogatories then interrogate the hostages particularly into the reasons and conditions of the ransom and be very circumspect as to the number of prisoners which may have been released and the place where the ship was discharged and the quality of their cargo and the time of their being released with the necessity for releasing the prisoners.

APPENDIX 6

ANSWERS TO INTERROGATIONS OF *LE ST AMAND*[1]

This is an example of the hundreds of documents stored from the legal proceedings involved in the High Court of Admiralty decisions. The two stamps of sixpence each which make this a legal document are imprinted at the top of the one sheet of paper, folded in half with the text on two and a half sides. The first page always has as an introductory two sets of text separated by a line, which is represented below.

The amount of detail disclosed by the interrogations of the three individuals is testament to the clever transition from personal data to revealing background history. This set of interrogations also highlights the fluidity of ownership. The vessel changed hands three times, and the London-born Thomas Oldfield was probably grateful to have been captured yet again.

***

Fryday the Seventh day of January 1757
Le St Amand whereof Louis Du Clos was master
Our sovereign Lord the King against the said ship
Her tackle apparel and furniture and the goods
therein taken and seized by his Majesty's ship
of war called the Happy whereof
Thomas Burnett Esq was Commander and brought
into the island of Guernsey and against all
Persons in general

on which day
Thomas Tyndall Esq
as Procurator
General as lawful
Proctor of our
Sovereign Lord
George the Second by the Grace of God of Great Britain
France and Ireland King Defender of the Faith
by all Lawfull ways and means, to all effects
of Law whatsoever alledged pleaded articulately
propounded as follows to wit:

[1] TNA HCA 32/168/18.

1. That on or about the seventeenth day of May 1756 War and Hostility was declared by his Majesty King George the Second against the French King his Subjects and Vassals. This was and is true publick and notorious and the party proponent doth alledge and propound of any other time and all and every thing joyntly and severally
2. That the said ship Le St Amand whereof the said Louis Du Clos was master on the fourth day of November 1756 being a French Ship belonging to the French King his vassalls or subjects having divers Goods Wares and Merchandize of the French King or his Subjects was by his Majesty's

2.

Said ship the Happy whereof the said Thomas Burnett was commander taken and seized and the party proponent doth alledge and propound as before

3. That the said ship and goods were and are the ship and goods of and belonging to the French King his vassals or subjects or others Inhabiting within his Countries Territories or Dominions and ought to be confiscated condemned and adjudged to be the good and lawful prize as being the ship and goods of the Enemies of the Crown of Great Britain and the party proponent prays the same may be adjudged and condemned accordingly and the party proponent doth alledge and propound as before
2. That all and singular the premises were and are true publick and notorious and thereof there was and is a publick voice fame & report of which legal proof being made the party proponent prays you the Right Worshipful Sir Thomas Salusbury Knight Doctor of Laws Lieutenant President and Judge of the High Court of Admiralty of England that right & Justice may be duly administered to him his party in the premises and that the said ship her tackle apparel furniture and the goods taken therein be pronounced to belong

3.

at the time of the capture of the same to the French King his Vassals Subjects or Others Inhabiting within his Countries Territories and Dominions and as Such or otherwise liable and Subject to Confiscation and to be adjudged and Condemned as and for good and lawful prize by you and your definitive sentence to be given in this behalf.
[signed] Geo. Hay

[On a separate piece of paper:]

Guernsey On the affair of the capture of the French snow called the St Amand whereof ....
was master taken by his Majesty's Ketch of war the Happy whereof Thomas Burnet Esq was and is commander, in company with his Majesty's ship of war the Lynn whereof James Kirk Esq was and is commander, and brought to the Island of Guernsey the fifth day of November in the year of our Lord one thousand seven hundred and fifty six

Thomas Burnet Esq Captain on board the said ketch of war the Happy, maketh oath that upon the taking the above mentioned french snow Louis Guyot Du Clos the french prize master delivered in to the hands of this Deponent the several parchments, papers, writings marked respectively from number one to two inclusive and hereto annexed to be transmitted into the hands of the Judge of the High Court of Admiralty of England, which said produced parchments, papers, writings, where all the Sea Briefs, Charterparty's, Bills of Loading, cockets, letters and other documents and writings as were delivered to this deponent by the said Louis Guyot Du Clos or found on board the said french snow, and which he has now delivered to me the underwritten Commissioner as they were received or taken without and fraud, addition, subduction and embezlement.

Sworn at Guernsey (where stamps are not used) before me the under written Commissioner this 6th day of November 1756 [signed] T. Burnett

[signed] Henry Budd Commissioner
and in the presence of me
[signed] Isaac Dobrée Not. Pub.
[The following sheets contain the series of interrogations]

1.

In the business of the prosecution in his	Depositions of Witnesses upon on the
Majesty's High Court of Admiralty on the	Interrogatories annexed to his Majesty's
behalf of our Sovereign Lord George the Second	Commission and of the High Court of

by the Grace of God of Great Brittain
France & Ireland, King Deffender of the Faith,
and so forth against the french snow called the
St Aman and her lading and touching and concerning
the taking and Seizing of the said
snow or vessel and her Lading as Lawfull Prize
by his Majesty's ketch of war the Happy
Thomas Burnet Esq Commander in company
with his Majesty's ship of war the Lynn

Admiralty to Peter Dobrée the younger,
William le Marchant, John le Mesurier,
Henry Budd and John Cornelius
Commissioners directed for the
examination of witnesses in all such
cases taken upon the oaths of the
respective witnesses at Guernsey at the
Publick offices of Isaac Dobrée Notary
Publick in the town of St Peter Port

in the Island of Guernsey the sixth day of November in the thirtieth year of his Majesty's reign by virtue of the said Commission in the Buisness aforesaid, before Henry Budd one of the said Commissioners, and thereunto first duely sworn

First Witness Louis Guyot Du Clos aged twenty years or thereabouts, a witness produced, Sworn and Examined Deposeth and sayeth as followeth:

1st to the first interrogatory. This deponent sayeth that he was born in St Malos where he has always lived, being a burgher of the place and a subject to the french King.

2nd to the second inter. This deponent sayeth that he was present and on board the snow or vessel called the St Aman concerning which he is now examined, at the time he was taken and seized by the Happy ketch of War, that he had a copy of captain Chevalier La Touraudée Commission, Commander of the Port Mahoon Privateer of St Malos, for carrying the said snow in france, the said privateer having taken her before from the English, who had taken her from the french.

3rd to the third inter. This deponent sayeth that on 26th day of October last he being a cruising, in the said french privateer the Port Mahoon about

[This page seems to be missing]

3.

Mariners were on board at the time she sailed from Bordeaux that when they took her from the possession of the English there were ten English men on board and two french men who were all sent on board the french privateer, except one English man they kept on board, and at the time they were taken by the Happy Ketch they were nine french men and all subjects of the french King.

6th to the 6th inter. This deponent sayeth that all the interest he and the rest of the crew on board had in the said vessel and lading was the Expectations of having their shares of the Prize money she should have produced had they got her safe in france, that he never saw her before they took her from the English, believes she is English built, and was on board in quality of prize master at the time they were taken by the Happy ketch.

7th to the 7th inter. This deponent sayeth that the name of the said snow is the St Aman, but does not know how long she has been called so, never knew her under any other name (knowing only her name by its written on her stern) that when he took possession of her the English officer carried all the papers on board the french privateer except one which he the deponent found in the cabin after parting with the privateer and that he has not found any other papers or writings on board, that he delivered the said paper to Captain Burnet at the time he was taken together with the Commission which had been given him for carrying the prize to france. That by the said paper she appears to be loaded with sundry sort of goods but doth not know the particulars.

8th to the 8th inter. This deponent knows nothing nor can depose thereto

9th to the 9th inter. This deponent sayeth that he doth not know who was the owner of the said snow and lading.

10th 11th 12th inter. To these interrogatories this deponent known nothing nor can depose thereto.

4.

13th to the 13th inter. This deponent sayeth that he has not seen any bills of lading nor any other papers whatsoever on board except that which he delivered to Captain Burnet.

14th and 15th To these interrogatories this deponent known nothing.

16th to the 16th inter. This deponent sayeth that he has seen no other papers on board but that which he delivered Captain Burnet and hereunto annexed that he has not seen or heard of any being burnt, torn, thrown over board, destroyed or concealed.

17th to the 17th inter. This deponent sayeth that he knows nothing nor can depose thereto.

18th to the 18th inter. This deponent sayeth that the loss he has sustained by being taken is the loss of some of his clothes, which he computes to be about thirty french livres, for which he has not received nor expect to receive any satisfaction.

19th and 20th inter. To these interrogatories this deponent knows nothing nor can depose thereto.

Taken subscribed and acknowledged [signed]
To be true before me Louis Guyot Du Clos
[signed] Henry Budd Commissioner
And in the presence of me [signed] Isaac Dobrée Not. Pub.

Second Witness Pierre le Raux aged twenty nine years or thereabouts a witness produced sworn and examined
deposeth and sayeth as follows:

1st to the 1st inter. This deponent sayeth that he was born in St Malos where he has always lived, being a free man of the place, a bachelor and subject to the french King.

2nd to the 2nd inter. This deponent sayeth that he was present and on board the said snow or vessel concerning which he is now examined at the time she was taken by the Happy ketch but doth not know if she had any commission.

5.

3rd to the 3rd inter. This deponent sayeth that being on a cruise in the Port Mahoon privateer of St Malo commanded by Chevalier de la Tauraudée on the 26th day of October last being about fifteen leagues to the westward of the Lizard, they brought to the said snow who immediately struck her English colours without fyring a gun, and that he the deponent on coming on board found she was called the St Aman of Bordeaux, bound from Bordeaux to America that she had been taken twenty one days before by the Bedford man of war, that when they took her from the English there was ten English men and two french men on board who were all sent on board the privateer except one English man which remained, and that being nine in number on board of the french privateer's crew under the command of Louis Guyot Du Clos (who was appointed prize master) with the said English man, they were ordered for the first port in france, but on the fourth day of this inst. being last Thursday at daybreak they were chased, and about eight o'clock that morning were taken by the Happy ketch of war Capt. Thomas Burnet in company with another man of war of forty guns, but doth not know her name, that he believes they had a proper commission from the king of England, that after being taken they were carried into this island where they arrived last evening.

4th to the 4th inter. This deponent sayeth that he doth not know the name of the person who was master of the said snow at her first setting sail from Bordeaux, that Louis Guyot Du Clos was prize master on board when they were taken by the Happy Ketch, and that Chevalier de la Tauraudée Captain of the Port Mahoon privateer appointed him prize master, and gave him a proper Commission for the purpose, that said Chevalier de la Tauraudée and the said Louis Guyot Du Clos both lives at St Malos are batchelors and subjects to the french king.

5th to the 5th inter. This deponent sayeth that the said snow concerning which he is now examined is about one hundred and thirty tuns burthen, that he doth not know what number of mariners were

6.

on board when they sailed from Bordeaux, that at the time they took her from the English they were ten English men and two french men on board, who were all except one put on board the Port Mahoon privateer, and that when they were taken by the Happy ketch they were nine french men and the English man before mentioned on board.

6th to the 6th inter. This deponent sayeth that neither he nor any of the officers and men on board had any part of the said snow or her lading, any more than they expected of prize money, had they got her safe into france, that he was second lieutenant on board the Port Mahoon privateer and second officer on board the prize, that he never saw her before they took her and believes she is English built.

7th to the 7th inter. This deponent sayeth that the name of the said snow is the St Aman, as appears by its being written in her stern, but doth not know how long she has been called so, that he has not seen any papers whatsoever on board, that she sailed as he is informed from Bordeaux bound for Americas and is loaded with sundry merchandizes but doth not know the particulars.

8th to the 8th inter. This deponent sayeth that he knows of some wine, some oyl and some soap on board but cannot tell the particulars of the cargo.

9th, 10th, 11th and 12th inter. To these interrogatory's this deponent knows nothing nor can depose thereto.

13th to the 13th inter. This deponent sayeth that he has not seen any bills of lading or any other papers whatsoever on board, and believes they were all carried by the English officer on board the Port Mahoon privateer.

14th and 15th inter. This deponent sayeth that he knows nothing nor can depose thereto.

7.

16th to the 16th inter. This deponent sayeth that he has not seen any papers whatsoever to have been found on board and that directly or indirectly he has not nor has he heard of any being burnt torn thrown overboard, destroyed or concealed.

17th to the 17th inter. This deponent knows nothing nor can depose thereto.

18th to the 18th inter. This deponent sayeth that all the loss he subtained by being taken is the loss of his cloathes which he computes to be about thirty French livres for which he has not received nor expect to receive any satisfaction.

19th and 20th inter. To these interrogatory's this Deponent knows nothing nor can depose thereto.

[signed] Pierre Leraux

Taken subscribed and acknowledged
to be true before me

[signed] Henry Budd Commissioner

And in the presence of me [signed] Isaac Dobrée Not. Pub.

Third witness Thomas Oldfield aged twenty four years of age or thereabouts a witness produced, sworn and examined, sayeth and deposeth as follows:

1st to the 1st inter. This deponent sayeth he was born in Covent Garden in London and has sailed from Jamaica for these nine years last past where his wife now lives and that he is a subject to his Majesty King George.

2nd to the 2nd inter. This deponent sayeth that he was present and on board of the snow concerning which he is now examined at the three several times she has been taken and that she had no

8.

commission of war as he believes.

3rd to the 3rd inter. This deponent sayeth that he belongs to his Majesty's ship the Bedford, commanded by James Douglas Esq. being a foremast man on board, and that on the 10th October last off of Cape Pinat on the coast of Galicia they brought too and took without any resistance the snow concerning which he is now examined which proved to be the St Aman of Bordeaux bound to St Domingo, loaded with sundry merchandises, and he the deponent being sent on board with one Olliver one of the mates of the man of war and nine men more being eleven English men in number, and three of the french crew (the rest being taken on board the man of war) they were ordered for Portsmouth but on the 26th of the said month at daybreak being in latitude 49 14m about twelve leagues to the north west of Ushant they were chased by a french privateer to whom they struck who proved to be the Port Mahoon of St Malos, that having taken all the English and the three french men on board the privateer except him the deponent, they sent nine of their men to take possession of her who parting with the privateer made sail for france and on the 4th inst. being last Thursday at daybreak being then in sight of the Seven Islands, they were chased by a large ship and a ketch whom brought them too about nine o'clock that morning and proving to be the Lynn man of war and the Happy ketch they struck to the ketch who manning her with her own hands and some from on board the Lynn made sail for this island were they arrived last evening.

4th to the 4th inter. This deponent knows nothing.

5th to the 5th inter. This deponent sayeth that the snow or vessel concerning

9.

which he is now examined is about one hundred and thirty tuns burthen, that at the time she was taken by the Bedford man of war there was some french passengers on board beside the crew, but doth not know the number of either not being on board at the time they were sent on board the man of war.

6th to the 6th inter. This deponent knows nothing

7th to the 7th inter. This deponent sayeth that by the name written in her stern she appears to be called the St Aman, but doth not know how long she has been so called, that he saw some papers carried on board the Bedford man of war, but doth not know what is become thereof, that he was informed by the french crew the said snow came from Bordeaux was bound to St Domingo, and further cannot depose to this interrogatory.

8th to 8th inter. This deponent sayeth he knows nothing nor can depose thereto.

To the 9th, 10th, 11th, 12th, 13th, 14th, 15th, 16th and 17th Knows nothing.

18th to the 18th inter. This deponent sayeth that he hath lost most of his cloathes, most of which were taken from him when taken by the Happy ketch being all the loss he has substained which he computes to about three pounds sterling for which he has not received nor expects to receive any satisfaction.

19th and 20th inter. To these interrogatorys this deponent knows nothing nor can depose thereto

Taken, subscribed and acknowleged to [signed] Thos. Oldfield
Be true Before me
[signed] Henry Budd Commissioner
and in the presence of Isaac Dobrée Not. Pub.

Right Worshipful

As one of the Commissioners appointed for the examination of witnesses relating to captures made upon the enemy and brought in this Island, I herewith transmit to your worship the Depositions concerning the capture of the french snow called the St Amand of Bordeaux, and also the papers found on board and thereunto annexed together with Captain Burnet's affidavit concerning the said papers as there was none of the french men brought in here which belonged to the said vessel at her setting sail from Bordeaux and at the time she was taken by the Bedford man of war I could not have them examined it seems they were all carried on board the said man of war, and on board the Port Mahoon french privateer which took her and having made a strict enquiry concerning the papers I have not been able to discover any more but those annexed to the Depositions, it appears to me they were carried on board the french privateer

I am with the greatest respect
Right Worshipfull
your worship's most humble
and most dutifull servant
Guernsey November 6th 1756 [signed] Henry Budd

To the Right Worshipfull Sir Thomas Salusbury Knight & Doctor of Laws Judge of the High Court of Admiralty of England, or his surrogate

11.

The execution of the Commission before mentioned as far as concerneth the taking and seizing of the French snow and her lading called the St Aman of Bordeaux appeareth in the Examinations and Depositions of Louis Guyot Du Clos and Pierre Le Raux belonging to the Port Mahoon privateer of St Malos, who had retaken the said snow from the Bedford belonging to the said man of war Bedford, (there being none of the people brought in her which belonged to her at the time of her being taken by the Bedford man of war aforesaid) and also the severall paper writtings hereunto annexed from Number one to two together with Capt. Burnet's affidavit concerning the said papers which said Depositions were taken by Isaac Dobrée Notary Publick (for that purpose substituted by George Bellas Esq Deputy Register of the High Court of Admiralty) before the underwritten Commissioner at the publick offices of the said Isaac Dobrée this 6th day of November 1756.

[signed] Henry Budd Commissioner

And the before named Isaac Dobrée Notary Publick by Royal Authority lawfully admitted and Sworn dwelling in Guernsey being personally present at all and singular the premises. In testimony of the truth thereof have hereto set my hand and seal of office at Guernsey Island (where stamps are not used) being thereunto required.

[signed] Isaac Dobrée Not. Pub

APPENDIX 7

CONDEMNATION OF *L'HEUREUX*

The final act of a condemnation took place in the dining room off the main chamber of Doctors Commons and was summarised in a relatively brief document. The legal phraseology might seem long-winded, and the clerks who copied the text, being paid by the copy, earned their fees.

- The captured ship and her master are named
- The captor/s are named
- No one has appeared to express interest in the capture
- This 'contumacious behaviour' has left the Judge no option but to condemn the captured ship
- This captured ship was a private ship of war with seventy-six men alive on board

***

In the name of God Amen. We Sir Thomas Salusbury Knight Doctor of Laws Judge President or Lieutenant of the High Court of Admiralty of England lawfully appointed having heard seen and understood and fully and maturely discussed the merits and circumstances of a certain business of taking or seizing of a certain ship called L'Heureux whereof Pierre Crespin formerly was Master but at the time of the capture Richard Thomas was commander, her tackle apparel and furniture and the goods therein by his Majesty's ships of war the Tartar whereof John Lockhart Esquire was Commander and the Happy whereof Thomas Burnett Esquire was commander and carried into the Island of Guernsey which lately was and still is depending in judgement before us on the part and behalf of our Sovereign Lord George the Second by the grace of God King of Great Britain France and Ireland against the said ship L'Heureux her tackle apparel and furniture and the goods taken therein and against all persons in general who have or pretend to have any right title or interest in the said ship or goods and We rightly and duly proceeding therein and our said Sovereign Lord the King appearing before us by his proctor who prayed sentence to be given and justice to be done to his party and all others in general having or pretending to have any right title or interest in the said ship or goods being heretofore duly and legally cited intimated called and not appearing but contumaciously absenting themselves and pronounced contumacious in pain of the contempt of the parties so cited and not appearing having first enquired into and duly considered of the whole proceedings had and done before us in the said business and having observed what by law ought to be observed in this behalf have thought fit and do think fit thus to proceed to the giving and promulging of our definitive sentence or final decree in the said business in manner and form following that is to say forasmuch as we have by the acts enacted deduced alledged pleaded propounded and proved in the said business found and thereby discovered that the proctor of our said Sovereign Lord the King have sufficiently founded his intention deduced in a certain allegation given in and admitted on his behalf in the said business and now remaining in the Registry of this Court which said allegation and other matters propounded exhibited and admitted We take and ought to be taken as if here read and inserted for us to pronounce for the condemnation of the said ship her tackle apparel and furniture and the goods therein as a ship and goods belonging to the French King his vassals or subjects enemies of the Crown of Great Britain as hereafter mentioned and that nothing at least effectual hath been accepted deduced alledged pleaded propounded or proved by any person whatsoever which may or can any ways defeat prejudice or weaken the intention of the proctor of our said Sovereign Lord the King therefore we Sir Thomas Salusbury Knight Doctor of Laws the Judge aforesaid first calling on the name of Christ and having God alone before our eyes and having heard Council learned in the law thereupon do hereby pronounce decree and declare that the said ship called L'Heureux and her tackle apparel and furniture and the goods therein were rightly and duly taken and seized by his Majesty's said ships of war the Tartar whereof John Lockhart Esquire was Commander and the Happy whereof Thomas Burnett Esquire was commander and the officers mariners and others then being in the service of the said ships the Tartar and Happy and that the said ship L'Heureux her tackle apparel and furniture and the goods therein did at the time of the capture and seizure thereof as far as appears to us belong to the French King his vassals or subjects enemies to the Crown of Great Britain and as such ought to be accounted and reputed liable and subject to confiscation and to be adjudged and condemned as and for good and lawful prize and we do also pronounce decree and declare that the said ship L'Heureux was and is a private ship of war and had a commission on board from the French King to act as such and that she was taken in fight by his Majesty's ships of war the Tartar whereof John Lockhart was commander and the Happy whereof Thomas Burnett Esquire is commander and that the said private ship of war L'Heureux had alive and on board her at the beginning of the engagement between them seventy six men and we do adjudge and condemn the said ship her tackle apparel and furniture and the goods therein taken as and for good and lawful prize as being a private ship of war and goods of the enemies of the crown of Great Britain or otherwise liable to confiscation by this our definitive sentence or final decree which we read and promulge by these presents.

Thomas Salusbury

Edward Simpson

This sentence was read promulged and signed by the Judge aforesaid on Thursday the fourth day of November in the year of our Lord one thousand seven hundred and fifty six in the dining room near the Common Hall of Doctors Commons London (the Court being adjourned from the said Hall) in presence of the two credible witnesses named in the act of Court
Which I attest
George Bellas Notary Publick
Deputy Registrar[1]

1 TNA HCA 34/37 55.

APPENDIX 8

DOCUMENTATION AUTHORISING PAYMENT OF HEAD MONEY[1]

Once the prize had been condemned, the agents were responsible for applying for the Bounty or Head Money due to their clients. They had to provide copies of the necessary documents:

- The proof of condemnation
- The proof of the number of men involved in the prize
- The Power of Attorney from both crews
- The certified muster lists from both crews
- A reminder of the Act by which Bounty was to be paid
- A statement by Samuel Seddon, the Admiralty's Solicitor, that the documentation was complete
- The Treasury confirming that no flag officer had claimed a share within the fifteen days' grace allowed
- The deposition by the master of *L'Heureuse* that there had been seventy-six men on board at the time of the capture

***

[On the cover of the little parcel of papers]
Received the 22nd April 1757
No 395 extra
William Redstone, James Bensley, Charles Brett and Philip Stephens
Bounty to the Tartar and Happy sloop for taking the Heureux a French privateer
£380 0s 0d

The state of the case of William Redstone, James Bensley, Charles Brett and Philip Stephens Esq claiming payment of Bounty Money at £5 per head for 76 men taken in the L'Heureuse a French privateer by his Majesty's ship

[1] TNA HCA 43/14.

the Tartar Captain John Lockhart Commander and the Happy sloop Captain Thomas Burnett Commander on 16th September 1756.
They have produced
The proof of condemnation dated the 20th December 1756
The Mayor of Plymouth's certificate for 76 men
Letters of attorney from the Captains, officers and companies of the Tartar and the Happy sloop appointing them agents
Lists of the said ship's officers and sloop's companies certified as usual.

To the Honourable Commissioners of his Majesty's navy
By a clause in the Act of Parliament passed in the 29th year of his majesty's reign (p571) it is directed that the Bill or Bills to be made out for the Bounty thereby granted to the Commanders, officers, seamen, marines, soldiers and others of his Majesty's ships of war for taking, sinking, burning or otherwise destroying any ships of war or privateer belonging to such person or persons as shall be authorised and appointed by the flag officers, ships, companies or ships company and others entitled thereunto, in like manner as is directed for the nominating and appointing agents for appraisements and sales and by the clause relating to the appointment of agents for appraisals and sales (p565 and 566) wares or merchandize as shall be taken by any of his Majesty's ships of war shall be made by agents or persons nominated and appointed in equal numbers by the Flag Officers or Flag Officer, captains or captain, officer or officer, ships companies or ships company and others entitled thereunto (that is to say) that if the Flag Officers or Flag Officer of any fleet or squadron of ships as shall take any such, shall nominate and appoint one or more person or persons, agent or agents to sell or appraise the same, then the Captains and Commanders or captain and commander entitled thereunto or the majority of them (if more than one) shall nominate and appoint the like number of persons or agents to act for them; and all the other officers under the degree of a captain and commander entitled thereunto or the major part of them shall also nominate and appoint the like number of persons or agents to act for them and all the crews of the several ships companies of the fleet or squadron, or ships company and others entitled thereunto or the major part of them shall likewise nominate and appoint the same number of persons or agents to act on their behalf in such appraisement or sale.
There is no appointment of an agent or agents by any Flag Officer produced in the present case nor is there a Flag Officer's name mentioned in any of the papers relating thereto. Query whether a Bill may be made out for their Bounty in the names of William Redstone, James Bensley, Charles Brett and Philip Stephens Esquires as agents of the captains, officers and companies of the Tartar and Happy sloop only.

I humbly certify that I have perused this state of the case, with the proofs of William Redstone, James Bensley, Charles Brett and Philip Stephens, claiming Bounty money for seventy six men taken in the L'Heureuse a French privateer by his Majesty's ship the Tartar, Captain John Lockhart Commander, and the Happy sloop, Captain Thomas Burnett Commander; and that I have no objection to any of the said proofs, nor to making out a Bill to the said Messrs William Redstone, James Bensley, Charles Brett and Philip Stephens, for the Bounty money claimed by them as agents only for the respective captains, officers and companies of the said ship Tartar and the said Happy sloop; provided no claim to any part of the said Bounty money shall be made and delivered to your Honour, by or on behalf of any Flag Officer, before such Bill shall be actually made out and delivered to the said Agents, pursuant to the directives of the abovementioned Act of Parliament, with respect to the time within which such Bill should be made out. I am with great respect, gentlemen, your Honours most humble and most obedient servant [signed] Samuel Seddon Pickadilly 29th March 1757.[2]

2 April 1757 The papers in support of the claim aforementioned having been delivered into this office upward of 15 days (the time prescribed by Act of Parliament for making out Bills for Head money) and no claim having been made to us on behalf of any Flag Officer for any part of this Bounty Let a Bill be made out for the same to Messrs William Redstone, James Bensley, Charles Brett and Philip Stephens as agents only for the Captains, Officers and Companies of the Tartar and Happy sloop agreeable to Mr Seddon's opinion. [initialled] GL. [George Lee, Commissioner 1742–44] JJ. GV.

Received back into my custody the lists of the Captors names with their letter of attorney appointing the agents aforementioned.

[On sheet of stamped paper]
Devon to wit Borough of Plymouth
I Thomas Bewes esquire Mayor of the Borough aforesaid in pursuance of a late act of parliament do hereby certify unto the Right Honourable the Commissioners of his Majesties navy that on this present day being the twenty third day of September in the year of our Lord one thousand seven hundred fifty and six Richard Thomas Bell late first captain Jacob Joseph Laterre late second captain and Jean Claude Pean late first lieutenant of a French privateer called the Heureuse late of St Malo came and personally appeared before me the said Mayor and did then and there freely and voluntarily by

2 Samuel Seddon was the Admiralty Solicitor, here authorising the payment of Head Money by the Treasury.

the interpretation of Orlando Manley of Plymouth aforesaid goldsmith in this behalf duly sworn severally depose and swear on the holy Evangelists of God in the manner following (that is to say) that the said ship Heureuse was on the sixteenth day of this instant September taken and seized as prize by his Britannick Majesties ship of war the Tartar under the command of John Lockhart Esquire by or in company with his Britannick Majesties sloop of war the Happy under the command of Thomas Burnett Esquire who have since sent in and brought these deponents with their said ship Heureuse into the port of Plymouth which was the first port these deponents were landed at after they were taken as aforesaid and that the said ship Heureuse was at the time of her capture a French privateer or a French private ship of war and these deponents were the chief officers then belonging to her and these deponents further say that there did really belong unto and were living on board the said ship Heureuse at the time of her being taken as aforesaid seventy six men with these deponents In witness thereof the said Mayor have hereunto subscribed my name and set my seal of office of Mayoralty this twenty third day of September in the year of our Lord one thousand seven hundred and fifty six.
[signed]
Richard Henry Bell Thomas Bewes Mayor
Jacob Laterre
J. Claude Pean
Orlando Manley
Interpreter

APPENDIX 9

POMPEY CONDEMNED AS A DROIT[1]

The court records compiled by William Burrell are indispensable to a researcher into the legal world of naval prizes in the eighteenth century. He provides the barest outline of the cases he quotes, but for each example there is just enough to give a flavour of the legal point at issue, and the justification behind the judgement.

In this case the master of the merchant vessel *Pompey*, smuggling goods from Monte Christi to Philadelphia, needed to conceal the fact that she was carrying contraband. He had made an agreement with the master of the privateer *Charming Sally*, to pretend that she had been taken, and was a prize. As a prize the *Pompey* would normally have been exempt from search by the small British squadron in the West Indies. John Lindsay, *Trent* (28), was suspicious and took possession of both vessels. He returned to Jamaica with *Pompey* and declared her his prize for having broken the law.

The law in this case was clear. The *Pompey* had colluded with the *Charming Sally* and had pretended to have been captured. The evidence that emerged in the interrogation of the master was damning. *Pompey* had been provided with a copy of *Charming Sally*'s commission. This however did not protect her, but was the evidence of her collusion.

The monition for John Lindsay's case to be heard in Jamaica was dated 21 December 1761. On 19 March 1762, only three months later, the vessel was confiscated and declared a Droit, with one half of the value of her sale going to the King, the other half to John Lindsay.

The owners of *Pompey* appealed, and in London on 9 July 1763 their appeal was rejected.

Exactly the same sequence of events occurred in the case of *Belle Savage*, whose appeal was rejected on the same day.

1 Burrell, *Reports of Cases*, 194–5.

The Pompey was taken by the Trent, man of war, on a voyage from Monte Christi to Philadelphia, and carried into Jamaica. 21st December, 1761, a monition issued at the suit of the captor to show cause why the ship and cargo should not be adjudged forfeited, one half to the King, one half to the captors, by reason of the master having suffered his ship and cargo to be taken by the Charming Sally, privateer, by collusion and contrary to the statute 29 Geo.2. A libel was filed by the Advocate-General, setting forth that by the said Act, "In case any ship or goods shall be taken by any privateer through context or clandestinely, or by collusion and contrivance, such ship and goods, and also such privateer, shall upon proof thereof made in His Majesty's Court of Exchequer, or in a Court of Admiralty, by declared to be good prize to His Majesty, one half to the use of His Majesty, one half to the use of such person who shall discover and sue for the same."

Claim was given by the master, who was examined in interrogatories filed for the informant, and deposed that, being apprehensive of being seized by an English privateer which was cruising off the harbour of Monte Christi, he applied to the master of another privateer which was lying off the harbour, and obtained from him a copy of his commission to protect him from capture but there was no real capture of his ship by said privateer, and that on his being brought to by the Trent, he produced said commission of the Charming Sally, privateer, and said that the Pompey was a prize to the Charming Sally, though in truth never taken by her, but it was a contrivance between the masters of the Pompey and Sally to protect the Pompey from being taken._

19th March 1762. The Judge of the Vice Admiralty Court at Jamaica decreed the sloop Pompey and her cargo to be confiscated, pursuant to 29 Geo., in the Libel recited, and condemned one-half to the King and one-half to the captor. 9th July 1763. On appeal, the Lords dismissed the appeal for want of jurisdiction.

The Belle Savage to the same purpose, 9 July 1763.

APPENDIX 10

APPEAL: CAPTAIN THOMAS BURNETT AND *THE TWO BROTHERS*

The first part (1) of this evidence comes from the files of Lord Colville, ADM 1/482. His papers are complete and give condemnation of the vessel, followed by the financial breakdown of the proceeds of the sale of *The Two Brothers* and her cargo, and also the costs involved.[1]

Burnett, perhaps having recognised the brothers Le Roy, Nicholas Le Mesurier and James Major from his years based in Guernsey acting against smugglers, seized the ship notwithstanding the customs dues paid. Despite permission having been given by Murray, the Governor of Quebec, for the cargo to be unloaded there, Burnett 'scuttled the decks' to remove the brandy, took the vessel to Halifax, out of Murray's jurisdiction, and libelled her in the Vice Admiralty Court in Halifax. There she was condemned and sold, as detailed below.

Instigated by Lloyd's, which had insured the vessel, the owners and master of *The Two Brothers* appealed 2 June 1762. The Judicial Committee in London reversed the sentence of condemnation, and the ship and cargo were ordered to be restored 16 March 1763. What happened next? Was Burnett ordered to refund the value of the vessel and her cargo? Not much of the brandy would have survived. Was the slush fund invoked?

Section (2) is from the printed reports of the Privy Council's Appeal cases on the shelves of the Reading Room in the National Archives.

1 This condemnation attracted the attention of a twentieth-century lawyer who chose to use this case as an exemplar of the high-handed behaviour of Britain in relation to her colonies. Renwick Riddell's argument was not that the 'bootlegging' he described was not punished, it was that the case was removed from a Canadian court to a British one so that Britain would benefit, claiming that 'the ultimate cause of this seizure was the same as the ultimate cause of the American Revolution itself'. William Renwick Riddell, LL.D., D.C.L., F.R.C.S. etc., 'Appeals to the Privy Council', in *The Empire Club of Canada Speeches 1927* (Toronto, 1928), 57–85.

(1)

Letter from Lord Colville 17 January 1762 to John Clevland, Secretary.[2]

Sir,

Captain Francis of the *Greyhound* ... brought with him to this place, a Brigantine and a Schooner, which he had detained on account of carrying on a clandestine or illicit trade. And Captain Burnett of the *Rochester*, at the Isle of Bic, took possession of a snow from Guernsey for Quebec, which he also brought into this place. All three were tried in the Court of Admiralty; and I enclose Copies of their Condemnation, as given me by Mr Collier, the Judge of that Court.

It has been customary in North America, for the Courts of the Admiralty to divide the Produce arising for these sort of Captures into three equal Parts and to adjudge one to the King, one to the captor and one to the Governour or Commander-in-Chief where the trial is held. The King's share has been claimed, sometimes by the Collector of the Customs, sometimes by the Governour and in 1755 Admiral Boscawen received Part of the Produce of some Vessels seized by Captains Rous and Hankerson at Newfoundland, when Captain Dorril was Governour of that Island. In the present Case the King's share of the Brigantine taken by Captain Francis was paid in deposit only, besides his own third, to Mr Belcher, Chief Justice and Commander-in-Chief of the Province; but the King's Third of the other Two at my request remains in custody of the Court.

I believe my Reasons for making this Address will be sufficiently obvious, without mentioning them. I humbly beg the Favour of their Lordships to recommend me to his Majesty, for his share of these three captures. The Bounty will be most thankfully received, and my Obligations to their Lordships ever gratefully remembered.[3]

Nova Scotia
Court of Vice Admiralty

In the name of God Amen
We John Collins, Esq., Judge of his Majesty's
Court of Vice Admiralty for the Province of
Nova Scotia aforesaid, and the Maritime part
thereunto belonging

2 ADM 1/482 correspondence of Lord Colville with the Admiralty; also available at http://ngb.chebucto.org/Articles/colville-1762.shtml

3 This was not the first request Lord Colville had made to be given some financial perquisite. He would have been very short of money, as he had status to maintain. When he returned to London he applied for his pay for the years from September 1759 until October 1762, and Clevland's response was 'Navy Board to pay it without a moments loss of time, his Lordship being ordered upon voyage. Let his Lordship know.'

Having heard, seen and maturely considered the merits and circumstances other certain libel exhibited to this court by William Nesbit Esq. his Majesty's Advocate General in the said Court in the name of Henry Newton Esq. Collector of his Majesty's Customs for the Province aforesaid for and on the behalf of his said Majesty, and of Thomas Burnett Esq Commander of his Majesty's ship *Rochester* against a certain Snow called the Two Brothers Nicolas le Mesurier Master and her Cargo seized in the Port of Halifax in the Province aforesaid, by the said Thomas Burnett for clandestine and illicit Trade having Imported (as in therein alleged) at the Isle of Bic in the River St Lawrence, a place now in his Majesty's Possession and within the Jurisdiction of this Court, a quantity of Wine and other Goods and Merchandise of the Growth, Produce or Manufacture of Europe, not having been ship'd in England Principality of Wales or Town of Berwick upon Tweed, contrary to the statute in that Case made and Provided, and all parties Concerned having been by due process informed of the said Libel and Cited to appear in the said Court at a day for that Purpose appointed, then and there to assert their rights to the said Snow and her Cargo, James Major Supercargo of the said Snow Two Brothers and her Cargo in his own proper person appeared in the said Court, and for and on the behalf of James le Roy Merchant, Native and Inhabitant of the Island of Guernsey Claimed all and every part of the cargo Laden on board said Snow, except 31 hogsheads of White Wine, one Case of Capers, one case of Olives, four bales of Almonds, five hogsheads of Red Wine, one box of Hungary Water, six small barrels of March, three butts of Cider, 50 dozen pair of Hose and four hogshead more of Red Wine, which the said James Major did claim as his own private property, with the reservation also of Claim for private Adventure, and the said Nicholas le Mesurier the master of the said Snow Two Brothers in his own proper person appeared in the said Court and for, and on the behalf of James Le Roy and John Le Roy of the Island of Guernsey Merchants claimed the said Snow Two Brothers with all her Guns, Rigging, Tackle, Apparel and Furniture as libel'd; as the Property of the said James and John Le Roy, with a reservation of Claim of private adventure as by the said Several Claims now on File may appear; and Sundry papers having been Produced and Exhibited, and several Witnesses having been Sworn and Examined in open Court, as well in Support of the said libel as by the said Claimants in Support of their Several Claims: it appear'd thereby to us that there had been imported in the said Snow Two Brothers at the Isle of Bic in the River St Lawrence, a place being in the possession of his Majesty, a quantity of Wines and other Goods, the Growth Produce or Manufacture of Europe, not having been ship'd in England, Principality of Wales or Town of Berwick on Tweed, as by Law is required; but in the Island of Guernsey aforesaid, in open and Manifest Violation of the Statute in that case and provided; and all matters and things requisite for a fair and Impartial hearing and Tryall of the Premises having been duly attended to –

We do pronounce this our Sentence and decree thereon as follows,

We do adjudge and decree this said Snow Two Brothers together with all her Guns, Tackle, Ammunition, Apparel and Furniture, as also all and Singular the Goods, Wares and Merchandize of the Growth, Produce or Manufacture of Europe: the Cargo thereof to be forfeited, and do Condemn the same as forfeited accordingly, and we do further order that the said Snow Two Brothers together with her Guns, Tackle, Apparel, Ammunition and Furniture, as also all the Several Goods and Merchandize, her Cargo by us Condemn'd as aforesaid, be sold by the Marshal of this Court or his Deputy at Public Auction, the said Snow and her appurtenances as also the several Goods and Merchandise, her Cargo being first appraised on Oath by three persons to be by us appointed, and the Monies arising by the Sales thereof, to be paid into the hands of the Register of the said Court, to be by him paid and distributed in manner following, (that is to say Court and Incident Charges first deducted) one third to the use of his Majesty his heirs and successors, one other third part thereof to the Honourable Jonathan Belcher Esq. Commander-in-Chief of this Province, and the Remaining third part thereof the said Thomas Burnett Esq. commander of his Majesty's ship Rochester aforesaid, the informer against the said Snow and her Cargo.
Given under our hand and the Seal of the said Court this 23rd day of September in the first year of his Majesty's reign, and in the year of our Lord 1761.

Signed John Collier.

Table 10. *Two Brothers* sale and receipts.

Amount received from sale of the *Two Brothers*

				£	s	d
The amount of Sales of the Snow Two Bothers				400	0	0
Marshall's commission 2 per cent				8	0	0
				392	0	0
Charges to be deducted						
Condemnation fees	20	0	0			
Poundage 5 per cent	19	12	0			
Balance Mariners wages	58	4	11			
To the Register, Settling and adjusting the Acc/t of wages, whole Amount being £93	2	6	6			
Warrant of appraisement	0	9	0			

3 appraisers 20/- each	3	0	0			
To Mr James Major for Pilotage	13	17	10			
Marshall's bill, Custody, wharfage labour etc	16	17	4			
Waiters bill custody from 3 Sep to 1 Oct at 5/per day	7	5	0			
Light money	2	10	0	143	12	7
				248	7	5
Settlement and distribution						
1/3 to his Majesty	82	15	9			
1/3 to the Governor or Commander in Chief	82	15	9			
1/3 to the prosecutor thereof	82	15	9			
				248	7	4

Allow'd
(Signed) John Collier

A true Copy examined
(Signed) Chas Morris jun'r Deputy Registrar

Table 11. Receipts from sale of cargo of *Two Brothers*, expended and distributed.

Sales of Cargo of *Two Brothers* amounts received, expended and distributed

				£	s	d
The Amount of Sales of the cargo of Snow Two Brothers				2960	2	2
Marshall's Commission 2 per cent				59	4	0
				2900	18	0
Charges to be deducted						
Condemnation fees 5 per cent	148	0	1			
Poundage 5 per cent	145	0	10			
Warrant of Appraisement	0	9	0			
Appraisers 8 days each	12	0	0			
Mr Gerrishe's bill Truckage	2	6	5			
Mr Creighton's bill ditto	6	10	9			
Mr McCulloch's bill ditto	1	6	7			

Mr MacNamarra's bill ditto	4	1	4			
Mr Gray's bill storage	9	16	5			
Mr Franklin's ditto	4	0	0			
Mr Heffernan's bill for Cooperage	5	4	0			
Mr England's bill ditto	2	14	10			
Mr Pierce's bill for gauging	5	5	8			
Cash paid by the Marshall for labourers	28	18	0			
Collectors bill	20	0	0			
Copying sundry papers for the use of the Prosecutors	3	6	8			
Advocate's fees 1 per cent	29	10	0			
James Brenton Proctor his bill	20	0	0	448	10	7
				2452	7	7
Settlement and distribution						
1/3 to his Majesty	817	9	2			
1/3 to the Governor or Commander in Chief	817	9	2			
1/3 to the prosecutor thereof	817	9	2	2452	7	7

Allowed
(Signed) John Collier J.A.

(2)
Acts of the Privy Council (Colonial)[4]
1762 2 June Nova Scotia
Reference to the Committee of the petition of James Major of Guernsey, for himself and James Le Roy of the same island, merchant, owners of the cargo of the snow *Two Brothers*, and of Nicholas Le Mesurier of the same island, late master of the said snow, for the owners James and John Le Roy, for a day for hearing their appeal from the condemnation of the vessel in the Vice Admiralty Court at Halifax, 23 Sept. 1761, at the instance of Henry Newton and Thomas Burnet.

1763 16 Mar.
On the committee report of 12 March, the sentence is reversed, and ship and cargo ordered to be restored. The case was heard *ex parte*, no appearance

4 This was obtained from the printed volumes of Acts of the Privy Council, 1762, 540–3.

having been made for the respondents. The petition set forth that the said snow is Plantation built, was duly registered and regularly manned and navigated according to Law and in May 1761 landed at Guernsey, a Cargo of Wine (part whereof was prize) some Brandy, Cider, and Stockings the produce and manufacture of Guernsey, and other things for Québec and for such goods as were Prize, the proper Certificate was obtained. That the said Snow sailed on 17th of May, but being by contrary Winds obliged to put into Plymouth, and finding the Antelope Man of War, Captain Le Mesurier put himself under her Convoy and was regularly searched paid the Port and other Charges, and Searchers Fees obtained the usual Permit and sailed with the Antelope, as far as the Banks of Newfoundland, and then steered the most direct course for the River St Lawrence, and on 19th of July 1761 arrived at the Isle of Beck in the said River but was prevented going higher by contrary winds whereupon Major agreed with one John Wynne of the Dolphin to come to the Isle of Beck for unloading the Snow of her Cargo (Brandys excepted) and on 29th July General Murray gave Wynne a Pass for that purpose and that Wynne went down and the Snows Cargo (Brandys excepted) on 1st August, began to be unloaded into his Sloop, when Captain Burnett of the Rochester Man of War came on board, and forceably seized the Snow and her Cargoe, though at the same time he was acquainted with the reason of unloading and shewn General Murrays permission and detained the Snow and her Cargo and that Captain Burnett carried her and her Cargo, out of the Jurisdiction where he seized her, to Halifax in Nova Scotia, And that on the 8th September 1761 Henry Newton ... exhibited a Libel against the Snow and her cargo in the Vice Admiralty Court at Halifax ... and ... prayed an order for the Snow and her cargo to be taken into Custody of the Marshall of the Court, and that the Snow was taken into the Marshall's Custody accordingly, and on 9th September, the Appellants, Major and Le Mesurier, claimed Ship and Cargo, and put in their answer to the Libel, insisting that the above Acts do not prohibit the importation of the Growth, Production or Manufacture of Europe, in Ships properly Navagated into any of His Majestys dominions subdued by Conquest for that during the present War Canada is not within the meaning of the Statutes, His Majesty not being restrained to rule it by any particular laws, but according to his pleasure, and that the Government of Canada had, from its conquest, been under the terms of Capitulation by such Proclamations, Military Rules, Orders and Regulations as his Majestys Governor there had thought proper for the Service of His Majesty. That the general not only permitted the importation of the Snows Cargo (Brandys excepted) but the Sale thereof, and that if it had been his Majestys Pleasure that the Acts of Trade should extend to this new Conquest, And that the Snow took in her loading at Guernsey a free port, where there is no Custom house Officer granting Coquets of clearances, and pursued the usual methods in loading the said vessel. And that the Captain did on his arrival at Plymouth, report to the Custom house there, his whole cargo, as in the Bill of Loading mentioned and paid all the fees in the port, And that there was no breaking of bulk or importation of any of the Cargo of the Snow until the above permission (vizt.) 1st of August 1761 and within the Jurisdiction of his Majesty's Governor at Québec and its dependencys and not within the Jurisdiction of the Court of Halifax, And that the Cause being at Issue, Captain Burnett on his Examination declared, that seeing the Sloop Dolphin alongside the Snow he went on board and was told they were unloading Wines out of the Snow into the Sloop by General Murrays orders, which were produced to him, together with the Light house Bill from Plymouth, and the Snows Register and other papers, and on his Cross Examination declared he did not see the Bulk broke before the first of August, but brought before that time, four dozen of Claret and three of Pruniac, and one of his Lieutenants told him the Master had informed him, they had been obliged to scuttle the Decks to get them. And that George Forbes Master of the Rochester, being examined confirmed the Captain's evidence, and said he had heard of some dozens of Wine coming on board the Rochester; that Captain Burnett did not tell him he seized the Snow for that Reason nor did he so understand it himself. That he heard the Master of the Sloop tell Captain Burnett he had orders from General Murray to take out of the Snow all her Cargo (Brandys excepted) and carry them to Québec and that on behalf of the Appellants sundry witnesses were examined who deposed as before stated, And that on 23rd of September 1761 the Judge decreed the ship and cargo forfeited and ordered the same to be sold at publick Sale by the Marshall of the Court, or his Deputy, having first been duly appraised ... And that the Snow and her Cargo have been sold pursuant to the Sentence and the Nett proceeds thereof amount to the sum of 3178 pounds 12 shillings 7¼ p Nova Scotia currency.

APPENDIX 11

THE SALE OF ELEMENTS OF THE CARGO OF *ST PIERRE*

The only agent's papers found were those of Richard Drakeford, but as these were so nearly contemporaneous and give a flavour of the many and varied elements of accounting required, the first five pages of an example are displayed here.[1]

The accounts were entered in a hard-backed ledger, with a very formal title:

> **St Pierre Accounts**
>
> Between W&B Jasper
>
> Mr Trevanion
>
> and myself
>
> 1744
>
> An Account of goods delivered to the Buyers of La St Pierre sold at Gosport by Publick Sale the 1st September 1744 taken by his Majesties Ship the Kinsale Robert Young Esq. Commander
>
> William and Benjamin Vaughan Brokers

On the cover of the ledger was recorded the prices:

> Price of indigo £4 1s per hundredweight; coffee £6 11s or £6 10s per hundredweight; sugar 5s per pound; cotton 16p per pound

- The cargo being sold here was sugar, coffee and indigo
- The quantities were hundredweights, quarters and pounds, where 112 pounds made 1 hundredweight, and 28 pounds made 1 quarter

1 Staffordshire Archives D1798/HM Drakeford 13.

- A pipe was a measure of wine, holding two hogsheads or 125 gallons
- Casks held liquid or solid goods
- 'Tare' indicates the weight of the barrel as opposed to its contents
- The agent charged 2½ per cent on the value of every sale
- The number of dealers, agents and associates is evidence of the wide network of businesses involved in trade
- The sale of the cargo took place on 1 September, with payment for the different elements coming in over subsequent weeks

Table 12. The prize agent's record of the receipts from *St Pierre*'s cargo.

Gosport September the 20th Anno 1744 Received of Mr Samuel Storke and Son for 4 lots indigo viz.

	cwts	**qtrs**	**lbs**	**tare**		**£**	**s**	**d**	**£**	**s**	**d**
Lot 77 a pipe	8	2	23	131							
	1		24	5	Draft						
	7	1	27		is 839 lbs at 4s 1d per lb				171	5	11
Lot 78 a cask	5	2	23	86							
ditto	2		26	48							
Lot 81 a cask	3		6	48							
ditto	2	3	5	59							
ditto	2	2	27	58							
Lot 82 ditto	1	3	18	54							
ditto	3		2	53							
ditto	3	2	0	52							
	24	3	23	468							
	4	1	3	11	Draft and Tare						
	20	2	20		is 2316 lbs at 4s 0d				463	5	0
									634	10	11
					Discount 2 ½ per cent				15	17	3
									618	13	8
Received deposit on 4 Lots						42	0	0			

Cash	105	0	0
Per Samuel Storke and his Bill on Spurling for	471	13	8
	618	13	8

Oct 6 1744 Received of Mr Samuel Storke by Mr John Rickman 1 Lott of sugar viz:

Lot 59 6 hogsheads	49	2	4							
			6	draft						
	49	1	26							
	6	0	21	Tare and Draft						
	43	1	5	neat sugar						
					At 65p per hundredweight			140	14	2
					Discount 2 ½ per cent			3	10	6
								137	3	8

Received deposits on the above Lot	10	0	0
per Arch. Bontoin Jn draft on John Walkinshaw			
to John Rickman at 3 days sight	31	10	0
per Holles Murray's draft on ditto to ditto			
at 3 days sight	21	0	0
per Robert Arnott's draft on Capt. Alexander Wilson			
to John Rickman at 3 days sight	35	0	0

per Maurice Tyrrol's draft on ditto to ditto			
at 3 days sight	17	0	0
By cash	22	3	8
	137	3	8

Oct 8 1744 Received from Mr Philip Titcher Jn for twenty barrels of coffee and two casks of indigo viz:

Lots No 69 and 71	33	0	0	574				
	5	1	26	40	Draft Tare and Super Tare			
	27	2	2		coffee at £6 10s per lb	180	4	10
Lot No 79 indigo cask	3	2	3	66				
	4	3	2	68				
	8	1	5	134				
	1	0	25	3	Draft and Tare			
	7	0	8		is 792 lbs at 4s	161	14	0
						341	18	10
					Discount 2 ½ per cent	8	11	0
						333	7	10

Paid Titcher bills on W. Stapps	222	0	0
Cash	111	7	10
	333	7	10

Oct. 25 1744 Received from Mr George Mackenzie for the ship St Pierre her tackle, apparrell and furniture

as per inventory				800	0	0
By his Bills on George ?? for deposit	200	0	0			
by ditto in full at 30 days date	600	0	0			
	800	0	0			

Nov 4 1744 Received of Mr William Vaughan for six Lots of coffee viz:[2]

Lots 61, 64, 65 68	65	1	5	756				
	6	3	22	22	Draft and Tare			
	58	1	11					
		1	5		Super Tare			
	58	0	6		neat coffee at £6 10s 0d per lb	377	7	0
Lots 73 and 74	35	3	1	629				
	5	3	25	40	Draft Tare and Super Tare			
	29	3	4		neat coffee at £6 10s 0d per lb	193	12	2
						570	19	2
					Discount 2 ½ per cent	14	5	6
						556	13	8

2 The original shows figures for separate Lots.

Received Deposits on the above 6 Lots	63	0	0
By Bank Post Bills	409	6	7
Mr Vaughan Deposit in Bank Post Bill	84	7	1
	556	13	8

APPENDIX 12

DISTRIBUTION OF PRIZE MONEY[1]

The document illustrated below is not in its final form, but it conveys sufficient information to enhance our understanding of the way in which this vital operation worked.

Once the sale of *St Pierre* and her cargo had been completed, the distribution of the proceeds could take place.

The Power of Attorney form provided the names of the officers and men on board the *Kinsale*. The muster book would provide the 'department' into which every individual was ranked. The agent organised the list into the 'departments' or rankings which received the shares.

Within each department the names were sorted alphabetically to make the distribution easier.

- Three eighths went to the captain: £2,343 17s 9d
- One eighth went to each of the lesser departments, the eighth being divided into smaller and smaller portions: Division 2 officers each received £192 15s 2¾d
- Division 3 warrant officers each received £96 7s 7¼d
- Division 4 petty officers each received £32 2s 6¼d
- Division 5 was the remainder of the crew. Their much larger numbers meant each received only £7 8s 11¾d

There were 245 names on the distribution list:

- Forty-two (seventeen per cent) received nothing:
- Six (two per cent) of these had died (DD) before taking the prize
- Twenty-two (seventeen per cent) had deserted (D) or (R)
- Two had been discharged to sick quarters (DSQ)

1 Staffordshire Archives D1798/HM Drakeford/11. Most readers will never have seen a farthing, and would not easily visualise the problems faced by the agent handling hundreds of those tiny quarters of a penny.

- Of the two supernumeraries, one received a share, the other did not
- Fourteen (six per cent) have nothing against their names
- Three have been entered as though eligible to receive prize money, without an attorney being named
- Only five (two per cent) individuals took possession of their own money
- Family members picked up shares sixteen times, between ten wives, two mothers, two fathers, a sister and a brother
- Attorneys were involved thirty-three times (13.5 per cent), many of those on behalf of further agents. What further deductions were made?
- Seventy-two men (thirty per cent) used J. Vincent
- Twenty-four (ten per cent) used Edward Jasper
- Twenty-two (nine per cent) used J. Malraven
- Seventeen (seven per cent) used B. Bechinoe
- Richard Drakeford was used once, as was James Henshaw and Oliver Toulmin
- The captain's brother, Hasden Young, despite being denied the entire agency, still collected for two senior warrant officers and was agent for a marine
- Francis Courtenay, Clerk, collected not only for himself but also for two others
- Six of the husbands whose wives collected for them were warrant or petty officers

Table 13. Distribution of prize money to *Kinsale*'s officers and crew.

Received of John Trevanion the several sums against our names expressed being our respective shares of the prize of the St Pierre we say received by our selves and representatives in full

Name	**Rank**	**Full sum**	**Paid before**	**Remainder**	**Collected by**
1					
Robert Young	Captain	2343 17s 9d		2343 17s 9d	as per his receipts
2					
Thomas Cross	1st Lieut.	192 15s $2^{3/4}$d		192 15s $2^{3/4}$d	Edward Jasper Attn
Charles Chasemore	3rd Lt.	192 15s $2^{3/4}$d		192 15s $2^{3/4}$d	E. Jasper Charles Chasemore
Thomas Foley	2nd Lt.	192 15s $2^{3/4}$d	17 16s $3^{1/4}$d	174 18s 6d	J. Vincent Attn
John Smith	Master	192 15s $2^{3/4}$d	81	111 15s $2^{3/4}$d	Margaret Smith Wife & Attn
3					
Dutton Richard	Boatswain	96 7s $7^{1/4}$d	96 7s $7^{1/4}$d		Edward Jasper
Jones Morgan	M. Mate	96 7s $7^{1/4}$d		96 7s $7^{1/4}$d	Hasden Young Attn
Hickes Israel	Gunner	96 7s $7^{1/4}$d	21	75 7s $7^{1/4}$d	J. Vincent for Geo. Orchard Attn
Kirks John	Surgeon	96 7s $7^{1/4}$d		96 7s $7^{1/4}$d	Robert Sporle Attn
Knowles Matthew	Lt. Marine	96 7s $7^{1/4}$d		96 7s $7^{1/4}$d	J. Vincent for J. Reynolds Attn
Lee John	M. Mate	96 7s $7^{1/4}$d	21	75 7s $7^{1/4}$d	B. Bechinoe for wife Hester Attn

Martin John	Carpenter	96 7s 7¼d	40	56 7s 7¼d	William Martin brother Attn
Parker Robert	Purser	96 7s 7¼d	21	75 7s 7¼d	J. Henshaw Ass
4					
Burthenshaw John (1)	Surgn mate	32 2s 6¼d		32 2s 6¼d	J. Vincent Attn
Benn John	Boats mate	32 2s 6¼d		32 2s 6¼d	Eliz. Hickman Executor
Becket John	Midshipman	32 2s 6¼d	10 10s	21 12s 6¼d	Edw. Jasper for Eliz. Strong Attn
Cox Edward	Coxswain	32 2s 6¼d		32 2s 6¼d	J. Vincent for John Elford
Cudlipp William	Midshipman	32 2s 6¼d	14 14s	17 8s 6¼d	B. Bechinoe for sister Amy Attn
Courtenay Francis	Clerk	32 2s 6¼d		32 2s 6¼d	Francis Courtenay
Drake John	Yeo. Powd. Room	32 2s 6¼d	4 4s	27 18s 6¼d	Grace Drake wife and Attn
Darracot Thom. Blyth	Midshipman	32 2s 6¼d		32 2s 6¼d	Hasden Young Attn
Dunfer Richard	Carp. mate	32 2s 6¼d		32 2s 6¼d	M. Allenby Assoc.
Dean Thomas	Sergeant	32 2s 6¼d		32 2s 6¼d	J. Vincent for M. Kirkes
Jackson Robert	Gunners mate	32 2s 6¼d	14 14s	17 8s 6¼d	J. Vincent Attn
Franklyn Matthew	Midshipman	32 2s 6¼d	13 13s	18 9s 6¼d	Matthew Coles Attn
Knight Elias	Q.M. Mate	32 2s 6¼d	2 2s	30 0s 6¼d	J Vincent for wife Elizabeth Attn
Lowfield William	Midshipman	32 2s 6¼d	30 0s 0	2 2s 6¼d	William Lowfield father and Attn

Masters Abraham	Quarter Master				DD
Owen John	Surgn mate	32 2s 6 1/4d		32 2s 6 1/4d	John Owen
Rabson John	Quarter Master	32 2s 6 1/4d	2 2s	30 0s 6 1/4d	J. Vincent for Roger Brockenton Asst
Saunders William	Corporal				R
Shean Joseph	Quarter Master	32 2s 6 1/4d		32 2s 6 1/4d	Margaret Shean Wife and Attn
Stump James	Q.M. Mate	32 2s 6 1/4d		32 2s 6 1/4d	Jean Stump Wife and Attn
Tole Thomas	Yeoman of sheets	32 2s 6 1/4d	4 4s	27 18s 6 1/4d	Edward Jasper Attn
White John	Q.M. Mate	32 2s 6 1/4d	3 3s	28 19s 6 1/4d	R. Drakeford for David Iver Ass
Williams William	Boats mate	32 2s 6 1/4d		32 2s 6 1/4d	Elizabeth Williams Wife and Attn
Young Robert (2)	Midshipman	32 2s 6 1/4d		32 2s 6 1/4d	Prudence Young Wife and Attn
5					
Adams Nicholas	Ab paid	7 8s 11 3/4d		7 8s 11 3/4d	Robert Sporle for Wm Brent Ass
Airs William	Ab				R
Abrill Goodroth	Ab	7 8s 11 3/4d		7 8s 11 3/4d	Robert Darling for Michael Kelly Ass
Adams Thomas	Capts. Cook	7 8s 11 3/4d		7 8s 11 3/4d	J Malraven for Hugh Dixey Ass
Allen William	Ab				DD
Allen Thomas	Ab	7 8s 11 3/4d		7 8s 11 3/4d	George Rogby Ass
Burgess John	Armourer	7 8s 11 3/4d		7 8s 11 3/4d	B. Bechinoe for Ant. Underwood Exec

Breach William	Carpenters Crew	7 8s 11$^{3/4d}$		7 8s 11$^{3/4d}$	Edward Jasper for wife Mary Attn
Bull John	Ab	7 8s 11$^{3/4d}$		7 8s 11$^{3/4d}$	B. Bechinoe for William Drake Ass
Buckle Robert	Ord S	7 8s 11$^{3/4d}$		7 8s 11$^{3/4d}$	John Newton for M. Newton Ass
Buckley Henry	Ab	7 8s 11$^{3/4d}$		7 8s 11$^{3/4d}$	Hannah Buckley wife and Attn
Brickleton Edward	Ab				D
Billing John	Cook	7 8s 11$^{3/4d}$		7 8s 11$^{3/4d}$	B. Bechinoe for widow Ann exec
Burtenshaw John (2)	Capt. Serv.	7 8s 11$^{3/4d}$		7 8s 11$^{3/4d}$	Jn. Vincent for father John Attn
Blanch James	Ab	7 8s 11$^{3/4d}$	2 2s	7 8s 11$^{3/4d}$	J. Malraven for wife Mary Attn
Baker John	Ab	7 8s 11$^{3/4d}$			R
Bynham John (1)	Ab	7 8s 11$^{3/4d}$	4 4s	3 4s 11$^{3/4d}$	Jn. Vincent for wife Dorothy Attn
Bynham John (2)	Capt. Serv.	7 8s 11$^{3/4d}$	4 4s	3 4s 11$^{3/4d}$	Jn. Vincent for M Reynolds Attn
Bacchus John	Carp. Serv.				
Bury William	Bosn Serv.	7 8s 11$^{3/4d}$		7 8s 11$^{3/4d}$	J. Malraven for Hugh Dixey Attn
Bolton James	Marine	7 8s 11$^{3/4d}$		7 8s 11$^{3/4d}$	Jn. Vincent for John Kirkes Ass
Burgess William	Marine	7 8s 11$^{3/4d}$		7 8s 11$^{3/4d}$	J. Malraven for Hugh Dixey Attn
Butler Maurice	Marine	7 8s 11$^{3/4d}$		7 8s 11$^{3/4d}$	Jn. Vincent for John Kirkes Ass
Broadhurst John					
Brittain Adam	Marine	7 8s 11$^{3/4d}$		7 8s 11$^{3/4d}$	Jn. Vincent for A. Crosscombe Exec

Broad Thomas	Marine	7 8s 11 3/4d		7 8s 11 3/4d	Francis Courtenay for Anne Broad Exec.
Bragg John	Marine				
Carpenter Thomas	Ab	7 8s 11 3/4d	1 2s	6 6s 11 3/4d	J. Malraven for Hugh Dixey Attn
Cross James	Capt. Serv.				DD
Collins James (1)	Capt. Serv.	7 8s 11 3/4d	4 4s	3 4s 11 3/4d	Edward Jasper Attn
Carline John	Ab	7 8s 11 3/4d			Edward Jasper for M. Young Ass
Cooper John	Ab	7 8s 11 3/4d			Jn. Vincent for John Kirkes Ass
Chicke Martin	Ab				DSQ
Criming Cornelius	Ab	7 8s 11 3/4d			Jn. Vincent for Jos. Sussey Att
Cudlip Richard	Capt. Serv.	7 8s 11 3/4d			Thomas Warren for Thomas Moody Attn
Christy John	Quart.m. gunner	7 8s 11 3/4d			Edw. Jasper for David Ivor Ass
Clarke John	Ab	7 8s 11 3/4d	2 2s	5 6s 11 3/4d	JW ???
Cox Benjamin	Lts Servant	7 8s 11 3/4d			Ben Cox
Carpenter Jos.	Ab	7 8s 11 3/4d			Ann Carpenter Wife and Attn
Carnegy David	Ab	7 8s 11 3/4d			Jn. Vincent for M Brent Ass
Cummins Nicholas (2)	Gunner's serv.	7 8s 11 3/4d			Jn. Vincent for John Kirkes Ass
Conselaing Peter	Ab				R

Coles Thomas	Marine	7 8s 11 3/4d			Jn. Vincent for John Kirkes Ass
Cock John	Marine	7 8s 11 3/4d			Jn. Vincent for John Kirkes Ass
Cleaves Robert	Supernumerary				
Dequeller John	Ab	7 8s 11 3/4d		7 8s 11 3/4d	Catherine Gall Mother and Attn
Doe James	Ord.	7 8s 11 3/4d	4 4s	3 4s 11 3/4d	
Densele William	Ab	7 8s 11 3/4d		7 8s 11 3/4d	Susan Densele Wife and Attn
Downey John	Ab	7 8s 11 3/4d	2 2s	5 6s 11 3/4d	J. Malraven for Hugh Dixey Attn
Dunkin John	Ab	7 8s 11 3/4d		7 8s 11 3/4d	Robert Darling for Michael Kelley Ass.
Drew Robert	Ab				DD
Dent Henry	Ab	7 8s 11 3/4d		7 8s 11 3/4d	Edward Jasper for David Ives Ass
Dyson William	Ab	7 8s 11 3/4d			
Dunn Michael	Piper				DSQ
Donovan Corn.	Ord	7 8s 11 3/4d		7 8s 11 3/4d	John Vincent for John Kirke Ass
Dove Thomas	Quarter gunner	7 8s 11 3/4d		7 8s 11 3/4d	Elizabeth Dove, Wife and Att
Davis John	Ab	7 8s 11 3/4d		7 8s 11 3/4d	John Vincent for John Kirke Ass
Davis Nathaniel	Quarter gunner	7 8s 11 3/4d	2 2s	5 6s 11 3/4d	Jn. Vincent
Drake Thomas (2)	Ab	7 8s 11 3/4d			Edward Jasper Att.
Davis Edwards	Ord	7 8s 11 3/4d		7 8s 11 3/4d	John Vincent for John Kirke Ass
Davis Thomas	Ord	7 8s 11 3/4d	4 4s	3 4s 11 3/4d	Jn. Vincent?

Diamond John	Ab	7 8s 11 3/4d		7 8s 11 3/4d	John Vincent for Jn. Harris Ass
Dunn Richard	Ab	7 8s 11 3/4d			John Vincent Att
Davis Samuel	Marine	7 8s 11 3/4d		7 8s 11 3/4d	John Vincent for John Kirke Ass
Dynch John	Marine	7 8s 11 3/4d		7 8s 11 3/4d	John Vincent for Jn. Harris Ass
Ford Thomas	Ab	7 8s 11 3/4d		7 8s 11 3/4d	J. Malraven for Thomas Redman Att.
Fairly George	Ord				R
Falhurst Abraham	Ab				TP ?
Foster John	Ab				R
Ford Thomas	Marine	7 8s 11 3/4d		7 8s 11 3/4d	John Vincent for John Kirke Ass
Gifford John	Ab	7 8s 11 3/4d		7 8s 11 3/4d	J. Malraven for M. Surby Ass
Gribble James	Ab	7 8s 11 3/4d		7 8s 11 3/4d	J. Malraven for Hugh Dixey Attn
Grey William	Ord	7 8s 11 3/4d	4 4s	3 4s 11 3/4d	Edw. Jasper Att 4 4s more
Gilbert Thomas	Ab				R
Gillard William	Ord				R
Garnush John	Ab	7 8s 11 3/4d		7 8s 11 3/4d	John Brown Attorney
Gardner Allen	Marine	7 8s 11 3/4d		7 8s 11 3/4d	J. Vincent for John Kirke Ass
Herbert Henry	Ab	7 8s 11 3/4d	4 4s	3 3s 11 3/4d	B. Bechinoe for John Derby Ass.
Hodgson John	Shipwright				R
Harvey Edmond	Carp. Serv.	7 8s 11 3/4d		7 8s 11 3/4d	B. Bechinoe for ? Delacombe Ass
Harris Henry	Ab	7 8s 11 3/4d		7 8s 11 3/4d	Henry Harris

Hugh Thomas	Ab	7 8s 11 3/4d	4 4s	3 3s 11 3/4d	John Vincent for wife Sarah Att.
Hooper John	Ord	7 8s 11 3/4d	4 4s	3 3s 11 3/4d	B. Bechinoe for wife Mary Arr
Hounsell Abraham	Ab	7 8s 11 3/4d	4 4s	3 3s 11 3/4d	J. Malraven for Hugh Dixey Att
Hickey Patrick	Ord	7 8s 11 3/4d		7 8s 11 3/4d	Robert Darling for Michael Kelley Ass.
Harvey Nicholas	Ab	7 8s 11 3/4d		7 8s 11 3/4d	Robert Sporle for Wm Brent Ass
Higgons Thomas	Ord	7 8s 11 3/4d	4 4s	3 3s 11 3/4d	Edward Jasper Att
Hawkins Edward	Ord	7 8s 11 3/4d		7 8s 11 3/4d	Jn. Vincent for John Kirkes Ass
Hill Richard	Ab				R
Hickson Jos	Ab				R
Hutchinson John	Ord	7 8s 11 3/4d	2 2s	5 6s 11 3/4d	John Vincent
Hyde Richard	Ord	7 8s 11 3/4d		7 8s 11 3/4d	John Vincent for Wm Brent Ass
Hely Edward	Pursers Serv.	7 8s 11 3/4d		7 8s 11 3/4d	Mary Parkinson mother and Arr.
Hutchins Samuel	Ab				R
Harneman John	Ab	7 8s 11 3/4d		7 8s 11 3/4d	John Newton for John Newton Att
Hodge John	Ab	7 8s 11 3/4d		5 6s 11 3/4d	John Vincent Att
Harper William	Ab	7 8s 11 3/4d	4 4s	3 3s 11 3/4d	Edward Jasper Att.
Hambly Nat.	Gunners Serv.	7 8s 11 3/4d		7 8s 11 3/4d	John Vincent for John Kirkes Ass
Hunt John	Bosw. Serv.	7 8s 11 3/4d		7 8s 11 3/4d	J. Malraven for Hugh Dixey Att
Harris William	Marine	7 8s 11 3/4d		7 8s 11 3/4d	John Vincent for John Kirkes Ass

Hodge Walter	Marine	7 8s 11$^{3/4d}$		7 8s 11$^{3/4d}$	John Vincent for John Kirkes Ass
Harbour Levi	Marine	7 8s 11$^{3/4d}$		7 8s 11$^{3/4d}$	John Vincent for John Kirkes Ass
Hicks John	Marine	7 8s 11$^{3/4d}$	2 2s	5 6s 11$^{3/4d}$	John Vincent for John Harris Ass
Hebdon Thomas	Marine	7 8s 11$^{3/4d}$		7 8s 11$^{3/4d}$	J. Malraven for Hugh Dixey Att
Hughes Thomas	Marine	7 8s 11$^{3/4d}$		7 8s 11$^{3/4d}$	John Vincent for Wife Ann Att.
Hollimore John	Marine	7 8s 11$^{3/4d}$		7 8s 11$^{3/4d}$	John Vincent for John Kirkes Ass
Hill Christopher	Marine	7 8s 11$^{3/4d}$		7 8s 11$^{3/4d}$	John Vincent for John Kirkes Ass
Hunt Henry	Marine	7 8s 11$^{3/4d}$		7 8s 11$^{3/4d}$	John Vincent for John Kirkes Ass
Hollet William	Marine	7 8s 11$^{3/4d}$		7 8s 11$^{3/4d}$	B. Bechinoe for Ann Dunn Ass
Jones David	Ord				R
Jones Benjamin	Ord	7 8s 11$^{3/4d}$	4 4s	3 3s 11$^{3/4d}$	B. Bechinoe for wife Honour Att
Johnson Joseph	Masters Serv.				
Jenkins William	Ab	7 8s 11$^{3/4d}$	2 2s	5 6s 11$^{3/4d}$	Edward Jasper Att.
Jones Charles	Ab	7 8s 11$^{3/4d}$		7 8s 11$^{3/4d}$	John Newton for John Newton Att
Jones Joseph	Carp. Serv.	7 8s 11$^{3/4d}$	2 2s	5 6s 11$^{3/4d}$	B. Bechinoe for father Ben Att
Jones Robert	Marine	7 8s 11$^{3/4d}$		7 8s 11$^{3/4d}$	B. Bechinoe for Susan Hill Att
Keast Richard	Ab	7 8s 11$^{3/4d}$		7 8s 11$^{3/4d}$	John Vincent for John Young Ass
Knipe William	Ab	7 8s 11$^{3/4d}$		7 8s 11$^{3/4d}$	George Rogby Ass
Lynn John	Ord	7 8s 11$^{3/4d}$	4 4s	3 3s 11$^{3/4d}$	Edward Jasper Att.
Loyall Thomas	Ord	7 8s 11$^{3/4d}$	4 4s	3 3s 11$^{3/4d}$	J. Vincent

Lewis William	Marine	7 8s 11$^{3/4}$d		7 8s 11$^{3/4}$d	Francis Courtenay Att for Francis Thomas
Luxon John	Marine	7 8s 11$^{3/4}$d		7 8s 11$^{3/4}$d	J. Malraven for Hugh Dixey Att
Millman Edward	Qtr Gunner	7 8s 11$^{3/4}$d	2 2s	5 6s 11$^{3/4}$d	John Fane Att to wife Mary Att
McDonald Allen	Ab				
Maen William	Qtr Gunner				
McDermott Jerm.	Ab	7 8s 11$^{3/4}$d	4 4s	3 3s 11$^{3/4}$d	J. Vincent
Manin John	Ab	7 8s 11$^{3/4}$d	4 4s	3 3s 11$^{3/4}$d	Joseph Brookes Att
Marshall John	Ab				DD EJ
Mark John	Ab	7 8s 11$^{3/4}$d	4 4s	3 3s 11$^{3/4}$d	Edward Jasper Att
Mark William	Ab	7 8s 11$^{3/4}$d		7 8s 11$^{3/4}$d	J. Vincent for John Kirkes Ass
Miller Thomas	Ab	7 8s 11$^{3/4}$d	4 4s	3 3s 11$^{3/4}$d	Edward Jasper Att
May Timothy	Cooks Serv.	7 8s 11$^{3/4}$d	2 2s	5 6s 11$^{3/4}$d	J. Vincent for John Wharhem Ass
Moor William	Ab	7 8s 11$^{3/4}$d		7 8s 11$^{3/4}$d	Mary Moor sister and Att
Mills William	Ab	7 8s 11$^{3/4}$d	3 3s	4 5s 6$^{3/4}$d	Paul Berthon for James Bucknall
Mockett John	Marine	7 8s 11$^{3/4}$d		7 8s 11$^{3/4}$d	J. Vincent for John Kirkes Ass
Moulton Joseph	Marine	7 8s 11$^{3/4}$d		7 8s 11$^{3/4}$d	J. Vincent for Joseph Newton Ass
Nelson Jacob	Capt. Serv.	7 8s 11$^{3/4}$d	4 4s	3 3s 11$^{3/4}$d	J. Vincent
Norwell George	Ord				
Nevil Thomas	Ord	7 8s 11$^{3/4}$d	2 2s	5 6s 11$^{3/4}$d	J. Vincent
Norris Richard	Ab				R

Nichols James	3rd Lt. Serv.	7 8s 11 3/4d		7 8s 11 3/4d	Charles Chasemon James Negro
Osborne James	Ab	7 8s 11 3/4d		7 8s 11 3/4d	J. Vincent for John Kirkes Ass
Osborne Henry	Carp. Clerk	7 8s 11 3/4d		7 8s 11 3/4d	B. Bechinoe for M Mary Att
Pearson William	Landsman				
Pellon Peter	Landsman	7 8s 11 3/4d		7 8s 11 3/4d	Peter Pellon
Poor Lawrence	Ord				
Pike Joseph	Ab				
Pattison James	Ord	7 8s 11 3/4d		7 8s 11 3/4d	John Newton for John Newton Att
Patton George	Ord	7 8s 11 3/4d		7 8s 11 3/4d	J. Malraven for Hugh Dixey Att
Page John	Marine	7 8s 11 3/4d		7 8s 11 3/4d	J. Malraven for Hugh Dixey Att
Payne Richard	Marine	7 8s 11 3/4d		7 8s 11 3/4d	J. Vincent for Abraham Pike Ass
Priddum Noah	Marine	7 8s 11 3/4d		7 8s 11 3/4d	
Reddish Joseph	Ab	7 8s 11 3/4d	4 5s	3 3s 11 3/4d	Edward Jasper Att
Rickens Edwards	Ab	7 8s 11 3/4d		7 8s 11 3/4d	J. Malraven for Thomas Redman Att
Robinson Thomas	Ord	7 8s 11 3/4d		7 8s 11 3/4d	John Christian father of Att
Ross John	Ab				
Richardson Henry	Ab				R
Rider John	Ab				
Robinson John	Ab	7 8s 11 3/4d		7 8s 11 3/4d	John Vincent for N. Brent Ass
Richards John	Capt. Serv.	7 8s 11 3/4d		7 8s 11 3/4d	J. Malraven for Hugh Dixey Att

Ridgeway William	Marine	7 8s 11$^{3/4}$d		7 8s 11$^{3/4}$d	J. Vincent for John Kirkes Ass
Sheppard Richard	Ab	7 8s 11$^{3/4}$d		7 8s 11$^{3/4}$d	George Rogby Att
Sole Edward	Ab	7 8s 11$^{3/4}$d		7 8s 11$^{3/4}$d	Mary Horsman Att
Salter Richard	Ab				R
Stevens Thomas	Quart Gunner	7 8s 11$^{3/4}$d		7 8s 11$^{3/4}$d	J. Malraven for Hugh Dixey Att
Scott William	Quart Gunner	7 8s 11$^{3/4}$d		7 8s 11$^{3/4}$d	Edward Jasper for David Iver Att
Sims William	Capt. Serv.	7 8s 11$^{3/4}$d	2 2s	5 6s 11$^{3/4}$d	Richard Darling for John Boulton Ass
Shepherd John	Ord	7 8s 11$^{3/4}$d		7 8s 11$^{3/4}$d	J. Malraven for Hugh Dixey Att
Smith Richard	Ab	7 8s 11$^{3/4}$d	2 2s	5 6s 11$^{3/4}$d	Edward Jasper Att
Symes Francis	Ord	7 8s 11$^{3/4}$d		7 8s 11$^{3/4}$d	John Newton for John Newton Att
Slater Robert	Ab	7 8s 11$^{3/4}$d		7 8s 11$^{3/4}$d	Thomas Birkley Att
Smith William	Steward				
Sams Robert	Ord	7 8s 11$^{3/4}$d		7 8s 11$^{3/4}$d	B. Bechinoe for Joseph Derby Ass
Sinclair Robert	Ab	7 8s 11$^{3/4}$d	4 4s	3 3s 11$^{3/4}$d	Edward Jasper Att
Saunders William	Marine	7 8s 11$^{3/4}$d		7 8s 11$^{3/4}$d	J. Vincent for John Kirkes Ass
Sampson Joseph	Marine	7 8s 11$^{3/4}$d		7 8s 11$^{3/4}$d	J. Vincent for John Kirkes Ass
Saunders Henry	Marine				R
Seaville John	Marine	7 8s 11$^{3/4}$d		7 8s 11$^{3/4}$d	J. Vincent for John Kirkes Ass
Stevens George	Marine	7 8s 11$^{3/4}$d		7 8s 11$^{3/4}$d	J. Vincent for John Kirkes Ass

Soaper John	Marine	7 8s 11¾d		7 8s 11¾d	J Vincent for William Brent Ass
Sommers John	Supernumerary	7 8s 11¾d		7 8s 11¾d	John Vincent for John Reynolds Att
Tomlyn Joseph	Ord	7 8s 11¾d		7 8s 11¾d	Robert Sporle for Wm Brent Ass
Tothill Henry	Ab	7 8s 11¾d		7 8s 11¾d	J. Malraven for Hugh Dixey Att
Thomas Benjamin	Ord	7 8s 11¾d		7 8s 11¾d	Robert Sporle for Wm Brent Ass
Townsend Moses	Ab				R
Taylor William	Ab	7 8s 11¾d	3 3s	4 5s 6¾d	John Vincent for Ann Cowan Ass
Tomsals Thomas Francis	Marine	7 8s 11¾d			J. Vincent for John Kirkes Ass
Threadwell Thomas	Marine	7 8s 11¾d		7 8s 11¾d	J. Vincent for John Kirkes Ass
Vineyard James	Ab				R
Williams James	Ab	7 8s 11¾d	4 4s	3 3s 11¾d	Edward Jasper for Ann Williams Att
Weams James	Ab	7 8s 11¾d	4 4s	3 3s 11¾d	Edward Jasper Att
Willey Samuel	Taylor	7 8s 11¾d		7 8s 11¾d	J. Malraven for Hugh Dixey Att
Webber Thomas	Ab	7 8s 11¾d		7 8s 11¾d	J. Malraven for Hugh Dixey Att
Waters George	Ab	7 8s 11¾d	4 4s	3 3s 11¾d	J. Malraven for Hugh Dixey Att
Whitford Thomas	2nd Lt. Serv.	7 8s 11¾d	3 3s	3 3s 11¾d	Oliver Toulmin for Ann Sambs Att
Winter William	Ab	7 8s 11¾d		7 8s 11¾d	B. Bechinoe for wife Jane Att
Wills William	Ord	7 8s 11¾d	4 4s	3 3s 11¾d	B. Bechinoe for wife Mary Att

Williams William	Ab	7 8s 11 3/4d	2 2s	5 6s 11 3/4d	Edward Jasper for Bridges Hatchman Ass
Whitaker William	Ab				R
Wilson John	Surg. Serv.	7 8s 11 3/4d		7 8s 11 3/4d	John Vincent for John Alford Ass
Wood John	Ab	7 8s 11 3/4d		7 8s 11 3/4d	Robert Darling for Michael Kelly Ass
Woodley Charles	Carp. Serv.	7 8s 11 3/4d	2 2s	5 6s 11 3/4d	B. Bechinoe Att
Wood Francis	Marine	7 8s 11 3/4d		7 8s 11 3/4d	J. Vincent for John Kirkes Ass
Webb John	Marine	7 8s 11 3/4d		7 8s 11 3/4d	J. Vincent for Hasden Young Att
Whenton John	Marine	7 8s 11 3/4d		7 8s 11 3/4d	Robert Sporle for Wm Brent Ass
Wills William	Marine	7 8s 11 3/4d	4 4s	3 3s 11 3/4d	EV
Warburton William	Marine				DD

Examined the 14th February 1745 and the original delivered to Mr Trevanion

APPENDIX 13

THE SAILOR'S DESCRIPTION OF A CHASE AND CAPTURE

The text found on Figure 3, *The Sailor's Description of a Chase and Capture* designed by Lt. John Sheringham, reads as follows:

> Why d'ye see 'twas blowing strong, & we were lopping it in forecastle under in Portland roads, when a sail hove in sight in the offing; we saw it with half an eye, she was an enemy's cruiser standing over from Cherbourg, better she couldn't come, so we turned the hands up and drew the splice of the best bower, but she not liking the cut of our jib hove in stays; all hands make sail ahoy; away flew the cable end for end & before you could say pease we had her under double reef'd top sails & top gallant sails, my eye how she walked licking it in whole green seas at the Weather chess tree & canting it over the lee yard arm pigs & live lumber afloat in the lee scuppers but just as we opened the bill standing through the tail of the race, by the holy ! I thought she'd have tipt us all the nines but she stood really well up under canvas while Johnny Crapaud was grabbing to it nigh on his beam ends so my boys we bowsed in the lee guns, gave her a Mugian reef & found she had as much sail as she could stagger under, we came up with her hand over fist & about seven bells she began to play long balls with her stern chasers, but overboard went her fore top mast her sails took aback & she fain would be off, but we twigging her drift let run the clew garnets ranged up to windward & gave her a broadside twixt wind and water as hard as she could suck it that dose was a sickner d--n the shot did she fire afterwards hard a starboard flew our helm & whack went our cathead into her quarter gallery with a hell of surge over board went her mizen mast in dashed our boarders & down came her colours to the Glory of Old England and the flying Saucy with three hearty Cheers !!!!

BIBLIOGRAPHY

Primary Sources

London Metropolitan Archives

CLC/B/227-100

NatWest Group Archives

Drummonds Accounts John Lockhart

NMM National Maritime Museum

ELL/400 John Elliot's letters
ADM 354

Staffordshire Archives

D 1798/HM Drakeford

TNA The National Archives

ADM 1 Captains' letters
ADM 2 Letters from Admiralty
ADM 6 Warrants and Commissions
ADM 36 Muster Books
ADM 43/12–22 Navy Board Head Money Vouchers 1750–69
ADM 49 Estimate of the debt of the Navy Board.
ADM 51 Ships' Logs
ADM 68 Greenwich Hospital prizes
AO 1 Declared accounts: Receiver of Prizes
FO Prize reports
HCA 30/16–19 Letters of Attorney: 1756–1830
HCA 31/35–49 Monitions to Prize Court: 1756–63
HCA 32/161–259 Papers for Prize Court: 1756–63
HCA 34/37–42 Sentences and interlocutaries: 1756–68
HCA 43/13–18 Head Money: 1756–83
HCA 45 High Court of Appeals for Prizes Case books: 1750–1818
HCA 47 Appeals from decisions of the High Court of Admiralty
HCA 48/45 High Court of Appeals for Prizes: 1672–1772
HCA IND 1 Database prepared at TNA
T Treasury Warrants

Other Primary Sources

Donnithorne, Chris, chris@navylist.org
George Marsh diary, Heath-Caldwell Family Archive, www.jjhc.info

Secondary Sources

Abell, Francis, *Prisoners of War in Britain 1756 to 1815* (Humphrey Milford, 1914)
Adkins, Roy and Lesley, *Jack Tar: The Extraordinary Lives of Ordinary Seamen in Nelson's Navy* (Abacus, 2008)
Anderson, Fred, *Crucible of War: The Seven Years' War and the Fate of the Empire in British North America 1754–1766* (Faber and Faber, 2000)
Anderson, Gary M. and Gifford, Adam Jn., 'Privateering and the Private Production of Naval Power', *Cato Journal* (Vol. 11 no. 1 1991)
Anderson, Olive, 'The Establishment of British Supremacy at Sea and the Exchange of Naval Prisoners of War, 1689–1783', *The English Historical Review* (Vol. 75 no. 294 January 1960), 77–89
Aspinall-Oglander, Cecil, *Admiral's Wife: The Life and Letters of Mrs Edward Boscawen 1719–1761* (Longman, 1940)
Barrow, Thomas C., *Trade and Empire: The British Customs Service in Colonial America 1660–1775* (Harvard University Press, 1967)
Baty, Thomas, 'Scottish Prize Decisions of the Seventeenth and Eighteenth Centuries', *The Yale Law Journal* (Vol. 27 no. 4 February 1918), 453–78, www.jstor.org/stable/786341
Baugh, Daniel, *British Naval Administration in the Age of Walpole* (Princeton, 1965)
—— *The Global Seven Years War 1754–1763* (Pearson, 2011)
Beatson, Robert, *Naval and Military Memoirs of Great Britain from the year 1727 to the present time* (Edinburgh, 1790)
Blom, Andrew, *Hugo Grotius (1583–1645)* (Internet Encyclopedia of Philosophy)
Boscawen, Hugh, *The Capture of Louisbourg 1758* (University of Oklahoma Press, 2011)
Bourguignon, Henry J., *Sir William Scott, Lord Stowell: Judge of the High Court of Admiralty, 1798–1828* (Cambridge University Press, 1987)
Brewer, John, *The Sinews of Power: War, Money and the English State 1688–1783* (Harvard University Press, 1990)
Brinkman, Anna, 'Spain and Neutrality', in *Co-dependent Empires during the Seven Years' War: Strategy, Spanish Neutrality and Law* (Imperial Entanglements, 2017)
Bromley, J.S., 'Prize Office and Prize Agency at Portsmouth 1689–1748', in *Hampshire Studies*, ed. J. Webb, N. Yates and S. Peacock (Portsmouth City, 1981), 169–99
Burgis, N., ed., Charles Dickens, *David Copperfield* (Oxford, 1981)
Burrell, Sir William, ed., *Reports of Cases determined by the High Court of Admiralty and upon appeal therefrom* (London, 1885)
Carter, Alice Clare, 'The Dutch as Neutrals in the Seven Years' War', *The International and Comparative Law Quarterly* (Vol. 12 no. 3 1963), 818–34, www.jstor.org/stable/756291

Clapham, Andrew, 'Booty, Bounty, Blockade and Prize: Time to Re-evaluate the Law', *International Law Studies* (Vol. 97 2021), 1200–68

Clark, Dora Mae, *The Rise of the British Treasury: Colonial Administration of the Eighteenth Century* (Yale University Press, 1960)

Clayton, Tim, *Tars: The Men Who Made Britain Rule the Waves* (Hodder, 2008)

Clowes, W. Laird, ed., *The Royal Navy: A History*, Vol. 3 (London, 1898)

Coleman, E.C., ed., *The Navy List March 1766* (Ancholme Publishing, 2001)

Collinge, J.M., *Navy Board Officials 1660–1832* (IHR, 1978)

Colombos, C.J., 'Some Notes on the Decisions of the French Prize Courts', *Journal of the Society of Comparative Legislation* (Vol. 16 no. 2 1916), 300–21, www.jstor.org/stable/752429

—— 'Ships and Their Owners in the Prize Courts of France, Great Britain, Italy, and China', *Journal of Comparative Legislation and International Law* (Vol. 2 no. 3 1920), 289–97, www.jstor.org/stable/752846

—— 'Cargoes in the Prize Courts of Great Britain, France, Italy and Germany', *Journal of Comparative Legislation and International Law* (Vol. 3 no. 4 1921), 286–302, www.jstor.org/stable/753298

Corbett, Julian S., *England in the Seven Years' War*, Vols I and II (Greenhill, 1992)

Costello, Kevin, 'The Court of Admiralty of Ireland, 1745–1756', *The American Journal of Legal History* (Vol. 50 no. 1 2008), 23–48, www.jstor.org/stable/25664482

Davey, James and Johns, Richard, *Broadsides: Caricature and the Navy 1756–1815* (Seaforth, 2012)

Davies, David James Llewelfryn, *Sir Leoline Jenkins* (Dictionary of Welsh Biography), https://biography.wales/article/s-JENK-LEO-1625

—— 'The Development of Prize Law under Sir Leoline Jenkins', *Transactions of the Grotius Society* (Vol. 21 1935), 149–60, www.jstor.org/stable/743068

Davis, Ralph, *The Rise of the English Shipping Industry in the 17th and 18th centuries* (David and Charles, 1962)

Deák, Francis and Jessup, Philip C., 'Early Prize Court Procedure Part 1', *University of Pennsylvania Law Review* (May 1934), 677–94

—— 'Early Prize Court Procedure Part 2', *University of Pennsylvania Law Review* (June 1934), 818–37

Dull, Jonathan R., *The French Navy and the Seven Years' War* (Nebraska, 2005)

Duncan, G.I.O., *The High Court of Delegates* (Cambridge, 1971)

Earle, Peter, *Sailors: English Merchant Seamen 1650–1775* (Methuen, 1998)

Ehrman, John, *The Younger Pitt: The Years of Acclaim* (London, 1969)

Erskine, David, *Augustus Hervey's Journal: The Adventures Afloat and Ashore of a Naval Casanova* (Chatham, 2002)

Gardiner, Richard, *An account of the expedition to the West Indies, against Martinico, Guadalupe and other the Leeward Islands* (London, 1759)

Gradish, Stephen F., *The Manning of the British Navy during The Seven Years' War* (London, 1980)

Green, Geoffrey, *The Royal Navy and Anglo-Jewry 1740–1820* (Green, 1989)

Gutridge, Tony, 'George Redmond Hulbert, Prize Agent', unpublished thesis, Portsmouth Polytechnic, 1981–82

—— 'Aspects of Naval Prize Agency 1793–1815', *Mariner's Mirror* (Society for Nautical Research, February 1994), 45–53

Gwyn, Julian, *The Enterprising Admiral: The Personal Fortune of Admiral Sir Peter Warren* (McGill-Queen's University Press, 1974)

Helfman, Tara, *Commerce on Trial: Neutral Rights and Private Warfare in the Seven Years' War* (Helsinki, 2011)

—— 'The Neutrality of Commerce in the Inter-State System', in Koen Stapelbroek, ed., *Trade and War* (Helsinki, 2011), 14–41

Hill, Richard, *The Prizes of War: The Naval Prize System in the Napoleonic Wars 1793–1815* (Sutton Publishing, 1998)

Horne, Thomas Hartwell, *A Compendium of the Statute Laws and Regulations of the Court of Admiralty relating to Ships of War, Privateers, Prizes, Re-captures and Prize Money* (London, 1803)

Hough, C.M., ed., *Reports of Cases in the Vice Admiralty of the Provinces of New York and in the Court of Admiralty in the State of New York 1715–1788* (New Haven, 1925)

Hoyt, Henry M., 'Recent Development and Tendency of the Law of Prize', *The Yale Law Journal* (Vol. 12 no. 5 March 1903), 306–17

Huberich, Charles Henry, 'The French Law of Prize', *The Yale Law Journal* (Vol. 24 no. 8 June 1915), 663–8

Huberich, Charles Henry and King, Richard, 'The Development of German Prize Law', *Columbia Law Review* (Vol. 18 no. 6 1918), 503–58, www.jstor.org/stable/1112252

Jenkinson, Charles, *A Discourse on the Conduct of Great Britain with respect to Neutral Nations* (London, 1758)

Jessup, Philip C. and Francis Deák, 'The Early Development of the Law of Contraband of War II', *Political Science Quarterly* (Vol. 48 no. 1 1933), 62–93, www.jstor.org/stable/2143040

Kemp, Peter, *The British Sailor: A Social History of the Lower Deck* (London, 1970)

Kert, Faye Margaret, *Prize and Prejudice: Privateering and Naval Prize in Atlantic Canada in the War of 1812* (Canada, 1997)

Lee, Richard, translation of Bynkershoek, *A Treatise of Captures in War* (London, 1759)

Lloyd, Christopher, ed., *Naval Miscellany IV* (Navy Records Society, 1952)

—— ed., *Above and Under Hatches* (London, 1957)

Long, W.H., ed., *Naval Yarns: Letters and Anecdotes, comprising accounts of sea fights and wrecks actions with pirates and privateers etc from 1606 to 1831* (Gibbings and Co., 1899)

Mackay, Ruddock, ed., *The Hawke Papers: A Selection 1743–1771* (Navy Records Society, 1990)

Mahan, Alfred Thayer, *The Influence of Sea Power upon History 1660–1783* (Boston, 1944)

Marcus, G.J., *Heart of Oak* (Oxford University Press, 1975)

Marriot, Sir James, *The Case of the Dutch Ships Considered* (London, 1758)

—— *A letter to the Dutch Merchants in England* (London, 1759)

Marsden, Reginald G., ed., *Reports of Cases Determined by the High Court of Admiralty and upon appeal therefrom together with Extracts from the Books and Records of the High Court of Admiralty and the Court of the Judges Delegates* (William Clowes, 1885)

—— *Law and Custom of the Sea*, Vol. I AD 1649–1767 (Navy Records Society, 1915)
—— 'Prize Law', *Journal of the Society of Comparative Legislation* (Cambridge University Press, 1915)
—— *Law and Custom of the Sea*, Vol II AD 1649–1767 (Navy Records Society, 1916)
McLeod, A.B., *British Naval Captains of the Seven Years' War* (Boydell and Brewer, 2012)
Murray, Mungo, *Treatise on shipbuilding and navigation: in three parts wherein the theory, practice and application of necessary instruments are perspicuously handled* (London, 1754)
Namier, Sir Lewis and Brooks, John, *The House of Commons 1754–1790* (HMSO, 1964)
O'Connell, D.P., *The Influence of Law on Sea Power* (Manchester, 1975)
Oxford Dictionary of National Biography
Pares, Richard, *War and Trade in the West Indies 1739–1763* (London, 1963)
—— *Colonial Blockade and Neutral Rights 1739–1763* (Philadelphia, 1975)
Piquet-Marchal, Marie-Odile, 'Revue Historique de Droit Français et Étranger (1922–)', *Revue Historique de Droit Français et Étranger (1922–)* (Vol. 65 no. 4 1987), 593–4, www.jstor.org/stable/43849113
Pritchard, James, *Louis XV's Navy 1748–1762* (McGill-Queen's University Press, 2009)
Raven G.J.A. and Rodger N.A.M., eds, *Navies and Armies: The Anglo-Dutch Relationship in War and Peace 1688–1988* (Edinburgh, 1990)
Richmond, Admiral Sir Herbert, *Statesmen and Sea Power* (Oxford, 1946)
Robinson, Sir Christopher, *Collecteana Maritima* (White and Butterworth, 1801)
Rodger, N.A.M., *Articles of War 1661, 1749 and 1866* (Mason, 1982)
—— ed., 'The Douglas Papers', *The Naval Miscellany 5* (Navy Records Society, 1984)
—— *The Wooden World: An Anatomy of the Georgian Navy* (Collins, 1986)
—— *The Command of the Ocean* (Penguin, 2004)
Roscoe, Edward Stanley, ed., *Reports of Prize Cases* (London, 1905)
—— *Lord Stowell – His Life and the Development of English Prize Law* (Boston, 1916)
—— *A History of the English Prize Court* (Lloyds, 1924)
Sainty, J.C., *Admiralty Officials 1660–1870* (IHR, 1975)
Senior, W., 'Ransom Bills', *Law Quarterly Review 34* (1918)
—— 'Sir Henry Penrice and Sir Thomas Salusbury', *Mariner's Mirror* (Society for Nautical Research, February 1927), 38–44
Spavins, William, *The Narrative of William Spavins, a Chatham Pensioner by Himself* (Chatham, 1998)
Spinney, David, *Rodney* (London, 1969)
Squibb, G.D., *Doctors Commons: A History of the College of Advocates and Doctors of Law* (Clarendon Press, 1977)
Syrett, David, ed., *The Siege and Capture of Havana* (Navy Records Society, 1970)
—— *Admiral Lord Howe a Biography* (Spellmount, 2006)
Tanner, J.R., *Samuel Pepys's Naval Minutes* (Navy Records Society, 1926)
Towns, Lydia, *The Role of British Privateers in the Seven Years' War* (Texas, 2015)

Tracy, Nicholas, *Manila Ransomed* (Exeter Press, 1995)
Truxes, Thomas M., *Defying Empire: Trading with the Enemy in Colonial New York* (Yale University Press, 2008)
Twiss, Sir Travers, transcribed, *The Black Book of the Admiralty* (The National Archives, 1871–76)
van Ittersum, Martine Julia, ed., Williams, Gwladys and Zeydel, Walter, trans., *Hugo Grotius, De Jure Praedae Commentarius* (Liberty Fund, 2005)
Watson, Michael, 'Judge Lewis Morris, the New York Vice-Admiralty Court, and Colonial Privateering, 1739–1762', *New York History* (Vol. 78 no. 2 1997), 117–46, www.jstor.org/stable/23181842
Williams, Gomer, *History of the Liverpool Privateers and Letters of Marque 1744–1812* (Liverpool, 2004)
Winfield, Rif, *British Warships in the Age of Sail 1714–1792* (Seaforth, 2007)
Winfield, Rif and Roberts, Stephen S., *French Warships in the Age of Sail 1626–1786* (Seaforth, 2017)
Wynne, William, *Life of Sir Leoline Jenkins* (London, 1724)
Young, G.V.C. and Foster, Caroline, *Captain François Thurot* (Isle of Man, 1986)

Contemporary newspapers

Aberdeen Press and Journal
Annapolis Maryland Gazette
British Spy or New Universal London Weekly Journal
Caledonian Mercury
Evening Advertiser
Gentleman's and London Magazine
Leeds Intelligencer
Lloyds Evening Post and British Chronicle
Lloyds List
London Annual Register
London Chronicle
London Evening Post
London Gazette
London Own Weekly Chronicle or Universal Journal
London Read Weekly Journal or British Gazetteer
The Newcastle Courant
Oxford Journal
Public Advertiser
Schofields Middlewich Journal
The Scots Magazine
Sussex Advertiser
Universal Chronicle and Weekly Gazette
Whitehall Evening Post

INDEX

I make no apology for the hundreds of ships listed in this index. In a time of naval war, vessels were at once the weapon and the target. Rif Winfield commented that captors and newspapers tended to overstate the strength of the opposition, and he and his books have helped me identify the number of guns on French privateers. It is still the case that the transcription of the French names of captured vessels caused problems: *Francis Lewis* instead of *François Louis*?

Printed and bound by CPI Group (UK) Ltd, Croydon, CR0 4YY
13/09/2026
14961003-0003

Rotenburg (Wümme) zur Zeit der Erzbischöfe von Bremen und der Könige von Schweden

Armin Schöne

Rotenburg (Wümme)

zur Zeit der Erzbischöfe von Bremen und der Könige von Schweden

Edition Falkenberg

Titelabbildungen:
Niedersächsisches Staatsarchiv, Standort Stade,
Archivsignatur Neu Nr. 13101

Königin Christina (17.12.1626 – 19.4.1689, Königin von Schweden (anfangs unter Vormundschaft) 1632 – 1654) Porträt aus Stadtarchiv Stade, Graphiksammlung 02, Nr. 68

1. Auflage 2019

ISBN 978-3-95494-185-8
www.edition-falkenberg.de

Inhalt

Geleitwort

Die Geschichte zu kennen ist wichtig, um die Gegenwart zu verstehen. Diese Erkenntnis ist nicht neu und sinngemäß schon durch Gelehrte des 18./19. Jahrhunderts wie Wilhelm von Humboldt und Johann Wolfgang von Goethe, aber auch von Politikern des 20. Jahrhunderts wie Winston Churchill formuliert worden. Diese Aussage trifft umso mehr für die Regionalgeschichte zu. Das Bistum und Stift Verden bzw. Erzbistum und Erzstift Bremen waren besonders im Mittelalter und der frühen Neuzeit für das Gebiet, das heute den Landkreis Rotenburg (Wümme) bildet, in vielfältiger Weise prägend. Später, nach der Säkularisierung, waren es die Herzogtümer Bremen und Verden.
Die Geschichte kann in diesem sehr heterogenen Raum eine verbindende Klammer durch die Zeiten bilden. In diesem Aufsatz widmet sich Prof. Dr. Armin Schöne dem Raum Rotenburg in der Zeit der Erzbischöfe von Bremen und der Könige von Schweden und deckt damit

einen Zeitraum von etwa 300 Jahren ab. Neben Bremervörde war Rotenburg als Sitz von Amt und Burg bzw. Schloss ein wichtiger Verwaltungsmittelpunkt. In Rotenburg kann man die Verwaltungsfunktion bis in heutige Tage nachverfolgen: Die Hauptgebäude der Verwaltung des Landkreises Rotenburg (Wümme) befinden sich auf dem Gelände, auf dem sich schon im 17. Jahrhundert der Hof des Amtes Rotenburg befand. Einige Gebäude aus dem 18. Jahrhundert sind hier noch erhalten und werden vom Landkreis genutzt. Von der namengebenden Burg in Rotenburg ist hingegen kaum noch etwas im Gelände zu erkennen. Wir sind somit auf die Erkenntnisse aus Geschichte und Archäologie angewiesen, um uns der Keimzelle der heutigen Stadt zu nähern. Die vorliegende Publikation unternimmt diese historische Annäherung in anschaulicher Weise. Ich wünsche allen Lesern viel Vergnügen und neue Erkenntnisse zur regionalen Geschichte.

Hermann Luttmann
Landrat des Landkreises Rotenburg (Wümme)

Anfänge der Nordwestdeutschen Regionalgeschichte

In der Regionalgeschichte, welche ich in den Büchern über die Erzbischöfe von Bremen, die Könige von Schweden und von Großbritannien, die Stadt Bremen und das Amt Langwedel auch in vielen Einzelheiten behandele, gehe ich immer wieder auf den Flecken und die Stadt, die Festung und das Amt Rotenburg (Wümme) ein. Nunmehr soll Rotenburg (Wümme) zentraler Gegenstand meiner folgenden Ausführungen sein. Wenn hierbei von den Erzbischöfen von Bremen die Rede ist, – das ist die Zeit bis zum Ende des Dreißigjährigen Krieges – dürfen die Bischöfe von Verden nicht vergessen werden. Hierbei waren häufig der Erzbischof von Bremen und der Bischof von Verden die gleiche Person. Wenn der Erzbischof von Bremen und der Bischof von Verden verschiedene Personen waren, gab es immer wieder politische Situationen, die eine enge Abhängigkeit der beiden Fürsten voneinander bewirkten. Dabei waren die Bischöfe von Verden, wie man sich denken kann, eher abhängig als umgekehrt.

Selbstverständlich stellt sich die Frage, wo der Anfang der begreifbaren Regionalgeschichte in Deutschland liegt. Dieses spätere Deutschland entwickelte sich allmählich aus den Herrschaften der Merowinger und Karolinger. Daneben sucht man nach Ansiedlungen von Menschen und hat herausgefunden, dass das Gebiet des heutigen Deutschlands im Laufe der Jahrhunderte von sehr unterschiedlichen Volksstämmen besiedelt war. Die archäologische Forschung lässt für Zeiträume bis zur Völkerwanderung geschlossene Siedlungsräume erkennen und getrennte Bevölkerungen abgrenzen. Man findet jedoch kaum Reste von früheren Siedlungen, aber häufig über viele Jahrhunderte verteilt Grabstätten, zum Beispiel Urnenfriedhöfe. Beschränkt man sich auf das engere Gebiet von Rotenburg, so gibt es Urnenfriedhöfe im Anschluss an Hügelgräber in Wohlsdorf (Scheeßel) und Waffensen (Rotenburg), einen Urnenfriedhof der älteren vorrömischen Eisenzeit in Bötersen (Samtgemeinde Sottrum), einen Fundplatz der älteren römischen Kaiserzeit bis zur Völkerwanderung und einen spätsächsischen Friedhof in Rotenburg-Luhne. Spätsächsisch bedeutete die Zeit des 7. bis 8. Jahrhunderts, die der karolingischen Zeit unmittelbar vorausging.

Gründung von Rotenburg (Wümme)

Fügt man vier Jahrhunderte hinzu, so befindet man sich kurz vor der Wende vom 12. zum 13. Jahrhundert. Es regierten Kaiser Friedrich I. Barbarossa (1152–1190) und dessen Sohn Heinrich VI. (1190–1197). Zur Zeit des Verdener Bischofs Iso von Wölpe ist die Rotenburg bereits erbaut. Iso ist am 12. August 1231 in Rotenburg verstorben. In Rotenburg, das als Residenz des Bischofs bezeichnet werden kann, hatte er am 27. Juli 1231 zwei umfängliche Urkunden ausgefertigt, mit denen Iso verschiedene vor allem im Stift und in der Diözese Verden gelegenen Besitztümer vergab und auch verschenkte. Darin sind die zahlreichen Verfügungen sehr detailliert behandelt.

Iso wurde erstmals um die Jahreswende 1296/97 als Dompropst zu Verden erwähnt. Wenn von Rotenburg gesprochen wird, so ist zunächst vor allem an die Stellung der Bischöfe von Verden gegenüber dem mächtigen Erzstift Bremen zu denken. Wer Bischof von Verden wurde und war, hatte diesen Nachbarn stets im Auge zu behalten und einen modus vivendi zu suchen und zu finden, wenn er fortlaufenden Streitigkeiten aus dem Weg gehen wollte. Allerdings erleichterten die bremischen Wirren vor dem Regierungsantritt des Erzbischofs Gerhard II. und dem Bau der Festung Langwedel dem Bischof Iso die Organisation der Verhältnisse im Stift und in der Diözese Verden.

Der Bau der Rotenburg an der Wümme und der Erwerb von Rechten als Landesherrn im Umfeld der neuen Burg wird dem unmittelbaren Vorgänger des Bischofs Iso, nämlich dem Verdener Bischof Rudolf I. (1188–1205) zugeschrieben. Rotenburg wurde als Bischofsburg gegen die Welfen gebaut. Hierdurch gewann das Verdener Domkapitel, das nun quasi allein in Verden residierte, eine größere Selbstständigkeit. Rudolf konnte dabei auch das Machtvakuum nutzen, das im Reich durch den Sturz Heinrich des Löwen entstanden war, und gleichzeitig auch seine Stellung als Angehöriger der Rechtskanzlei unter Kaiser Heinrich VI. (1191–1197). Zieht man die Grenzen des 13. Jahrhunderts in Betracht, so lag die Rotenburg an der nordwestlichen Grenze des im Vergleich zur großen Diözese Verden recht kleinen Stiftes Verden. So wie Langwedel gerade außerhalb des Stiftes Verden lag, so lag die Rotenburg gerade noch innerhalb des Stiftes Verden.

Übergang vom 14. zum 15. Jahrhundert

Im weiteren Verlauf der Geschichte zeigen sich auffallende Zusammenhänge zwischen dem Bistum Verden und dem Erzstift Bremen. Im Bistum Verden war um die Jahreswende 1388/89 Otto von Braunschweig-Lüneburg als Nachfolger des Bischofs Johannes von Zesterfleth als Bischof gewählt worden. Otto war ein Neffe des Bremer Erzbischofs Albert II. Man nimmt an, dass Otto als Bischof von Verden sich stets um Einvernehmen mit seinem Onkel Albert bemüht hatte. Nach dem Tod von Erzbischof Albert II. im Jahr 1395 wurde der Verdener Bischof Otto Erzbischof von Bremen (1395–1406). Als Bischof von Verden war Rotenburg seine Residenz gewesen. Darauf wollte Otto auch als Erzbischof von Bremen nicht verzichten. Im Jahr 1399 kam es wegen der Herausgabe von Langwedel an den Erzbischof Otto zu einem umfassenden Vergleich, an dem unter anderem Johann von Slamstorp, der spätere Bremer Erzbischof Johann II. von Slamtorp, beteiligt war.

In diesem Vergleich waren auch verschiedene Vereinbarungen wegen Rotenburg (Wümme) geschlossen worden. Damit Erzbischof Otto die Rotenburg in seinem Besitz halten konnte, sollte die Rotenburg sowohl durch zwei Angehörige des Verdener Domkapitels wie auch zwei Angehörige der Verdener Ritterschaft verwaltet werden. Dadurch sollte sichergestellt werden, dass von der Rotenburg aus niemandem ein Schaden zugefügt wurde. Der Nachfolger von Otto als Bischof von Verden wurde nach zwei Unterbrechungen Konrad II. von Soltau (1399–1400, 1402–1407), dem es auch gelang, sich in den Besitz von Rotenburg zu setzen (1406?). Ansonsten liest man Feststellungen, dass dieser Bischof nicht fähig war, das Stift Verden ordnungsgemäß zu verwalten.

Beim Regierungsantritt des Bischofs Johann III. von Asel (1426–1470) im Jahr 1426 befand sich das Schloss Rotenburg im Besitz von Brüdern, genannt Klencken, die dafür fast 12.000 Rheinische Gulden aufgewendet hatten. Johann III. von Asel war Doktor des Kirchenrechts sowie Kämmerer und Sekretär des Papstes Martin V. Johann III. Ihm gelang es, vor allem durch Verkauf und Verpfändung verschiedener Güter das Geld zur Wiedergewinnung der Rotenburg aufzubringen. Allerdings war das Schloss in verschiedenen Gebäudeteilen verfallen. Im Laufe einer langen Zeit gelang es Johann III., sich in den Besitz des Schlosses Rotenburg zu bringen und die Gebäude wiederherzustellen. Eine Stütze fand er in Otto, Herzog von Braunschweig und Lüneburg[1]. Johann III. regierte bis zu seinem 90. Lebensjahr und trat dann zurück.

---

1 Vermutlich Otto IV., von 1434 bis 1446 Fürst von Lüneburg.

Die Erzbischöfe Johann Rode, Christoph und Georg im 16. Jahrhundert

Mit Beginn des 16. Jahrhunderts war unter Erzbischof Johann Rode (»Wer Langwedel besitzt, beherrscht das Land«) Herzog Christoph von Braunschweig-Lüneburg-Wolfenbüttel als Koadjutor bestellt worden (1500). Im Jahr 1505 wurde Christoph zum Bischof von Verden bestellt. Bis zum Tod von Johann Rode im Jahr 1511 residierte Christoph in Langwedel und Rotenburg, ab 1511 in vor allem in Rotenburg, daneben in Bremervörde (Voerde) und in Langwedel. Ähnliches gilt auch für den auf Christoph folgenden Erzbischof Georg. Das »wesentliche Hoflager« befand sich unter den Erzbischöfen Christoph und Georg in Rotenburg. Die »Hofhaltung« der Erzbischöfe konnte sich durchaus auch an anderen Orten befinden, also nicht nur an den genannten drei Orten (Rotenburg, Voerde, Langwedel), sondern gelegentlich auch in einem anderen befestigten Ort im Erzstift oder irgendwo im Reich, zum Beispiel dort, wo gerade ein Reichstag stattfand. Im Jahr 1558, unmittelbar nach dem Tode von Erzbischof Christoph, hat man in einem Gewölbe zu Rotenburg unter dem Nachlass des Erzbischofs das Johan Roden Bok gefunden, das »Registrum« (»Registrum Bonorum et Iurium Ecclesiae Bremensis«) des Erzbischofs Johann Rode. Dieses geschah im Zusammenhang mit der Inventarisierung des in den »Kammern« in Rotenburg, Voerde und Langwedel vorhandenen Nachlasses des Erzbischofs Christoph.

Im 14. und 15./16. Jahrhundert sind verschiedene Angehörige derer von Staffhorst in leitenden Stellen überliefert. 1348 ist ein Heinrich von Staffhost Vogt von Rotenburg (Wümme). Johann von Staffhorst, der zuvor in der Grafschaft Hoya tätig war, ist zwischen 1512 und 1522 erzbischöflicher Drost und Rat in Langwedel und Offizial des Bremer Domkapitels.

Das Amt des Hofmarschalls findet man im Erzstift Bremen erstmals im Jahr 1519. In diesem Jahr setzt im Auftrag des Erzbischofs der Hofmarschall Ambrosius Rabitz den Kanzler Gabriel Eisenhofer im Turm zu Rotenburg gefangen. Gabriel Eisenhofer war zunächst Sekretär gewesen und im Jahr 1517 zum »steten Kanzler« bestellt worden. Wegen angeblicher Untreue im Wurster Feldzug wird Eisenhofer fast ein

Jahr lang in Rotenburg eingekerkert. Am 21. Januar 1521 schwört er dem Erzbischof Urfehde und reist mit ihm zum Wormser Reichstag. Amtmann (Rentmeister) in Rotenburg in den Jahren 1512–1525 war Wigand Rauch.

An sich traf man die Voerder Kanzlei (also auch den Kanzler) häufiger in Rotenburg als in Voerde. Die Verdische Kanzlei befand sich sowieso in Rotenburg.

In den Jahren 1520 bis 1547 war Stephan Hopfensteiner bei unterschiedlichen Herren als Beamter tätig. 1535 musste er sich in Brüssel wegen angeblicher Verbindungen zum Lübecker Bürgermeister Wullenwever verantworten. Wullenwever wurde 1536 von Klaus Hermeling während der sogenannten Grafenfehde Lübecks gegen Dänemark beim Ritt nach Hadeln gefangen und zum Erzbischof nach Rotenburg gebracht. Bei seiner peinlichen Befragung nannte Wullenwever Stephan Hopfensteiner als Mitwisser.

Unter dem Erzbischof Christoph war es nicht ungebräuchlich, dass die Beamten des Erzbischofs sich persönlich verpfändeten. Der Landdrost Burghard von Kramm (Voerde) und der Rotenburger

Amtmann Stephen Harder (»Stephen Lamstedt«) mussten sich für eine vorgestreckte Summe bis zur Bezahlung dieser Summe dem Herzog Heinrich dem Jüngeren von Braunschweig-Wolfenbüttel »mith glubden unnd eiden verwandt« machen, sich also in den Dienst des Herzogs begeben und standen demnach in Voerde und in Rotenburg nicht zur Verfügung.

Die Überlieferung der Protokolle der Landtage im Hochstift Verden beginnt im Jahr 1531, als der Bruder Heinrich der Jüngere, Herzog von Braunschweig-Lüneburg, des Bremer Erzbischofs Christoph, zugleich Administrator des Hochstifts Verden, in verschiedenen Streitfragen zwischen Christoph, den Verdener Ständen und einzelnen Personen einen Vergleich vorschlug. Soweit Rotenburg betroffen war, wurde festgelegt, dass immer dann, wenn der Bischof durch Reisen abwesend war, Mitglieder des Domkapitels nach Rotenburg abgeordnet werden sollten. 1532 wurde beschlossen, dass Geld, das von den Steuereinnahmen im Stift Verden für einen Zug gegen die Türken vorgesehen war und übrig bleiben sollte, für Baumaßnahmen an der Rotenburg verwendet werden sollte.

Beamte in Rotenburg zur Zeit der Erzbischöfe Christoph und Georg waren 1537 Henning Eckeleff als Rentmeister, Stephan Harde (Stephan Lamstedt) 1544–1553 als Befehlshaber (Vogt) und Heinrich Clüver 1562–1565 (?) als Drost. 1562 war Klaus von Eppen Rat und Hauptmann auf Haus Rotenburg und zugleich Gläubiger des Erzbischofs.

Dem Heer der im Schmakaldischen Krieg zwischen Kaiser Karl V. und den im Schmakaldischen Bund vereinten protestantischen Fürsten gelang am 23. Mai 1547 unter Führung des Grafen Albrecht von Mansfeld und des Grafen Christoph von Oldenburg bei Drakenburg an der Weser ein überlegener Sieg über ein kaiserliches Heer. Dieses stand unter dem Herzog Erich II. von Braunschweig-Lüneburg-Kalenberg, der zunächst Bremen belagern wollte, dann aber den Protestanten im Raum Hoya entgegengezogen war. Das kaiserliche Heer war zum größten Teil aufgerieben worden, Herzog Ernst konnte sich nur durch die Weser schwimmend retten. Nach der Schlacht von Drakenburg nahm das schmalkaldische Heer am 1. Juni 1547 Rotenburg, am 2. Juni Langwedel und innerhalb weniger Wochen auch Ottersberg und Bremervörde (Voerde) ein. Die Stadt

Bremen übergab, so wurde überliefert, das Erzstift Bremen und das Stift Verden dem Grafen Albrecht von Mansfeld als einem der beiden Heerführer des schmalkaldischen Bundes. Der Graf Christoph von Oldenburg hatte sich, da er auch Bremer Domherr war, zurückgehalten.

Der Erzbischof Christoph war während dieser Ereignisse zum Kaiser geritten in der Hoffnung, er würde dort Hilfe gegen die Truppen der Protestanten erhalten. Nach seiner Rückkehr vom Kaiser bestellte er den Hofrat Franz von Halle des Herzogs Heinrich dem Jüngeren als Kriegskommissar. Trotz der schwachen Kräfte, über die Christoph und von Halle verfügten, gelang es ihnen, zunächst Verden und auch Langwedel zurückzuerobern. Wegen der feindseligen Einstellung der Stände kam Christoph bei der Rückeroberung des Erzstiftes zunächst nicht weiter. Erst 1549 gelang ihm ein Vergleich mit den Ständen, durch den Christoph wieder als Landesherr anerkannt wurde. Einzelheiten wurden am 13. Juni 1549 im Landtag von Daverden (unmittelbar bei Langwedel) vereinbart. Bis dahin hatten die Stände die Ämter Voerde (Bremervörde) und Neuenhaus in ihrem Besitz gehabt, Rotenburg aber offenbar nicht.

Haus und Amt Langwedel hatte Christoph in den Jahren 1539–1548 an eine Gruppe von Edelherren in einer komplizierten Rechtskonstruktion verpachtet. Der Erzbischof erhielt einen großen Geldbetrag, für den verschiedene Bürgschaften abgegeben worden waren.

Über die Besetzung der Rotenburg hatten die Stände des Hochstiftes Verden schon am 15. Mai 1548 beraten. Sobald der Graf von Mansfeld das Haus Rotenburg geräumt habe, solle Dietrich Bere als Drost von Rotenburg eingesetzt werden. Die Burg soll dem Bischof (und Erzbischof) jederzeit mit beliebig vielen Pferden zugänglich sein, wie dieses schon immer die Regel gewesen war. Am 8. Oktober 1548 beschließen die Stände ergänzend, der Bischof solle die verschiedenen Geschütze auf der Rotenburg, welche bei benachbarten Herrschern entliehen worden waren, diesen zurückgeben, wann immer dieses verlangt werde. Am 24. Januar 1549 befassten sich die Verdener Stände wieder mit der Rotenburg, da die Abreise des Erzbischofs und Bischofs Christoph bevorstand. Daher sollte Rotenburg an mehrere Domherren und Adelige des Stifts übergeben werden. Die Stände rechneten mit weiteren Aufwendungen für die Burg und verlangten die Zusage, dass solche Aufwendungen, vor allem wenn sie durch Schulden gegenüber Dritten entstünden, zurückgezahlt würden.

Etwa ab 1550 unmittelbar nach dem schmalkaldischen Krieg führte die Adelserhebung in Niedersachsen und die »Fürstenverschwörung« zu erbitterten Kämpfen, in deren Mittelpunkt zeitweise vor allem die Festung Langwedel stand, während Rotenburg offenbar von Erzbischof Christoph gehalten werden konnte. Eine zentrale Rolle bei diesen Auseinandersetzungen spielten der Kurfürst Moritz von Sachsen, der Markgraf Albrecht Alcibiades von Brandenburg-Kulmbach und Herzog Heinrich der Jüngere von Braunschweig-Lüneburg-Wolfenbüttel. Der eigentliche Adelskrieg in Niedersachsen brach im Jahr 1552 aus. Claus Barner wurde vor Alfeld verwundet. Heinrich der Jüngere flüchtete zunächst zum Kaiser. Langwedel als Zentrum der Adelserhebung wurde anfangs von Klaus von Rottorf gehalten. Zu Beginn des Jahres 1553 griffen Truppen des Herzogs Heinrich dem Jüngeren unter dem Kommando seines Sohnes Prinz Philipp Magnus zuerst die Burg Hülsede des Klaus von Rottorf an und rückten nach deren Eroberung über Hoya und Rethem gegen Langwedel vor. Rottorf musste flüchten, Philipp Magnus legte eine starke Besatzung auf die Festung Langwedel.

Inzwischen hatte Claus Barner den Markgrafen Albrecht Alcibiades überredet, sich an den Auseinandersetzungen in Niedersachsen zu beteiligen. Auf der anderen Seite standen der Kurfürst Moritz von Sachsen und Herzog Heinrich der Jüngere. Anfang Juli 1553 musterte der Markgraf in Verden und ließ drei Regimenter auf Langwedel vorrücken, konnte aber die unter dem Kommando von Zitterd von Arnim stehende Festung nicht nehmen. Gleichzeitig sammelten beide Seiten Truppen, wobei der niedersächsische Adel hauptsächlich auf der Seite des Markgrafen stand. Am 9. Juli 1553 kam es bei Sievershausen östlich von Hannover zur Schlacht, bei der sich Heere von jeweils etwa 20.000 Mann gegenüberstanden. Entschieden wurde die Schlacht durch die kursächsische Reiterei. Kurfürst Moritz erlitt durch einen Gewehrschuss eine zunächst anscheinend nicht schwere Verwundung, an der er jedoch nach zwei Tagen verstarb. Die Söhne Philipp Magnus und Karl Victor des Herzogs Heinrich dem Jüngeren sowie ein Prinz von Braunschweig-Lüneburg-Celle fielen. Unter dem niedersächsischen Adel wurde ein Blutbad angerichtet.

Endgültig siegte Herzog Heinrich der Jüngere im September 1553 bei Geitlingen. Claus Barner auf der Seite des Markgrafen kam bei dieser Schlacht ums Leben. Klaus von Rottorf lieferte sich einen erbitterten Zweikampf mit Wisberg und floh hinterher ins Bremische. Wegen Langwedel kam es zu einem bis 1616 währenden Rechtsstreit zwischen von Rottorf und dessen Erben mit dem Erzstift Bremen vor dem Reichskammergericht, bei dem es um den »Pfandschilling« von 6.700 rheinische Gulden ging.

Der in Rotenburg residierende Erzbischof Christoph überwachte die Finanzen in den Ämtern des Erzstiftes selbstverständlich auch aus Rotenburg. Aus dem Jahr 1555 ist ein Schriftwechsel des Erzbischofs aus Rotenburg mit dem Rentmeister Johann Stude zu Voerde und dem »Renthmeister zum Neuwenhauß« wegen dortiger Schatzsammlungen überliefert.

In dem Bau der Festungsanlagen war mit dem Aufkommen der Geschütze in der frühen Neuzeit ein grundlegender Wandel eingetreten, unter anderem dadurch gekennzeichnet, dass die Festungen nun mit Wällen gebaut wurden. Für die Festungen Langwedel und auch Rotenburg gilt als verlässliche Überlieferung, dass der Baubeginn des einfachen Hauptwalls im 16. Jahrhundert stattfand. Für Burgschanze an der Lesum und Hoya ist hingegen zweifelhaft, dass mit diesem Bau schon im 16. Jahrhundert begonnen worden war. Sicher hingegen ist für Hoya der Baubeginn im Jahr 1618, also bei Beginn des Dreißigjährigen Krieges. Grundsätzlich ist davon auszugehen, dass an den Festungen ständig Baumaßnahmen stattfanden, vor allem auch an der Festung Langwedel und der Festung Rotenburg (Wümme).

Die Aufstellung von Truppen zur Landesverteidigung war noch zu Lebzeiten des Erzbischofs Christoph im Jahr 1557 Gegenstand einer »Satinge«, womit die bremische Landschaft Truppengrößen festsetzte. »Bremische Landschaft« bedeutete, dass das Stift Verden und insbesondere Rotenburg (Wümme) von derartigen Festsetzungen nicht betroffen waren. Bei den im Erzstift Bremen zu stellenden Truppen wurde zwischen Berittenen und Fußvolk unterschieden. Von den insgesamt 341 Berittenen sollten die Ritterschaft 268 Berittene, die Städte Bremen, Stade und Buxtehude 50 Berittene und die fünf »Häuser« Langwedel, Hagen, Stotel, Thedinghausen und Ottersberg 23 Berittene stellen, davon Langwedel sieben Berittene. Das Fußvolk war mit 3650 Mann festgesetzt worden, davon für das »Land Wursten« 800 Mann, das »Gericht zwischen Langwedel und Bremen« (Achim) 80 Mann, das »Amt Thedinghausen« 40 Mann, das »Amt Ottersberg« 80 Mann. Voerde (Bremervörde) war von den verschiedenen Festsetzungen nicht betroffen, also weder als »Haus« noch als »Amt«, was seltsam ist.

Für das Stift Verden und insbesondere für Rotenburg (Wümme) sind so spezielle Festlegungen zur Landesverteidigung nicht zu finden. Bekannt ist jedoch die Musterung vom 22. Januar 1606 im Amt Ottersberg und einschlägiger Schriftwechsel über die Frage, wer unter das Erzstift Bremen und wer unter das Stift Verden und speziell Rotenburg falle[2].

Der Erzbischof Christoph verstarb auf der Rückreise von seinem Besuch bei Kurfürst Joachim von Brandenburg am 22. Januar 1558 in Tangermünde und wurde im Dom zu Verden bestattet. Da die Verdener Stände auf den in Rotenburg, Voerde und Langwedel liegenden Nachlass des verstorbenen Erzbischofs keinen Zugriff hatten, beschloss ein Landtag

---

2 Musterung der Landfolgepflichtigen, Schöne, Die Erzbischöfe von Bremen, S. 336; Dörfler, Herrschaft und Landesgrenze, S. 400–404.

von 1558, für die Zeit während der Sedisvakanz für die Burg Rotenburg 1000 Rthr. auszuleihen.

Sein Bruder Georg und Nachfolger als Erzbischof zu Bremen und Bischof zu Verden residierte häufig in Rotenburg, aber wohl auch in Langwedel. Verstorben ist er zwei Tage nach dem Landtag vom 2. Dezember 1566 zu Basdahl in Bremervörde. Bestattet wurde er wie sein Bruder im Dom zu Verden.

Der Amtmann Heinrich Meier in Langwedel hatte schon unter Erzbischof Christoph die Zollfreiheit Bremer Bürger in Langwedel nicht beachtet und er tat es auch unter dem neuen Erzbischof Georg nicht. Der Schriftwechsel ergab, dass die Bremer Bürger in Langwedel ihr Recht auf Zollfreiheit belegen mussten und bestimmte Erklärungen über ihre Zollfreiheit (sogenannte Zollzettel) mitzuführen hatten. Außerdem mussten die Bremer Bürger unter Eid versichern, dass die mitgeführten Waren ihre eigenen waren.

Nachdem der Erzbischof am 1. April 1560 mit Abgesandten von Bürgermeister und Rat der Stadt Bremen im »Dorf Sottrum« westlich von Rotenburg im Erzstift Bremen zusammengekommen war, schrieb der Erzbischof Georg am folgenden Tag aus

Bild 1a: Brustbild des Erzbischofs Georg, Herzog von Braunschweig-Lüneburg-Wolfenbüttel (1558–1566), von vorn auf Doppeltaler 1560

Bild 1b: Porträt des Erzbischofs Georg, Herzog von Braunschweig-Lüneburg-Wolfenbüttel, 16. Jh., Maler unbekannt (Sächsische Landesbibliothek – Staats- und Universitätsbibliothek Dresden Mscr. Dresd. H. 193 Bl. 50 r)

Rotenburg (Wümme) an das Domkapitel in Bremen und an den Amtmann Heinrich Meier in Langwedel. Der Erzbischof teilte »seinem lieben Getreuen« Meier mit, dass die Stadt Bremen sich beklagt habe, dass Meier die vorgelegten Zollzettel nicht anerkenne. Da der Erzbischof auch in Langwedel nicht immer anwesend war, bekam der Amtmann von Langwedel vom erzbischöflichen Verordneten Jobst Behr in einem folgenden Brief den Auftrag, bei Abwesenheit »unseres gnädigen Fürsten und Herrn« sich um das Haus und die Haushaltung zu kümmern. Entsprechendes hätte auch für Rotenburg verordnet werden müssen.

Die Festungsanlagen der damaligen Zeit mussten ständig repariert und verbessert werden. Dafür benötigte man billige Arbeitskräfte. So ist vom Erzbischof Georg überliefert, dass nach seiner Bestimmung die Meier und andere Bauern im Amt Rotenburg die notwendigen Dienstleistungen beim Festungsbau zu erbringen hatten. Auf diese Bestimmung des Erzbischofs Georg hat man sich auch unter den nachfolgenden Bischöfen von Verden berufen.

Der »Ausschusstag« der Abgeordneten der Stände des Erzstifts Bremen wegen der Rückgabe von Ottersberg an das Erzstift , wie schon beim Landtags vom 14. März 1561 in Basdahl erörtert, fand unmittelbar bei Langwedel (»beim Langwedell«) am 19. März 1562 in Daverden statt. Am Rande ging es auch um zwei Geschütze, die von der Stadt Bremen an das Erzstift zurückgegeben werden sollten.

Verdener Bischöfe Eberhard und Philipp Sigismund

Nachfolger von Erzbischof Georg als Bischof (Postulierter) von Verden war Eberhard, Konfirmierter Bischof zu Lübeck, Herr zu Lüneburg (Verden 1566 – 1586). Im Zusammenhang mit einer neuen kirchlichen Organisation im Stift Verden wurde 1570 das Stift in die Superintendanturen Verden und Rotenburg eingeteilt. In Rotenburg wurde dem Prediger Johann Macke die Inspektion übertragen.[3]

Unter Bischof Eberhard entschieden die Verdener Landstände am 3. April 1576, dass die Baumaßnahmen auf Burg Rotenburg zunächst einzustellen wären, bis die Schatzeinkünfte vorlägen. Am 21. Juni 1581 befassten sich die Stände mit einer Reihe die Burg Rotenburg betreffenden Befestigungsanlagen. Der Bischof hatte Geschütze, Pulver und Kugeln auf die Rotenburg gebracht. Er ersuchte die Stände, diese in Augenschein zu nehmen und deutete

3 Mathias Nistal, Immunität und Landesherrschhaft, S. 182.

zugleich an, dass er Teile davon dem Stift schenken wolle. Die bewilligten Baumaßnahmen auf der Rotenburg wären weitgehend abgeschlossen. Die Kosten habe der Bischof teils als verzinstes Darlehen aufgenommen, teils aus eigenem Geld beglichen. Er bittet darum, über diese Zahlungsvorgänge genau Buch zu führen. Die Kapelle auf der Burg sei bisher aus Holz gebaut. Stattdessen solle ein Neubau (vermutlich aus Stein) errichtet werden. Weiterhin solle auch ein starker Zwinger errichtet und der Schlossgraben vertieft werden. Bisher biete der Graben keinen ausreichenden Schutz.

Am 5. Juli 1582 mussten sich die Stände in Gegenwart des Domdechanten Andreas von Mandelschlo wieder mit der Rotenburg befassen. Der Bischof hatte schon vor einem Jahr eine Aufstellung der in Rotenburg entstandenen Baukosten übergeben, die sich ungefähr auf 20.870 Rthr. beliefen. Davon habe der Bischof schon einen beträchtlichen Teil selbst übernommen und er biete weitere 2.000 Taler an. Das Baugeld war größtenteils bei Dritten gegen Zinsen aufgenommen worden. Die Stände sollten die Einnahme des fehlenden Geldes über einige Jahre veranschlagen und berücksichtigen, dass durch die Türkensteuer[4] große Verpflichtungen auf das Stift zukämen. In Rotenburg müsse noch ein Pforthaus (offenbar nach dem Vorbild von Langwedel) errichtet werden, das gleichfalls zu finanzieren sei. Nach dem Tod von Bischof Eberhard waren im Januar 1587 noch etwas mehr als 6.500 Taler Baukosten für die Rotenburg offen. Dieses Geld sollte gemäß Beschluss der Stände durch zwei jährliche Landschatzungen aufgebracht werden. Bischof Eberhard ist am 5. Juli 1586 auf einer Reise von Rotenburg nach Lübeck in Lüneburg verstorben, wo er die Reise aus gesundheitlichen Gründen unterbrochen hatte. Er wurde in der Kirche des Lüneburger Michaelisklosters bestattet.[5]

Im Bistum Verden war am 26. September 1586 Philipp Sigismund, Herzog von Braunschweig-Lüneburg, zum Bischof gewählt worden. Wenn er sich im Hochstift Verden aufhielt, residierte er meistens in Rotenburg. Dort ließ er den von Eberhard

---

4 An das Reich abzuführende Steuer, mit der ein Feldzug gegen die Türken finanziert wurde.
5 Mathias Nistal, Immunität und Landesherrschaft, S. 184.

von Holle begonnenen Schlossbau im Renaissancestil vollenden. 1590 brannte in der Burg Rotenburg ein offenbar sehr großes Gebäude ab. Der Bischof erreichte, dass die Verdener Landstände (das waren das Domkapitel, die Ritterschaft und die Städte) ihm am 31. Juli 1593 die beachtliche Summe von 7.000 Rthr. aus den Kontributions- und Landsteuereinkünften zur Durchführung der Reparaturen auf der Burg Rotenburg bewilligten. Der Bischof hatte bereits mit den Reparaturen an der Rotenburg begonnen, doch hatte sich inzwischen herausgestellt, dass die notwendigen Bauarbeiten noch beträchtlichen Umfang hatten. Das Geld sollte der Bischof in den Jahren 1594 und 1595 zwischen Martini und Weihnachten, zu zwei unterschiedlichen Terminen erhalten.

Um das Jahr 1596 war zwischen den Ämtern Ottersberg (Erzstift Bremen) und Rotenburg ein Grenzstreit ausgebrochen. Aus diesem Anlass wurden zwei Lageskizzen (»Ortssignatur«) angefertigt (Bild 2 und Bild 3).

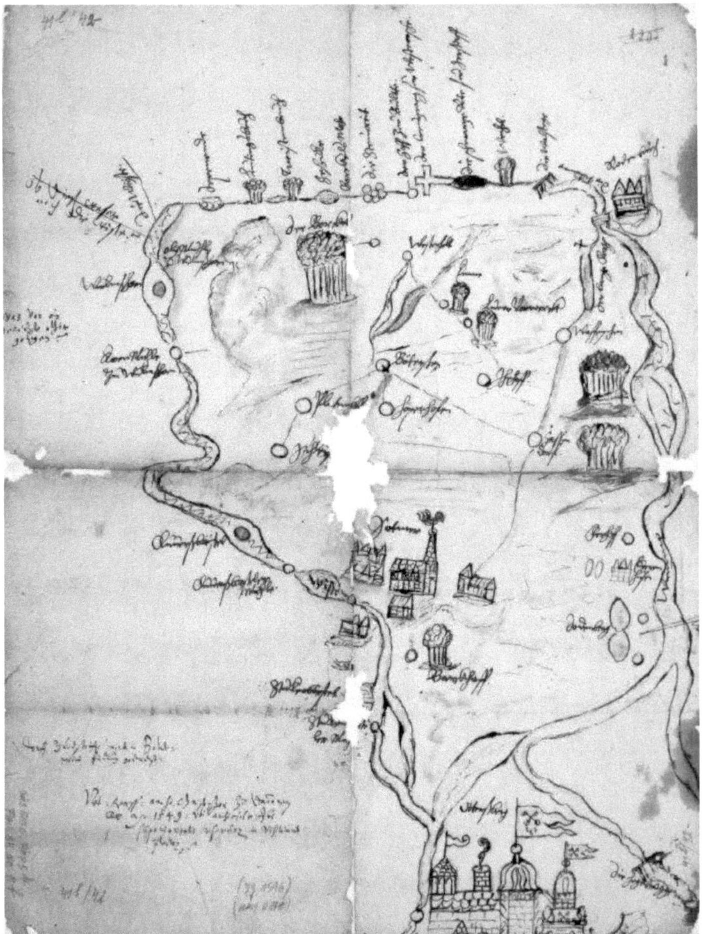

Bild 2: »Ortssignatur« Schloss Rotenburg und Ottersberg, um 1596
Nieders. Landesarchiv, Standort Stade, Archivsignatur Neu Nr. 13122

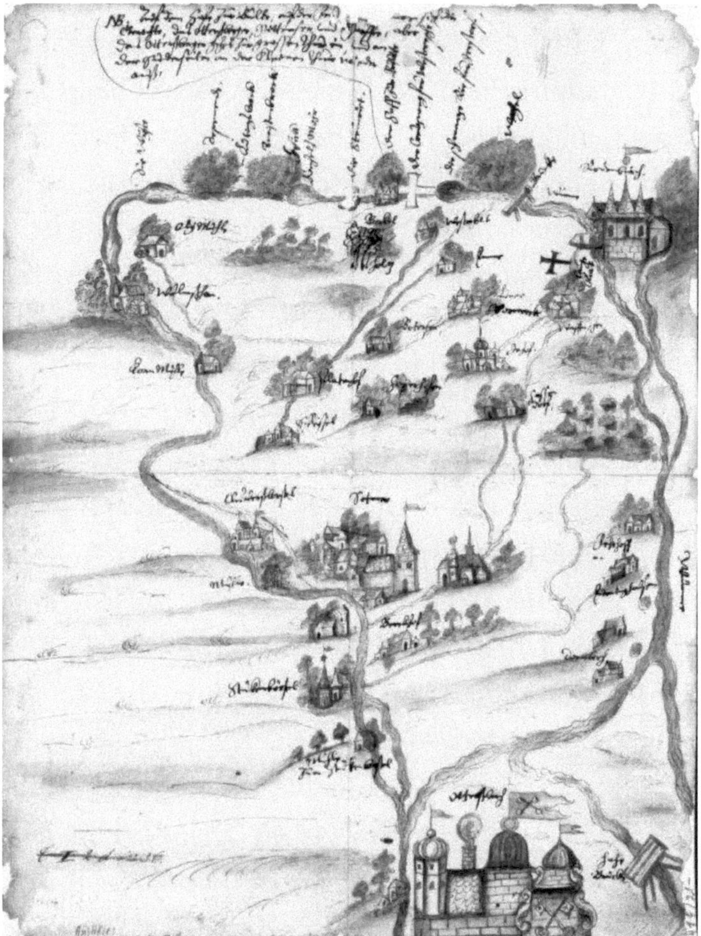

Bild 3: »Ortssignatur« Schloss Rotenburg und Ottersberg, um 1596
Nieders. Landesarchiv, Standort Stade, Archivsignatur Neu Nr. 13101

Im Jahr 1608 ließ Bischof Philipp Sigismund in Rotenburg eine Schlosskirche (Schlosskapelle) errichten. Die Orgel in der Schlosskirche baute Hans Scherer der Ältere (ca.1535–1611). Es handelt sich um die letzte der verschiedenen von Hans Scherer bekannten Orgeln. Der Orgelprospekt stammt von Ludwig Münstermann und ist allein erhalten geblieben. Heute befindet sich dieser Prospekt im Bremer Focke-Museum.

Im Jahr 1609 stiftete Philipp Ferdinand in Rotenburg eine Schule[6]. Rentmeister zu Rotenburg am Anfang des 17. Jahrhunderts war Johann Badenhop. Seine Tochter Irmgard heiratete den am 6.1.1617 geborenen Christoph Gabel, der am 23. April 1639 zum erzbischöflichen Kammerschreiber bestallt wurde. 1648 ist er königl. dän. Kammerschreiber, 1664 im dän. Reichsadelsstand.

Im Jahr 1620 ist inzwischen allenthalben von Krieg die Rede. Auf Vorschlag des Bischofs Philipp Sigismund beschließt der Landtag am 31. August 1620, auf die Rotenburg zwölf tüchtige Soldaten und

---

6 Mathias Nistal, Immunität und Landesherrschaft, S. 186.

Bild 4: Prospekt der Orgel in der Schlosskapelle von Rotenburg von Ludwig Münstermann, 1608. Prospekt befindet sich heute im Focke-Museum, Bremer Landesmuseum für Kunst und Kulturgeschichte

einen erfahrenen Korporal zu legen. Rotenburg sei der einzige Festungsort im Stift Verden.

In der Kipper- und Wipperzeit war bei Münzprägungen verbreitet Missbrauch üblich geworden. Um diesen Missbrauch abzustellen, erließ Bischof Philipp Sigismund am 10. August 1621 in Rotenburg (Wümme) eine Bischöflich Verdische Münzordnung.

Diese sollte als Interims-Münzordnung gelten, bis man sich im Reich oder den benachbarten Reichskreisen, d.h. dem niedersächsischen und dem niederländisch-westfälischen Reichskreis auf neue Münzordnungen verständigt hatte. Geprägt wurden Kupfermünzen als Doppelschillinge, Grote, halbe Grote und Schware. Für den Geldwert der Kupfermünzen wurde festgesetzt:

24	Verder Doppelschillinge	= 1 Reichstaler
72	Verder Grote	= 1 Reichstaler
144	Verder halbe Grote	= 1 Reichstaler
360	Verder Schware	= 1 Reichstaler

Im Handel war niemand verpflichtet, von diesen Münzen mehr als 9 Grote anzunehmen.

In Rotenburg sollte eine Wechselbank eingerichtet werden, welche das Kupfergeld in Reichsgeld umzutauschen hatte. Es wurden 13 verschiedene Münzarten festgesetzt, in welche das Kupfergeld eingetauscht werden konnte. Vermutlich erfolgten auch die Münzprägungen in Rotenburg.

Bischof Philipp Sigismund starb im Jahr 1623. Als Nachfolger wählte am 5. Mai 1623 das Verdener

Domkapitel den Koadjutor Friedrich, Prinz von Dänemark, Sohn des Königs Christian IV von Dänemark. Zu seiner Zeit ist um den 19. April 1633 Caspar Schulte, erbgesessen zu Kuhmühlen, Burgmann zu Horneburg, königlich schwedischer Drost auf dem Haus und Amt Rotenburg. Seit Herbst 1634 ist er in königlich Dänischen Diensten und betreibt die Wahl von Friedrich zum Erzbischof von Bremen. Seit 1637 war Dietrich Schulte Rat und Drost auf Rotenburg (gestorben 1641). Vom 1. November 1640 mindestens bis 1645 ist Dietrich von der Recke Drost in Rotenburg. 1657 ist er Rat des Herzogs Christian Ludwig von Braunschweig-Lüneburg und Oberhauptmann zu Harburg.

Nach der Niederlage von König Christian IV. von Dänemark am 27. August 1626 in der Schlacht am Barenberge besetzten die Truppen des kaiserlich-katholischen Heerführers Graf Johann Tserclaes von Tilly das Stift Verden vollständig. Der Flecken Rotenburg mit samt der Kirche wurde 1626 von kaiserlichen Soldaten niedergebrannt[7]. Tilly blieb fast

---

7 Mathias Nistal, Immunität und Landesherrschaft, S. 188. Geschichte des Landes zwischen Elbe und Weser, Bd. 3 Michael Ehrhardt zur Sozial und Wirtschaftsgeschichte im 17. Jahrh., S. 256.

während eines ganzen Jahres vor der Festung Langwedel stehen[8]. Der König von Dänemark hatte das Feldlager seines Heeres gegen die von Tilly besetzte Stadt Verden durch Befestigungsgatter gegen mögliche Allerquerungen geschützt und auch die Einmündung der Aller in die Weser befestigt. Die Rückseite des Feldlagers lehnte sich mit befestigten Übergängen an die Festung Langwedel an.

Die dänischen Truppen vor Langwedel wurden zunächst durch verbündete Holländer, Engländer und Franzosen weiter verstärkt. Der Ausbruch der Pest im Herbst 1627 könnte die Ursache gewesen sein, dass diese Truppen die Befestigungen um Langwedel und dann die Achim-Linie hastig räumten. Die Ligisten unter Fürst Anhalt rückten rechts der Weser an Bremen vorbei bis zur Lesum vor. Die vor Bremen lagernden Flüchtlinge ergossen sich in die pestverseuchte Stadt Bremen.

Mitten im Dreißigjährigen Krieg zu Zeiten des Erzbischofs Johann Friedrich hatte sich so im Jahr 1630 die Situation ergeben, dass das Erzstift Bremen

---

8 Schöne, Die Erzbischöfe von Bremen, S. 472–474.

immer noch weitgehend von ligistischen Truppen, also den kaiserlichen Truppen, besetzt war. Am 14. August 1630 sah sich Johann Friedrich sehr im Gegensatz zu den sonst üblichen Gepflogenheiten gezwungen, nicht nur seinen Regierungssitz, sondern auch seine Zentralverwaltung in die Stadt Bremen zu verlegen. Die Ruhr, die seit 1629 in Bremen geherrscht hatte, war anscheinend dabei abzunehmen. Zur Unterbringung der Verwaltung mussten neben dem Pallatium auch zwei Domkurien belegt werden.

Als dann Schweden unter König Gustav Adolf in den Krieg eingriff und die kaiserlichen Truppen unter Tilly am 17. November 1631 bei Breitenfeld besiegte, war mit dem baldigen Ende der kaiserlichen Hegemonie in Norddeutschland zu rechnen. Erzbischof Johann Friedrich begann frühzeitig, Truppen aufzustellen und das Erzstift zurückzuerobern. Erzbischöfliche Truppen eroberten schon am 29. September 1631, also vor der Schlacht bei Breitenfeld, Langwedel zurück. Ein Rückschlag für den Erzbischof war, dass es den Ligisten gelang, am 14. Dezember 1631 Langwedel wiederzugewinnen. Nunmehr drängte der Erzbischof die Ligisten systematisch zurück. Am 13. Januar 1632 eroberten erzbischöfliche Verbände das Haus Hagen und unmittelbar darauf nahmen sie auch Langwedel wieder ein und am 22. Februar 1632 Ottersberg. Wenig später konnten erzbischöfliche Truppen Buxtehude erobern. Am 5. Mai 1632 räumten die kaiserlichen Truppen Stade und händigten dem Erzstift Bremen die Schlüssel sämtlicher von Katholiken besetzten Kirchen und Klöster aus.

Johann Friedrich nahm schließlich von Langwedel aus, wo er starke Truppenverbände angesammelt hatte, am 31. Mai 1632 auch die Stadt Verden ein und am 2. Juni 1632 Rotenburg (Wümme).

Aufgrund seiner Siege über die Ligisten wurde Erzbischof Johann Friedrich am 27. Juli 1632 in der Stadt Bremen mit Salutschüssen empfangen. In Langwedel feierte der Erzbischof seinen Sieg mit dem Auftreten eines Musikkorps.

Bild 5: Erzbischof Friedrich II. von Bremen (Erzbischof 1634–1646/48, Bischof Verden 5.5.1623–1646/48), als Friedrich III. König von Dänemark 1648-70

Erzbischöfe Johann Friedrich und Friedrich II., Prinz von Dänemark

Nach dem Tod des Bischofs Philipp Sigismund am 19.3.1623 war, wie erwähnt, auf dem Landtag vom 5. Mai 1623 des Stiftes Verden von den Ständen des Stifts der bisherige Koadjutor Friedrich von Dänemark, Sohn des Königs Christian IV. von Dänemark, zum konfirmierten und legalisierten Bischof des Stiftes Verden gewählt worden. Später sahen die Stände sich veranlasst, in ihrem Beschluss vom 22. April 1630 das kurze Zwischenspiel des katholischen Bischofs Franz Wilhelm von Wartenberg[9] zu akzeptieren.
Zu dieser Zeit ist im Erzstift Bremen noch der Erzbischof Johann Friedrich an der Regierung. Der im Hochstift Verden seit 1623 im Amt befindliche Bischof Friedrich ist im Erzstift Bremen noch Koadjutor von Johann Friedrich.

---

9 Franz Wilhelm von Wartenberg, Bischof von Osnabrück, nach verschiedenen Wirren vom Papst am 26.1.1630 zum Verdener Bischof bestimmt, am 18. März 1631 vom (katholischen) Verdener Domkapitel als Bischof akzeptiert (Mathias Nistal, Verdens evangelische Bischöfe als Landesfürsten bis 1648, S. 190).

Bild 6: Königin Christina (17.12.1626 – 19.4.1689, Königin von Schweden (anfangs unter Vormundschaft) 1632 – 1654)

Auf dem am 9. Oktober 1636 in Rotenburg gehaltenen Landtag hatte sich der Bischof Friedrich II. durch den Landdrosten und Kanzler Caspar Schulte uff Khumuhlen Erbgesessen und Dietrich Reinkingen, Doktor des Rechts, vertreten lassen. Die Stände beschlossen, das Fürstliche Haus und Amt Rotenburg dem Obristen Josias Rantzowen gegen 16.000 Rtlr. abzutreten, wobei 4.000 Rtlr. am künftigen Martini zu bezahlen seien. Über die Aufbringung der weiteren 12.000 Rtlr. müsse noch entschieden werden. Weiterhin beschlossen die Stände, dass man das fürstliche Haus Rotenburg und die Stadt Verden nicht ungeschützt lassen könne. Eine Kompagnie von 100 Soldaten sei erforderlich, die je zur Hälfte nach Rotenburg und nach Verden zu legen sei. Über den Unterhalt dieser Soldaten stellte der Verdener Landtag am 28. Februar 1637 fest, die Soldaten seien bisher weitgehend durch Mittel des Erzbischofs und Bischofs unterhalten worden. Die vom Bischof verauslagten Mittel sollten diesem jetzt ersetzt werden. Die noch offenen 1.200 Rtlr. hätte der König von Dänemark dem Hochstift Verden geliehen. Die Stände wollten sich überlegen, wie sie dieses Darlehen zurückzahlen könnten. Die

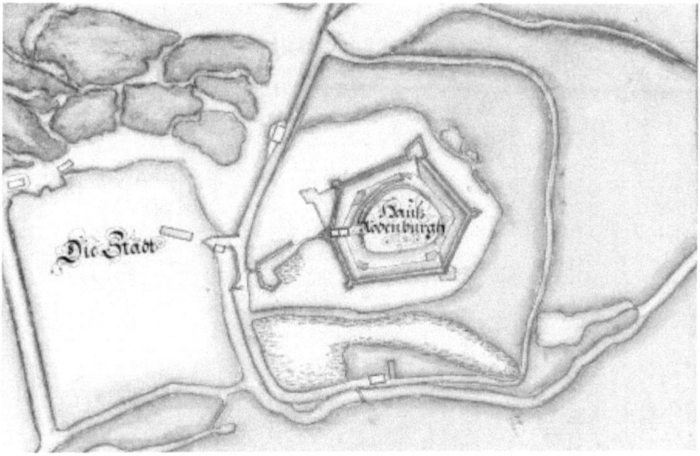

Bild 7: »Erik Dalberghs Rit Bok«, Rotenburg ca. 1648. Riksarkivet Stockholm, Schwed. Kriegsarchiv

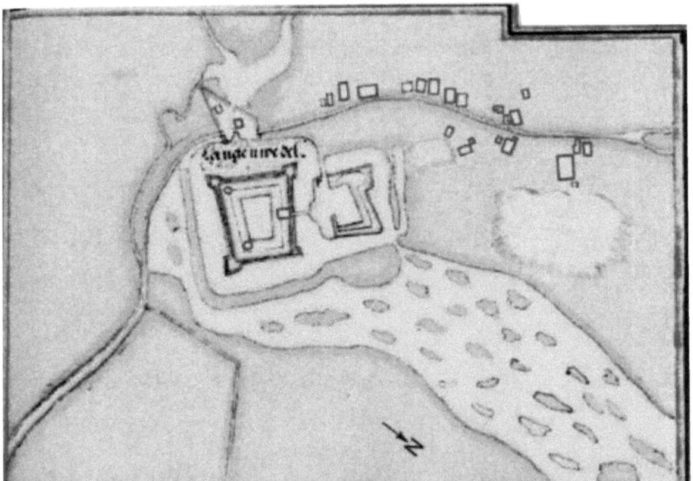

Bild 8: Erik Dalberg, maßstäbliche Zeichnung der erzbischöflichen Festung Langwedel einschließlich Hornwerk von 1632

genannten Zahlungsvorgänge legen nahe, dass das Schloss Rotenburg im Dreißigjährigen Krieg nach 1623 auch häufig Residenz von König Christian IV. von Dänemark war.

Im Jahr 1645 hatte Hans Christoph von Königsmarck[10] nach unterschiedlichen Kämpfen um die Festung Langwedel im Jahr 1644 das Erzstift Bremen und das Stift Verden für Schweden erobert. Königsmarck wurde Generalgouverneur der eigentlich noch geistlichen Fürstentümer Bremen und Verden und sicherte die schwedische Herrschaft in diesen Fürstentümern. Der Westfälische Friedensvertrag vom 24. Oktober 1648 bestätigte den Besitz des bisherigen Erzstifte Bremen und des Hochstiftes Verden durch das Königreich Schweden.

Im Friedensvertrag heißt es unter anderem, dass *»der Kaiser mit Zustimmung des ganzen Reiches der Königin und ihren Erb- und Nachfolge-Königen und dem Königreich Schweden«* das Erzbistum Bremen und das Bistum Verden mit Stadt und Amt

10 Hans Christoffer von Königsmarck (1605–1663), 1643 schwedischer Generalmajor, 1645 Generalgouverneur Herzogtümer Bremen und Verden.

Bild 9: Hans Christoffer von Königsmarck (12.12.1605 – 20.2.1663), Porträt aus Stadtarchiv Stade, Graphiksammlung 02 Nr. 32

Wildeshausen »*und allen Rechten, welche den letzten Erzbischöfen von Bremen in Kapitel und Diözese Hamburg zustanden, mit allen kirchlichen und weltlichen Gütern und Rechten unter allen Titeln und allem, war irgendwie zu Landes oder zur See irgendwo dazugehört* als ewige und unmittelbares Reichslehen unter den gebräuchlichen Abzeichen, jedoch mit dem Titel eines Herzogtums gewährt«. Die Reichslehenschaft bedeutete, dass der Huldigungseid geleistet werden musste, dass zukünftige schwedische Könige als Lehnsträger jeweils um Lehenserneuerung nachsuchen mussten und dass mit den beiden Herzogtümern jeweils die Reichs- und Kreisstandschaft verbunden war.

Da das Erzstift Bremen und das Hochstift Verden verschiedenen Reichskreisen angehört hatten, ergab sich hieraus die Mitgliedschaft der nunmehrigen Herzogtümer Bremen und Verden in zwei unterschiedlichen Reichskreisen, dem Niedersächsischen Kreis (Herzogtum Bremen) und dem Niederrheinisch-Westfälischen Kreis (Herzogtum Verden).

Herzogtümer Bremen und Verden unter Königen von Schweden

Bei der Übernahme der Herzogtümer Bremen und Verden (des bisherigen Erzstiftes Bremen und des Hochstiftes Verden) hatte Königin Christina etwa 150 Donationen vergeben. Die weitaus wertvollsten hatte Graf Hans Christoph von Königsmarck erhalten, der Generalgouverneur der Herzogtümer Bremen und Verden. Dazu gehörten im Jahr 1645 vor allem Amt und Schloss Rotenburg. Inwieweit die Familie Königsmarck Rotenburg selbst bewohnte, ist unklar, da Königsmarck 1652 für seine Frau Barbara Maria Agathe von Lehsten (8.4.1608–1671) das Schloss »Agathenburg« bei Stade erworben und unter diesem Namen ausgebaut hatte. Dort ist Agathe 1671 verstorben.

Zu Beginn der Übernahme der Herzogtümer Bremen und Verden durch Schweden gibt es eine Zeichnung von Rotenburg von Erik Dahlberg (Bild 7), die deutlich von Dahlbergs Zeichnung von Langwedel abweicht (Bild 8). Die verschiedenen Einzelheiten der Rotenburg gehen weitaus genauer aus dem

Protokoll der Übergabehandlung vom 1. Juli 1681 hervor (vgl. unten).

Hans Christoph von Königsmarck und Agathe von Lehsten hatten die Söhne Kurt (Cord) Christoph Graf von Königsmarck und Otto Wilhelm Graf von Königsmarck und die Tochter Beata Elisabeth von Königsmarck (1637–1724), die seit 1655 mit Pontus Frederic de la Garde (1630–1692) verheiratet war. Kurt Christoph von Königsmarck war mit Maria Christine von Wrangel (geb. 28.8./7.9.1638) verheiratet. Aus dieser Ehe stammten die Kinder Karl Johann (geb. 5./15. Mai 1659), Philipp Christoph, (1665–1.7.1694) Maria Aurora[11], (geb. vermutlich 1663), Wilhelmine Amalie.

Der Generalgouverneur Hans Christoph von Königsmark war im Oktober 1656 in polnische Gefangenschaft geraten. In dieser verblieb er bis zum Frieden von Oliva vom 3. Mai 1660 in der Festung Weichselmünde. In diesen Jahren hat sich wahrscheinlich seine Frau Agathe um die Verwaltung

11 Beate-Christine Fiedler, Maria Aurora von Königsmarck, die schwedische Gräfin aus Stade. Stader Jahrbuch 1991/92, S. 138–153 (Sohn Moritz von Sachsen, französischer Heerführer).

Bild 10: Fürstbischof Christoph Bernhard Graf von Galen (12.10.1606 – 19.9.1678, Fürstbischof Münster 1650 – 1678, zuvor Domküster Münster)

von Rotenburg gekümmert. Hans Christoph von Königsmarck ist am 20. 2. (8. 3.) 1663 in Stockholm an Blutvergiftung verstorben.

Graf Kurt Christoph von Königsmarck wurde ab 17. 9. 1664 Vizegouverneur der Herzogtümer Bremen und Verden. Diese Stellung gab er 1672 an seinen Bruder Otto Wilhelm ab und war als Generalleutnant in nicht genau zu klärenden holländischen Diensten. Am 31. 10. 1673 traf ihn bei Bonn eine Kanonenkugel, woran er verstarb.

Graf Otto Wilhelm von Königsmarck übernahm das Amt des Vizegouverneurs am 23. 5. 1672. Schon zuvor war Otto Wilhelm durch seine ruhmreichen Teilnahmen an Kriegszügen bekannt. In die Zeit der Tätigkeit von Graf Otto Wilhelm von Königsmark für Schweden fällt die Reichsexekution gegen Schweden in den Jahren 1675/76 bis Anfang 1680.

Reichsexekution gegen Schweden

Die Aggressionen des französischen Königs Ludwig XIV. im Rheinland und gegen die Niederlande hatten ab 1672 zu militärischen Auseinandersetzungen geführt, an denen auch der »Große Kurfürst« gegen Frankreich und der zwischen unterschiedlichen Bündnissen schwankende Fürstbischof Christoph Bernhard Graf von Galen beteiligt waren. Schweden stand auf der Seite Frankreichs. Die politische Situation führte allmählich zu einer Annäherung von Münster (Fürstbischof Christoph Bernhard) an den deutschen Kaiser. Die Verhandlungen für den Kaiser Leopold führte Freiherr Franz Paul von Lisola. Am 22. April 1674 wurde in Köln der Kölner Frieden zwischen dem Fürstbistum Münster und den Generalstaaten geschlossen. Über einen Bündnisvertrag zwischen dem Fürstbistum Münster und dem Kaiser wurde danach noch ein Jahr lang verhandelt. Bündnisverhandlungen mit dem Kaiser durch den münsterschen Hofrat Dr. Ham und Gespräche mit Frankreich wurden von Münster wechselweise geführt. Nach verschiedenem Hin und Her schloss das Fürstbistum Münster am 7. Juni 1675 einen Bündnisvertrag mit Kaiser Leopold, der sich an den im August 1673 am Reichstag zu Regensburg verlesenen kaiserlichen Aufruf an die Reichsstände zum Krieg gegen Ludwig XIV. anlehnte. Die Ratifizierung des Vertrages zwischen dem Kaiser und Münster erfolgte seitens des Fürstbischofs von Galen am 29. Juni 1675, seitens des Kaisers Leopold am 7. September 1675.

Der Angriff auf die Herzogtümer Bremen und Verden wurde auf der Westseite weitgehend durch Münstersche Truppen durchgeführt. Dazu zog Münster seine Truppen aus dem Elsass nach Westfalen ab. Die Münsterschen Truppen waren den wenigen noch in den Herzogtümern Bremen und Verden stehenden schwedischen Truppen weit überlegen. Nachdem Münster ohne besondere Anstrengungen die Weser überquert hatte, fiel ein zentraler Ort nach dem anderen weitgehend kampflos. Langwedel fiel am 27. September 1675, die Festung nahezu kampflos. Auch die Stadt Verden fiel Ende September 1675 in Münstersche Hände. Der Fürstbischof Christoph Bernhard hatte seinen Obristen von Twickel den Befehl zur Einnahme der Stadt am 25. September 1675 mit der ausdrücklichen Anordnung gegeben, die Bevölkerung möglichst unbehelligt zu lassen. Burg an der Lesum ergab sich am 28. September. Rotenburg (Wümme) wurde am 30. September 1675 genommen, nach anderen Pressemeldungen schon am 27. September. Heftiger war der Kampf um Ottersberg.

Die angreifenden Mächte sahen sich frühzeitig veranlasst, die Herzogtümer Bremen und Verden unter sich aufzuteilen. Die erste Vereinbarung wurde schon am 10. Oktober 1675 in Rotenburg und Walsrode zwischen Münster, Braunschweig-Lüneburg-Celle und Braunschweig-Lüneburg-Wolfenbüttel getroffen. Nach dieser Vereinbarung fielen unter anderem »Burg« bei Bremen, Langwedel, Rotenburg und Ottersberg unter Anrechnung des Münsterschen Quartanteils an Münster. Wenn Fürstbischof Christoph Bernhard sich in den Herzogtümern Bremen und Verden aufhielt, residierte er überwiegend in Rotenburg.

Die Münstersche Regierung hatte ihren Sitz in Verden. An der Spitze dieser Regierung stand der Präsident Nikolaus von Zitzwitz. Außerdem gehörten der Oberhauptmann Conrad Peper und die Regierungsräte von Schwann und Moritz von der Lippe zur Regierung. Im Oktober 1678 zeichnete Grany Marschalck statt Moritz von der Lippe als Regierungsmitglied. Kabinettsitzungen mit Teilnahme des Fürstbischofs fanden anscheinend vor allem in Rotenburg statt. Von einer Sitzung vom 4. September 1677 in Rotenburg gibt es ein Kabinettsprotokoll. An dieser Sitzung hatten außer dem Fürstbischof auch Zitzwitz, der »Domküster« und weitere Personen teilgenommen. Der Fürstbischof trug vor, dass die katholischen Geistlichen in Wort und Lebensführung den Nichtkatholiken Vorbilder zu sein hätten. In katholischen Gottesdiensten sei deutsch zu singen. Der Katechismus sei sorgfältig zu lehren. Den Armen seien Almosen zu geben. Man habe darauf zu achten, dass keine unwissenden und ungelehrten Prediger tätig seien.

Als Verwalter in Langwedel setzte Münster anfänglich, also ab Herbst 1675, den Amtsschreiber Johann Erich Wittneben ein. In der Verwaltung der Einkünfte richtete sich Wittneben nach den Unterlagen, die er von der schwedischen Verwaltung vorfand. Er stellte zwei Vögte ein (Samuel Schwer und Johan Franck Müller). Am 2. September 1676 übertrug der Fürstbischof das Amt Langwedel dem Erbkämmeramt des Hochstiftes Münster. Wittneben wurde nach Rotenburg versetzt. Als Amtsschreiber des Erbkämmeramtes kam Otto Ziegeler nach Langwedel. Ziegeler arbeitete bis zum Tod des Fürstbischofs Christoph Bernhard von Galen für das Erbkämmeramt. Unter dem Fürstbischof Ferdinand von Fürstenberg unterstand er der von Münster in Verden eingesetzten Regierung.

Die Festungen in dem von ihm in den Herzogtümern Bremen und Verden verwalteten Gebiet hatte Münster offenbar ohne Zerstörungen übernommen. Darauf weist eine Liste der von Münster in diesen Festungen besoldeten Artilleristen, also von Soldaten mit Spezialausbildung hin: Bremervörde 10 Köpfe, Rotenburg 6 Köpfe, Ottersberg 5 Köpfe, Carlsburg 3 Köpfe, Burg 4 Köpfe, Langwedel 1 Kopf.

Christina gibt die Insel Öland für Rotenburg und andere Besitzungen

Die Grafen von Königsmarck hatten im Jahr 1680 oder auch schon zuvor gegen Ende des Jahres 1679, eventuell schon vor der Übernahme der Herzogtümer Bremen und Verden durch Schweden, Schloss und Amt Rotenburg zurückbekommen. Das hieße, Otto Wilhelm von Königsmarck hätte eine diesbezügliche Absprache mit dem Fürstbischof Ferdinand von Fürstenberg getroffen. Otto Wilhelm von Königsmarck verlor das Amt Rotenburg und damit auch das Haus Rotenburg schon im Jahr 1681. Die frühere schwedische Königin Christina hatte die Insel Öland abgetreten und erhielt als Entgelt verschiedene Eigentumsrechte in den Herzogtümern Bremen und Verden, vor allem das Amt Rotenburg. Öland ist eine Insel vor der Küste Südschwedens von 137 km Länge und einer Fläche von 1.347 km^2. Die Insel ist heute ein beliebtes Urlaubsziel an der Ostsee.

Die Übertragung des Amtes Rotenburg an die Beauftragten von Christina fand am 1. Juli 1681 statt. Christina war kurz nach ihrem Rücktritt als Königin katholisch geworden und lebte in Rom, wo sie am 19. April 1689 starb.

Die Übergabeverhandlung vom 1. Juli 1681, durch die die Donation Rotenburg der früheren Königin Christina übergeben wurde, fand in der Amtsstube des Schlosses Rotenburg statt. Diese befand sich im gut erhaltenen Gartenhaus des Schlosses. Die verfassten Aufstellungen bezogen sich auf alle Einzelheiten des Schlosses und seiner unmittelbaren Umgebung, nicht jedoch auf das »Amt Rotenburg«. An der Übergabehandlung nahmen teil:

- Der Resident Emanuel Teixera und der Kommissar Johan Philip Silbercron als Beauftragte der Königin Christina,
- der Amtmann Jonas Zipfel als Beauftragter des Feldmarschalls und bisherigen Inhabers von Rotenburg, Otto Wilhelm von Königsmarck,
- der Kanzler der Herzogtümer Bremen und Verden, Esaias von Pufendorf als Vertreter der Krone Schwedens,
- der neue Drost Johann Philipp von Langen, der aus dem an Braunschweig-Wolfenbüttel übertragenen Thedinghausen kam und dem jetzt offenbar das Amt Rotenburg unterstand,

- der Land- und Kriegskommissar Andreas Scharnhorst
- und der Sekretär Möller aus Hamburg.

Es wurden weitere Personen hinzugezogen, so der Bürgermeister von Rotenburg Jost Ho(h)mann, der Ratsherr Marten Frantz, der Zimmermann Barthold Eggers und der Maurer Jost Bahr.

Die Einzelheiten der Bestandsaufnahme vermitteln den Eindruck, so wird im Protokoll behauptet, dass die Schlossanlagen in der letzten Zeit kaum noch im Gebrauch gewesen seien. Am besten seien die Kellerräume erhalten geblieben. Dagegen spricht, dass der Fürstbischof von Münster die von ihm eroberten Teile der Herzogtümer Bremen und Verden, vor allem das Herzogtum Verden mit dem Schloss und Amt Rotenburg, behalten wollte und Münster in den Jahren 1675–1679 die militärischen Befestigungen ausbaute. Das Protokoll vom 1.7.1681 nennt von den oben angeführten Personen nur einige wenige, die durch das Schloss gegangen waren.

Es werden verschiedene Räume aufgeführt, die zum Schloss gehörten, auch die Kirche. Bei der Kirche wird die Orgel erwähnt, deren Pfeiffen größtenteils beschädigt waren, und der Altar. In der Jägerkammer befanden sich wenig brauchbare Netze zum Fangen von Wild bei Treibjagden. Die besten fünf Netze hatte der Bischof von Münster mitgenommen. Ein Trinkgefäss fällt auf, das der Dr. Jur. Eberhard Graffenthal hatte anfertigen lassen, der 1670 Regierungsrat in den Herzogtümern Bremen und Verden, seit 1671 schwedischer Resident in Hamburg und 1687 Kanzler in den Herzogtümern Bremen und Verden war. Das Schloss besitzt zwei Türme, an denen eine Zwei-Stunden-Glocke und eine Reiterglocke angebracht war. Das Uhrwerk war nicht in Betrieb. Verschiedene sonst im Schloss auffallende Einrichtungen werden genannt. Der Amtmann Jonas Zipffel (er ist nur 1681 als Amtmann nachzuweisen) stellte ein Verzeichnis der vorhandenen Vorräte auf.

Zur Zeit der Besetzung der Herzogtümer Bremen und Verden durch die Okkupationsmächte hatte der schwedische König Karl XI. im Jahr 1677 erneut Donationen an Persönlichkeiten vergeben, die er an Schweden binden wollte. So hatte Graf Otto Wilhelm von Königsmarck in Ergänzung zu Rotenburg das gesamte Herzogtum Verden als Donation erhalten.

Der Verlust seiner Donationen in den Herzogtümern Bremen und Verden, zu denen zwischenzeitlich nicht nur Rotenburg, sondern das ganze Herzogtum Verden gehörte, veranlasste Otto Wilhelm, im großen Türkenkrieg in kaiserlichen Dienst zu treten. 1682 heiratete er die Gräfin Katharina Charlotte de la Gardie, eine Tochter des Grafen Magnus Gabriel de la Gardie, der Oberst der Leibgarde der Königin Christina gewesen war, verschiedene hohe schwedische Regierungsämter besessen hatte und unter König Karl XI. 1672 schwedischer Kanzler (Lord High Chancellor) gewesen war.

Graf Otto Wilhelm von Königsmarck vollbrachte auch in den Türkenkriegen zahlreiche militärische Großleistungen. Bei der Belagerung der Stadt Negroponte (heute Chalkis) auf der Insel Euboea verstarb er am 15. September 1688 trotz der Pflege durch seine Frau an der grassierenden Pest. Eine Porträtbüste von Otto Wilhelm von Königsmarck ließ der Senat von Venedig durch Enrigo Merengo aus Marmor anfertigen. Die Porträtbüste wurde im Arsenal von Venedig aufgestellt. Am 19. (29.) Januar 1691 wurde Otto Wilhelm von Königsmarck in Stade bestattet.

Es wird vermutet, dass Christina sich um das Amt und Haus Rotenburg kaum gekümmert hat. Gleiches wird vom Drost Johann Philipp von Langen angenommen, der bis 1690 hätte in Rotenburg tätig sein sollen. Nach dem Tod von Christina im Jahr 1689 folgte von 1690 bis 1706 auf Langen der Amtmann Erich Prytz-Claßon. Ähnlich wie im Fall von Langwedel wurde Rotenburg in diesen Jahren ausgeschlachtet. Blei und Eisen gingen an das Stader Zeughaus. 1704 gingen Holz und etwa 200.000 Mauersteine von Rotenburg nach Ottersberg. Nach dem Tod von Christina im Jahr 1689 waren Amt und Schloss Rotenburg wieder an die schwedische Regierung gefallen.

Der Große Nordische Krieg und Übergang an das Kurfürstentum Hannover und Großbritannien

Nachdem Schweden im Großen Nordischen Krieg anfangs große Erfolge erzielt hatte, wendete sich nach der verheerenden Niederlage von König Karl XII. im Jahr 1709 bei Poltawa das Blatt. Im Jahr 1712 waren die Herzogtümer Bremen und Verden zunächst teilweise an Dänemark und ab 1715 bzw. 1719/20 (mit einer wenig durchsichtigen Übergangszeit zwischen 1712/15 und 1719/20) weitgehend an Braunschweig-Lüneburg bzw. an Großbritannien gefallen. Im Jahr 1714 unterstanden die schwedischen Beamten Haddorf und Behling in Rotenburg wie auch der Zollverwalter Richter in Langwedel und der Amtsvogt Knütel in Ahausen dem schwedischen Generalgouverneur Vellingk, der seinen Sitz von Stade nach Bremen hatte verlegen müssen[12]. Rotenburg muss demnach zu den erst 1719/20 an

12 Schöne, Vom Westfälischen Frieden bis zum Wiener Kongress, S. 274. NLA StA Stade Rep. 5 g Nr. 123.

Braunschweig-Lüneburg gefallenen Gebietsteilen gehört haben. Allerdings war dann die neue braunschweig-lüneburgische Regierung in Stade noch einige Jahrzehnte damit beschäftigt, sich mit den verwirrenden Zuständigkeiten der schwedischen Zeit irgendwie abzufinden und dann im Laufe der Jahre klare Organisationformen zu schaffen.

Bilder

Bild 1a: Brustbild des Erzbischofs Georg, Herzog von Braunschweig-Lüneburg-Wolfenbüttel (1558 – 1566), von vorn auf Doppeltaler 1560

Bild 1b: Porträt des Erzbischofs Georg, Herzog von Braunschweig-Lüneburg-Wolfenbüttel, 16. Jh., Maler unbekannt (Sächsische Landesbibliothek – Staats- und Universitätsbibliothek Dresden Mscr. Dresd. H. 193 Bl. 50 r) aus: (Die Erzbischöfe von Bremen, Bild 6 b, S. 279)

Bild 2: Niedersächsisches Staatsarchiv, Standort Stade, Archivsignatur Neu Nr. 13122

Bild 3: Niedersächsisches Staatsarchiv, Standort Stade, Archivsignatur Neu Nr. 13101

Bild 4: Prospekt der Orgel in der Schlosskapelle von Rotenburg von Ludwig Münstermann, Orgel von Hans Scherer der Ältere, 1608. Prospekt befindet sich heute im Focke-Museum, Bremer Landesmuseum für Kunst und Kulturgeschichte

Bild 5: Erzbischof Friedrich II. von Bremen (Erzbischof 1634 – 1646/48, Bischof Verden 5.5.1623 – 1646/48), als Friedrich III. König von Dänemark 1648-70 aus: Die Erzbischöfe von Bremen, Bild 18, S. 516)

Bild 6: Königin Christina (17.12.1626 – 19.4.1689, Königin von Schweden (anfangs unter Vormundschaft) 1632 – 1654) Porträt aus Stadtarchiv Stade, Graphiksammlung 02, Nr. 68 aus: (Vom Westfälischen Frieden bis zum Wiener Kongress, Bild 2, S. 43)

Bild 7: »Erik Dalberghs Rit Bok«, Rotenburg ca. 1648, Riksarkivet, Stockholm, Schwed. Kriegsarchiv

Bild 8: Erik Dalberg, maßstäbliche Zeichnung der erzbischöflichen Festung Langwedel einschließlich Hornwerk von 1632 aus: (Die Erzbischöfe von Bremen, Bild 14, S. 491).

Bild 9: Hans Christoffer von Königsmarck (12.12.1605 – 20.2.1663), Porträt aus Stadtarchiv Stade, Graphiksammlung 02 Nr. 32 (Anderes Porträt in »Geschichte des Landes zwischen Elbe und Weser« Band III, S. 179) aus: (Vom Westfälischen

Frieden bis zum Wiener Kongress, Bild 1, S. 21)

Bild 10: Fürstbischof Christoph Bernhard Graf von Galen (12.10.1606 – 19.9.1678, Fürstbischof Münster1650 – 1678, zuvor Domküster Münster) aus: (Vom Westfälischen Frieden bis zum Wiener Kongress, Bild 9, S. 135).

Literatur

Hans-Eckhard DANNENBERG, Heinz-Joachim SCHULZE (Hrsg.) mit Michael EHRHARD und Norbert FISCHER, Geschichte des Landes zwischen Elbe und Weser, Band III Neuzeit. Landschaftsverband der ehemaligen Herzogtümer Bremen und Verden, Stade 2008.

Beate-Christine FIEDLER, Maria-Aurora von Königsmarck, die schwedische Gräfin aus Stade. Stader Jahrbuch 1991/92 (Stader Archiv – Neue Folge 81/82.) S. 138 – 153.

Beate-Christine FIEDLER, Die Entwicklung der schwedischen Staatsform im 17. Jahrhundert und ihre Auswirkungen auf die deutschen Provinzen Bremen und Verden. Heinz-Joachim Schulze (Hrsg.), Landschaft und regionale Identität. Landschaftsverband der ehemaligen Herzogtümer Bremen und Verden, 1989.

Arend MINDERMANN, Zur Frühgeschichte des Hochstiftes Verden. Bernd Kappelhoff, Thomas Vogtherr (Hrsg.), Immunität und Landesherrschaft. Landschaftsverband der ehemaligen Herzogtümer Bremen und Verden, Stade 2002.

Arend MINDERMANN (Hrsg.), Die Landtagsabschiede des Erzstiftes Bremen und des Hochstiftes Verden. Veröffentlichungen der Historischen Kommission für Niedersachsen und Bremen. Verlag Hahnsche Buchhandlung Hannover 2008.

Matthias NISTAL, Die Reichsexekution gegen Schweden in Bremen-Verden. Heinz-Joachim Schulze (Hrsg.), Landschaft und regionale Identität. Landschaftsverband der ehemaligen Herzogtümer Bremen und Verden 1989.

Matthias NISTAL, Verdens evangelische Bischöfe als Landesfürsten bis 1648. Bernd Kappelhoff, Thomas Vogtherr (Hrsg.), Immunität und Landesherrschaft. Landschaftsverband der ehemalischen Herzogtümer Bremen und Verden. Stade 2002.

Karl H. SCHLEIF, Regierung und Verwaltung des Erzstiftes Bremen zu Beginn der Neuzeit (1500–1645). Hamburg 1972.

Armin SCHÖNE, Die Erzbischöfe von Bremen und ihr Haus und Amt Langwedel. 2. Auflage, Bremen 2016. Edition Falkenberg.

Armin SCHÖNE, Vom Westfälischen Frieden bis zum Wiener Kongress. Europäische Machtpolitik um Langwedel und Bremen. 1. Auflage, Bremen 2016. Edition Falkenberg.

Herbert SCHWARZWÄLDER, Rotenburg 1681. Heinz-Joachim Schulze (Hrsg.), Landschaft und regionale Identität. Landschaftsverband der ehemaligen Herzogtümer Bremen und Verden 1989.

Wolf-Dieter TEMPEL, Zur Siedlungsentwicklung im Raum Rotenburg-Stade. Heinz-Joachim Schulze (Hrsg.), Landschaft und regionale Identität. Landschaftsverband der ehemaligen Herzogtümer Bremen und Verden 1989.

Thomas VOGTHERR (Hrsg., Kommentator), Chronicum episcoporum Verdensium, Die Chronik der Verdener Bischöfe. Bernd

Kappelhoff, Hans-Eckard Dannenberg (Hsgb.), Schriftenreihe des Landschaftsverbandes der ehemaligen Herzogtümer Bremen und Verden, Band 10. Stade 1998.

Thomas VOGTHERR, Iso von Wölpe, Bischof von Verden (1205–1231), Reichsfürst, Bischof, Adliger. Eine Biographie. Landschaftsverband der ehemaligen Herzogtümer Bremen und Verden. Stade 2008.

Ortsregister

Personenregister

Der Autor

Prof. Dr. Armin Schöne, emeritierter Professor der Universität Bremen und außerplanmäßiger Professor der Rheinisch-Westfälischen Technischen Hochschule Aachen, ist Autor zahlreicher Veröffentlichungen über Messtechnik, Regelungstechnik und Systemtechnik, aber auch über die Regionalgeschichte Nordwestdeutschlands. In den Ingenieurwissenschaften hat er sowohl zahlreiche Fachaufsätze wie auch eine größere Reihe von Fachbüchern zu unterschiedlichen Themen verfasst.

In der Regionalgeschichte stammen von ihm nicht nur zahlreiche umfangreiche Aufsätze, sondern neuerdings zwei sehr umfassende Bücher, in denen die Geschichte von Stadt, Erzstift und Herzogtum Bremen einen Schwerpunkt bildet.

Ein weiteres Werk ist die 2017 erschienene Biografie Friedrich von der Decken, in der die Lebensgeschichte einer ungewöhnlich herausragenden Persönlichkeit wiedergegeben wird, welche die Geschichte des Kurfürstentums und Königreichs Hannover mit der Großbritanniens zur Zeit der Personalunion Hannover/Großbritannien verbindet, sowie 2018 ein Beitrag zur Geschichte der Reformation in Norddeutschland: »Die reichsunmittelbare Grafschaft Diepholz im 16. Jahrhundert«.

Die Geschichte des Großraumes Bremen und die einschlägige Nordwestdeutsche Geschichte hat Prof. Dr. Armin Schöne in zwei umfassenden Büchern behandelt, nämlich unter »Die Erzbischöfe von Bremen und ihr Haus und Amt Langwedel« (etwa die Jahre 1200 bis 1650) und »Vom Westfälischen Frieden bis zum Wiener Kongress – Europäische Machtpolitik um Langwedel und Bremen« (etwa die Jahre 1640 bis 1820).

Katrin Steengrafe

Mord an der Wümme

Ein Krimi in HB und ROW

244 S., Taschenbuch 14 x 19 cm
9,90 Euro
ISBN 978-3-95494-126-1

Der 20-jährige Sven Hartmann wird am Borgfelder Deich tot aufgefunden. Weder ein Motiv noch weitere Hintergründe des Mordes sind erkennbar. Die Kommissarin Rieke Senger tappt bei ihrem ersten Fall in Bremen völlig im Dunkeln. Welche Rolle spielt der Verein »Helfende Hände e.V.«, bei dem Hartmann gerade eine Ausbildung absolvierte und Carmen Schütte ihre Stelle antritt? Die einzige Zeugin, ein depressives Mädchen, hüllt sich in Schweigen …

Andreas Mundt

Hühnerhorst

Eine seltsame Reise ans Nordkap

Roman
148 S, Taschenbuch 14 x 22 cm
9,90 Euro
ISBN 978-3-95494-146-9

Eigentlich war es ja seine Frau, die sich am Nordkap die Polarlichter ansehen wollte. Doch die hatte es zu Lebzeiten nicht geschafft. Woran Horst nicht ganz unschuldig war. Also macht er sich nun auf den Weg. Stellvertretend sozusagen.

Und weil er die beiden Hühner Helene Fischer und Renate nicht alleine zurücklassen kann, nimmt er sie einfach mit. Und weil das Auto gerade kaputt ist, fahren die drei mit dem alten Mofa los. Werden sie ihr Ziel im hohen Norden erreichen?

Kauzig, komisch, kurios:
Beste Unterhaltung mit skurrilem Humor – nicht nur für Schwedenliebhaber.